MEDIEVAL CHRISTIAN
PERCEPTIONS OF ISLAM

MEDIEVAL CHRISTIAN PERCEPTIONS OF ISLAM

EDITED BY
JOHN VICTOR TOLAN

ROUTLEDGE
NEW YORK AND LONDON

First paperback edition published in 2000 by
Routledge
29 West 35th Street
New York, NY 10001

Published in Great Britain by
Routledge
11 New Fetter Lane
London EC4P 4EE

Routledge is an imprint of the Taylor & Francis Group

Library of Congress Cataloging-in-Publication Data

Medieval Christian perceptions of Islam / edited by John Victor Tolan.
    p.   cm.
    Includes bibliographical references index.
    ISBN 0-8153-1426-4(alk. paper)
    ISBN 0-415-92892-3(pbk.)
    1. Islam — Relations — Christianity. 2. Christianity and other
religions — Islam. 3. Islam — Public opinion. 4. Public opinion —
Europe. I. Tolan, John Victor, 1959-.
BP172. M396 1996
261.2'7'09—dc20   94-5298
                                            CIP

Printed on acid-free, 250-year-life paper
Manufactured in the United States of America

10 9 8 7 6 5 4 3 2 1

In fond memory of Braxton Ross

Contents

Abbreviations

AASS	Acta Sanctorum.
BT	Babylonian Talmud.
CM	*Crónica mozárabe de 754.* José Eduardo Lopez Pereira, ed. Zaragoza, 1980.
COD³	*Conciliorum oecumenicorum decreta.* 3rd ed., G. Alberigo et al., eds. Bologna, 1972.
CSCO	*Corpus Scriptorum Christianorum Orientalum.* Leuven, 1903– .
CSEL	*Corpus Scriptorum Ecclesiasticorum Latinorum.* Vienna, 1866– .
CSM	*Corpus scriptorum muzarabicorum.* Juan Gil, ed., 2 vols., Madrid, 1973.
De con.	*De consecratione,* the third part of Gratian's *Decretum.*
EI¹	*Encyclopedia of Islam.* 1st ed. Leiden, 1913–1938.
EI²	*Encyclopaedia of Islam.* 2nd ed., Leiden, 1960– .
EETS	Early English Text Society.
GCS	*Die griechischen christlichen Schriftsteller.* Berlin, 1897– .
HB	*Historia diplomatica Friderici secundi.* Compiled by J. L. A. Huillard-Bréholles. 6 vols., Paris, 1852–1861.
Henry	MS Oxford Bodl. Laud misc. 85.
MGH	Monumenta Germaniae Historica.
MGH AA	Monumenta Germaniae Historica, Auctores.
MGH Epist Saec.	XIII Monumenta Germaniae Historica, *Epistolae saeculi XIII e Regestis Pontificum Romanorum.*

ix

MGH SS	Monumenta Germaniae Historica, *Scriptores.*
PG	J.P. Migne, ed. *Patrologiae graecae cursus completus.* 162 vols., Paris, 1857–1886.
PL	J.P. Migne, ed. *Patrologiae latinae cursus completus.* 217 vols., Paris, 1844–1864.
PO	*Patrologia orientalis.* Paris, 1907– .
RHC, Arm	*Recueil des historiens des croisades, Documents Arméniens*, ed. et trad. E. Dulaurier and C. Kohler, Paris, 1906.
St. B.	MS Holy Name College 69.

Introduction

John Tolan

For medieval Christians, Islam presented a series of disquieting challenges. Militarily, most of the Christian world fell into Muslim hands in the seventh and eighth centuries, and much of the rest of it succumbed to the expansion of Muslim dominion by the sixteenth century. Intellectually, Muslim science and philosophy were built on an edifice of Greek, Persian, and Hindu learning inaccessible (until the twelfth and thirteenth centuries) to the Latin West.[1] The Muslim world developed a thriving trade-based economy; Italian and Byzantine merchants saw the Muslim lands as opulent and sophisticated. Theologically, Islam presented a series of quandaries: Were Muslims pagans? Were they heretics or schismatics?

There were never any clear, monolithic answers to these questions. Individual Christians, depending on their own experience with Muslims, their interests, prejudices, and preoccupations, portrayed Islam in very different ways. Polemicists wrote theological refutations of Islam; historians attempted to explain Islam's origins and expansion; lawyers defined the legal status of Muslims living in Christian lands; exegetes defined Islam's role in the divine plan; diplomats vilified or apologized for Muslims, depending on what kinds of alliances they were trying to justify; epic poets imagined Muslim warriors as embodiments either of demonic hostility or of chivalric ideals.

Few of these writers used the words "Islam" or "Muslim"; instead they spoke of "Saracens," "Hagarenes," "Arabs,"

"Turks," "Pagans," "Moors," or simply, those who follow the Law of Muhammad. Christians defined Muslims as they defined themselves: through a complex (and not often distinguished) mix of ethnic, linguistic, and religious definitions. Islam is both a rival civilization and a rival faith (or Law, *lex*, to follow the most common Latin usage).[2]

The medieval texts treating Islam are many and varied: It is beyond the purpose of this collection to give a thorough catalogue of these works.[3] Rather, the authors of these essays provide a series of vignettes, of discrete examples of medieval Christian perceptions of Islam. In choosing the articles that make up this collection, I have been driven by two fundamental principles. First, I wanted each article to acquaint readers with new, unfamiliar texts (unfamiliar at least to students of Muslim–Christian relations); hence I preferred essays on the "Tathlîth al-waπdânîyah" or the legal documents of Manuel I Comnenus to analyses of Dante, the *Chanson de Roland*, or Peter the Venerable. Second, I wanted the collection to reflect the wide range of medieval Christian interest in (or preoccupation with) Islam. The texts that our authors analyzed vary widely in genre (travelogue, miracle accounts, history, epic, polemic, exegesis, and so on), in language (Arabic, Syriac, Armenian, Latin, Greek, Italian, French, Spanish, and Dutch), and date of composition (from the seventh to the sixteenth centuries). The variety of Christian response to Islam will become clear, as will the persistence of several key themes.

The first generations of Christians to face Muslim invasions see Muslims as a formidable political and military force, but know and care little about their religious beliefs. It is only in the following generations, as the Christian majority assimilate to Arabic culture and convert in large numbers to Islam, that Islam becomes a religious threat; then and only then do Christians feel a need to confront the religious challenge of Islam, to fit it into the context of divine history, and to refute it through polemic. This same pattern occurs in two very different societies at opposite ends of the Mediterranean, as we see in Chapters 1 and 4 by John Lamoreaux and Kenneth B. Wolf, respectively.

Christians of the eastern Mediterranean had contact with Arabs long before the rise of Islam; the earliest Christian authors who discuss the Muslim conquest are largely ignorant of the religious nature of the dramatic military successes that they describe in detail. This is as true of chroniclers writing in Armenian, Syriac, or Greek in the seventh century as of those writing in Latin in the eighth century. While some writers consider the Muslim conquest divine punishment for Christian sins, they are unaware that their Muslim conquerors are not the Arab pagans familiar from texts of the Roman era.

As Arabic becomes the dominant language of the new Muslim empire and as conversion to Islam facilitates entry into government service, growing numbers of Christians convert to Islam.[4] Leaders of the Christian communities look on with alarm and seek ways both to explain and to stem this tide of conversions. Hence the need for anti-Muslim polemic, written not for a Muslim audience, but in order to convince Christians not to convert: Islam needs to be explained to the Christian faithful, its dramatic successes have to be placed logically in the context of a (Christian) divine plan, and Islam itself has to be shown to be some form of diabolical error.

Again, the articles of Lamoreaux and Wolf show a strikingly similar picture in seventh-century Syria and eighth-century Spain. In both cases, Christian polemicists explain Muslim success by putting it into an apocalyptic context (in the eastern Mediterranean, Maximius, Sophronius, Pseudo-Methodius, and the anonymous *Doctrine of Jacob Recently Baptized*; in Spain, Eulogius and Paul Alvarus). Various apocalyptic traditions had long predicted mass conversions to a "false" Judaism or Christianity, a sect of error with the outward appearance of piety; just as Jews had used these traditions to explain the successes of Christianity, now both Christians and Jews employ them to explain those of Islam. Muhammad (or Islam) is a manifestation of Antichrist.

This leads to defamatory biographies of the Prophet, something that soon becomes a staple of anti-Muslim polemic. Some of these biographies show familiarity with Muslim traditions; some reflect earlier polemics against heresiarchs such as Arius; some reflect—more than anything else—their authors' abilities to create wild images of depravity and perversity.[5]

Conversions and their concomitant tension at times lead to martyrdom. In the East, prominent Muslim converts to Christianity (such as Anthony of Ruwah) become martyrs. This conversion in the face of death is held up to local Christians as a testimony to the truth of Christianity. The cult centered at the new martyr's tomb gives focus and cohesion in the face of pressures to assimilate; the hagiographer, of course, writes of miracles produced at the tomb. In Córdoba, Christians seek martyrdom by deliberately attacking Islam and its prophet before a Muslim judge (*qadi*); the majority of Córdoba's Christians oppose this movement, and even its apologists admit to a lack of miracles produced by these new saints. These martyrs and their apologists are unsuccessfully trying to convince their compatriots that Islam is a diabolical heresy.

In northern Europe, far from the threat of Muslim invasion, ignorance about Islam—and indifference toward it—helps create the fantastic, diabolical, anti-Trinitarian Saracen idolatry of the chansons de geste. In the *Chanson de Roland*, the Saracens of Zaragoza worship a trinity of golden idols: Mahomet, Apollin, and Tervagant. They destroy the golden idol of Mahomet when it fails to prevent their defeat at the hands of Charlemagne. The Muslim here is the quintessential other, the ideal enemy. The basic outlines of this Saracen paganism are found in many other French epics.[6]

As northern Europe developed increasing contacts with the Muslim world (through trade, crusades, and translation of Arabic texts into Latin), a more thorough response to Islam became necessary. Two Latin authors of the late eleventh and early twelfth centuries responded by crafting defamatory verse biographies of Muhammad: Embrico of Mainz and Gauthier de Compiègne.[7] Embrico, weaving together elements of the eastern Christian polemical biographies of Muhammad and a sort of inversion of the *topoi* of hagiography, created a crude heresiarch that his readers could love to hate and whose followers they could safely hold in contempt. Tutored by a heretical Christian Magus, Muhammad preaches lechery and incest, stages bogus miracles, and puts to death Christians who oppose his new law.

After God punishes him with epilepsy, he explains away his fits by saying that his soul had left his body to commune with God. God kills him for his impieties and his corpse is devoured by pigs. The wily Magus places Muhammad's remains in an iron casket which is suspended by magnets, making the people believe that it floats through divine favor.

While authors north of the Pyrenees created an imaginary Islam that they could safely hold in contempt, those in Spain were forced to confront the real Islam; the most accurate information on Islam in medieval Europe comes from Spain. The ignorance about Islam that Wolf describes in some of the early Latin texts gives way as Christians learn Arabic. In the ninth century Paulus Alvarus, one of the Latin apologists for the Córdoba martyrs, complains that Andalusian Christians are more interested in learning Arabic than Latin.[8] Thomas Burman (in Chapter 5) demonstrates that by the twelfth century these Arabicized Christians, or Mozarabs, develop a new breed of anti-Muslim polemic that combines knowledge of three distinct textual traditions: Muslim holy writings (in particular Qur'ân and *Hadith*), Eastern anti-Muslim polemic, and Latin theology. Petrus Alfonsi, an Andalusian Jew who converted to Christianity in 1106, composed his *Dialogi contra Iudaeos* in 1110. In the fifth chapter of the *Dialogi* Alfonsi attacks Islam, following—to a large extent—the Arabic text attributed to 'Abd al-Masih b. Ishâk al-Kindî.[9]

In 1142 Peter the Venerable, abbot of Cluny, traveled to Spain to meet with Alfonso VII, king of Castile and León.[10] In the course of this voyage, it seems, Peter conceived a plan to forge a new, comprehensive, rationalist attack on Islam. He put together a team of translators and had the Qur'ân, the *Risala* of al-Kindî, and other texts translated into Latin. He also composed two polemical texts of his own. Later Spanish Christians, writing in the vernacular or in Latin, continued to have a knowledge of Islam superior to that of their northern contemporaries; in the fifteenth century, this fact is clear in the writings of Paul of Burgos and Juan de Segovia, as Philip Krey shows in Chapter 7.

Yet the old perceptions of Islam as idolatry die hard, not only in the Latin East but even in Byzantium. In Chapter 3, Craig L. Hanson examines a Byzantine polemical tradition that equates

Islam with idolatry and shows how Emperor Manuel I
Comnenus (1143–80) becomes embroiled in a controversy with
the orthodox ecclesiastical hierarchy when he argues that this is
inaccurate.

The twelfth and thirteenth centuries bring Islam more
prominently to the consciousness of northwestern Europeans,
both through the crusades and—perhaps more important—
through the arrival of Arab philosophy and science in European
centers of learning. Not surprisingly, this leads to new
apocalyptic speculation about the role of Islam in the divine
plan. Krey shows in Chapter 7 that some Latin theologians, such
as Alexander Minorita and Pierre Auriol, see the crusades as the
beginning of the end of Islam; Nicholas of Lyra argues, on the
contrary, that the Christian successes in the Crusades are but
minor impediments to an ever-expanding Islam. Apocalyptic
tradition had long predicted that an alliance of Christians,
Eastern and Western, would fight an international alliance of
Muslims, pagans, and heretics. Hence it is with foreboding that
Joachim of Fiore reports the rumored alliance between Muslims
and Cathars (as shown by David Burr in Chapter 6).

The invasions of the Mongols in the thirteenth and
fourteenth centuries lead to new apocalyptic speculations. Some
Christian exegetes identify the Mongols with Gog and Magog (as
Burr shows). Some Western Christians hope to unite with the
Mongols to form an anti-Muslim alliance;[11] some know that
there are Christians among the Mongol subjects. There are
stories that conversion of key groups of Muslims to Christianity
has already begun, and that these groups are ready to help
Christians recover Jerusalem (as William Patrick Hyland shows
in Chapter 9). When the Mongols convert to Islam, Christians in
both the East and West explain this in apocalyptic terms. It
seems (to the less cautious) that the world is uniting against the
Christians, that the forces of Gog and Magog have been
unleashed.

Apocalyptic scenarios are less common, it seems, in
Eastern Christian responses to Islamization of the Mongols. One
Armenian scribe, in a fourteenth-century colophon, identified
Muhammad as a forerunner of the Antichrist; another colophon
describes the Muslim Mongol leader Öldjaytu as resembling the

Antichrist. More commonly, however, persecution and conquest were seen as punishment for Christian sins (as David Bundy shows in Chapter 2).

An author's perceptions of Islam or of particular Muslims often depends on his political and military alliances. Bundy shows that Het'um II, a fourteenth-century king of Cilician Armenia, justified his alliance with the Muslim Mongol Il-Khan because he was the enemy of the Egyptians, and (Het'um claimed to believe) he intended to conquer Jerusalem and restore it to the Christians. The sixteenth-century speculations that the Shiite leader Isma'il Safavi was a crypto-Christian are informed by the same sort of political concerns (as Palmira Brummett shows in Chapter 15). Political purposes can work the other way, as well: John Phillip Lomax (Chapter 8) examines how Pope Gregory IX accuses Emperor Frederick II of Muslim sympathies in order to justify excommunicating him.

In their attempts to make sense of Islam, these medieval authors could draw on the theological tracts of earlier polemicists, from the defamatory biographies of Muhammad, and the apocalyptic passages of the Bible, to the Saracen idolatry of the French Epic tradition, and—occasionally—the experience of travelers to Muslim lands. Many authors combined two or more of these traditions in a single text: either awkwardly juxtaposing them or deftly weaving them together. In Chapter 10, Geert H.M. Claassens shows how Vincent of Beauvais, in his *Speculum historiale* (composed between 1246 and 1253) made use of both the polemical works of theologians and the defamatory biographies of Muhammad. When Jacob van Maerlant creates a Dutch version of Vincent's work, the *Spiegel Historiael* (1283–88), he rearranges Vincent's material in order to create a livelier narrative focused on the life of Muhammad.

Gloria Allaire (Chapter 11), in her analysis of the *Guerrino il Meschino* by Andrea da Barberino (c. 1371–1431), shows Andrea's curious blending of various and contradictory elements. At several points Andrea depicts Saracens worshiping Muhammad as a god and at times as part of the standard idolatrous trinity of the chansons de geste. Yet elsewhere he distinguishes clearly between paganism and Islam and condemns Muhammad as a false prophet. The protagonist

Guerrino sees Muhammad tortured in hell (in a passage reminiscent of Dante's *Inferno*, xxviii, 22–33) and reports seeing his casket suspended by magnets at the mosque in Mecca. Guerrino is both hostile to and dismissive of the religious practices of Saracens. Yet these polemical elements are secondary for Andrea: Guerrino is a mercenary fighting for Muslims, and at one point defending Mecca against a Turkish attack. Andrea's descriptions of religious practices (like those of eating habits) are more exotic than polemical.

This same spirit of exoticism pervades *Mandeville's Travels*, as we see in Chapter 12 by Frank Grady. The fictitious Sir John, like Andrea's Guerrino, is a Christian mercenary fighting for Muslims. Absent here, however, are the elements of the epic tradition; instead, Sir John throughout recognizes the monotheism of Islam and Muhammad's role as prophet. He admires the piety of Muslims, implying that it is superior to that of most Christians. This brings the *Travels* uneasily close to seeing Islam as a legitimate alternative to Christianity. The author avoids this by putting an apocalyptic prophecy in the mouth of the Muslim Sultan: Islam will end, and soon, through mass conversions of Muslims to Christianity. The end of Islam is clearly written in the divine plan, and Christian readers can generously indulge in their admiration of Muslim piety and culture.

Such confident magnanimity becomes impossible as Turkish armies march into the heart of Europe; clearly, Islam is not disappearing. Sixteenth-century Western writers exude fear of an expanding Islam and call, in many cases, for European military action against the Ottomans.

Gonzalo de Arredondo y Alvarado's *Castillo inexpugnable de la fe*, written at the behest of Charles V in 1528, is a call for renewal of crusade against the Turk and for Christian unity behind Charles. In Chapter 13, John S. Geary shows how Arredondo portrays Turks as barely human: violent, cruel, lustful, and bent on converting Christians to error. Since this is a call to war, portrayals of Islam as a religion can only be hostile. Drawing on a variety of medieval anti-Islamic texts, including the corpus of Peter the Venerable, Arredondo portrays Muhammad as a follower of the devil.

Muslims within the Spanish kingdoms also caused difficulties for Spanish rulers. In the newly conquered lands of Granada, conquest and forced conversion of Muslims sparked several Morisco revolts, which were in turn violently quelled. Ginés Pérez de Hita sympathized with the oppressed Moriscos, though he is forced to express these sympathies indirectly in his *Guerras civiles de Granada*, as Rhona Zaid shows in Chapter 14. He attacks violence and greed on the part of Spanish mercenaries, while he overlooks incidents of Morisco violence and avoids portraying the war as a conflict of religions: For example, he does not mention that the Moriscos had destroyed several churches and monasteries. Differences between Christian Spaniards and Moriscos are downplayed in order to emphasize their common humanity.

Europeans long hoped for an Eastern ally to aid in their fight against Islam: Prester John, the Mongols. In the early sixteenth century, a Shiite Türkmen arouses similar hopes: Isma'il Safavi. In Chapter 15, Palmira Brummett analyzes the growth of the European myth surrounding Isma'il: A potential ally against the Ottomans, his Shiism is made into a crypto-Christianity. While Europeans can no longer view Sunni Ottomans with the same kind of sympathy that one sees in *Mandeville's Travels*, Shiism is distant and exotic enough for such admiration. Some authors give the boy Isma'il an Armenian monk as his tutor; one even says that his mother was an Armenian Christian. These portrayals serve both to justify military allegiances with a non-Christian and to fuel hopes that some sort of apocalyptic solution to the problem of expanding Islam is at hand. Apocalyptic speculation is always tinged with a mix of hope and fear, hence some authors' ambivalence towards Isma'il: Is he Christian or Antichrist? Parts of the legend have him set himself up as a god, worshiped by his troops.

Throughout this period, we find a wide variety of Christian responses to Islam: from friendly to hostile, from condescending to fearful, from calls for crusade to plans for alliance. There is no unified Christian response to Islam, no universally accepted explanation of the role of Islam in the divine plan. Both as a rival religion and as a rival civilization,

Islam was tremendously successful. It was hence appealing, intriguing, and frightening. The attraction of Muslim learning, Muslim culture, and Muslim sophistication was extremely strong; it is what Maxime Rodinson has called "la fascination de l'Islam."[12] But the more Christians were attracted to Islam, the stronger others felt a need to condemn it—for it was this attraction, more than the might of Muslim armies, that was most threatening to Christendom. It is not unusual to see both this attraction and this repulsion expressed by the same author.

To a large extent, one's opinion of Islam is a product of how much one knows about Islam and of how much contact one has with Muslims. Perhaps even more important, though, are the needs and interests of the Christian author. If the Saracen (or Moor, or Turk) is the Other, he is an Other who may conveniently be deployed to fit the needs of each Christian author.

NOTES

1. On the translation and transmission of Arabic science to the West, see Lindberg, "The Transmission of Greek and Arabic Learning to the West," 52–90. His bibliography should be supplemented with several more recent works: D'Alverny, "Translations and Translators," 421–462; and Beaujouan, "Transformation of the Quadrivium," 463–497; and the articles in *La diffusione delle scienze islamiche nel medio evo europeo*.

2. Hodgson (*Venture of Islam* 1:57–60) distinguishes between these two ideas by using "Islam" only to refer to the religion and "Islamdom" to refer to Muslim civilization (on an analogy with "Christendom").

3. The most extensive bibliography of texts dealing with Christian-Muslim relations is Caspar et al., "Bibliographie du dialogue islamo-chrétien." For texts of Latin polemic, see Daniel, *Islam and the West*. The best introduction of Western Christian views of Islam remains Southern, *Western Views of Islam in the Middle Ages*. See also the recent survey by Berriot, "Remarques sur la Découverte de l'Islam par l'Occident," 11–25. The present collection is meant to complement two

recent collections of essays in the field: Gervers and Bikhazi, eds., *Conversion and Continuity: Indigenous Christian Communities in Islamic Lands, Eighth to Eighteenth Centuries*; Powell, ed., *Muslims under Latin Rule, 1100–1300*. The basic works on the Byzantine tradition are those of Adel-Théodore Khoury (listed in the Bibliography). For an overview of the situation in Spain, see Ron Barkai, *Cristianos y musulmanes en la España medieval*.

4. See Glick, *Islamic and Christian Spain in the Early Middle Ages*, 33–35, who presents a curve of conversion based on a series of informed hypotheses. No hard demographic data on conversion is available for this period.

5. I am currently writing a history of Christian biography of Muhammad.

6. The bibliography on the Saracen paganism of the chansons de geste is extensive; the most important recent works are those of Norman Daniel and Paul Bancourt. (Daniel, *Heroes and Saracens*. See bibliography for Bancourt's works.)

7. Embrico of Mainz, *Vita Mahumeti*; Gauthier de Compiègne, *Otia de Machomete*. D. M. Stone is in the process of translating both of these texts into English; see *Speculum* 66 (1991): 263, 267; 68 (1993): 290, 293. On Embrico's *Vita Mahumeti*, see Tolan, "Anti-Hagiography: Embrico of Mainz's *Vita Mahumeti*."

8. Paulus Alvarus, *Indiculus Luminosus*, sect. 35, in CSM 1:314–15.

9. On Alfonsi's work, see Tolan, *Petrus Alfonsi and His Medieval Readers*.

10. See Kritzeck, *Peter the Venerable and Islam*.

11. Southern, 42–52.

12. Rodinson, *La Fascination de l'Islam*.

I. Eastern Christian Responses to Islam

CHAPTER 1

Early Eastern Christian Responses to Islam

John C. Lamoreaux

In the seventh century the Muslims swept into the lands of Eastern Christianity; overnight a good portion of Orthodox believers lost their Christian empire.[1] Although the conquests were unexpected, they could not go unexplained. There was a need to account for the success of the Arabs and the apparent defeat of the Christians. This was especially true insofar as patristic authors had tended at times to identify religious truth with political success. One church father, for example, declared to the Jews that because they had sinned against their creator in crucifying Christ, their "good fortune has [been] transferred to the Romans."[2] For "if the Lord is righteous in all his ways and you, as you say, do not go astray, why has your people, your city, and your temple . . . received wrath like this?"[3] Such arguments were easily thrown back upon the Christians. The new prophet Muhammad declared, "The Jews and the Christians say: We are the sons of God and his beloved. Say: Why then does he punish you for your sins?"[4] Above and beyond such concerns, the Christians needed to find a way to live in the new and sometimes hostile environment ushered in by the Muslim invasions. Numerous texts produced by the Christians living under Islam addressed themselves to these concerns. Some were composed by Melkite (Orthodox) believers, others by Jacobites and Nestorians. In what follows the former will be of primary concern, though the latter will be touched on for the sake of contrast.

3

The Muslim Conquest and Its Aftermath

In the century preceding the Muslim conquests the Byzantine Empire had been growing ever more intolerant of its religious minorities. This intolerance was directed primarily against Jews, Samaritans, and Jacobites. The Nestorians had by then established themselves in Persia, and were thus little influenced by Byzantine policies. This persecution resulted in discontent and disloyalty among the religious minorities. In the sixth century the Samaritans led a number of revolts that were put down by the Byzantines only with great difficulty.[5] The Jews assisted the Persians during their invasion in the early seventh century and participated in the massacre and exile of tens of thousands of Christians.[6] One chronicler states that they killed more Christians than did the Persians.[7] Furthermore, from the middle of the sixth century the Jacobites had begun to organize an alternative ecclesiastical hierarchy that stood in opposition to that of the state-supported Melkites.[8]

The Melkite church of Syro-Palestine on the eve of the Muslim conquests had very little popular support. This was true especially in the Patriarchate of Antioch where its rival, the Jacobite church, could draw upon the support of villages, nomadic Arabs, and rural monasteries.[9] It was only in the Patriarchate of Jerusalem that there was significant popular support for the Melkites, but even there it seems to have been confined to urban centers. In addition, they were there opposed by the Jews and Samaritans who perhaps accounted for some 10 to 15 percent of the population.[10] To some extent the Melkite church leaders were looked upon as foreigners by the indigenes. The culture of Syro-Palestine had never been fully assimilated into the mold of the Hellenistic world.[11] The Jacobite church, on the other hand, was closer to the "roots" of local society, a fact reflected in its use of Syriac for liturgical purposes. There was, furthermore, a deep resentment on the part of the indigenes (whether Melkites or Jacobites) to Byzantine attempts at doctrinal compromise, especially the heresy of Monotheletism, which was first coming to be an issue of contention on the eve of the Muslim conquests.

And then the Muslims came. In 634 the Byzantines met the Arabs in battle at Ajnādayn, the ancient Yarmūth in the vicinity of Wādī al-Simt, some twenty-five kilometers southwest of Jerusalem.[12] The battle was hard fought, but eventually the Byzantines were routed and their commander killed. Again in 636 the opposing forces engaged at the battle of Yarmūk. The fighting was fierce, so that at first even the Muslim women were required to participate. Eventually, however, the Muslims gained the upper hand and inflicted a decisive defeat upon the Byzantines, many of whom were killed in the fighting and subsequent retreat. The courses of these two battles show that when the Byzantines met the Arabs on the field of battle, the former still proved a formidable enemy: their army was anything but moribund. The fighting was intense and the battles were lost only as a result of "divisions between the commanders and unfavorable terrain."[13] Nevertheless, although the Byzantines could not match the Arabs on the field, it would at least be expected that they could maintain their defenses in the cities, especially as the Arabs had little experience in siege warfare and lacked siege engines. Khâlid b. al-Walîd, for example, had to borrow ladders from a monastery in order to climb the walls of Damascus.[14] And yet, apart from Damascus and Caesarea, the cities put up little resistance. In most cases there was a token effort at defense (to receive favorable terms) or no effort at all. There seems to be no option but to conclude that the Byzantines lost Syro-Palestine because the towns did not resist the invaders. This unexpected defeat, as Gibbon with characteristic trenchancy once suggested, is indicative of changes that had taken place in Byzantine society: for "the empires of Trajan, or even of Constantine or Charlemagne, would have repelled the assault of the naked Saracens, and the torrent of fanaticism might have been obscurely lost in the sands of Arabia."[15]

It has been argued that the most probable explanation for this seemingly needless capitulation is to be found in the extensive demographic decline and economic weakness to which the cities of Syro-Palestine had been subject since the fifth decade of the sixth century.[16] It was no longer the land of cities with spacious agoras and thriving commerce, but "a country in fact more similar to Merovingian Gaul than to second- or fifth-century Syria."[17] The evidence for the decline of urban centers is impressive and hard to dispute. But here let us treat it as the background upon which danced the shadows of a more ethereal change: the breakdown of the ideals of *romanitas*. As will be argued in what follows, at the time of the Muslim conquest many inhabitants of the Byzantine empire no longer felt themselves subject to the demands of *romanitas*. Allegiance to one's religion or sect thereof weighed heavier on the conscience than duties to either city or state.[18] The religious character of the age is more redolent of Ottoman millets than of Constantine's or Theodosius's late antiquity.

Very little disruption of Melkite church life occurred during the conquests. The leaders of the Muslims were men who had long been used to the settled life; they were merchants who knew that the infrastructure of the conquered territories must be maintained. Archaeological evidence for church destruction is almost nonexistent. At Rihāb, Christians were able to dedicate two churches in the year 635, in the midst of the conquests and apparently unhindered by them.[19] Indeed, Orthodox building activity was greater between the years 635 and 640 than in the years following the Byzantine reconquest of Syro-Palestine from the Persians.[20] In general, it was in the Muslims' own interest to maintain the conquered communities intact, insofar as they provided a stable economic base for the nascent Muslim empire—as 'Alî, Muhammad's son-in-law, said with respect to the non-Muslims of the Sawād, "Leave them to be a source of revenue and aid for the Muslims."[21] Administrative papyri from Egypt, which date from within a few years of the conquests, give evidence for the remarkable degree of bureaucratic continuity maintained during the transition from Byzantine to Arab rule.[22] Later the stability of Syro-Palestine was subject to increasing strains with the shift of the Islamic capital to Baghdâd, a general economic decline, and an increase in nomadization, but these events fall outside the temporal limits of our present concern.[23]

However, life for the Melkites did not continue as before. Now that the sources and means of coercion had been removed from Christian hands, there came about a leveling of the various sects: all now stood equal as religious minorities in an Islamic land—minorities not with respect to numbers, but rather in their legal status. In effect, the Melkites lost their privileged position vis-à-vis the Jacobites and Nestorians, not to mention the few remaining communities of Montanists, Bardesanites, and Marcionites. This change is illustrated by the fact that it was only during the reign of the Umayyad caliphs that the first Nestorian monasteries appeared in Palestine—Tell Masos was founded sometime before 700, and the Monastery of the Mount of Olives is first attested in 739.[24] Similarly, in Egypt, the original sites of Egyptian monasticism which were in decline by the sixth century due to Byzantine persecution, underwent a revival in the context of stability provided for the Monophysites by the Muslims.[25] In much the same way, it was only under the Muslims that the Jews were able to transfer the Sanhedrin from Tiberias to Jerusalem, an action which would have been unthinkable under Byzantine rule.[26]

A second long-term consequence of the Muslim invasions: The Melkites under Islam were for all practical purposes cut off from their compatriots in Rome and Constantinople. Many of the Greek-speaking Christians and leaders fled before the Muslim conquerors to lands still held by Christians; they left behind a church in which the majority of believers were Syriac speakers, who, although Orthodox, would have considered much of Greco-Roman culture as foreign. This had the long term effect of semiticizing the Melkite church under Islam, with a concomitant recovery of their Syriac heritage and eventually their adoption of Arabic as a liturgical and theological language.[27] Offhand references in the life of St. Stephen of Mar Sabas show that by the late eighth century, Greek was all but unknown in the great monastery of Mar Sabas, its place having been taken by Syriac and Arabic.[28] Moreover, following the death of Theodore Abū Qurrah in 820, we know of few Greek compositions originating from the Melkite Church under Islam.[29] Theodore himself composed the majority of his works in Syriac and Arabic. He also wrote a number of Greek tracts, but these were short and some were even translations from Arabic originals.

Once the Arabs were able to establish a working bureaucracy in Syro-Palestine, they quickly imposed land and head taxes upon all non-Muslim inhabitants.[30] The Muslims were subject to a different and lighter set of religious taxes.[31] Our sources often speak of the burdensome nature of these taxes and the inducement they gave Christians to convert to Islam. One Syriac chronicler writes:

> The extortions and the poll tax on the Christian people were intensified beyond measure and began to bring about devastation on the earth. . . . The Christians, however, lest the tributes in the Arab epoch become more and more heavy, beyond their endurance, and [lest] the evils of the bitter extortions suddenly suffocate them, and [since] they had not yet learned to escape from one place to another, and [since] here the gate into paganism [i.e., Islam] opened to them—all the wanton and slack slipped into the pitfall and the well of perdition.[32]

The sheer terror raised by tax season is well seen in the *Vita* of St. Stephen of Mar Sabas where the beatings and threats of the tax collector caused even a church official to seek refuge in the protection offered by conversion to Islam.[33] Muslim sources report a similar state of affairs. The governor of Egypt, for example, wrote to 'Umar II (717–720) and informed him that Christians were converting to Islam in order to escape their taxes.[34]

Added to these general fiscal burdens, Christians were subject to various social indemnities meant to emphasize their subordinate status in Islamic society. Many of the restrictions on Christians that appear in later literary sources seem to belong to the last half of the Umayyad period. In the reign of 'Abd al-Malik (685–705) many Christians were dismissed from administrative posts in the Muslim bureaucracy when the language of the state registers was changed from Greek to Arabic.[35] At the same time there was initiated a public campaign for the destruction of images offensive to Muslim sensibilities.[36] It was also at this time that archaeological evidence begins to suggest that a moderately widespread destruction of images was taking place in the churches of Syro-Palestine.[37] A decade or so later, in the reign of 'Umar II, it was reported that Christians were forbidden to pray loudly in their churches, to ride horses with saddles, to ring the bells in their churches, and to dress like Arab soldiers.[38] 'Umar II is also said to have ruled that if an Arab killed a Christian, that Arab must pay a blood price of five thousand dirhems, but that he could not be executed for his crime.[39] The total effect of all these incidents is best illustrated by the fact that Christians were using only one-half the number of churches in 750 that they had used in 600.[40]

The changing circumstances of the late seventh century would naturally have tended to impress upon the Melkite Church leaders the danger that Islam was beginning to pose to Christianity. Here was a threat to the popular base of the church, the first since the accession of Constantine. Furthermore, and more significant, the various restrictions imposed by the Muslims would have had great effect upon the hierarchy of the church and its ability to function independently under Muslim rule, as well as upon its ability to provide spiritual and material relief for its flocks.

Roman Views of the Pre-Islamic Arabs

Before turning to the earliest Christian responses to the Muslims, it should be remembered that the Romans were not unfamiliar with the Arabs prior to the Muslim conquests. For centuries late-Roman authors had drawn upon the reservoir of Jewish, pagan, and biblical writings, and on the basis of this material had formulated an image of the Arabs as a race of people with an innate ferocity and proclivity to heresy. Ammianus Marcellinus (d.c. 400), for example, in describing the battle of Adrianople which took place in 378 and in which the Romans were aided by Arab mercenaries, wrote:

> The contest was long and drawn out, both sides separated on equal terms. But the [Arabs] had the advantage from a new event, never before seen. One of them, a man with long hair, naked except for a loin-cloth, uttering hoarse and dismal cries, with drawn dagger rushed into the thick of the Gothic army, and after killing a man applied his lips to his throat and sucked the blood that poured out. The [Goths], terrified by this strange and monstrous sight, after that did not show their usual self-confidence.[41]

Reports such as this, which mention the fierceness of the Arabs as warriors and as the "robbers of Arabia," abound in both pagan and Christian literature.[42] Unless by chance they had converted to "the rational flock of Christ," as indeed many did, they were but the "wolves of Arabia."[43]

Pre-Islamic authors also associated the Arabs with the characters of Judeo-Christian sacred history. On the basis of the book of Genesis they often described the Arabs as the descendants of Abraham through Hagar. This allowed the Christians to understand the various names by which the Arabs were known, even before the rise of Islam. They were called "Saracens" because Hagar had been sent away from Sarah empty *(Sarra-kenê)*. They were called "Ishmaelites" insofar as they were descended from Ishmael. They were called "Hagarians" due to Ishmael's birth from Hagar. These fictitious genealogies could sometimes be called upon to serve theological duty. For example, concerning St. Euthymios's treatment of Arab converts to Christianity, Cyril of Skythopolis, abusing Paul's Epistle to the Galatians, said that

> [St. Euthymios] kept [the Arab converts] with himself for forty days, illuminating and confirming them with the word of God. He then allowed them to depart, no longer Agarenes and Ishmaelites, but descendents of Sarah and heirs to the promises, by baptism transferred from servitude to freedom.[44]

Such identifications as these date back at least to the first century before Christ. We find them in Jewish authors such as Josephus, as well as in the writings of pagan authors.[45] Molon, for example, a Greek historian from the first century B.C., whose work survives only in fragments, told how Ishmael went off to Arabia with his twelve sons and became a ruler there. This, he said, accounts for the fact that there are twelve kings of Arabia who bear the names of Ishmael's first twelve sons.[46]

With respect to the religion of the Arabs, here also information abounds in pre-Islamic Christian, Jewish, and pagan literature. Clement of Alexandria and Arnobius, among others, inform us that the Arabs worshiped a stone.[47] Josephus and Sozomen speak of the Arabs' Jewish customs. They are circumcised at the age of 13, because "Ishmael, the founder of their race, born of Abraham's concubine was circumcised at that age."[48] They abstain from pork and practiced many other Jewish customs, indeed, "many among them still live in a Jewish fashion."[49] Certain pagan authors saw the Arabs as a source of arcane knowledge.[50] Similarly, and in a more sinister fashion, there are accounts in Jewish and Christian literature of Arab customs such as child sacrifice, demon worship, and magic. In the Talmud, for example, with reference to Genesis 25:5–6 ("Now Abraham gave all that he had to Isaac; but to the sons of his concubines, Abraham gave gifts while he was still living, and sent them away from his son Isaac eastward, to the land of the east.") Rabbi ben Abba says that the only gifts which were imparted by Abraham to the Ishmaelites were the "unholy arts" of magic.[51] The land of Arabia also had a reputation as something of a breeding ground of heresy. John of Skythopolis, an early sixth-century commentator on the works of Pseudo-Dionysius, in reference to a text in the writings of Dionysius wherein Elymas the magician is mentioned, says rather offhandedly that Arabia has many like unto Elymas who profess various Christological heresies.[52]

Examples like these could be multiplied endlessly; but the point, I think, is clear. The Christian authors who first encountered the Muslims would not do so *tabula rasa*; rather, they would bring to their first interpretations of Islam and its place in sacred history a whole series of unfavorable stereotypes. This is especially true insofar as many of these authors, in particular the Melkite ones, were unable or unwilling to distinguish between Arabs and Muslims.

The Religious Minorities and Islam

The earliest responses to the Muslims on the part of religious minorities were in general quite favorable. In 634, on the eve of the conquests, the Emperor Heraclius issued an edict which commanded that all Jews in the Empire be baptized.[53] In order to escape forced conversion Palestinian, Syrian, and Egyptian Jews fled in large numbers both to the protection of Persia and to the invading Muslims.[54] Sebēos likewise reports that certain Jews acted as guides for the Arabs in their invasion of Palestine.[55] Furthermore, we are told by the Muslim historian al-Balâdhurî that a certain Jew named Joseph led the Arabs through a secret passage under the walls into Caesarea, thus facilitating its downfall.[56] The Samaritans of Palestine aided the invading Muslims to such an extent that they were later exempt from certain taxes.[57] Al-Balâdhurî also reports that, like the Jews, they supported the Arabs as spies and guides.[58] By 639 the Samaritan council and high priest were reestablished, and this with the permission of the Caliph Abû Bakr. As a result, it was for some time popular for Samaritans to name their children after their new patron.[59]

There are but few sources originating from the hands of Jews or Samaritans that allow us insight into their own perceptions of the Islamic conquests, and those that are extant are difficult to use. One such source is a piyyū t or liturgical poem that was composed after the initial Arab victories but before the fall of Jerusalem and Caesarea.[60] In this work it is clear that Jewish perceptions of the conquests were initially extremely positive, indeed, were imbued with an apocalyptic fervor which understood the conquests as presaging the coming of the Messianic age.

> The king of the West and the king of the East
> Will be ground against one another,
> And the armies of the king of the West will hold firm in
> the Land.
>
> And a king will go forth from the land of Yoqtān
> And his armies will seize the Land,
> The dwellers of the world will be judged
> And the heavens will rain dust on the earth,
> And winds will spread in the Land.[61]

In this passage the author refers first to the battles between Byzantium and Persia in the early seventh century that resulted in the devastation of the Persian army and territory, and then speaks of the armies of Yoqtān, one of the sons of Eber known from the book of Genesis (10:25–30), the eponymous ancestor of the southern Arabian tribes. This and similar sources, although lacking in historical detail, tell us at the very least that there was present in the Jewish community at the time of the Muslim invasions the hope that these events would at last free the Jews from the yoke of infidel rule and usher in the Messianic age.[62]

When we examine the earliest non-Melkite Christian sources we find a similar enthusiasm, but without the strong apocalyptic overtones present in Jewish responses to the Muslims. Īšō'yaw III, Nestorian Catholicos in the 650s, in his fourteenth epistle wrote with respect to the Muslims:

> These Arabs, whom God has now given sovereignty over the world, are disposed towards us as you know. They are not opposed to Christianity. Indeed, they respect our religion and honor the priests and the saints of our Lord and they give aid to the churches and monasteries.[63]

This is more than rhetoric: As was mentioned above, Nestorian monasteries first began to appear in Palestine only under the Muslims. Clearly, the rule of the Muslims was for the Nestorians a better state of affairs than had been the rule of the Byzantines. Similarly, when the Arabs were forced to abandon Emesa due to Byzantine advances under Theodore, they returned to the inhabitants taxes that had been collected insofar as they were now no longer able to give their protection to the inhabitants. At this moment the residents said that they preferred the Arabs to the tyranny of the Byzantines. This is probably more than propaganda: the story is recorded in both Christian and Muslim sources.[64] In 661 the Monophysite Armenian bishop Sebēos wrote of Muhammad that he was learned in the law of Moses, that he taught the Arabs to know the God of Abraham, and that for their part by "abandoning the reverence of vain things, they turned toward the living God, who had appeared to their father Abraham."[65] He further explained that God intended to fulfill in the Arabs the promises made to Abraham and his descendants, for which reason the Arabs were to possess the territory that God had granted to Abraham.[66] Thus, they left the desert and with God's help overcame the armies of Byzantium.[67] The Monophysite chronicler John of Nikiu in the last decades of the seventh century wrote of the conquests that God, "the guardian of justice," allowed the Islamic conquests for the sake of his persecuted people, the Monophysites, and as punishment upon those who "had dealt treacherously against Him," to wit, the

Orthodox.[68] A later Monophysite chronicler explained that the Byzantines had been given over to the Muslims "as a punishment for their corrupt faith," and because of their heretical acceptance of the decrees of the Council of Chalcedon.[69] In the early eighth century, when the Muslims were seeking to consolidate their control over Caucasian Albania, they were aided by factions from within that did not want the Monophysite Albanian church to submit itself to the authority of the Byzantine Orthodox church.[70] The uniform nature of the responses of the non-Melkites, whether Jews, Samaritans, Monophysites, or Nestorians, although understandable given the realities of the social and political developments outlined, is even more striking when contrasted with the equally unanimous and diametrically opposed Melkite responses to the Muslim invasions.

The Earliest Melkite Views of Islam

Between the years 634 and 640 Maximus the Confessor, while staying in Alexandria, wrote a letter to Peter the Illustrious.[71] In the course of the letter Maximus exhorts Peter to pray and remain awake.[72]

> And especially when . . . nature herself teaches us to take refuge in God, when she uses the present dire circumstances as a symbol. For what could be more dire than the present evils now encompassing the civilized world? . . . To see a barbarous nation of the desert overrunning another land as if it were their own! To see our civilization [*politeia*] laid waste by wild and untamed beasts who have merely the shape of a human form![73]

Maximus goes on to describe the Arabs as "a Jewish people who . . . delight in human blood . . . whom God hates, though they think they are worshipping God."[74] The author hints at how the Arabs are "announcing the advent of the Antichrist" and storing up wrath against themselves on the day of judgment.[75] He then explains the cause of the Arabs' success—Christian sins!

> For we have not conducted ourselves in a manner worthy of the Gospel of Christ. . . . We have all acted like wild

> beasts towards one another, ignorant of the grace of God's
> love for humans, and the mystery of the sufferings of the
> God who became flesh for our sakes.[76]

And finally he exhorts his readers to remain fast in their orthodoxy, to avoid persecution as long as possible, and if necessary, to suffer death for their faith.[77] In general, although Maximus hints at the conquests as announcing the advent of the Antichrist, his emphasis is on its function as a temporary divine chastisement for Christian sins. The impression one gets from the letter is that all that needs to be done in order to turn back the Muslim tide is a sincere communal repentance.[78]

Another source for early Melkite views of Islam is the writings of Sophronius, Patriarch of Jerusalem (d. 639).[79] He mentions the Arabs in three contexts: a Christmas sermon of 634,[80] a synodical epistle of 634,[81] and an Epiphany sermon of 637.[82] Though much of his ink is spilt recounting Saracen misdeeds—"Why is the flow of blood continual? Why are bodies prey for the birds of the sky? Why are churches destroyed and the cross insulted?"[83]—at times he attempts to understand the significance of what was then beginning to happen. He claims that the Christians were experiencing these tribulations because of their own wickedness, and like Maximus he thought that repentance would turn the Muslim advances.[84] At the same time we find in his works the beginnings of an apocalyptic understanding of Islam. In his Epiphany sermon he calls the Arabs the "Abomination of Desolation predicted by the prophets."[85] We are further told by Theophanes the Chronicler (whom Gibbon calls "the father of many lies") that when 'Umar first entered Jerusalem, Sophronius cried out, "Verily, this is the Abomination of Desolation established in the holy place, of which the prophet Daniel spoke," and that with many tears the white-haired champion of Orthodoxy "lamented over the Christian people."[86] Absent from the works of Sophronius, as well as from those of Maximus, is any sense that the Arabs were spurred by a new religion. He refers to them as "filled with all diabolical savagery," "godless Saracens," "godless and impious," and so on[87]—a tirade worthy of Cyril of Alexandria. He has no concept of the religious nature of the conquests.

A third early reference to the conquests occurs in a rather unusual work entitled *The Doctrine of Jacob Recently Baptized*, which dates from within a few years of the onset of the Muslim invasions.[88] Although most likely a work of theological fiction, the text purports to be a dialogue taking place in July of 634 between a Jew recently converted to Melkite Christianity, by the name of Jacob, and his Jewish friend, Justus, both of whom had arrived at Carthage from Palestine in that year.[89] Jacob had come first, been forcibly baptized, thrown into prison, and while there become convinced of the truth of Christianity through reading the scripture. He then argued with the other Jews of Carthage and convinced them that Jesus was the Messiah. When Justus arrived he condemned Jacob for what he had done. There follows in the text an account of the dialogue between Jacob and Justus. Justus is not convinced that the Messiah has already come, because the fourth beast of Daniel 7:23ff. (the Roman Empire) has not yet fallen to the ten horns, nor has the little horn, Hermolaus Satan, yet come. Eventually Justus agrees that the fourth beast has fallen, the ten horns have come, and that the little horn has arisen, for "truly we can see a diminution of the empire of the Romans."[90] The clinching argument is given by Justus himself, whose brother, Abraham, had written to him from Caesarea that "a deceiving prophet has appeared among the Saracens."[91] At his coming the Jews rejoiced, for his Saracen followers had killed the hated Byzantine official, Sergius the *candidatus*.[92] It is further reported by Abraham that this prophet was preaching the advent of "the Coming One, even Christ."[93] When Abraham referred this matter to a learned Jewish scribe, he was told that this prophet "is a deceiver, for prophets do not come with swords and chariot, do they?"[94] Abraham goes on to say that he has heard from those with this prophet that "you can find nothing true in the so-called prophet, except the slaughter of men."[95] This is more than enough evidence to convince Justus that this new prophet is indeed the little horn, Hermolaus Satan, and that the Christ whom the Christians worship is the true Christ.

In the accounts examined the outline of a clear pattern has begun to emerge. All felt called to give explanations of the Arab's success. The Melkites, those who had lost their empire, ascribed the success of the Muslims to Christian sins. After the fashion of the Deuteronomic cycle, the Arabs are seen as a temporary divine chastisement intended by God to bring the Christians back to a righteous manner of life. At the same time there is a hint of apocalypticism in the works of Maximus and Sophronius, although its significance is tempered by the more general themes of chastisement and repentance, and this to such an extent that one is almost tempted to see it as more rhetoric than serious sentiment. The case is otherwise with the *Doctrine of Jacob*. Hermolaus Satan (i.e., Muhammad) is seen as a deceiving prophet whose coming has brought about the end of the Roman Empire. He is the final piece in the eschatological puzzle, the little horn of Daniel. Our anonymous author's whole framework for understanding the Muslim conquests is apocalyptic. Furthermore, none of the three authors we have examined sees any positive value in what was beginning to happen. The Arabs were either without religion, or were under the sway of a false prophet. Our authors, especially Maximus, constantly contrast the civilization of Christian Byzantium to the beastly character of the Arabs. Unlike Īšōʻyaw III they cannot hope for increased freedom, and unlike Sebēos they cannot see anything positive in the new religion of the Arabs.

In the case of Jews and Samaritans, although we have few accounts from their own hands, their actions would seem to suggest that they welcomed the Muslims, or at the very least, that they aided the Muslims to the best of their ability, limited though it was as a result of various Byzantine indemnities. At the same time there seem to have been present in the Jewish community Messianic expectations which saw the defeat of the Byzantines and Persians as a harbinger of the eschatological age. This really should not be surprising, given the high degree of Messianic fervor present in the Jewish community at the time of the Persian conquests in the early seventh century. Jacobites and Nestorians also appear to have looked upon the Muslim conquests with a guarded hope for increased freedom. At the same time, there were some who, like Sebēos, saw positive religious value in the new monotheism of the Arabs and who ascribed to this monotheism a place in the sacred history of Judaism and Christianity. Other Monophysite authors, mostly of a later date, saw the defeat of the Byzantines as a punishment for their heresy and their persecution of the Monophysites.

The responses of the religious minorities taken as a whole show that the Muslim invasions were looked upon as a generally positive state of affairs by the non-Melkite inhabitants of Syro– Palestine—not usually because of some inherent value attached to Islam *per se*, but rather insofar as the events were seen as playing an important role in the maintenance and furtherance of the communities of the religious minorities themselves. The bonds and duties of the Christian empire of Byzantium were no longer of cardinal importance; they had been replaced by the religious communities themselves as the primary locus of identity and obligation. A change has taken place. In order to appreciate its extent and significance consider, for example, Joshua the Stylite's account of the Persian war of the early sixth century. He saw the devastation wrought by the Persians as a chastisement from the hand of God to bring back his chosen people, the Christians of Byzantium, to a holy manner of life. [96] In his understanding of the significance of the Persian invasion the bonds of city and state remain strong. Joshua's devotion to Anastasius, "the believing emperor," is still very much in the fashion of the earlier age of Constantine and Theodosius. [97] Furthermore, civic pride and trust in the fact that Edessa is "the city of Christ" are strong themes in the work. [98] This is even more striking when we remember that Joshua was himself a Monophysite and that he wrote in the vicinity of Edessa, a stronghold for the non-Chalcedonian traditions. In his work the bonds of *romanitas* are immeasurably stronger than they were to be a little over one hundred years later when the Muslims invaded Syro-Palestine.

Melkite Reassessments of Islam

In time, these early explanations are no longer satisfying. The liberated find that they have not been liberated, whereas those who have lost their power find that they have not lost as much as they thought. When the Christians realize that the Muslims are there to stay, new strategies must be devised to account for the continuing presence of the Muslims and to provide a way of living under their rule. The element of explanation is not as strong in these later responses. Its place has been taken by an almost tacit acceptance of the fact that the Muslims' presence is permanent, at least until the apocalyptic end is ushered in. Of paramount importance in these later responses is rather the need to establish the religious legitimacy of Christianity. Above and beyond the rising tides of conversion to Islam, the mere existence of Islam and its claims to have succeeded Christianity represented a challenge to the leaders of the Christian communities.

Toward the end of the seventh century there was a massive surge of apocalyptic activity among the Jews and Christians living under Islam. Among the Jews, for example, Abû'Îsâ of Isfahan in the late seventh or early eighth century claimed to be a prophet and harbinger of the Messiah.[99] He revolted against the Muslims and was joined by numerous Persian Jews. Although eventually he was killed and his army defeated, his followers claimed that he was not dead, but instead had entered a cave and disappeared. The movement that he had founded (the Isunians or Isfahanians) is known to have continued in existence as late as the tenth century.[100] At about the same time there began to appear among Christians and Jews a number of apocalyptic works dealing with Islam. These include the apocalypses of Pseudo-Athanasius,[101] John the Less,[102] Esdras,[103] Samuel,[104] and Rabbi Simon ben Yōhay.[105]

Another such text is the *Apocalypse of Pseudo-Methodius*, an extremely popular work which was early on translated into Greek and from which, in turn, Slavonic and Latin versions were made.[106] The original Syriac text was composed between 685 and 692. Its author was probably Orthodox, although his work was widely read by the Jacobites and Nestorians as well.[107] In what follows the Syriac version is utilized. Therein it is stated that the Muslims were given to rule over the Christians for their punishment and purification, until "few from many will be left over who are Christians," not because God loved the Muslims, but because the Christians had sinned exceedingly.[108] In this way Christians will be "tried and the believers be separated from the unbelievers ... because that time [will] indeed [be] a testing furnace."[109] But then suddenly a king of the Greeks will come forth in wrath and reduce the Muslims to a servitude one hundred times more severe than their own.[110] A time of incomparable peace will be established, until the Alexandrian Gates of the North will be shattered and the nations hitherto held in abeyance will descend upon the civilized world for one week.[111] The king of the Greeks with angelic help will destroy them in one hour, allow his diadem to ascend to heaven, and then die.[112] After this, the Son of Perdition will be revealed, but quickly delivered into Hellfire, while the saints enter into the heavenly kingdom, where they "shall offer up praise and honor and veneration and exaltation now and at all times for ever and ever."[113] In the apocalypse of Methodius we find not so much a giving up of earlier views of Islam, but an incorporation and expansion of those views. The invasions are still seen as punishment for Christian sins, but this punishment is now placed firmly within an apocalyptic framework that interprets all events in terms of cosmic history and an imminent end.

A second type of new response consisted of initial attempts at doctrinal refutation, which is to say, polemics.[114] This activity can be found among all sects of Christians. Our earliest Melkite example is Anastasius of Sinai (d.c. 700), a monk and polemicist against the heresy of Monotheletism. In his third sermon he connects the success of the Arabs with Constans II's (641–48) exile of Pope Martin I (d. 655) for his resistance to the *Ekthesis* and *Typos*.[115] Elsewhere he attempts to refute the Muslims—though seldom by name, speaking instead of "unbelievers" or "certain men."[116] Occasionally he refers to Quranic stories and Islamic doctrines such as Satan's refusal to bow down to Adam[117] or Muslim rejections of the Trinity.[118] In general, he seldom attempts an outright refutation of specific Islamic doctrines, but contents himself with assimilating those doctrines to earlier theological errors, whether of the Jews, Manichaeans, Severian Monophysites, or Samaritans.[119]

Among the Melkites the project started by Anastasius really only began to blossom some fifty years later in the works of John of Damascus (d. 749) and still later in those of Theodore Abū Qurrah (d.c. 820).[120] Characteristic of these later works is their pastoral intent. The treatises are directed toward the

Christian community itself: they are written in simple Greek or Arabic and the format is such that they provide easily remembered arguments that could be used by Christians challenged with the claims of Islam. It seems likely that bishops and monks were composing such treatises in an effort to stem the growing tide of conversion that was at that time first beginning to threaten the Christian communities. As an example of this sort of text and their polemic strategy, as well as their pastoral intent, consider the following *opusculum* that Theodore Abū Qurrah composed in the late eighth century.[121] It is in dialogue form and opens with an Arab asking a Christian the following question:

> A.   [Arab] Tell me, is Christ your God?
> X.   [Christian] Yes.
> A.   Do you have another God besides Him?
> X.   No.
> A.   Are then the Father and the Spirit of absolutely no value to you?
> X.   Listen! Your scripture in reality stands here, having come down from heaven, as you claim. I ask you, do you have any other scripture besides this?
> A.   I answer that I have no other.
> X.   Do you therefore disown all other scripture?
> A.   Yes.
> X.   What? If another book were present, having the same scripture, would you disown that scripture?
> A.   It is not a different scripture, but the same, even if it exists in different books.
> X.   Well then, I also say that the Father and the Spirit are not different things besides the Son, even if He is found in a different hypostasis.

Clearly not a terribly sophisticated argument! Taken by itself, it would lead one to suspect that the Persons of the Trinity are really nothing more than reflections of some archetypal Godhead—a teaching not likely to pass muster in the sophisticated theological environment of Abû Qurrah's day. Nonetheless, one can well imagine the aged bishop of Harrān teaching his beleaguered congregation such arguments in an effort to shore up the community against the tides of conversion.

Another way that the Christians under Islam attempted to reconcile themselves to the continuing presence of the Muslims was through the production of new hagiographical texts and the promotion of new cults. The *passiones* of these neomartyrs, whether or not they record historical events, play a subtle role in the Christians' attempt to acquire religious legitimacy. These texts are in many respects exercises in Christian polemics against Islam.[122] They often contain extended discourses on the legitimacy of Christianity. Many of them attempt to portray in the sharpest colors the contrasts between Christian perseverance and Islamic roguery. Consider, for example, the life of St. Anthony Ruwah, who was martyred under Hārūn al-Rashīd on Christmas Day 799.[123]

Our soon-to-be saint was of the Arab nobility and a member of the tribe of Quraysh, the same tribe from which Muhammad himself had sprung. Later church tradition goes further and makes him a close relative of Hārūn al-Rashīd.[124] He lived near Damascus in a monastery dedicated to St. Theodore, which the Muslims had confiscated and converted into a government palace. Although the monastery had been confiscated, the Christians were apparently still allowed to hold services in the sanctuary. Our earliest account of his life records that Ruwah was wont to steal the elements of holy communion, vandalize the crosses and coverings of the altar, and terrorize the priests when they prepared mass.[125] One day when the church was empty, Ruwah shot an arrow at the icon of St. Theodore; miraculously, however, the arrow returned and pierced his own hand instead.[126] A few days later, as Ruwah watched the priests prepare communion, instead of the elements of bread and wine, he saw a "lamb whiter than snow kneeling and above it a white dove fluttering."[127] That night as Ruwah lay pondering what he had seen, he was visited by St. Theodore, mounted and in arms, who chastised him for his behavior toward the priests and the church.[128] As dawn was breaking "faith in our Lord Jesus Christ fell upon his heart like fire."[129] He then proceeded to travel to Jerusalem, where he asked the Patriarch to baptize him.[130] The Patriarch, however, refused for fear of Muslim reprisals and instead sent him to the river Jordan where Christ would baptize him in secret.[131] Two days' journey brought him to the river

Jordan—more precisely, to the very spot upon which Christ himself had been baptized—and there he met two monks who baptized him and clothed him in the monastic habit.[132] When he returned to Damascus, his family denounced him to the chief judge of Damascus for his apostasy.[133] Eventually, after severe trials and a long imprisonment, he was brought before the Caliph Hârûn al-Rashîd.[134] When Ruwah refused the Caliph's offer of money and honor in exchange for his reconversion to Islam, he was beheaded and crucified on the banks of the Euphrates.[135] While the body hung from its gibbet, signs appeared in the sky at night; thus the Caliph was forced to intern the body in a place called "the Convent of the Olives," but to no avail, for many had already come to believe in Christ.[136]

The general course of events here is much the same as in other texts: for example, the *passiones* of St. Abo of Tbilisi (d. 786),[137] St. Pachomios (d.c. 800),[138] and St. 'Abd al-Masîh (d.c. 860).[139] In each case it is an Arab and former Muslim who is martyred. Also, the Muslim is usually presented as being either a government official or at least someone very learned in the Islamic religion. Such a representation increases the polemical value of the texts. If highly placed members of your religious opponents convert, the legitimacy of your own religion is thereby increased—even more so if they are Arabs by birth and learned enough to know what they are rejecting. The value of such saints is further emphasized by the almost immediate propagation of their cults. St. Anthony Ruwah, for example, was venerated within a few years of death, as is clear from an offhanded reference in Theodore Abû Qurrah's tract on the veneration of icons:

> In our own day there was a famous martyr, a convert of the [Arab] nobility. His account is well known. May Christ remember us by means of his prayers! His name was Mar Anthony. He was wont to tell everyone whom he met that he had come to believe in Christianity only because of a miracle which he had seen respecting the icon of St. Theodore."[140]

Ruwa, though himself a Melkite, came eventually to be venerated among the Maronites and Monophysites. Further, his cult was celebrated in Ethiopia, Georgia, and Syro-Palestine.[141]

New saints, such as St. Anthony Ruwah, clearly fulfilled a need that older saints were unable to meet—that of establishing religious legitimacy for the Church under Islam.

Conclusion

Early Christian responses to the Muslims were far from monolithic: various strategies were employed by different authors at different times. In part, this diversity was a result of the social and political realities with which the Christians had to deal both before and after the Muslim conquests. The religious minorities welcomed the change of rulers, whereas the Melkites, those who had connected their fate with that of an empire, looked upon the new state of affairs with fear and trembling. Despite this marked diversity, however, in every case the need to account for the Muslims is manifest. A category for them had to be found; a place in sacred history had to be assigned. Only thus were the Christians able to maintain their worldview intact and find a way of living in the new milieu ushered in by the Muslim conquests. At the same time, during this crucial period of transition it is possible to detect a far subtler change, the breakdown of *romanitas* and the duties that it entailed vis-à-vis civic and imperial loyalty. Religion and one's sect thereof had begun to displace the empire as a locus of identity.

On the basis of the few sources that remain, I have attempted to outline the various types of Christian responses to the Muslims in relation to their very concrete and often bitter contexts. But it must be emphasized that these are intellectual responses. What we do not know, what would really illuminate the nature of early Eastern Christian perceptions of the Muslims, is the day-to-day religious life of the Christians in relation to their new Muslim overlords. What happened, for example, to monastery landholdings? How did the loss of imperial support affect the church's ability to maintain its properties, charities, and missionary work? We would further like to know how lay views of the hierarchy changed when the Muslims began to interfere in the election of church officials and to depose recalcitrant leaders for more malleable candidates. Though we have glimmers of the high ecclesiastical and monastic responses to the Muslims, the effect of the conquests upon the day-to-day functioning of the Church and upon the great majority of Christian believers remains in near-total darkness.

NOTES

1. This is a revised version of a paper presented at the 26th International Congress on Medieval Studies, May 1991.

2. *Disputation of Sergius the Stylite against A Jew*, CSCO 338/339 (1973), 70 (T = text), 69 (V = version).

3. Ibid., 72 (T), 70 (V).

4. Sūrah 5, 18.

5. Crown, "The Samaritans in the Byzantine Orbit," 127–138.

6. Avi-Yonah, *The Jews of Palestine*, 266.

7. Eutychius, *Das Annalenwerk des Eutychios von Alexandrien*, 128 (T), 108 (V).

8. Frend, "Severus of Antioch and the Origins of the Monophysite Hierarchy, 261–275"; idem, *The Rise of the Monophysite Movement*.

9. On the relative distribution of Christian sects, see Honigmann, *Évêques et évêches monophysites d'Asie antérieure au VIe siècle*; idem, *Le Couvent de Barsauma et le patriarcat Jacobite d'Antioche et de Syrie*; Kennedy, "The Melkite Church from the Islamic Conquest to the Crusades: Continuity and Adaptation in the Byzantine Legacy," 325–343.

10. Avi-Yonah, *The Jews of Palestine*, 241.

11. Hitti, *History of Syria*, 417: "At its thickest Hellenistic culture was only skin-deep, affecting a crust of intelligentsia in urban settlements."

12. Donner, *The Early Islamic Conquests*, 129.

13. Kennedy, "The Last Century of Byzantine Syria," 145.

14. al-Balādhurī, *Kitāb Futūh al-Buldān*, 121.

15. Gibbon, *The Decline and Fall of the Roman Empire*, 3:134.

16. Kennedy, "The Last Century of Byzantine Syria," 180–83. There is an enormous literature on this still controversial topic, see Kazhdan and Cutler, "Continuity and Discontinuity in Byzantine History," 427–441; Foss, "Archaeology and the Twenty Cities of Byzantine Asia," 469–486; Hodges and Whitehouse, *Mohammed, Charlemagne and the Origins of Europe*, 54–72; Russell, "Transformations in Early Byzantine Urban Life: The Contributions and Limitations of Archaeological Evidence," 137–154; Mango, *Byzantium: The Empire of New Rome*, 60–74.

17. Kennedy, "The Last Century of Byzantine Syria," 149.

18. See the comments on "the disintegration of the citizen-body of the Graeco-Roman city state into religious and racial groups" in Liebeschuetz and Kennedy, "Antioch and the Villages of Northern Syria in the Fifth and Sixth Centuries A.D: Trends and Problem," 86.

19. For the Menas Church, see Lux, "Der Mosaikfussboden der Menas-Kirche in Rihāb," 34-41; Mittmann, "Die Mosaikinschrift der Menas-Kirche in Rihāb," 42–45; for the Church of the Prophet Isaiah, see Avi-Yonah, "Greek-Christian Inscriptions from Rihâb," 70. The Metropolitan Theodore mentioned in the dedicatory inscription of this church can now be dated, Mittmann, "Die Mosaikinschrift," 42.

20. Schick, "The Fate of the Christians in Palestine during the Byzantine/Umayyad Transition, 600–750 A.D.," 107.

21. Al-Balādhurī, *Kitāb Futūh, al-Buldān*, 266. See also the comments of the chief Qādī of Hārūn al-Rashīd, Abū Yūsuf Kitâb al-Kharâj, 140–141.

22. For example, see Grohmann, "Greek Papyri of the Early Islamic Period in the Collection of Archduke Rainer," 5–40.

23. Ashtor, *A Social and Economic History of the Near East in the Middle Ages*, 9–35; Levtzion, "Conversion to Islam in Syria and Palestine and the Survival of Christian Communities," 289–311.

24. Fritz and Kempinski, *Ergebnisse der Ausgrabungen auf der Hirbet el-Mšāš (Tēl Māōs), 1972–1975*, 182–5; Baramki and Stephan, "A Nestorian Hermitage between Jericho and the Jordan," 84.

25. Evelyn White, *The Monasteries of the Wadi'n Natrun* 2:265–329; Bridel, ed., *Le Site monastique copte des Kellia*, 327.

26. Avi-Yonah, *The Jews of Palestine*, 237.

27. See Griffith, "Greek into Arabic: Life and Letters in the Monasteries of Palestine in the Ninth Century: The Example of the *Summa Theologica Arabica*," 128, 130.

28. Leontius of Mar Sabas, *Vita S. Stephani Sabaitae Thaumaturgi Monachi*, 569, 597.

29. Blake, "La Littérature grecque en Palestine au viiie siècle," 367–380; Griffith, "The Monks of Palestine and the Growth of Christian Literature in Arabic," 1–28.

30. On Christian and Jewish indemnities under Muslim rule, see Fattal, *Le Statut legal des non-musulmans en pays d'Islam*; Tritton, *The Caliphs and Their Non-Muslim Subjects: A Critical Study of the Covenant of 'Umar*; Khoury, *Toleranz im Islam*; Paret, "Toleranz und Intoleranz im Islam," 344–365.

31. See Simonsen, *Studies in the Genesis and Early Development of the Caliphal Taxation System*; Dennett, *Conversion and the Poll Tax in Early Islam*; Løkkegaard, *Islamic Taxation in the Classical Period.*

32. Pseudo-Dionysius of Tel-Mahrē, *Chronicle* 2.381.18–20, as cited in Witakowski, *The Syriac Chronicle of Pseudo-Dionysus*, 44.

33. Leontius of Mar Sabas, *Vita S. Stephani Sabaitae*, 575–577.

34. al-Tabarī, Ta'rīkh al-Rusul wa al-Mulūk, II/1354.

35. Al-Balādhurī, 193.

36. *Chronicon ad A.C. 846 pertinens*, 234 (T), 178 (V).

37. Schick, 363.

38. Bar Hebraeus, *The Chronography of Gregory Abu'l Faraj*, 117 (T), 108–9 (V).

39. *Chronicon ad A.C. 1234 pertinens*, 307–308 (T), 239–240 (V).

40. Schick, 369.

41. Adapted from Ammianus Marcellinus, *Res gestae* 31.16.5–6 (3:501–503).

42. For the "robbers of Arabia," see Julian the Apostate, *Orations* 1.21B (1:52).

43. Cyril of Scythopolis, *Life of Euthymius*, 24.

44. Ibid., 21.

45. Josephus, *Antiquities of the Jews* 1.12.2, in *Flavii Iosephi opera omnia*, 1:40–41.

46. As cited in Eusebius, *Preparatio evangelica* 9.19, GCS 8 (1954), 505.

47. Clement of Alexandria, *Protrepticus* 1.4.46, GCS 1 (1905), 35; Arnobius, *Contra nationes* 6.1, CSEL 4 (1875), 222.

48. Josephus, 1.12.2, 1:40–41.

49. Sozomen, *Church History* 6.38, PG 67, 1412C.

50. Porphyry, *Life of Pythagoras* 11–12 (41).

51. BT Sanhedrin 91a.

52. *Scholia*, PG 4, 360CD. Perhaps a reference to the Monophysitism of the Arab tribes of Ghassān.

53. On the forced baptism of Jews in the seventh century, see Blumenkranz, *Juifs et chrétiens dans le monde occidental*, 97–138.

54. Michael the Syrian, *Chronique* 4:413 (T), 2:414 (V).

55. Sebēos, *History*, 123.

56. Al-Balādhurī, 141.

57. Ibid., 158.

58. Ibid.

59. Crown, "The Byzantine and Moslem Period," 78.

60. Hebrew text in Ginzberg, *Geniza Studies in Memory of Doctor Solomon Schechter*, 310–312; translation and commentary by Lewis, "On That Day: A Jewish Apocalyptic Poem on the Arab Conquests."

61. Lewis, "On That Day," 199.

62. It is important to remember that at the time of the Persian invasion Messianic expectations were already rife among the Jews of Palestine, as is witnessed by the attempts to restore temple services, *The Midrash of Elijah*, and *The Book of Zerubbabel*. For details, see Avi-Yonah, *The Jews of Palestine*, 160–169.

63. Išōʾyaw III, *Liber epistularum*, 251 (T), 182 (V). For his life and works, see Fiey, " Išōʾyaw le Grand."

64. Al-Balādhurī, 137; *Chronicon ad A.C. 1234 pertinens*, 229 (T), 195–196 (V).

65. Sebēos, 122.

66. Ibid., 123.

67. Ibid., 123–124.

68. John of Nikiu, *Chronicle*, 186.

69. Severus, *History*, 492–493.

70. Hitchins, "The Caucasian Albanians," 243–244.

71. For the date, see Sherwood, *An Annotated Date-List of the Works of Maximus the Confessor*, 40.

72. PG 91, 538. With language echoing the Olivet Discourse.

73. Ibid., 540.

74. Ibid. Maximus' reference to the Muslims/Arabs as a "Jewish people" is not necessarily indicative that he was aware of the "irredentist and messianic character of the conquests," as has been

suggested by Crone and Cook, *Hagarism*, 155 n. 27. It could just as easily be accounted for in terms of pre-Islamic views of the Arabs, such as were discussed above.

75. PG 91, 540.

76. Ibid., 541.

77. Ibid., 541–544.

78. It is interesting, if not ironic, to note that Maximus' hostile Syriac biographer attributed the conquests to the sins of Maximus himself. "For following the wicked Maximus the wrath of God punished every place which had accepted his heresy." Brock, "An Early Syriac Life of Maximus the Confessor," 313 (T), 318 (V).

79. For his life and works, see von Schönborn, *Sophrone de Jérusalem*, 51–118.

80. Sophronius, "Weihnachtspredigt," 500–516.

81. "Epistola Synodica," PG 87, 3148–3200.

82. Sophronius, "Logos eis to Hagion Baptisma," 151–168; on the dates for these three works, see Schönborn, *Sophrone de Jérusalem*, 102–104.

83. Sophronius, "Logos," 166.

84. Sophronius, "Weihnachtspredigt," 506–507, 514–515. Cf. "Epistola Synodica," PG 87, 3197D.

85. Sophronius, "Logos," 166.

86. Theophanes, *Chronographia*, 339.

87. Sophronius, "Weihnachtspredigt," 507, 514; "Epistola Synodica," PG 87, 3197D.

88. *Doctrina Iacobi nuper baptizati*; the text is also preserved with some variations in Ethiopian, Grébaut, ed. and trans., *Sargis d'Aberga*.

89. In the introduction to his Greek edition of part one of this text F. Nau suggests 640 as a date of composition, *La didascalie de Jacob*, 715. Because of the text's "lack of hindsight in respect of the outcome of the Arab invasion," Crone and Cook have suggested with some plausibility that Nau's date is too late, *Hagarism*, 152. It is extremely unlikely that the text preserves Jewish views of the Muslims, as has been suggested by Moorhead, "The Earliest Christian Theological Responses to Islam," 272 n. 4. Neither should it be considered a "Jewish document," as is stated by Meyendorff, *Imperial Unity and Christian Diversity*, 342 n. 25.

90. *Doctrina Iacobi*, 63.

91. Ibid., 86.

92. Ibid.

93. Ibid.

94. Ibid.

95. Ibid., 87.

96. Joshua the Stylite, *Chronicle*, 3–4. See also the account of the miraculous egg upon which was written "The Greeks shall conquer," ibid., 57. On Joshua, see Gelzer, "Josua Stylites," 34–49.

97. Ibid., 6.

98. Ibid., 52–53.

99. Zvi Averni in the *Encyclopaedia Judaica* (Jerusalem, 1971), s.v. "Abū 'Īsā."

100. Similarly, the movement of the enigmatic Maruta seems to have had Christian apocalyptic overtones, see *Chronicon ad A.D. 846 pertinens*, 179–180 (T), 234 (V).

101. Early eighth century Egyptian, for Coptic and Arabic versions, Martinez, "Eastern Christian Apocalyptic."

102. Late seventh or early eighth century from northern Mesopotamia, *Gospel of the XII Apostles* 15–21 (T), 34–39 (V).

103. Seventh-century Syrian, "L'Apocalypse d'Esdras touchant le royaume des Arabes."

104. Early eighth century, "L'Apocalypse de Samuel, supérieur de Deir-el-Qalamoun."

105. The "Secrets of Rabbi Simon ben Yōhay" probably dates from the mid-eighth century, Jellinek, *Bet ha-Midrasch*, 3:78–82. For discussion and partial translation, see Lewis, "An Apocalyptic Vision of Islamic History," 308–338.

106. For Syriac text and translation, Martinez, "Eastern Christian Apocalpytic in the Early Muslim Period"; for Greek version, Pseudo-Methodius, *Die Apokalypse des Pseudo-Methodios*; for bibliography, see Reinink, "Der Edessenische Pseudo-Methodius." In what follows I quote from the translation of Alexander in *The Byzantine Apocalyptic Tradition*.

107. Brock, "Syriac Sources for Seventh-Century History," 34; idem, "Syriac Views of Emergent Islam," 18–20

108. Alexander, *The Byzantine Apocalyptic*, 44, 47.

109. Ibid., 48.

110. Ibid., 48–49.

111. Ibid., 49–50.

112. Ibid., 50.

113. Ibid., 51.

114. On the rise of this activity, see Abel, *Les Caractères historiques*; Khoury, "Apologétique byzantine contre l'Islam (viiie–xiiie siècle)"; Sdrakas, *Hê kata tou Islam polemikê tôn Buzantinôn Theologôn.*

115. Anastasius of Sinai, "Sermo III," PG 89, 1156.

116. Anastasius of Sinai, *Interrogationes et responsiones*, PG 89, 776.

117. Ibid.

118. Anastasius of Sinai, *Viae Dux*, CCSG 8(1981), 9.

119. Ibid., 113.

120. On John of Damascus, see Sahas, *John of Damascus on Islam*; on Theodore Abū Qurrah, see I. Dick's introduction to *Maymar fī wujūd al-Khāliq wa al-Dīn al-Qawīm*, as well as the comments of Joseph Nasrallah, "Regard critique."

121. Theodore Abū Qurrah, "Opusculum 8," PG 97, 1528.

122. Abel, "La Portée apologétique," 229–240.

123. Edited and translated by I. Dick, "La Passion arabe de S. Antoine Ruwah néo-martyr de Damas," 109–133.

124. al-Birūnī, *Les Fêtes des Melchites*, 299.

125. Dick, "La Passion arabe," 119.

126. Ibid., 120-1.

127. Ibid.

128. Ibid., 122.

129. Ibid.

130. Ibid.

131. Ibid., 123.

132. Ibid., 123–124.

133. Ibid., 124.

134. Ibid., 124–125.

135. Ibid., 125–126.

136. Ibid., 126.

137. Schultze, "Das Martyrium des heiligen Abo von Tiflis."

138. PG 100, 1199–212.

139. *Passion of 'Abd al-Masîh*, 360–74.

140. Theodore Abū Qurrah, *De cultu imaginum*, 33 (T), 34–35 (V).

141. For details on his cult, see Dick, "La Passion arabe," 109–111; Peeters, "S. Antoine le néo-martyr," 410–416.

CHAPTER 2

The Syriac and Armenian Christian Responses to the Islamification of the Mongols

David Bundy

The Arab Caliphate in Baghdad was ill-equipped to offer an effective response to the Mongols who arrived in Northern Mesopotamia during the middle part of the thirteenth century. The fall of the Islamic state was quick and hard, as had been the experiences of others who had faced the same foe earlier in the Caucasus. When the Mongols arrived, there were Muslims in their ranks; indeed, the Golden Horde farther north had already become Muslim. However, there were also significant numbers of Shamanists, Buddhists, and Christians. In the areas invaded, all peoples suffered, irrespective of the coreligionists among the invaders.

Among the victims of the Mongol invasion were large numbers of Syriac Christians, both east (Nestorian) and west (Jacobite) Syrian Christians in Mesopotamia, as well as Armenians and Georgians in the Caucasus. For some Syriac and Armenian Christians who survived the initial invasion, the presence of Christians among the invaders was a consolation and a cause for hope. For the Georgians, confronted already by the Golden Horde, the situation was even more complex and their situation is beyond the scope of this essay. Over a period of time, the Mongols of the Il-Khanate converted to Islam. The purpose of this chapter is to explore the response of the Armenian and Syriac Christians to this process of islamification.

To do that it also explores the expectations of the these groups regarding Mongol rule, to reexamine the thesis of J.-M. Fiey, who has argued that the Armenians and Syriac speaking Christians "opted" for the Mongol cause against their Islamic-Arab countrymen.[1]

The Islamification Process

The Mongol conversion to Islam was not instantaneous. It was a process that began in the steppes of Central Asia and would accelerate as contact with Islam intensified in the decades of conquest and rule, in the Central Asia of the Muslim Turkomens and, after the 1230s, in the Middle East. In Central Asia, the Mongols had been animists with a shamanist tradition that was tolerant of and supportive of Islam, Buddhism, Manichaeism, and Nestorian Christianity. The Turkomens, and later the majority indigenous Islamic population, steadily but slowly absorbed the Mongol minority, partly because of similar cultural experience but also because of the political realities facing the Il-Khanate both as conqueror-administrators and as principals in international politics vis-à-vis Mamluk Egypt.[2]

When the Mongols arrived in the Middle East, there were many Nestorian Christians in the Il-Khanid hierarchy, some of whom, including the wife of Hulagu, personally promoted Christian interests.[3] Through her efforts, many Christians in Baghdad were spared during the 1258 devastation of Baghdad by the forces of Hulagu. This imperial solicitude led to unwarranted and ill-advised triumphalism on the part of the East Syrian (Nestorian) leaders.[4] To make matters more complex, the Mongols, using the age-old technique of divide and conquer, frequently appointed both Armenian and Nestorian Christians as administrators and/or advisors, in addition to Muslim from outside the traditional power structures.

That Teguder, a son of Hulagu who had been baptized Nicholas as a Christian, converted to Islam in 1282 to reign briefly (1282–1284) as Ahmad was considered an aberration;[5] and under the eclectic tolerant Arghun (1284–1291), Rabban

Sawma could say to the Catholic Cardinals in Rome during his 1287 visit that,

> Many Mongols are Christians, many of the queens and sons of Mongol kings have been baptised and confess Christ. They have established churches in their camps. They honor the Christians and many among them are believers.[6]

However, by 1295, the *Continuator* of the Syriac polymath Grigor Abu-l- Farağ (Barhebraeus) observed, "Both the nobility as well as the common people, all have become Muslim."[7] Baydu (April–September 1295) publicly embraced Islam, although Barhebraeus suggests it was a conversion of expedience because he neither fasted nor observed the prayer system.[8] Finally, in September 1295, Ghazan (d. 1304), a convert from Buddhism to Sunni Islam, became the Il-Khan. He established Islam as the state religion and decreed that Christians and Jews were to wear distinctive dress.[9] Political realities, especially hope for Western aid against the Mamluk Egyptians who were not impressed by his conversion, led to a more moderate policy as his reign progressed. Then Öldjäytü (1304–1316) grandson of Arghun, who had also been baptized as Nicholas (whether according to the Latin or Nestorian rite is uncertain) converted to Shiite Islam, a decision that would have perpetual consequences for both Christians and Muslims in what is now Iran.[10]

This *Tendenz* of islamification is well documented. What is less known is the reaction of the Armenian and Syriac Christians to the islamification process. The Armenian and Syriac sources need to be considered together for the following reasons:

1. Both groups were relatively powerless in the international and interfaith situations in which they found themselves.
2. The geographical and demographic boundaries overlapped (the Armenian official presence extended at least as far east as Tabriz and the West Syrians [Jacobites] had a church in the Armenian capitol of Sis).
3. Both groups flourished or suffered according to the Mongol political-religious stance at least in part because of shared socio-religious features.

However, the Armenians, West Syrians (Jacobites), and the East Syrians (Nestorians) had different national experiences, and it is important to distinguish sources and traditions. Even though they often witnessed, and were influenced by the same events, the perspective is often different. This was due in part to the fact that the Kingdom of Cilician Armenia was able to maintain a degree of territorial integrity during the first half of the Il-Khanate period. The Syriac Christians had never been a majority or dominant force in Mesopotamia and had neither sought nor been accorded a state of self-determination. Therefore this chapter reflects the individual writer's presentation of the Mongols and the perception of islamification process in light of the national religious and historical experience.

Relations between Armenian and Syriac Christians

Armenian-Syriac relations during the thirteenth and fourteenth centuries, a subject little studied but for the observations of J.-M. Fiey and the not very helpful work of Ter-Minassiantz.[11] The geographical overlap of Armenian, West Syrian, and East Syrian Christians has been noted previously. It would appear that the West Syrians, especially, found refuge within Armenian controlled areas from the ravages of Mamluk incursions and the molestations of Damascene rulers. This relationship was expedited by the refusal of both Armenians and West Syrians to accept the Council of Chalcedon (351) and the identification of the theological articulations of both groups as monophysite by their antagonists.

Thus, it was not unexpected that Grigor Abu-l-Farağ (Barhebraeus) should be ordained *Maphrain* at Sis, in the presence of King Het'um I of Cilician Armenia in 1264:[12]

> And the Patriarch together with the bishops came to Sis,
> and there present were also King Het'um and his sons and
> nobles, and certain bishops and doctors of the Armenians,
> and a great crowd of people, in the Catholic Church of the
> Mother of God and Grigor was proclaimed Maphrain of

the East . . . [he] himself preached on the headship of the priesthood. . . . And T'odoros of Smakri' translated into Armenian.

Barhebraeus would spend most of his later years in or near Tabriz and there would be Nestorians, Greeks, and Armenians at his funeral (1286) in Maraga, but few of his fellow Jacobites who were nearly exterminated by this time.[13]

Relations between Armenians and East Syrian (Nestorian) Christians were more complicated. An Armenian historian gloats over the looting of East Syrian churches and monasteries by Armenian soldiers in the service of the Mongols.[14] Georgian soldiers, also culturally and by profession Christian joined with Armenian troops in the sack of Baghdad and pillaged Christian sites.[15] However, later Cilician Armenian King Het'um II would intercede to the Il-Khan on behalf of the East Syrian (Nestorian) Catholicos, Mar Yaballah III.[16] Making common cause at the Court of the Il-Khan appeared to be the limit of contacts between East Syrians and Armenians after the fall of Baghdad.

The Armenians and the Mongols

The Armenian experience of the Mongols from circa 1220–1320 can be described in three stages: (1) contact and submission; (2) forced service; and finally, (3) the period of withdrawal due to the acceptance of Islam by the Mongol leadership and the simultaneous waning of Mongol political and military power in Asia Minor, Syria, and the Caucausus.

The historian Kirakos of Ganjak presents a lengthy and detailed account of the arrival of the Mongols on the scene in Greater Armenia, Georgia, and then Cilician Armenia.[17] A witness to much that he reports, and a disciple of Johannes Vanakan, he recounts how the Georgians were defeated by Mongol armies as early as 1220 C.E. (§12), and defends his decision to write this history already discussed by other writers because, "the evil caused by the Tatars (Mongols), conquerors of the Universe, surpasses all accounts . . . as each warm season they disperse for their journeys of devastation (§21)." He describes the sack of Lori (§26), Ani (§28), Khatchen (§31), Karin

(Erzerum) (§35), and many other villages. He notes that the Prince of Awag perceived the hopelessness of resistance and submitted to the Mongols (§27) and his city was spared for a time (§30). The Mongols continued their drive south and engaged the Sultan in battle (§ 36) and would have turned on Cilician Armenia except that King Het'um I surrendered two women, the wife and daughter of the Sultan, who had sought refuge in his lands (§37). Both Kirakos and the *Chronique du Royaume* insist that this breach of etiquette was caused by a justified fear for the safety of his kingdom.[18] Greater Armenia was ravaged (§41) and the Mongols imposed taxes on the Muslim minority there (§45). Then, the Georgian King went before the Khan (§46) to submit. Het'um I sent his brother Smbat a year later (1248–1250 C.E.) and would himself make the pilgrimage (§59) as the devastations continued in neighboring regions.[19] Contemporary Armenian historians leave no doubt as to the motivation of this submission. Grigor of Akanc' observed:[20]

> Thus the Christ crowned and pious King Het'um, when he heard of all this fury which had been wreaked in the upper districts of the east, out of love for the Christians, but even more because of his own land went with much treasure to the Kanku Gan and took care that this country should not be exposed to such outrages.

Part of this submission was the obligation to provide troops and logistical support for the Mongol forces as they fought across a front extending from Jerusalem to Baghdad. Kirakos of Ganjak tells of Het'um's campaigns in Syria (§60) and describes the sack of Baghdad and the special treatment accorded the Christians (§61), an aspect of the struggle not mentioned by Grigor of Akanc', perhaps because he wanted to gloat over the spoils taken from East Syrian (Nestorian) churches by the Armenian and Georgian troops at Mayyafariqin.[21]

The next half-century would find Armenian (and Georgian) troops committed to the Mongol cause, and the sources reflect some change in attitude as the heady wine of occasional victory leads to expansive and probably exaggerated accounts of Armenian participation and prowess in the *Chronique du Royaume*. The *Chronique* as well as Grigor of Akanc' and

Samuel of Ani Continuator all suggest, however, that there was a grim side to the cooperation.[22]

This cooperation, obligatory as it was, had for Cilician Armenia the following positive results:[23]

1. It brought most Mongol incursions and molestations to an end;
2. it provided an alliance against the Egyptians (although this also brought Mamluk anger to focus on Cilician Armenia); and,
3. it gave the country greater leverage against the importunities of the Roman Church which disapproved of the alliance but was militarily and politically incapable of intervening.

The respectful tone of the Armenian church toward Rome, expressed for example in the acquiescence of the Synods of Sis of 1243 and 1251 to demands from the Papacy,[24] would become more independent. A meeting at Acre between Mxit'ar Skewṙac'i and the Pope's legate, Bishop John of Jerusalem, provided a context for a bold assertion of Armenian ecclesiastical (and by implication, political) independence (from Rome, but not from the Mongols!).[25] A similar statement would be made when the Armenian church declined to be represented at the Council of Lyons (1274) even though Mongol observers were present.[26] The ecclesiastical relations were considered an aspect of foreign policy and Cilician Armenia was, in essence, part of the Mongol Empire. Seen from this perspective, the reason for the deposition of Catholicos Kostandin II in 1289 by Het'um II, allegedly because of his presumed submission to Rome, is clear.[27] The Mongols were in charge of the international relations of the Empire. Indeed, it is Arghun (1284–1291) who appears to have initiated the 1289 embassy of John of Monte-Corvino (a Franciscan from Tabriz), carrying a letter from Het'um to the Pope.[28] The change of the date of Easter in the Armenian church calendar to coincide with that of Rome at the Synod of Hromkla (1292) may well have been part of the same diplomatic offensive.[29] No other serious initiatives would be made until the Council of Sis, 1307, and by then the political and military situation in the Middle East was quite different.[30]

Armenian hopes of national prominence, independence, and identity that had been nurtured in the brief period of stability were to disintegrate with a resounding crash in the military disasters of 1295, 1303, and 1307. In 1295, the Il-Khan Ghazan embraced Islam.[31] The armies of Ghazan (including Armenian contingents) were defeated in Syria in 1303.[32] In 1307, the Armenian hierarchy was decimated in the massacre by Bulargu.[33]

It would appear from the sources at our disposal from this period (the colophons, the chronicles, the *Anonymous Life of Gēorge Skewṙac'i*, and *La flor des estoires* of Het'um) that the Armenians were very aware of their precarious position vis-à-vis the Mongols and aware of the tendency toward islamification. Het'um (Hayton) develops carefully the entire process from Ahmad to Ghazan. He describes the conversion of Teguder, and asserts that, ". . . at the time of this Ahmad Khan, were converted to the faith of the Sarassins a great multitude of Mongols."[34]

The results of this conversion from the Armenian perspective as articulated by Het'um were that (1) he persecuted the Christians; (2) Islam was preached everywhere; and (3) there were peace initiatives toward Egypt.[35] Het'um notes that Ghazan came to power on a groundswell of Islamic sentiment, that, "all those who kept the law of Mohammed left and went to Ghazan," but that later he moderated his policies and states the improbable that Ghazan wished to, "recover the Holy Land and give it to the Christians."[36] Het'um's thesis is that Egypt is the enemy and that the Mongols are willing to ally themselves with Christian forces against the Mamluks. He theorized that perhaps a victory over Egypt could reverse the trend toward islamification. His essay perceptively points to the political and military aspects of the attractiveness of Islam for the Mongol leadership.[37]

The colophons, especially those from Greater Armenia, present a less dispassionate view and reflect the grimness of the reign of Öldjäytü for the Armenian population. A colophon by a certain Daniel of Alt'amar in 1306 laments:[38]

> . . . the nation of archers . . . converted to the false faith of
> Mohammed, which will lead them directly into perdition.

> And they coerce everyone into converting to their vain
> and false hope. They persecute, they molest, and they
> torment, some by confiscating their possessions, some by
> tormenting them, some by slandering, by insulting the
> cross and the church. . . .

Or, as another anonymous colophon writer expressed it:[39]

> For the savage . . . Nation of Archers abandoned their
> native faith and followed the evil sect of the forerunner
> Antichrist, Mahmet, and they subjected the Christians to
> more intense anguish and persecution. . . .

Other colophons mention the registration of the
population,[40] the imposition of levies and taxes,[41] and the
enforcing of the wearing of the opprobrium, a distinctive black
or blue cloth across the shoulders.[42] Already by 1310, there is the
report of individuals fleeing their ancestral lands in the face of
oppression.[43] Daniel of Alt'amar, in another manuscript, copied
in 1307, asserts, ". . . they make every effort to efface Christianity
from the earth."[44]

The interpretation of the islamification and the adverse
effects on Armenian life is consistent. The tone is fatalistic,
frustrated, and fearful. It is asserted that both the cause and
effect are the earned results of national and personal sin. This
apocalyptic theme in twelfth-fourteenth century Armenian
thought has yet to be studied, but suffice it to say it was constant.
Vahram of Edessa in the *Rhymed Chronicle* lamented, "Is it just,
they said, that punishment has struck us? Are we greater sinners
than the other peoples of the world?"[45]

This is echoed in the manuscript colophons. Daniel of
Alt'amar follows his description of the taxes and opprobrium
with the explanation, ". . . all of this on account of our sins."[46] An
anonymous scribe was more explicit:[47]

> And because of our impenitence His (God's) wrath was
> not abated; rather, His hand is still raised to punish and
> chastise us. Yet we are still unrepentant; we have become
> feeble and lean, emaciated and languished, and we are
> nearing death and hell.

However, perhaps the most poignant expression of the
theme of self-reproachment is found in the poem attributed to

Het' um II, whose desperate duty it was to preside over Cilician Armenian fortunes from 1288–1307.[48] Here one finds the writer trying to comprehend the political and ecclesiastical difficulties of the period. This may in fact indicate the reason for Het'um's vows as a Franciscan and his periodic withdrawals from the government for meditation. It was consistent with Armenian thought that he should feel morally and personally responsible for the nation's reverses and that he should attempt to "repent" to regain divine favor.

Thus it can be argued that the Armenians were very aware of the conditions of their cooperation with the Mongols from the beginning. It was a submission and a forced cooperation born of the desperate circumstances in which they found themselves. They had not the military strength to resist the invaders from Central Asia. There is no evidence that the Armenians ever considered the Mongols to be "Christians," although they noted with relief that there were Christians within their ranks. Nor does it appear that they were surprised when the Mongol leaders gave approbation to the tendency toward islamification and became Muslim themselves. The past to which the writers hearkened, observing that later Mongol leaders "forgot" or "abandoned the way of their fathers," was a past marked by pluralism and by toleration of different religious expressions and views. It was the religious policy that had existed in the camps of Central Asia but which was no longer tenable for the rulers of an Islamic majority population.

The Syriac Christians and the Mongols

As has been noted, the Mongols arrived in the Middle East at a moment when the local Abbasid government was ill prepared to organize its resources to counter their threat. Georg Warda, a Syriac Christian churchman and hymnographer, described the devastation of Karamlaiss in 1235–1236.[49] He recounted the fear of the Mongols in the streets as of "panthers and lions (§7)," described the casualties, each house having one or two deaths (§23) with no one being able to aid or rescue their loved ones from the whims of the invaders (§40), and told of the sorrow and emptiness of the ravaged city (§§49–50). Nowhere does he suggest that Christians in the villages and monasteries received special dispensation. In fact the monasteries seem to have been singled out for particularly severe treatment.[50] The anonymous *Chronicon ad A.C. 1234 pertinens* describes the Mongols as "pagans and assassins," but notes that they were more severe with the Muslim than the Christian population: "Thus they undertook to kill, especially to annihilate the Turks of those regions more than the Christians; the Muslim more than the Jews; they had pity for no one."[51]

These experiences must have tempered the relief and joy felt generally at having been spared during the destruction of Baghdad in 1258 C.E. because of the intervention of their coreligionists among the Mongol aristocracy, although as we have seen, the official attitudes did not prevent a certain amount of looting by the Armenian and Georgian contingents of the Mongol forces.

The East Syrian Catholicos was given palaces in Baghdad by Hulagu in 1258 and Christian triumphalism may have bloomed briefly, but by the patriarchate of Denha I (1265–1281), the Patriarch was forced to leave Baghdad and then Arbeles for the Mongol royal camps in hope of gaining an audience with the Mongol overlords.[52] It was only initially and briefly that the Mongols found Nestorian Christians (and other minority groups as well) to be useful administrators.

The appointment of Mar Denha's successor indicates that the situation must have soon looked grim to the East Syrians. In 1281 they elected Yaballah III to be their Catholicos. Yaballah was a Uigur monk (Markos) from Khan-balik (Beijing) who had no connections to Middle Eastern seats of political or ecclesiastical power. He also knew no Syriac, the Nestorian liturgical and canonical language. His biographer honestly asserts that his primary qualification was to be able to speak the language of the Mongols: "The kings who held the reins of government of the world were the Mongols and there was no one other than Mar Yaballah who knew their manners, customs, their policy of government and their language."[53]

This patriarchal election was clearly an effort to use the results of their Central Asian missions to alleviate the pressures of the local majority population on their momentarily liberated position. It must be noted that even at this point the sources suggest that the Syriac-speaking Christians were aware of their dependence upon a few individuals among the Mongols who were Christian and that the situation was very fluid.

The anonymous biographer(s) of Mar Yaballah III and his mentor Rabban Sawma is (are) our best source(s) for an East Syrian perspective on the entire period. The conversion of Ahmad is recounted: "He lacked education and knowledge and much persecuted the Christians because of his association with the Hagaraye (Muslim) toward whose religion he leaned."[54] This religious orientation is given as his reason for believing the accusations of certain Syriac Bishops against the Catholicos: "Now the King lacked wisdom in that he had cast God aside . . . "[55] resulting in the Catholicos' imprisonment for a time. He was saved by the intervention of the Il-Khan's mother, Qutai Khatun, a Christian. Ahmad's death was interpreted as a judgement of God.[56]

The period of Arghun's reign (1284–1291) is recalled in positive terms, but after his death, "the people of the Arabs aroused to take vengeance on the Church and its children for the destruction which the father of these kings (Arghun) had inflicted upon them."[57] By 1295, "a rumor was heard of the flight of Khan Baydu and of his destruction, and with it came the proof, that in very truth, the abandonment of (the Church by) God had taken place."[58]

The rest of the biography focuses on the tribulations of the Christians. The writer comments in words from the lectionary attributed to St. Ephrem:[59]

> Because we have despised the way, and have regarded it with great contempt, (God) has made us a reproach to those who are outside; that we may drink of the cup of their mockery. The filthy ones have ruined our churches, because we have not prayed in them in a right manner; they have defiled the altar which is before him (because) we have not ministered there with a pure service.

This introspective, apocalyptic note becomes one of the primary interpretative themes for the narration of the period 1295–1316 as the author describes the massacres at Maraga,

Arbeles and Baghdad, the widespread Arab-Syriac misunder-
standings and conflict, the imposition of a distinctive dress for
Christians and the gradual disenfranchisement of the Christian
population. The other main interpretative focus is that the Il-
Khans were seduced from the "ways of their fathers" to
adherence to Islam.[60] This islamification led to a "kind of hatred
of the Christians" [61] on the part of the Il-Khan Öldjäytü. Thus, in
this text the process of assimilation of the Mongols to Islam is
seen as a punishment for the sins of the Christian population and
because of the seduction of the minds of Mongol leaders by
influential Muslim in the employ of the Il-Khanate. The painful
reduced situation in which the Catholicos and his "flock" find
themselves is graphically and poignantly portrayed.

When one discusses the second important work for the
Syriac perspective on these events, one is in fact dealing with
two writers, Grigor Abu-l-Farağ (Barhebraeus) and his
Continuator, perhaps his brother. The precise relationship
between their contributions to the *Chronography* has not yet been
analyzed but a profitable starting point might be the respective
views of the two writers with regard to the Mongols. For
example, Barhebraeus gives a brief description of the Mongols,
discussing their religion and noting the influence of the Uigurs:[62]

> Since the Mongols had neither literature nor writing,
> Chingiz Khan commanded the scribes of the Uigurs and
> they taught the children of the Tatars their books, and they
> wrote the Mongol language with Uigur letters . . . and they
> wrote down the following laws . . . Let the Mongols
> magnify and pay honor to the modest, and the pure and
> the righteous and to the scribes and wise men, to whatever
> nation they might belong . . . the Mongols loved the
> Christian people greatly at the beginning of their
> kingdom.

Then there is appended the following statement, probably
from the *Continuator*: "But their love has turned to such intense
hatred that they cannot even see them with their eyes
approvingly, because they have all alike become Muslims,
myriads of people and peoples."[63]

Barhebraeus describes in detail the devastations of the
Middle East by the conquering Mongol armies.[64] He observes

that during the sack of Baghdad the Christians took refuge in "the church of the third bazaar" and were spared, but that within months the troubles caused by being caught between Muslim majority and conquerors began.[65] He does not mention the intervention of the Mongol queen at Baghdad, but does note that she intervened on behalf of the Christians at Maraga in a dispute over liturgical practices[66] and reports several "diplomatic" visits of Mongol royalty to Christian churches.[67]

Ahmad's rule is discussed without reference to his conversion to Islam. It is suggested that he was generous to the Christians:[68]

> And he looked upon all peoples with a merciful eye, and especially the heads of the Christian faiths, and he wrote for them patents which freed all the churches, and the religious houses, and the priests and monks from taxation and imposts in every country and region.

The reason for his deposition by Arghun was that ". . . he was incapable of ruling."[69] In fact, much of the account in the *Chronography* indicates a radical breakdown in social control during this time. Christians, and others, suffered as bands of marauding Kurds and Arabs terrorized villages, monasteries, and churches. On an official level, the Mongols became more and more influenced by Muslim advisors as they endeavored to control the situation. Barhebraeus accuses those advisors of "stirring up persecution and wrath against the hated Christians. . . ."[70] He perceived this as being due to the "abandonment of God"[71] and lamented:[72]

> The persecution and wrath which these . . . suffered during these . . . months, neither tongues can describe nor the reed write. Wake up and sleep not, O Lord, and look on the blood of thy servants which is being poured out without mercy, and be sorry for thy church which is being rent in pieces by the persecution.

The remainder of the *Chronography* continues in this tone. Barhebraeus' *Continuator* does point out that other religious groups also suffered:[73]

> Now this persecution had not dominion over our people alone, but also over the Jews, and it was twice as fierce,

many times over, on the priests who were worshippers of idols. . . . And a very large number of pagan priests, because of the way they were persecuted, became Muslims.

The persecutions, which had been more or less spontaneous socioreligious phenomena, became government ordered and sanctioned destruction: "Mongol messengers were sent to every country and town to destroy the churches and to loot the monasteries." Those who were spared were those able to pay sufficient ransom.

Barhebraeus and his *Continuator*, more than the other sources examined, were aware of the social and religious demographic problems involved with the islamification of the Mongols. This is especially clear in their analysis of the short reign of Baydu:[74]

And because at this time the Mongols, both the nobles and the inferior folk had become Muslim, and had already been circumcised, and had been well instructed in ablutions, and prayers, and the special customs and observances of the Muslims, since it was pleasing to them, Baidu became a Muslim and all of the nobles rejoiced exceedingly.

However, he continued to use Christians in his administration and the historians suggest that the position of Baydu became intolerable because of suspicions by the Arab population of his Christian connections. Barhebraeus's *Continuator* may well not have survived the pogroms against the Christians and Christian institutions throughout the Il-Khanate after the installation of Ghazan as the Il-Khan of Persia.[75] In any case, their narrative stops at this point. Part of the persecution of the Christians was the purge of the administration by Ghazan of non-Muslim elements at the beginning of his reign, although there was a gradual relaxation of hiring regulations as his reign became more secure.

The *Chronography*, more than any other literature of the period, reflects a sensitive understanding of the social and political issues involved in the islamification of the Mongols. That does not mean that the writers were any more happy about it. When they reflected on the trend in theological terms, it was also in apocalyptic categories of fatalism, divine punishment, and "abandonment." Less than the Armenians, or even the biographer of Mar Yaballah III, did they expect that there would be the possibility of "restoration." For them the trend of Middle Eastern history was clear and they had little hope for a future.

Conclusion

One sees, even in the limited number of sources available, divergent reports of the character of the reigns of individual Il-Khans. However, as the tendency of islamification becomes clearly definitive, both Armenian and Syriac Christian analysts respond using the same interpretative foci. They consider it an "abandonment by God" for which they are partially responsible. It is their national and personal sin which has led to the disaster. Islamification is a punishment by God. The Mongols are not responsible. They have been seduced by their Muslim advisors. The tone of these interpretations is one of fear. They have little hope for the future. This fear probably explains the overwhelming pessimism and probably exaggerated accounts of devastation, for we do know that Armenian manuscript production would increase throughout the 1340s and the arts of manuscript illumination and architecture would continue to flourish.[76]

The sources clearly indicate that the Syriac and Armenian writers were aware, from the beginning, of their tenuous situation. Unfortunately some church leaders, especially the Patriarch Mar Makkika of Baghdad, thought otherwise. Tabriz became the center of intrigue as the Nestorian Catholicos, the West Syriac (Jacobite) Maphrain, Armenian representatives, and spies (and businessmen) competed for the attention and protection of important court figures. They were aware that to call their relationship to Mongol power an "alliance" was to put the best interpretation on what was abject submission. There was no other viable alternative to submission and service. Fiey's thesis that they "opted" for the Mongol cause is untenable, as is the myth of the diplomatic offensive of Het'um and his wise alliance with the Mongols perpetuated in the manuals of Armenian history.

As islamification progressed, the Cilician Armenian historians were very aware of the military difficulties and the international political necessities brought on by an aggressive Mamluk Egyptian government to the south and the Papacy (Latins) to the west. They hoped that peace with Egypt or Egypt's defeat could halt or at least slow the process of religious and social assimilation to Islamic culture. The Syriac writers were more aware of the internal sociopolitical matrix of the Il-Khanate, and their writings reflected little concern for international relations. The most pessimistic sources are those of Greater Armenia, where the Armenian population had little significant possibility of self-determination.

Similarly, the three groups of sources reflect different levels of despair. Those from Greater Armenia exhibit anger with the Mongol government and their own impotence. The Syriac authors are more fatalistic and resigned. The Syriac culture was decimated and there are almost no sources for any aspect of Syriac Christian life for the larger part of the fourteenth century. The Cilician Armenian sources are more extensive and diverse than the others. The range of feeling and analysis expressed is wider but also dominated by the apocalyptic fears being realized in their country. They would struggle and retain their lands and property as well as some self determination and territorial integrity for another half century before their kingdom would fall into the maelstrom of Middle Eastern history.

NOTES

1. Fiey, *Chrétiens syriaques sous les mongols*. For two significantly different analyses of the period, see Bedrosian, "The Turco-Mongol Invasions and the Lords of Armenia," which focuses on the narratives of the historians of Greater Armenia, and the more detailed analysis on the basis of a wider selection of texts by Limper, "Die Mongolen und *die Völker des Kaukasus*." Neither Bedrosian nor Limper venture into

Northern Mesopotamia and its Syriac and Arabic sources. The same is true of Babayan, *Sotial'no-ekonomicheskaia i politicheskaia istoriia Armenii.* More concerned with Cilician Armenia is Sukiasyan, *Istoria kilikiiskogo armonskogo gosudarstra i prava IX–XIV BB.*

2. On the Mongols, see *The Saljuk and Mongol Periods* in Boyle, *The Cambridge History of Iran,* vol. 5.

3. Barhebraeus, *Chronography,* 491 [text], 419 [trans.].

4. For all the sources regarding the appropriation by East Syrian Patriarch Makkikha II of the Caliph's palace, see Fiey, *Chrétiens syriaques,* 24. The circumstances of this event are less than clear, but apparently had repercussions for the already fragile Islamic-Christian relations.

5. Het'um, *La Flor des estoires* (RHC, Arm. II, 185–186; and Fiey, *Chrétiens syriaques,* 41–43. It must be remembered, however, that Het'um was a less than impartial observer as he recounted these events a quarter of a century later. It was to his advantage to portray the overall *Tendenz* of the Mongols to be either Christian or deceived by advisors. On this text, see Bundy, "Het'um's 'La flor des Estoires de la Terre d'Orient.'" Cf. Krause, "Das Mongolenreich nach der Darstellung des Armeniers Haithon," 238–267.

6. *Mar Yaballah,* 64. The naive conclusions both pro and con drawn in the West on the basis of this type of information have been discussed by Sinor, "Les relations entre les Mongols et l'Europe jusqu'a la mort de Arghun," 39–62. Cf. Pelliot, "Les Mongols et la Papauté," and especially the insightful work of von den Brincken, *Die "Nationes Christianorum Orientalium" im Verständnis der Lateinischen Historiographie.* See also Lupprian, *Die Beziehungen der Päpste zu islamischen und mongolischen Herrschern.*

7. Barhebraeus, *Chronography,* 593 [text], 505 [trans.].

8. Ibid.

9. Zayat, *Signes distinctifs des chrétiens et des juifs en Islam.*

10. Fiey, *Chrétiens syriaques,* 74–79.

11. Ibid., *passim;* Ter-Minassiantz, *Die armenisches Kirche in ihren Beziehungen zu den syrischen Kirchen.*

12. Barhebraeus, *Chronicon Ecclesiasticum,* II, cols. 749–752.

13. Ibid., III, cols. 475–476. In 1282, Barhebraeus describes the ruin of West Syrian (Jacobite) centers mentioning by name Antioch, Gumya, Allepo, Mabbug, Calonicus, Edessa, Harran, and Melitene.

14. Grigor of Akanc', 335.

15. Barhebraeus, *Chronography*, 505 [text], 431 [trans.].

16. *Mar Yaballah*, 103–104.

17. *Kirakos;* text is cited in the body of the essay according to the paragraph numbers. See Bedrosian, *Turco-Mongol Invasions*, passim, and especially Boyle, "Kirakos of Ganjak on the Mongols."

18. Kirakos, 37.

19. Cf. RHC, Arm, I, 460 (Chronography of Samuel of Ani) as well as "Samuel d'Ani, Tables Chronologiques," *in* Brosset, *Collection d'historiens arméniens*.

20. Grigor of Akanc', 324–325.

21. Ibid., 334–335.

22. RHC, Arm, I, 656–664; Grigor of Akanc', 348–377; Samuel of Ani, *RHC*, Arm, I, 462–467.

23. RHC, Arm, II, 163–168; also, ibid., I, 691.

24. Tournebize, *Histoire politique et religieuse de l'Arménie*, 287–289.

25. RHC, Arm, I, 691–698.

26. Guiard and Cadier, *Les Registres de Gregoire X et Jean XXII*, nos. 304–305; Hefele, *Histoire des conciles d'apres les documents originaux* 6,1, 174.

27. There are discrepancies of chronology and various causes postulated by the sources. The *Chronique du Royaume* (RHC, Arm, I, 653) places the ascendency of Het'um II in 738 (= 1238) and asserts that Kostandin II was falsely accused. Samuel of Ani Continuator (RHC, Arm, I, 462–463) gives the charge (secret Roman alliance), states that Kostandin II was exiled by Het'um in 737, but also suggests Het'um became king only in 738.

28. Golubovich, *Bibliotheca bio-biografica*, I, 301–309; II, 440; Langois, *Les Registres de Nicolas IV*, no. 2229; Delorme and Trautu, *Acta Romanorum Pontificum ab Innocento V ad Benedictum XI (1276–1304)*, no. 85.

29. E. M. Baghdassarian (Baldasaryan), "La Vie de Georges de Skevra," 399–435; See Bundy, "The 'Anonymous Life of Georg Skewr̄ac'i' in *Erevan 8356*."

30. D. Bundy, "The Council of Sis, 1307."

31. However, he is remembered by Armenian sources as a protector of the Christians, who provided a modicum of sociopolitical stability (see RHC, Arm, I, 191); Xac'ikyan, *XIV Dari Hayeren Jeragreri Hisatakaranner*, no. 28, 30, of which an English translation can be found in Sanjian, *Colophons of Armenian Manuscripts, 1301–1480*, 48, 49. It was

Öldjäytü (Karbanda Khan) who would be seen as the first Mongol oppressor of the Arménians, see Arak'el, "Livre d'histoires," trans. by Brosset, 568–569.

32. RHC, Arm, I, 656–664 (*Chronique du Royaume*).

33. Ibid., I, 490 (Het'um), 466 (Samuel of Ani), 664 (*Chronique du Royaume*).

34. Ibid., II, 185–186. On this problematic text, see Bundy, "Het'um's 'Flor,'" 223–235.

35. RHC, Arm, II, 185–187.

36. Ibid., II, 190, 191, 199.

37. Ibid., II, 237–253 passim.

38. Xac'ikyan, *XIV Dari*, no. 54; Sanjian, *Colophons*, 50–51. On Oldjaytu, see ibid., 373. Another colophon writer (Xac'ikyan, no. 61; Sanjian, 52) described him as "a young one-eyed man, who looked like the Antichrist who is to arrive someday. . . . Xarbanda which means the slave of a donkey."

39. Xac'ikyan, no. 65; Sanjian, 55–56; related to Xac'ikyan, no. 239; Sanjian, 65–66.

40. Xac'ikyan, no. 136; Sanjian, 58.

41. Xac'ikyan, nos. 55, 61, 62, 89, 125, 126, 135, 204; Sanjian, 51–53, 55, 57–58, 63.

42. Xac'ikyan, no. 178; Sanjian, 60 (blue); Xac'ikyan, no. 62; Sanjian, 53–54 (black).

43. Xac'ikyan, no. 89; Sanjian, 55–56.

44. Xac'ikyan, no. 62; Sanjian, 53–54.

45. RHC, Arm, I, 532.

46. Xac'ikyan, no. 62; Sanjian, 52–53 (1307) = Xac'ikyan, no. 89; Sanjian, 55–56 (1310).

47. Xac'ikyan, no. 65; Sanjian, 54 (1307). The same lines are found in a manuscript from 1315, Xac'ikyan, no. 150; Sanjian, *Colophons*, 57.

48. RHC, Arm, I, 550–555.

49. Deutsch, *Edition drier syrischen Lieder*, 10–13 [text], 15–22 [trans.]; and H. Hilgenfeld, *Ausgewählte Gesänge des Giwargis Warda*, 20–27 [text], 49–59 [trans.]. On George Warda, see Bundy, "George Warda," 668–669.

50. Hilgenfeld, *Ausgewählte Gesänge*, passim.

51. *Chronicon ad A. C. 1234 pertinens* (CSCO 109, Syr. 56 [text], CSCO 354, Syr. 154 [trans.], 236 [text], 179 [trans.].

52. Fiey, *Chrétiens syriaques*, 35.

53. Mar Yaballah, 33–39.

54. Mar Yaballah, 39. This was apparently a sensitive political issue. Mar Yaballah was accused of having said, "This man [the Il-Khan] has abandoned the ways of his fathers and become Muslim," and was imprisoned for his impropriety (41–42).

55. Ibid., 41.

56. Ibid., 44.

57. Ibid., 99.

58. Ibid., 99.

59. Ibid., 102.

60. Ibid., 33–41.

61. Ibid., 125.

62. Barhelbraeus., 411 [text], 354 [trans.].

63. Ibid.

64. Ibid., 444–599 [text], 381–509 [trans.].

65. Ibid., 505, 507 [text], 431, 433 [trans.].

66. Ibid., 539–540 [text], 460 [trans.].

67. Ibid., 547 [text], 466 [trans.].

68. Ibid., 548 [text], 467 [trans.].

69. Ibid., 553 [text], 471 [trans.].

70. Ibid., 564 [text], 481 [trans.].

71. Ibid.

72. Ibid., 566 [text], 482 [trans.].

73. Ibid., 596 [text], 507 [trans.].

74. Ibid., 593 [text], 505 [trans.].

75. See the description of the period by Fiey, *Chrétiens syriaques*, 66–73. However, Fiey homogenizes the Syriac and Armenian sources and thereby distorts the analysis. There is no recognition of the perspectives and arguments of the individual texts.

76. Kakovkin, "Historical-Literary Data Concerning the Jewelry Craftsmanship of Cilician Armenia," 164–165; Moutzegyan, "Money Circulation in Armenia during 9th–14th Centuries," 41–60; Ismaylowa, "The Syunik School of Armenian Miniatures,"182–190; Kouymjian, "Dated Armenian Manuscripts as a Statistical Tool for Armenian History," 425–438.

CHAPTER 3

Manuel I Comnenus and the "God of Muhammad": A Study in Byzantine Ecclesiastical Politics

Craig L. Hanson

Toward the end of his reign the Byzantine emperor Manuel I Comnenus (1143–1180) precipitated a bitter controversy with his ecclesiastical hierarchy over traditional Orthodox perceptions and portrayals of the "God of Muhammad." Since at least the ninth century a series of twenty-two anathemas against Islamic beliefs had been incorporated into a "Formula of Abjuration," which was used as part of the required rituals of conversion (or reconversion) for Muslims wishing to join the Christian Church. The anonymous author of this formula made use of earlier Byzantine polemical literature written by such figures as John of Damascus, Theodore Abu-Qurra and Nicetas of Byzantium, as well as contemporary sources. One of the more striking anathemas was that directed against the deity worshiped by Muhammad and his followers: "And before all, I anathematize the God of Muhammad about whom he [Muhammad] says, 'He is God alone, God made of solid, hammer-beaten metal; He begets not and is not begotten, nor is there like unto Him any one.'"[1] It was this anathema that lay at the heart of the controversy involving Manuel and his ecclesiastical officials in the year 1180. The emperor ordered the deletion of this anathema from the Church's catechetical texts, a measure that provoked vehement opposition from both Patriarch and bishops. The purpose of this chapter is to offer a detailed assessment of the entire controversy, furnishing necessary background on traditional Byzantine perceptions of the "God of Muhammad," the character and possible motivations of Manuel, and the theoretical and practical considerations of "conversion" and diplomacy in the age of the Comneni. In order to understand the origins, course, and significance of the dispute it is first necessary to examine the Christian-Muslim environment as seen from the Byzantine point of view. Byzantium had come to feel the military might of Islam early in its history. Indeed, from the seventh through the ninth century the very survival of the empire often seemed in doubt. This "military" aspect of Byzantium's encounter with the new religion was to color and even dominate its perceptions of and attitudes toward Islam in the future.[2] The continuing threat of an aggressive Islam remained uppermost in the minds of the rulers of Constantinople, and their preoccupation was, in turn, reflected in Byzantine society generally. To be sure, as Daniel Sahas has recently noted, the Byzantines did not develop a monolithic approach to the Muslim religion, but rather responded according to varying personal, cultural, and political circumstances.[3] Nonetheless, certain attitudes did predominate during the course of the Middle and Late Byzantine eras, especially those that were actively promoted by the official civil, military, and ecclesiastical hierarchies. In part it was the military confrontations and the defeats Byzantium suffered at the hands of Arab (and later, of Turkish) armies that made Islam the enemy. Any such threat to the "God-centered realm of the Romans" was viewed in religious as well as military terms:

> Both civilizations thus confronted were, to a large extent, shaped by their respective religious ideologies, and each side interpreted the attitudes and actions of the other as motivated by religion. If the Qurran appealed to a holy war against "those who ascribe partners to God"—i.e., Christians who believe in the Trinity—the Byzantine retaliated, after the example of St. John of Damascus, by considering Islam as a "forerunner of Antichrist.". . . There was an abyss between the two religions which no amount of polemics, no dialectical argument, no effort at diplomacy, was able to bridge. Insurmountable on the spiritual and the theological level, this opposition from the

very beginning also took the shape of a gigantic struggle
for world supremacy, because both religions claimed to
have a universal mission, and both empires world
supremacy. By the very conception of its religion, Islam
was unable to draw a distinction between the "political"
and "spiritual," but neither did Byzantium ever want to
distinguish between the universality of the Gospel and the
imperial universality of Christian Rome. This made
mutual understanding difficult and led both sides to
consider that holy war was, after all, the normal state of
relations between the two Empires.[4]

According to Byzantine imperial ideology, Orthodox Christianity represented the world's one "true" faith, exclusive and
unique in character, and Byzantium itself, the inspired earthly
approximation of God's kingdom. Thus, a Byzantine military
defeat, however minor, necessitated a religious explanation, for
Muslim victory would seem to imply the "truth" of Islam. The
fundamental question for Orthodox believers was the following:
If God allowed his chosen community to suffer at the hands of
Muslim armies, how were Christians to understand his motives
and message? Various explanations were possible, but two major
themes emerged. Perhaps God was using the Muslims to
chastise his people for their sins. Or perhaps he was
demonstrating his love by testing their fidelity, even preparing
them for greater things in the future. Each viewpoint, often
stated with subtle variations, attracted its supporters over the
centuries.[5]

It was also Islam's often-perceived status as a Christian
heresy that made this religion especially insidious and hateful.
According to Orthodox theologians and polemicists (beginning
with John of Damascus in the eighth century), since the Qur'ân
itself admitted the revealed character of both Judaism and
Christianity, the Muslim faith was to be treated as merely
another in a long line of heretical teachings. The criteria to be
applied in judgment were Orthodox, and the topics for
discussion traditional Christian ones. In particular, Islam was
linked to past heresies already condemned by Church councils.
For example, Muhammad himself was singled out as a latter-day
manifestation of Arius of Alexandria because he denied the
divinity of the Logos and of the Holy Spirit.[6] From the Byzantine

perspective Muhammad and his followers had the opportunity to accept Christ in the correct manner, but had consciously denied him.[7] Hence, the association of Muhammad and Islam with the Antichrist.[8]

Modern scholars have argued correctly that the initial encounter of Christianity and Islam did not involve the imperial Church so much as the Nestorian and Monophysite communities of Arabia, Syria, Mesopotamia, and Egypt, which represented the bulk of the Christian populations there.[9] Among these the Muslims found many who preferred, at least in the beginning, Islamic rule to Chalcedonian oppression. Thus, as might be expected, the first polemical reference to Islam came from Orthodox theologians "trapped" in enemy territory, individuals such as John of Damascus and Theodore Abu-Qurra.[10] For them the new foe was not the Arab whose traditional culture they shared in the Near East, but the Muslim.[11] And in the state of war that existed between Byzantium and Islam all means available were to be used by Christian loyalists living in Muslim-dominated lands: acts of confrontation; oral and written polemic; group education; community insulation and isolation; in essence, everything short of military warfare itself. For such Christians the Byzantine emperor was still the legitimate ruler of their lands. The losses suffered by his armies were considered temporary aberrations. And the empire's triumphal return was eagerly anticipated.[12] The honorary status of *dhimmi* accorded them by Muslim authorities to distinguish them from other conquered peoples only served to remind them of their true allegiances. For those Byzantine Christians who did not live under direct Arab rule the range of options was, of course, wider, with direct political and military intervention possible. While the early literature produced by *dhimmi* Christians was characterized by a sense of immediacy (even urgency), directness of language, and relative nonviolent tone, that generated from within the empire, beginning slightly later, was more academic, indirect, and overtly hostile. It is possible that the former was often intended to convince, if not actually convert, Muslim opponents; the latter could only serve to ridicule or embarrass the foe. More importantly, anti-Islamic polemic served to defend the principles of Christianity against its detractors, both real and imagined, while fortifying believers in their traditional faith of Orthodoxy. Although both *dhimmi* and non-*dhimmi* Christian polemicists were experienced theologians, well-trained in dialectic, most were poorly informed about Islam, particularly its historical origins, motivations, ethical values, and spiritual content.[13] Notwithstanding, numerous detailed treatises were produced over the centuries,[14] often following standard format and content guidelines:

> The typical Christian heresiological technique had always been the exposition of a heresy vis-à-vis the Christian orthodoxy. This was done usually in the form of actual or fictitious dialogues. The same technique was used against Islam. In "dialogues" like those "between a Christian and a Saracen" by John of Damascus, Abu Qurrah, Patriarch Timothy, Nicetas of Byzantium, Arethas and others, the Saracen finds himself in a difficult position to defend convincingly his faith under Christian questioning. The Christian treats the Muslim as a Christian and uses his own sources, especially the Bible, as well as his Christian thinking and arguments, to judge Islam. This approach places the Muslim seemingly in a nondiscriminatory, but nevertheless in a disadvantageous position.[15]

Topics for discussion often included the Orthodox doctrines of the Trinity and the Incarnation, the authenticity of revelation in the Bible and the Qur'ân, the prophecy of Muhammad, the nature of Islamic cult practices, and the morality of Muslim ethics.[16] As the Muslims themselves became more adept in theological matters and more knowledgeable about the techniques and arguments of Christian polemics, the situation was sometimes reversed with Arab scholars taking the offensive.

While Islam was confronted by Byzantium, on the one hand, with political and military force, and on the other, with intellectual and theological polemic, it is the process of "conversion" as an instrument of imperial policy that merits our closest attention. Faced with a successful and aggressive new religion in the Near East and the reality of widespread Christian apostasy in Muslim-held territories, Byzantine authorities were pressed to deliver on the ancient pledge of "converting the barbarians." To their credit, an attempt was made over the

centuries to regain the offensive in this regard;[17] it was thought
that conversion, especially of prominent and powerful Muslims,
would ease and even end the conflict with Islam.[18] The
cooperation of the Byzantine civil, military, and religious
hierarchies was crucial and, for the most part, produced positive
if unspectacular results.[19] In their effort to gain converts and
"reconverts" from Islam, Byzantine authorities were forced to
view and appreciate the realities of Muslim religion and life.
Often these realities were at variance with the images
popularized by Orthodox polemicists. Where the polemical
images held sway as reality, there was strong opposition to any
accommodation or compromise with the "infidel," whether this
meant temporary coexistence with Muslim states or the
relaxation of strict regulations governing the conversion process
itself. Where Christian polemic was viewed as a necessary but
rhetorical complement to other policies, the attitude was more
flexible. Thus, occasionally the common goal of Muslim
conversion could be obscured by differences of perception and
approach by Byzantine authorities. The controversy involving
Manuel I Comnenus and his ecclesiastical officials informs us as
to the seriousness and dangers of such disunity.

   John Meyendorff has observed that it was the Byzantine
polemical tradition that "largely determined the official canonical attitude of the Church towards Islam, an attitude which is
reflected in the rites of reception of Moslem converts to
Christianity."[20] One of the earliest and most widely used of such
ritual tracts is the so-called "Formula of Abjuration."[21]
Traditionally attributed to the civil servant and historian Nicetas
Choniates (ca. 1155–1215), the text in reality derives from the
ninth or possibly even the eighth century.[22] Its author is
unknown. The rite consists of a brief statement of affirmation
vis-à-vis Orthodox dogmas (termed the *syntaxis* or "concur-
rence") and a series of twenty-two anathemas against Muslim
beliefs (termed the *apotaxis* or "renunciation"). Each portion was
to be recited by the initiate, phrase by phrase, following the
priest's promptings, or "if he [the initiate] happens to speak no
Greek," by his consent and through an interpreter.[23] If the
convert was a child, the godparent would serve as the interpreter. These recitations were apparently followed by a series

of prayers.[24] At the close of the ceremony the initiate became one of the catechumens, ready to enter into the next stage of the Orthodox conversion process.[25] The ceremony itself took place in the presence of other Christian faithful in the baptistery of a church. The text seems to indicate that both people who wished to become Christians for the first time and those who had apostasized were the intended subjects for the ritual.[26] Norman Daniel has noted that "the formula takes an unusually severe attitude in condemning whatever a Muslim believes, including the whole of what he believes about God and about Christ, although some of that is true according to the Christian faith."[27] The initiate was required to anathematize Muhammad, all of the Prophet's relatives (each by name), all of the caliphs through Yazid (680–683), the Qur'ân and its doctrines and traditions, the Muslim conceptions of paradise and predestination, the practice of polygamy, the "angels" of Muhammad, his interpretation of the Old and New Testaments, and many other aspects of Islam.[28] Although it is apparent that the author of the formula knew more about Islam than many of his contemporaries and had firsthand knowledge of the Qur'ân (in translation), he often confuses Islam with pre-Islamic Arab paganism.[29] There is also strong evidence to suggest that he drew on earlier Muslim, Jewish, and Manichaean "conversion" texts.[30] The anathemas reproduce many of the Byzantine polemicists' traditional attacks on Islam, and it is clear from the official ecclesiastical sanction given it and its widespread use from at least the 800s A.D. that the Orthodox Church, for its part, maintained a rigorist stance vis-à-vis Islam and the conversion process over the centuries.

It is the final anathema, No. 22, that is pertinent to the present inquiry. It reads as follows:

> And before all, I anathematize the God of Muhammad, about whom he [Muhammad] says, "He is God alone, God made of solid, hammer-beaten metal; He begets not and is not begotten, nor is there like unto Him any one."[31]

The author's basic reference here is to Sura 112 of the Qur'ân. This section, known as *al-Tawhid* ("The Unity"), proclaims the absolute unity of God as the basis for the Islamic faith.[32] As such, *al-Tawhid* also represented a challenge to Christian theologians

seeking to explain and defend the mystical doctrine of the
Trinity to Muslims. It was charged that Christians, by their
attribution of "partners" to God, were polytheists. For if they
could associate two with God, why not more? Christological
concerns were also prominent in the debates. How could Jesus
Christ be anything but a man, for how could God be born from a
woman? And finally, couldn't and wouldn't God have saved
humans by some other means than that of the Incarnation? As
Speros Vryonis has pointed out,

> The Byzantine replies to these attacks were a curious
> mixture of clever philological arguments and propositions
> attained as a result of faulty translation from the Arabic of
> the Koran. First, the prophets who spoke of Christ referred
> to Him as the Son of God, as God, and as One who would
> be incarnate. Second, the Muslims themselves accepted the
> fact that Jesus is the *logos* and *pneuma* of God and that
> these are in God. For to argue the contrary is to say that
> God is *alogos* and *apnous* (thoughtless and breathless), and
> this would reduce God to dead matter. Therefore the spirit
> and the *logos* have always been with God. And Christ, as
> being born of the Virgin, is also man, as the prophets
> prophesied. How his birth came about is a mystery, but to
> deny God's incarnation as an impossibility is to admit that
> God is not omnipotent. God became incarnate in order to
> save man, and it is useless to inquire why He did not seek
> to save man in some other manner for this is beyond the
> comprehension of man.[33]

Byzantine polemicists countercharged that Muslims worshiped a
material God, who was both *alogos* and *apnous*.[34] For
confirmation they declared that the Qur'ân itself characterized
Allah as being "made of solid, hammer-beaten metal." This
Christian interpretation was based entirely upon a translation
into Greek of the Arabic word *samad* in Sura 112.2. The word
samad in Qur'ânic usage means "solid, massive," or more
figuratively, "permanent, everlasting, eternal."[35] In order to
understand how and why the Greek translation became an
accepted and integral part of the Byzantine anti-Islam polemical
and "conversion" traditions, one must look back to the eighth
and ninth centuries.

The earliest Orthodox theologian (whose work is extant) to comment on the phenomenon of Islam and the Qur'ân was John of Damascus, who was probably born about fifty years after the Hijra.[36] Although some scholars have questioned the authenticity of various of his anti-Islamic treatises, the chapter entitled "On the Heresy of the Ishmaelites" in his *De haeresibus* appears authentic.[37] Here John closely examines key aspects of the Qur'ân as well as topics of contention between Christianity and the new faith. Regarding Sura 112, he has this to say: "He [Muhammad] says that there is one God, *creator of all*, who is neither begotten, nor has begotten."[38] The italicized words above indicate his translation and understanding of the crucial word *samad*. Though modern translators of the Qur'ân have not rendered *samad* in this fashion, the essential point is that John (who was a native Arabic speaker) even in his role as theological opponent attempts here to understand and to transmit accurately Qur'ânic language and concepts to his readers.[39] Accordingly, we must look elsewhere for the origins of the "polemical" translation of *samad*. Theodore Abu-Qurra (ca. 750–825), like John of Damascus, was born in Muslim-occupied territory. In later life he was appointed Orthodox bishop of Harran in northern Mesopotamia, a city known for its religious diversity, and there he became an active anti-Islamic writer.[40] And like John, Theodore was interested in understanding as well as refuting his religious opponents. His treatises, although negative in tone, are marked by a seriousness of purpose and real insights into the Christian-Muslim debate. In discussing the Muslim concept of God, Theodore translates *samad* rather figuratively with the Greek word σφυρόπηκτος, which means "hammered together, consolidated, indivisible."[41] It is clear that Theodore, like his predecessor, attempts to translate *samad* faithfully for his audience. And it is here we find the technical origins of, or rather, the inspiration for the later, negative interpretation. In the middle of the ninth century a Byzantine scholar, the philosopher Nicetas of Byzantium, initiated the tradition of anti-Islamic polemics within the empire.[42] Unlike his *dhimmi* predecessors Nicetas was unfettered by the restraints of an environment of Muslim rule and also less interested in entering into a potentially productive dialogue with Byzantium's enemies. His intent was to offer a systematic refutation of Muslim beliefs as expressed in the Qur'ân. Although it is probable that Nicetas, as an academic living in Constantinople, had little personal contact with Muslims, his extensive knowledge of the Qur'ân and of earlier Byzantine polemicists is apparent. Today three of his polemical writings are extant.[43] His principal work, commissioned by the emperor Michael III (842–867), is entitled *Refutation of the Book Forged by Muhammad the Arab* and represents a detailed analysis and critique of the Qur'ân.[44] In his discussion there of the Muslim conception of God and of Sura 112, Nicetas translates *samad* initially as ὁλόσφαιρος ("all-spherical")[45] and later as ὁλόσφυρος ("made of solid, hammer-beaten metal").[46] Clearly Nicetas is familiar with Theodore Abu-Qurra's earlier figurative interpretation of *samad*, and has chosen to advance this imagery along more negative lines.[47] This, in turn, allows him to ridicule Islam as an alien, even pagan, religion espousing a materialist conception of God—a God who is unable to see, hear, comprehend, or act without assistance.[48] Thus, it is with Nicetas of Byzantium that we find the origins of the "polemical" tradition regarding the Arabic word *samad*. Modern scholars agree that Nicetas' writings subsequently became the most influential and popular source for Orthodox polemicists, particularly on the subject of the nature of the "God of Muhammad."[49] And it was the descriptive epithet ὁλόσφυρος that was transmitted to later authors. More importantly for our purposes, Nicetas' interpretation of *samad* as ὁλόσφυρος became an accepted, integral part of the official Byzantine conversion ritual for Muslims wishing to join the Christian church. And this ritual was in use during the twelfth century, at the time of the emperor Manuel I Comnenus.

The reign of Manuel (1143–1180) is fairly well-documented in the sources of the period, thanks principally to the work of the historians Nicetas Choniates and John Cinnamus. One of the most energetic and intriguing of the Byzantine rulers, Manuel presided over an eventful, turbulent era in the history of the Eastern empire.[50] Beset on all sides by enemies, Christian and non-Christian, Manuel successfully maintained his realm with a diplomatic and military dexterity that impressed his contemporaries. Whether he was dealing with Norman, German, or Papal threats from the West, delicate negotiations with Hungary, Serbia, Russia or Venice, military instability caused by Turkish or Crusader ambitions, or internal dissension in Constantinople itself, Manuel exhibited a clear sense of purpose and the ability to act quickly with firm resolve. It is his relationship with the Orthodox Church and his viewpoint and policies regarding the matter of Muslim conversion that merit our attention here. Like his Comnenian predecessors, Manuel adopted what may be described as a "domineering" attitude and approach to the Church, and like them also he developed a taste for theological debate and controversy.[51] Our sources record, not without criticism, that the emperor even presented occasional public lectures on theological topics. Whatever Manuel's true personal interest in such activities,

> in good Comnenian fashion he used theological disputes to establish his credentials as a defender of orthodoxy and to confirm his mastery of the church. . . . Critics of Manuel may have complained that he went close to wrecking the harmony that was supposed ideally to exist between church and emperor in Byzantium, because of the way he meddled in matters of dogma. Yet the truth is that over the last part of his reign he was able to master any opposition to his interference with comparative ease. In other epochs of Byzantine history his conduct would have called forth bitter and sustained action from sections of the church, but this was noticeably absent.[52]

The only exception to this last trend arose from the ὁλόσφυρος controversy in the final months of his life, and even in this instance Manuel eventually won his point.

Concerning the issue of conversion of Muslims and other "barbarians," Manuel viewed a process of "inclusion" as an imperial necessity, and implemented it as an active policy. Indeed, with the general successes of Byzantine armies during most of his reign, chances were significantly improved for positive results in this regard. Both Turkish Muslims and former Christians converted to Islam were the objects of Manuel's missionary attentions.[53] Particularly noteworthy from a politico-military standpoint was the sizable number of Turks who were recruited to serve in the imperial army. Such men were offered employment in this capacity with the stipulation that they first renounce Islam and pledge themselves to Christianity. As Speros Vryonis has observed, "Their military qualities made of them highly desirable additions to the empire's military strength, and we see them in the armies of Alexius I, John II, and Manuel I, and, by the thirteenth and fourteenth centuries, the Tourkopouloi had become standard contingents of the Byzantine armies."[54] It was therefore only natural for Manuel to support measures that would strengthen the empire through the creation of additional Christians, soldiers or not. This goal Manuel and the Church of his day shared. It was in their approach and in their methods of attaining such a goal that contention arose.

Our principal source for the ὁλόσφυρος controversy is the *Historia* of the imperial civil servant and polymath Nicetas Choniates (ca. 1155–1215).[55] Two Greek chroniclers also refer to the affair, but offer little beyond what is provided in this account.[56] As a well-educated and fair-minded insider writing soon after the reign of Manuel, Nicetas Choniates offers much of interest to the reader.[57] That he was also something of a theologian in his own right and apparently had access to the archives of Hagia Sophia makes what he has to say about the controversy even more compelling.[58] Although Nicetas clearly believed that Manuel overstepped his authority in this and in other ecclesiastical matters and that his theology was misguided here, he does indicate this in his account, and there is no reason to doubt his basic narration of the events.

The ὁλόσφυρος controversy seems to have begun in February of 1180, in the last year of Manuel's reign.[59] According to Nicetas, the emperor proposed to have the final anathema (No. 22) of the "Formula of Abjuration" for Muslims, which was directed against the God of Muhammad, "expunged from all the catechetical books, beginning with the codex of the great church [i.e., Hagia Sophia]."[60] The patriarch, Theodosius Boradiotes (1179–1183),[61] accordingly was summoned to the palace along with other learned churchmen resident in the city. Most likely this group comprised the so-called "permanent" or patriarchal synod of Constantinople, or at least representatives of it.[62] Manuel proceeded to explain his ideas to them. Nicetas characterizes his approach and style as "bombastic," though elsewhere in his chronicle he notes that the emperor was "gifted with a silver tongue and an innate grace of expression."[63] The assembled hierarchy reacted negatively to the proposals, considering them "slanderous and detracting from the most true glory of God."[64] It was explained to the emperor that it was not the Christian God who was being anathematized "but the ὁλόσφυρος god fabricated by the deluded and demoniacal Muhammad and who was neither begotten nor did he beget."[65] It is interesting to observe here that Nicetas indicates that the opposition stemmed as much from the group's reaction to these latter attributes of the Muslim God as from the epithet ὁλόσφυρος itself.[66] Manuel is also described as not knowing the meaning of the Greek word ὁλόσφυρος. Although use of the term was rare in this and other periods of Byzantine history, surely Manuel in the preparation of his case would have thoroughly researched its usage and traditions, since its meaning was the very basis for his proposed change in the ritual text.[67] It is likely that Nicetas here is referring to the manner in which the emperor presented the word—in opposition to that of the Church hierarchs.

Thwarted in this, his first attempt to garner support for his ideas, Manuel now took another tack. With the assistance of certain learned members of the imperial court (Nicetas characterizes them as being "opportunistic" as well) the emperor produced his own "tome," or civil decree, setting forth his proposals in formal, written form and criticizing "former emperors and members of the hierarchy . . . for being so stupid and thoughtless as to suffer the true God to be placed under anathema."[68] Nicetas's declaration that Muhammad's ideas concerning God were upheld in the imperial tome is simply his own negative reaction to the general contents of the document. The decree was duly delivered to the residence of Patriarch Theodosius to be read publicly before the church officials gathered there. Accompanying the tome on its journey to the patriarchal palace was a sizable contingent of supporters, eminent civil officials all ("leaders of the senatorial council, the senate, and the learned nobility").[69] No doubt they were sent by Manuel to help create a positive environment for the proceedings and for the edict's reception. Indeed, Nicetas reports that this group was so enthusiastic in its sentiment as to appear unseemly—"like a band of youths."[70] But even he grudgingly admits that Manuel's written arguments were powerful and persuasive:

> So plausible did reason make the doctrine appear, not with the words which the Holy Spirit teaches but in the enticing words of man's wisdom,[71] that it was very convincing by virtue of the diverse scope of the issue, the attractiveness of its elaborate arguments, and in the careful examination of the meaning of its contents."[72]

Very likely the discussions and debate that ensued were lengthy and difficult. Nicetas gives primary credit to the redoubtable Theodosius for his stubborn refusal to accept "the introduction of novel doctrines" and his ability to prevail upon the majority of those gathered "to suspect these as being noxious."[73] Manuel, who apparently did not attend the sessions, reacted to the rejection of his proposals angrily, calling the church officials "foolish things of the world."[74] Nicetas notes that it was possibly Manuel's serious illness (which was to take his life a few months later) that contributed to his ill-tempered reaction. The emperor, denied once again, set about revising and strengthening his written proposals. Ultimately, a second, shorter version was produced and publicly issued.[75] Because Manuel was at that time residing at the Scutari palace in Damalis "to benefit from its mild climate and gain relief from the crowds of people while receiving thorough medical care," again the church hierarchy as well as "all those who were honored because of their learning" were summoned to meet.[76] Possibly Manuel hoped that his own presence, despite his weakened condition, together with the new, imperial setting would improve his chances. And it is probable that he intended the latter group of visitors, containing various of his own palace theologians and ecclesiastical advisors, to help win the day. Unfortunately, when the assemblage arrived the emperor was too ill to receive them. Instead of allowing the discussions to take place without his presence, Manuel sent one of his trusted undersecretaries, Theodore Matzoukes,[77] to inform them that he was indisposed and to deliver to them two documents to be read then and there. One was the new, shorter tome prepared by Manuel. It was his intent "that the assembled bishops should affix their signatures with dispatch."[78] The other was a strong critique of the patriarch and synod's earlier opposition to his request; Nicetas describes its tone and language as being "neither moderate nor elegant."[79] More important, in this document Manuel threatened to convoke a full church council to address the issues, and even to confer with the Pope himself if need be. This proved too much to bear for at least one of those listening. The metropolitan bishop of Thessalonica, Eustathius, normally an imperial supporter[80] and a man renowned for his learning and even temper,

> was filled with indignation by what was read and could not suffer the true God to be called ὁλόσφυρος , the fabrication of a demoniacal mind, [and] said, "My brains would be in my feet and I would be wholly unworthy of this garb," pointing to the mantle covering his shoulders, "were I to regard as true God the pederast who was as brutish as a camel and master and teacher of every abominable act."[81]

Nicetas goes on to report that "the bishops were nearly struck dumb by what they had heard, for he had shouted out these words, visibly shaken by pious zeal."[82] Perhaps they were more shocked by Eustathius' misunderstanding of Manuel's position on the issues at hand and its implications vis-à-vis the emperor than by his lapse of decorum in the presence of an imperial representative. The commotion caused by Eustathius can only be imagined, and Theodore Matzoukes, in a state of shock, returned to the palace, his mission brought to an abrupt end. It may well be that the other document, the shorter dogmatic tome, was never read before the group.

Manuel, for his part, determined to make the most of this slip by one of his leading foes in the controversy. Nicetas provides the following details:

> Manuel, perturbed by the report of what had been said, gave an artful defense of his position, commending forbearance as never before. He counted himself among the most orthodox of Christians and asserted that he came from most holy parents, while shunning the censorious and the scoffers. He urgently appealed that a judgment be made between him and the archbishop of Thessalonica, for

he said that if he should be absolved of believing in a god
who is a pederast and of distorting the faith, then a just
punishment should be imposed upon him who belched
out blasphemies against the anointed of the Lord.
However, should he be condemned as glorifying another
god than Him whom Christians worship, then he would
learn the truth and be deeply grateful to the one who
should convert him from error and initiate him into the
truth.[83]

Clearly Manuel entertained here the possibility of discrediting
and even punishing a leader of the opposition, making
Eustathius serve as an example of what might happen to other
clerics involved[84] and, as a result, organized resistance to his
viewpoint might dissipate. But fortunately for the archbishop of
Thessalonica, Patriarch Theodosius, drawing on his past
relationship with Manuel and using all of his charm, prevailed
upon the emperor to forgive his colleague, a man who had
hitherto served his ruler faithfully. Manuel agreed to pardon
Eustathius, in Nicetas' words, "for speaking amiss."[85] Days later
(Nicetas does not say exactly when) those invited to the aborted
conference were reassembled, again at Scutari it seems, and the
shorter dogmatic tome was read publicly. The chronicler reports
that everyone present praised its contents "as being reverently
orthodox in its teaching" and gladly affixed their signatures to
the document.[86] Nicetas clearly attributes this surprising change
of heart to the elaborate alterations and embellishments that
characterized the second tome.[87] Possibly, too, the palace setting,
the presence of Manuel himself, the well-remembered affair of
Eustathius, and behind-the-scenes political maneuvering by the
emperor's men all contributed to the outcome. Nevertheless,
according to Nicetas—who may be attempting to present the
most positive interpretation of this reversal of fortune—"The
bishops departed exulting in the fact that in opposing the
emperor they had won out over him, while he rejoiced in having
bent them to his will, having achieved with a few words what he
had been unable to do with the earlier prolix tome."[88] On the
following day, when officials sent by Manuel requested that the
Church hierarchs put into effect the agreed-to provisions,
opposition arose again. It may be that the synod somehow
believed the emperor would be content with their mere approval

of this tome and would not demand implementation as well. Meeting now in the patriarchal palace, the bishops "were no longer of the same mind but again shook their head in denial, contending that the written decree still contained certain reprehensible words which should be excised and replaced by others that would give no offense whatsoever to correct doctrine."[89] Which exact words were judged "reprehensible" are not identified by Nicetas. Understandably, Manuel was outraged and according to the chronicler, "charged that their inconstancy and fickleness plainly showed that they were devoid of any intelligence."[90] There the matter stood for probably several weeks. Nicetas' following statements on the whole affair are perhaps the most revealing in his entire account:

> After a long delay, they [the bishops] barely agreed to remove the anathema of Muhammad's god from the catechetical books and to write in the anathema of Muhammad and of all his teachings. Having proclaimed and confirmed this doctrine, the many synods and assemblies came to an end.[91]

Here the chronicler admits that Manuel won the day and attained what had been his goal all along: the deletion of the final anathema and the striking of the offensive epithet ὁλόσφυρος from the traditional Orthodox "Formula of Abjuration." It is significant that he does not offer reasons for Manuel's victory, considering the amount of space he devotes to this episode in his general account of the emperor's ecclesiastical policies. It is of little consolation to Nicetas, at least, that another anathema condemning Muhammad and all his teachings was substituted for the previous one; perhaps this is because several other sections of the "Formula of Abjuration" already covered the same ground.

Nicetas goes on to recount the final months of Manuel's life and reign. He begins by describing the revered figure of Nicetas, bishop of Chonai in Asia Minor. This man, he says, was renowned both for his virtue and for his oracular powers.[92] The elder Nicetas many years before had predicted, against the opinion of most observers, that the young, newly crowned Manuel Comnenus would defeat his brother Isaac for the throne and exceed his illustrious grandfather, Alexius I, in the number of years he would rule.[93] More ominously, it was prophesied that near the end of his life he would go mad. The chronicler further notes that

> this prophecy was known to me, the author Nicetas, together with many others, for the seer was my godfather in holy baptism. As to what this madness would be and how it would be manifested, no one could contribute to the prediction; some related the forecast to his madness for gold, while others believed he would fall victim to some frailty of the flesh."[94]

The historian's intent here becomes obvious with his next statement:

> When the controversy over the above-mentioned doctrine was initiated and the emperor recklessly contended for the first time that the god glorified by Muhammad as ὁλόσφυρος, who is neither begotten nor begets, is the true God, everyone agreed that this was the fulfillment of the prophecy because this doctrine, being wholly the opposite of the truth, was truly and absolutely the worst kind of madness.[95]

Nicetas, of course, has the last word in the affair and stresses that Manuel's ideas and actions were quite simply manifestations of the madness predicted for him, the tragic fulfillment of a prophecy. It is interesting to note that Nicetas maintains that "everyone" recognized this, an interpretation which seems at odds with his own account of the controversy. Nicetas finally closes his record of Manuel's ecclesiastical policies with the following words:

> The controversy was resolved around the month of May, and with the coming of September the emperor came to the end of his life. He had achieved nothing very notable for the empire and had made no provisions or arrangements for events following his death because he in no way would accept that death was near, for he contended that he had certain knowledge that another fourteen years of life was to be freely given him.[96]

The purposeful linking of the prophecy and the emperor's role in the controversy to his imperial failures and lack of wisdom in other matters is obvious.

Three questions remain. First, what were Manuel's beliefs and motivations and how are his actions to be interpreted? Second, what were the results of the ὀλόσφυρος controversy, both immediate and long-term? And third, what importance should be attached to this episode in Byzantine church-state relations? Nicetas certainly furnishes his own general explanation for Manuel's actions. But apart from this, the historian does offer other, more specific observations regarding the emperor's beliefs and conduct. A brief review of these materials is in order here. In his description of the initial days of the controversy Nicetas records that:

> Manuel proposed to have the anathematization expunged from all the catechetical books beginning with the codex of the great church. The reason was specious: he contended that it was scandalous that the Agarenes [Muslims],[97] when being converted to our God-fearing faith, should be made to blaspheme God in any manner.[98]

Later he writes that:

> Manuel let the opposition perish and set forth his own tome with the assistance of those members of the imperial court whom he knew to be opportunistic as well as learned, in which Muhammad's babbling (for I cannot call it theology) was upheld and former emperors and members of the hierarchy were thoroughly upbraided for being so stupid and thoughtless as to suffer the true God to be placed under anathema.[99]

When noting the reception of Manuel's first tome by the clergy Nicetas says, "Perhaps the ὀλόσφυρος god about whom Muhammad spoke so foolishly would have been glorified as the true God had not the patriarch resisted so strenuously."[100] And later he quotes Manuel from the polemical document that caused Eustathius to react so vehemently: "'I would be an ingrate and a fool,' said he, 'if I did not return to him who made me emperor, the God of all, a fraction of the good things I have received from him and did not make every effort to prevent the true God from

being subjected to anathema.'"[101] Finally, in describing Manuel's
prophesied madness he writes:

> When the controversy over the above-mentioned doctrine
> was initiated and the emperor recklessly contended for the
> first time that the god glorified by Muhammad as
> ὁλόσφυρος, who is neither begotten nor begets, is the
> true God, everyone agreed that this was the fulfillment of
> the prophecy because this doctrine, being wholly the
> opposite of the truth, was truly and absolutely the worst
> kind of madness.[102]

In each instance, Nicetas asserts that Manuel identified the "God
of Muhammad" with his own deity, the Christian God; it was
inconceivable to him that either one should be anathematized.
Hence, his proposal to delete the final anathema of the "Formula
of Abjuration" from the catechetical books of the Orthodox
Church. The ecclesiastical opposition, including his own
patriarch, viewed the emperor's ideas as a radical departure
from the established patterns of belief (Nicetas calls them "novel
doctrines"). But it may be argued that Manuel's motivations,
beliefs, and policies were more consistent with the older,
dominant Byzantine tradition concerning Islam than those of his
foes. For it was precisely because Islam had for centuries been
regarded by leading Byzantine theologians as a Christian heresy
that Manuel could and did accept Islam as a religion that
believed ultimately in the same God. Beginning with John of
Damascus in the eighth century, Orthodox writers had treated
the Muslim faith as a hostile, dangerous, flawed, but ultimately
understandable sect within the general fabric of Christianity.
And it was the recognition of this that allowed Manuel to
propose his canonical changes with a free conscience. There is
some irony in the fact that while Manuel was accused of
theological "innovation," always a serious charge in Byzantium,
he was merely advancing to their logical conclusions traditional,
mainstream arguments regarding Islam. His opponents, on the
other hand, drawing upon the more recent work of Nicetas of
Byzantium as transmitted in the "Formula of Abjuration,"
viewed the "God of Muhammad" as having no commonality
with the Christian deity, and Islam as an alien, pagan faith. As

such, it certainly merited no concessions or compromise on the part of either emperor or imperial Church.

Manuel was also motivated, of course, by his commitment to the evangelization of Muslims. Undoubtedly knowledgeable Muslims, potential converts or not, had long objected to the blatant, derogatory mistranslation of the divine epithet *samad* as "made of solid, hammer-beaten metal." Manuel recognized that the conversion of such individuals would be made easier by the removal of the final anathema from the ritual text.[103]

As a result of the ὁλόσφυρος debate and the eventual agreement between emperor and Church, the traditional final anathema in the "Formula of Abjuration" was dropped. In its place, a new anathema was substituted. The offensive translation of *samad* was deleted, the common monotheism of Islam and Christianity recognized, and the conversion process made less objectionable to Muslims. But both sides could claim to have been vindicated. Manuel accomplished all that he had sought. And the opposition in the Church hierarchy could argue (but perhaps only privately for a time) that implicit in the new anathema was a condemnation of the very same teaching of Muhammad about his God, that is, that Allah was ὁλόσφυρος. In addition, there was still the matter of implementation of the imperial initiative throughout the empire. It is certainly conceivable that the opposition in the Orthodox hierarchy, led by the patriarch himself, was slow to authorize and supervise the required textual changes in all catechetical books of the realm. And although the twenty-second anathema in later editions of the patriarchal *Euchologion* does read, "Anathema to Muhammad, to all his teaching and all his inheritance," the manuscript tradition of the excised anathema text may indicate that it continued to be used in some circles.[104] Finally, it must be remembered that Manuel himself, the ultimate guarantor of the revised oath for Muslims, died only a few months after the compromise solution was reached. Unfortunately, since the issue receives no mention in our sources for the empire's later history, it is difficult to judge how effective and long-lasting his efforts were. But, then, the significance of this affair does not lie merely in the impact of Manuel's ideas on his society or in the effectiveness of his imperial decrees. Rather, the ὁλόσφυρος controversy brings into perspective once again the dynamics of the church-state, or church-emperor relationship in Byzantium. And here too we see the profound effect that Islam had not only upon the military and diplomatic workings of the empire, but also on its internal religious and spiritual life as well. Islam represented a perennial challenge to the Christian inhabitants of the "God-centered realm of the Romans." The ways the Byzantines individually and collectively attempted to understand and deal with this "enemy faith" reveal much about their very human attempts to make sense of their world.

NOTES

1. Montet, "Un rituel d'abjuration des musulmans dans l'Église grecque," 155; cf. PG 140:133.

2. Gibb, "Arab-Byzantine Relations under the Umayyad Caliphate," 221, says

> The wars between Islam and Byzantium occupy so prominent, indeed almost exclusive a place in our history books and in the chronicles on which they draw, that the student of medieval history may be excused for taking the rubric 'Arab-Byzantine Relations' as a record of little more than continual warfare.

3. Sahas, "The Art and Non-Art of Byzantine Polemics," 55.

4. Meyendorf, "Byzantine Views of Islam," 115, 129.

5. Sahas, "Art and Non-Art," 64; Speros Vryonis, *The Decline of Medieval Hellenism in Asia Minor and the Process of Islamization,* 421, 435.

6. Daniel, *Islam and the West,* 4–5; Meyendorff, 119; Sahas, "John of Damascus on Islam. Revisited," 108.

7. Sahas, "Art and Non-Art," 57–58.

8. See the comments of John of Damascus in his *De haeresibus* (PG 94:764).

9. See John Lamoreaux's chapter in this collection; see also Moorhead, "The Earliest Christian Theological Response to Islam," 265–

274; *idem,* "The Monophysite Response to the Arab Invasions,"579–591; Kaegi, "Initial Byzantine Reactions to the Arab Conquest," 139–149.

10. On John of Damascus and Theodore Abu-Qurra, see Lamoreaux, Meyendorff, 116–121, and Daniel, 3–4.

11. Cf. Sahas, "Art and Non-Art," 61: "For the earliest Arab–Byzantine polemicists the 'Arab' ingredient represents the element of continuity, while Islam represents the element of abnormality, and, thus, of conversion."

12. See Meyendorff's comments (pp. 117–118) concerning John of Damascus.

13. See Norman Daniel's insightful observations (p. 2) on the consequences of such ignorance.

14. Scholars have paid increasing attention to such literature in recent years. See Khoury's excellent two-volume survey, *Les théologiens byzantins et l'Islam.*

15. Sahas, "Art and Non-Art," 63.

16. Cf. Vryonis, 422–436

17. On the dating of the earliest Byzantine conversion texts directed at Muslims, see Montet, 146–147.

18. Meyendorff, 123, 129; Sahas, "Art and Non-Art," 69.

19. Vryonis, 424–425, 440–443.

20. Meyendorff, 123.

21. This text was originally edited and published by Friedrich Sylburg (Heidelberg, 1595) and republished in PG 140:123–136. A new edition of the anathemas only (with French translation and commentary) by Edouard Montet appeared in 1906 (see n. 1). Cf. Ebersolt, "Un nouveau manuscrit sur le rituel d'abjuration des Musulmans dans l'Église grecque," 231–232/ Further bibliography in Beck, *Kirche und theologische Literatur im byzantinischen Reich,* 622.

22. On the dating of this text, see Montet, 146–147; Daniel, 3; and Meyendorff, 124.

23. PG 140:124.

24. Ibid.

25. Cf. Ebersolt, 232.

26. For example, the title refers to those "who are returning" to the Christian faith. Cf. Montet's comments, 147.

27. Daniel, 3.

28. Montet, 148–155 (text); 156–163 (commentary).

29. Daniel (p. 3) observes that

> it is true that Islam at that date may have seemed to overcivilised Syrian-Greek ecclesiastics to be only a temporary manifestation by simple desert-dwellers apt to revert to ancient superstition. The formula, however, definitely confused Islam itself with pre-Islamic paganism, and associated an idol of "Aphrodite" with the Ka'bah; there is no suggestion that such an idol had been removed. The formula's editor, Montet, describes it well when he calls it "at once exact and mistaken."

30. Interesting parallels and precedents can be found particularly in earlier Jewish "conversion" texts. See Starr, *The Jews in the Byzantine Empire, 641–1204*, 2, 24–25, 136–38, 173–80.

31. "Καὶ ἐπὶ πᾶσι τούτοις ἀναθεματίζω τὸν θεὸν τοῦ Μωάμεδ, περὶ οὗ λέγει ὅτι υἱὸς ἐστι θεὸς εἷς θεὸς ὁλόσφυρος, οὐκ ἐγέννησεν οὐδὲ ἐγεννήθη οὐδὲ ἐγένετο ὅμοιος αὐτῷ" (Montet, 155; PG 140:133).

32. See Blanchère, *Le Coran*, 670–671.

33. Vryonis, 430–431.

34. This tradition can be traced back to John of Damascus.
See Daniel, 4; and especially Abel, "La polémique damascénienne et son influence sur les origines de la théologie musulmane," 65.

35. صمد

Modern English translators of the Qur'ân have varied in their exact understanding of *samad* in this passage, but most have rendered it according to the latter, figurative meaning.

36. Concerning John of Damascus and Islam, see Sahas, *John of Damascus on Islam*.

37. Cf. Meyendorff 116–118; Vryonis, 422.

38. "Λέγει ἕνα θεὸν εἶναι ποιητὴν τῶν ὅλων μήτε γεννηθέντα, μήτε γεγεννηκότα" (PG 94:765).

39. Sahas, *John of Damascus*, 76, believes that here "John of Damascus conveys rightly the Qur'anic teaching."

40. On Theodore Abu-Qurra, see Dick, "Un continuateur arabe de saint Jean Damascène: Théodore Abuqurra"; and Graf, *Die arabischen Schriften des Theodor Abû Qurra, Bischofs von Harrân (ca. 740–820)*. Additional bibliography in Graf, *Geschichte der christlichen arabischen Literatur*, 2:7–11.

41. "σφυρόπηκτος." "Ὁ θεὸς, μουνὰξ, ὁ θεὸς, σφυρόπηκτος, ὅς οὐκ ἐγέννησεν, οὐδὲ ἐγεννήθη οὐδε γέγονεν αὐτῷ ἀντιμεριστής τις." (PG 97:1545) Cf. Sophocles, *Greek Lexicon of the Roman and Byzantine Periods,* 2:1062.

42. On Nicetas, see Meyendorff, 120–122; and especially Khoury 1:110–162. Further bibliography in Beck, 530–531.

43. Meyendorff, 121–122.

44. Ibid.

45. "ὁλόσφαιρος." For Nicetas's use of this word vis-à-vis the "God of Muhammad," see his *Refutation,* PG 105:705–708.

46. "ὁλόσφυρος." For his use of *this* word, ibid., 776, 784–788. Cf. Lampe, *A Patristic Greek Lexicon,* 950; and Sophocles 2:803.

47. Cf. Sahas, *John of Damascus,* 77: "The misunderstanding of Nicetas is not simply an oversight of one word, but actually the result of a biased attitude and wrong interpretation of the Qur'anic proclamation of Allah."

48. Meyendorff's provocative comment (p. 122) regarding this matter is worth noting:

> On the other hand, it can be asked whether, in some instances, such Byzantine interpretations of Islamic doctrine as the alleged belief in the spherical shape of God or the leech as the origin of men, did not, in fact, come from some forms of popular Arab religion— distinct, of course, from orthodox Islam—which were known to the Byzantines.

49. For example, this imagery and argumentation reappears in the later writings of such authors as Bartholomew of Edessa (ninth century; PG 104:1385, 1453), Euthymius Zygabenus (eleventh century; PG 130: 1348), and Emperor John Cantacuzenus (fourteenth century; PG 154:692), to name only three of the most prominent.

50. A good, recent survey of Manuel's reign is provided by Angold, *The Byzantine Empire, 1025–1205: A Political History,* chapters 10–12. The older standard work of Ferdinand Chalandon, *Les Comnène: Études sur l'empire byzantin au XIᵉ et au XIIᵉ siècles,* vol. 2: *Jean II Comnène (1118–1143) et Manuel I Comnène (1143–1180)* is still valuable.

51. Nicetas, *Historia,* 210, criticizes Manuel's activities in the area of theology.

52. Angold, 230, 233.

53. See Chalandon, 660–661; and Constantine G. Bonis, "Ό Θεσσαλονίκης Εὐστάθιος καὶ οἱ δύο 'τόμοι' τοῦ αὐτοκράτορος Μανουὴλ Α' Κομνηνοῦ," 162–164.

54. Vryonis, 441.

55. On Nicetas Choniates's career and writings, see the introduction to Magoulias's translation of the *Historia*, ix–xxviii; and esp. van Dieten, *Niketas Choniates*. I have here used Magoulias's translation, with a few slight adjustments.

56. *Synopsis Chronike*, 303–307; and Dositheos Notaras, Παραλειπόμενα ἐκ τῆς 'Ιστορίας περὶ τῶν ἐν Ἱεροσολύμοις πατριαχρθευσαντῶν, 247–249. Cf. also Euthymius Zigabenus' *Panoplia dogmatica*, chapter 26, cited in van Dieten's critical apparatus for the *Historia*, 213–219.

57. See Magoulias, xvi–xviii.

58. Magoulias (xvi) reports that Nicetas composed a theological treatise of some value for historians, the Δογματικὴ Πανοπλία (PG 139:1101–1444; but still partly unpublished). Concerning his access to the records of Hagia Sophia, see Magoulias, xvii.

59. Nicetas himself furnishes this information: *Historia*, ed. van Dieten, 220. A few modern scholars have opted for the year 1178 (Bonis, 161; Chalandon, 660; Meyendorff, 124). But cf. Magoulias, 121, 124; and Brand, *Byzantium Confronts the West*, 25.

60. *Historia*, 213.

61. On the background and career of Theodosius Boradiotes, see Chalandon, 660.

62. See Meyendorff, 124; cf. *Historia*, ed. van Dieten, 216.

63. *Historia*, ed. van Dieten, 213, 220.

64. Ibid., 214.

65. Ibid.

66. In the very next sentence Nicetas stresses: "For Christians believe God to be a father and it was these absurd and frivolous words of Muhammad which they utterly proscribed" (*Historia*, 214).

67. Bonis (164, n. 2) comments, "It is to be noted that the word 'ὁλόσφυρος' is non-standard linguistically and does not appear in other standard writers." Cf. Sophocles, 803; and Lampe, 950.

68. *Historia*, 214. On Manuel's "court theologians," ecclesiastical advisors, and general relations with the Church, see Angold, 228–242.

69. *Historia*, 214.

70. Ibid.

71. Cf. 1 Corinthians 2:4, 2.:13.

72. *Historia*, 214.

73. Ibid., 215.

74. Ibid. Cf. 1 Corinthians 1:27.

75. "Expatiating on the former tome, he resorted to discrepant elaboration and rhetorical embellishments which he then epitomized, and thus again making the doctrine enticing, he publicly posted a second tome" (*Historia*, 215).

76. *Historia*, 215.

77. On Theodore Matzoukes, see Chalandon, 662 n. 1.

78. *Historia*, 216.

79. Ibid.

80. On Eustathius's ties to the imperial court and his role in the affair generally, see Bonis, passim.

81. *Historia*, 216–217. On the alleged sexual immorality of Muhammad, see Vryonis, 431–433; and Daniel, 4.

82. *Historia*, 217.

83. Ibid.

84. Regarding Manuel's aggressive tactics in other theological controversies, see Angold, 230–232.

85. *Historia*, 218.

86. Ibid.

87. Cf. *Historia*, 215.

88. Ibid., 218.

89. Ibid.

90. Ibid.

91. Ibid., 218–219.

92. Ibid., 219.

> There was a certain eunuch by the name of Nicetas who presided as bishop over the city of Chonai and who was the habitation of every virtue; indeed, such were his oracular powers, his ability to foresee the future, that he was reckoned as one of the greatest seers and deemed a marvel by those who knew him. While ours was a wicked and adulterous generation, we were fortunate to have such a good man.

93. Magoulias (386 n. 594) reminds us that "actually both Alexios I (1081–1118) and Manuel I (1143–1180) reigned for 37 years."

94. *Historia,* 219–220.

95. Ibid., 220.

96. Ibid. Nicetas's account of Manuel's activities in his final months has been questioned in some aspects; see Brand, 24–25.

97. On the use of the word *Agarenes,* see Sahas, "Art and Non-Art," 60–61.

98. *Historia,* 213.

99. Ibid., 214.

100. Ibid., 215.

101. Ibid., 216.

102. Ibid., 220.

103. Modern scholars agree that this consideration was vital to Manuel's proposal and subsequent actions: Angold (p. 232); Bonis (p. 164); Brand (p. 25); Chalandon (p. 661); Meyendorff (p. 124); and Vryonis (p. 442). Also see Hussey, The Orthodox Church in the Byzantine Empire, 153; Kazhdan and Constable, *People and Power in Byzantium: An Introduction to Modern Byzantine Studies,* 148; and Runciman, *The Byzantine Theocracy,* 133–134.

104. See Montet, 145–146; Ebersolt, 231–232. Also, it should be noted that later Byzantine writers continued to employ the ὀλόσφυρος epithet and imagery, perhaps indicating their reliance directly upon Nicetas of Byzantium, but possibly also their familiarity with contemporary abjuration oaths. Indeed, one of these later writers was John Cantacuzenus, an emperor himself (see n. 49).

II. Spanish Anti-Muslim Polemic: Eighth to Twelfth Centuries

CHAPTER 4

Christian Views of Islam in Early Medieval Spain[1]

Kenneth Baxter Wolf

Historians run a number of risks when trying to assess medieval Christian views of Islam. One of these is the danger of defining the subject too narrowly, that is, of limiting the scope of inquiry to observations about Islam as a religion. As logical as it may seem to us to regard Islam in this way, it is important to realize that it was not the religious identity of the Arab conquerors that first struck European observers. What made them sit up and take notice was the speed and the extent of the conquest itself, which, in a few short decades, resulted in Arab domination of the eastern, southern, and western shores of the Mediterranean. Thus, we have the seventh-century Burgundian authors of the so-called *Chronicle of Fredegar* reporting on the Arab advances in the East and across Africa almost as they were happening, yet saying very little about the religious framework within which the Arab armies operated. Given the fact, then, that the earliest recorded impressions that the Latin Christians had of the Muslims cast them in military and political terms, it would seem appropriate to broaden our working definition of Islam and, by extension, amplify our notion of what constitutes a proper view of Islam. By so doing we stand a better chance of treating the subject honestly, working within the categories used by the Christian observers themselves rather than attempting to impose our own. Moreover, by considering Islam to be a political as well as a religious phenomenon, we find ourselves in a better position to appreciate the special circumstances under which views of

Islam *as a religion* actually appeared when they did indeed appear.

A second potential danger is that of treating a view of Islam without considering the particular context within which the "viewer" operated.[2] At one level, it is a matter of taking into account the specific historical circumstances that led particular Christian observers to record their perceptions about Islam when, where, and how they did. At another level, it is a matter of appreciating the *mentalité* of the observers, that is, the mental categories that they had at their disposal for framing something like Islam. This is not as difficult a task as it might seem at first glance, given the fact that virtually every early medieval European who recorded his impressions of Islam had been educated according to the same basic monastic (or monastically derived) curriculum, a curriculum whose general contours we can easily reconstruct. The scriptural and patristic focus of this curriculum, combined with a highly cultivated appreciation of the role of divine providence in history, determined that early medieval observers of something new like Islam would describe it in terms of age-old categories and patterns found in the Bible and the writings of the church fathers. Thus, it should come as no surprise that medieval views of Islam bear a strong structural resemblance to earlier views of the "other." To treat views of Islam *sui generis* is to fail to see that, from a medieval Christian perspective, Islam was only one species of a genus that included every perceived threat to Christendom from the very beginning of Christian history.

Each of these considerations assumes particular importance when we turn our attention to Spain and the views of Islam produced by Christians living there in the first century and a half after the Muslim invasion of 711. As we shall see, the earliest impressions that the Muslims made on Spanish Christian observers were military and political ones. Over time and under very particular circumstances, some Spanish Christians began to characterize Islam in religious terms. When they did, the views of Islam that they produced were structurally similar to views of previous threats to Christendom.

The earliest Spanish Christian references to the Muslims in Spain are to be found in two anonymous Latin chronicles dating from 741 and 754.[3] These chronicles, written by Christians living under Muslim rule, were conceived of by their authors as installments in the universal chronicle begun by Eusebius but continued by Jerome, Prosper of Aquitaine, Victor of Tunnuna, and John of Biclaro.[4] Faithful to the pattern established by their predecessors, the chroniclers of 741 and 754 focused on the political history of the Mediterranean and the various challenges to the maintenance of imperial hegemony in that region. Thus the *Chronicle of 741*, which begins with the death of Reccared in the west and the accession of Heraclius in the east, provides a great deal of information about the progress of the Muslim armies in Syria and across Africa. It has, however, very little to say about Islam as a religion. The chronicle describes Muhammad as the prince of the Saracens, "born of the most noble tribe of his people, a prescient man, a foreseer of some future events."[5] The author's succinct observation that "today the Saracens worship Muhammad with great honor and reverence as they affirm him to be an apostle of God and a prophet in all of their sacraments and scripture," exhausts his description of the new religion.[6]

The *Chronicle of 754* is much longer and far more informative about the conquest of Spain itself, but is even less forthcoming about the religious identity of the invaders. For the year 618—which the author incorrectly assigned to the initial Saracen military campaigns in the East—he simply recorded that they "appropriated for themselves Syria, Arabia, and Mesopotamia, more through the trickery than through the power of their leader Muhammad, and devastated the neighboring provinces. . . ."[7] Only once in the seven times that Muhammad is mentioned in the text is he identified as a prophet.[8] From time to time, the author referred to the caliph in Damascus as *amir almuminin* ("leader of the faithful") which, if he had translated it correctly, would have suggested that the Muslim *regnum* had a religious dimension; instead he rendered it, "carrying out all things prosperously."[9] Occasionally there is an oblique reference to a distinct Muslim religious tradition, such as when the author identified Mecca: "the home of Abraham, *as they assert* [emphasis mine]."[10] But it is hard to imagine an uninitiated Latin reader putting these bits and pieces together into anything even vaguely resembling the actual religious contours of Islam.[11]

Nor did the chronicler of 754 draw religious lines when recounting Muslim-Christian military encounters.[12] He relied exclusively on ethnic designations when referring to the various populations he discussed. For the Muslims he used *arabes*, *sarraceni*, and *multitudo* (or *plebs* or *grex*) *Ishmahelitarum* interchangeably, and *mauri* when referring specifically to the Berbers who made up the bulk of the occupation forces. Terms such as *pagani, ethnici, gentiles*, and *infideles* do not appear. Likewise, the author preferred the terms *gothi* and *franci* to *christiani* when referring to the peoples that the Muslims encountered in Europe.[13] Finally, in his summaries of the reigns of the Muslim caliphs of Damascus and governors of Córdoba, the author characterized the rulers according to their effectiveness in imposing order and suppressing rebellion, ignoring the whole issue of their religious affiliation or their treatment of subject Christian peoples.[14]

But would we expect much information about the religious component of Islam from chroniclers who, true to their genre, were more interested in military and political events? Perhaps not. But on the other hand, none of the previous continuators of Eusebius's universal chronicle were silent when it came to earlier religious challenges to Catholic Christianity. For that matter even the *Chronicle of 754* includes information about other peninsular religious novelties in the postinvasion period. In the year 721, the chronicle reports that a man named Serenus claimed to be the Messiah and called upon his fellow Jews to sell their property and leave with him for the promised land.[15] At the end of the entry for 744 is a reference to a Sabellian heretic.[16] Under the year 750, the author mentioned a book written by Deacon Peter of Toledo for the edification of certain Christians in Seville who were celebrating Easter on the wrong date.[17] He even noted a case of Islamic deviance when reporting that one of the Andalusian governors had suppressed certain rebels and heretics "whom they call *Arures*."[18] It is remarkable that a Christian living in Muslim Spain should have found these religious aberrations worthy of record while ignoring altogether the subject of Islam.[19]

The author of the *Chronicle of 754* was not the only Andalusian Christian visibly bothered by religious heterodoxy yet silent about Islam.[20] Around the year 730, Archdeacon Evantius of Toledo wrote to reprimand certain Christians in Zaragoza for claiming that animal blood and the meat of strangled animals was unclean.[21] Similar concerns about Judaizing prompted Bishop Felix of Córdoba in 764 to inquire about some local Christians who had suggested celebrating a joint fast with the Jews on the Day of Atonement.[22] Twenty years later, Bishop Elipandus of Toledo drafted a series of polemical and apologetic letters after being accused by Bishop Etrerius of Osma and Beatus of Liébana of holding Adoptionist Trinitarian views.[23] His preoccupation with his own defense did not stop him from reprimanding Migetius, a heretic in the vicinity of Seville, who not only espoused his own distinctive Trinitarian views, but selected twelve apostles and prophesied about his own resurrection.[24] At roughly the same time, at the other end of peninsula, Christians who denied both the Assumption of Mary and the uncorruptibility of the bodies of the saints evoked the consternation of the Asturian bishops Ascaricus and Tusaredus.[25]

How are we to account for the fact that despite the evidence for widespread concern about threats to Christianity, both internal, in the form of heresy, and external, in the form of Jewish law, the subject of Islam should remained untouched? It could simply be an illusion created by spotty documentation. It could be a function of the conceptual difficulty that domination by a non-Christian power posed for Spanish Christians versed in Old Testament notions connecting political power and divine favor.[26] Or it could reflect an overriding sense that the religion of the conquerors did not constitute much of a threat to the religion of the conquered. If at first glance it seems hard to believe that a Migetius could have appeared more threatening to eighth-century bishops than a Muhammad, let us back up a bit and consider the circumstances surrounding the Muslim conquest.

The speed with which the Muslims absorbed the Iberian peninsula was not entirely, or even principally, a function of their military strength. It was a product of their willingness to offer remarkably attractive terms of surrender to the towns and local lords they encountered. The *Chronicle of 754* refers to one such agreement worked out between 'Abd al-Aziz, the son of Musa ibn Nusayr, and the Christian Count Theodemir.[27] An independent Arabic source confirms that the Muslim general offered the count the opportunity to continue ruling the area around Murcia without any diminution of his power, property, or religious freedom, in exchange for his recognition of the Muslim regime and the payment of a yearly tax (*jizya*).[28] This was by no means unusual. Pacts or *dhimam* (singular: *dhimma*) of this sort were used to secure Islamic authority from one end of the growing empire to the other.[29]

Why were the Muslims so willing to come to terms with the peoples they encountered? Because the Muslims were so few in number. They simply could not have provoked military confrontations with the local populations every step of the way without seriously depleting their forces and thereby stalling their advance. They only fought when they had to, preferring to rely on the threat of force to encourage the peoples they encountered to accept terms that required a minimum of personal sacrifice. Typically, as in the case of Theodemir, the Christians retained their property and liberties in exchange for the payment of the *jizya*. Only those towns that resisted or those individuals who fled were victims of confiscation.

Aside from retaining their land and possessions, the Christians were allowed substantial religious freedoms. The theoretical basis of this policy was the Qur'ân, which protected "peoples of the book" as monotheists.[30] But scripture was not the only, or even the most significant, factor influencing Muslim policy toward subject religious communities. Again, the discrepancy in numbers between the Muslims and the Christians they encountered in the Mediterranean basin limited their options. Even if the Qur'ân had commanded it, they could not have effected mass conversions of local populations. Quite the contrary, their policies indicated that Muslim rulers and jurists were more concerned about protecting their own people from the potentially polluting effects of physical proximity to Christians. In Spain's case, the large percentage of recently converted Berbers in the invading force only made the Muslim leaders more wary of the religious climate.

One way to limit unwanted acculturation was to segregate the Muslim minority. To this end, the conquerors sometimes established garrisons outside of Christian urban centers.[31] Such garrisons not only made sense from a military standpoint, but they minimized potentially harmful religious contact with indigenous peoples.[32] More universally, the Muslims relied on legal rather than physical barriers to maintain their distance. In an attempt to give Christianity a public face commensurate with its subordinate status, the jurists prohibited bell ringing and processions, as well as church building and decoration. They also acted to limit social interaction by restricting intermarriage and forbidding the elevation of Christians to positions of public authority.[33] One of the by-products of these restrictions and the attitudes that gave birth to them, was the remarkable degree of autonomy exercised by the Christian communities.[34] The political prominence of the bishop, already pronounced in Visigothic times, was heightened not only by virtue of the fact that the conquest had removed much of the secular Christian elite, but because the bishops were the natural spokesmen for a *dhimmi* community that far outnumbered the Muslims.

While the particular circumstances surrounding the Muslim occupation of Spain may have helped to forestall Christian concerns about Islam, the conquest itself probably served to augment Christian fears about heresy and Judaizing. For with the fall of the Visigothic monarchy, the Spanish church lost its access to a secular authority disposed toward the enforcement of its conciliar decrees against heretics and Jews. Whether or not the threats posed by these groups actually increased after 711, it is quite possible that Spanish churchmen felt more vulnerable to them. It is also conceivable that the threat of Judaizing seemed more ominous by virtue of the fact that the Christians of Spain had been essentially "demoted" to the status of Jews, that is, as a protected but subordinated community within a community. The unfamiliar sensation of living "in diaspora" may have made Christian leaders more wary of maintaining their sense of distance from and superiority over the Jews.

In short, favorable capitulation terms meant that most Christians were largely unaffected by the change of regime in 711. Moreover, as a result of the fears of the Muslim leadership, contact between Christians and Muslims was restricted. Only within this context of a ruling minority trying to maintain both its political authority and its religious integrity, do the seemingly insignificant religious concerns of subject clerics make any sense. Only within this context could the anxiety provoked by Trinitarian heretics or by Christians who wanted to celebrate Yom Kippur eclipse the fear of Islam.

As it turned out, the walls that the early Muslims built between themselves and the Christians began to crumble shortly after they were put into place. Within a century of the conquest, the sources reveal a high degree of assimilation and acculturation in both directions, especially toward Islam. Among the forces at work in undermining the efforts of the jurists were the pragmatic political concerns of the governors and emirs. For they, like their Eastern counterparts, quickly recognized the advantages of appointing to government posts Jews and Christians whose lack of tribal affiliation rendered them more vulnerable and therefore theoretically more loyal than Muslims. By at least the ninth century, Christians and Jews were regularly employed by the emirs as tax collectors, ministers, and even bodyguards.[35] A more significant factor behind the increased assimilation of Christians into Islamic society was the attraction of participating in a culturally sophisticated and economically prosperous commercial empire that linked Spain with Africa, the Near East, and Central Asia. Many Christians became successful merchants on both a local and international scale.[36] Others studied Arabic and immersed themselves in a rich and fresh literary tradition.[37]

As favorable as this situation might have been for Andalusian Christians from a political, economic, or cultural standpoint, such assimilation posed some potentially serious problems of religious identity, analogous to those that occupied the Muslim jurists in the wake of the conquests. From the end of the eighth century on, an increasing number of Christians converted to Islam.[38] More typically, Christians retained their religious identity, but did all they could to melt into the dominant society by avoiding anything that might, on the one hand, draw undue attention to their inferior religious status, and on the other, offend the religious sensibilities of their hosts. In short, they dressed like Muslims, spoke like Muslims, and lived like Muslims. While this process of acculturation contributed to the well-being of many Christians, others looked on with suspicion. With each new generation born into Andalusian society, the cultural barriers that had originally separated the Christians from the Muslims became more and more porous. By the early ninth century, the perception of a passive but steady encroachment on the part of Islam was strong enough to prompt Andalusian ecclesiastics to address for the first time the problem of Islam as a rival religious phenomenon.[39]

Unfortunately, the very earliest such Latin treatments of Islam are obscured by a lack of information about either their authors or their contents. The first of these works, the *Disputatio Felicis cum sarraceno*, survives only as a title mentioned in one of Alcuin's letters to Charlemagne, although we can be fairly certain that its author was Bishop Felix of Urgel, better known for his support of Elipandus during the Adoptionist controversy.[40] A second *disputatio*-style treatise against the Saracens, composed in the 820s or 830s by a Cordoban abbot named Speraindeo, apparently to be used as a "primer" for the education of local clerics, fared only slightly better, a single paragraph having been preserved in a quotation in a later work.[41]

A third assessment of Islam, a short and singularly unsympathetic life of Muhammad known as the *Istoria de Mahomet*, still exists in its entirety, but without any indications as to authorship.[42] We know that the *Istoria* had to have been written sometime before 850, when it was discovered by a visitor to the Navarrese monastery of Leyre.[43] Its prologue, with references to church construction in Toledo and Andújar, would suggest that it was written in one of those two places.[44] The *Istoria* covers the entire span of Muhammad's life. It tells how Muhammad, orphaned at an early age, was placed in the service of a certain widow, whom he later married "in accordance with some barbaric law." He became an "avaricious usurer," and, in the process of plying his trade, came into contact with Christians. Attending some of their religious services, he memorized sermons and refashioned them to deliver to his people, thus becoming the "wisest of all among the irrational Arabs." Shortly after he was visited by a golden-mouthed vulture, claiming to be the angel Gabriel. Ordered by this apparition to pass himself off as a prophet, Muhammad complied and "made headway as [the Arabs] began to retreat from the cult of the idols" and worship God. He commanded his followers to fight on his behalf and they defeated the Greek army in Syria and made Damascus their new capital. Muhammad fabricated "psalms" about a number of biblical figures as well as about animals. He issued a law that would allow him to exercise his lust on the divorced wife of one of his followers. Finally he prophesied that he would rise from the dead after three days. When, after his death, three days passed and nothing had happened, a pack of dogs, attracted by the smell of his decomposing body, devoured most of it. His followers buried the rest. The biography ends with the observation that "it was appropriate that a prophet of this kind fill the stomachs of dogs, a prophet who committed not only his own soul, but those of many, to hell."[45]

Though crude and deprecatory, the *Istoria* nonetheless reveals a remarkable familiarity with Islamic tradition and doctrine. Muhammad was indeed an orphan who worked for and later married Khadijah. The *Istoria* accurately depicts Islam as monotheistic and acknowledges its missionary success among the Arabs. Its author must have known that the Qur'ân contains references to biblical figures and that many of its suras are identified by reference to individual animals. He even paraphrased the Qur'ânic account of the divorce of Zayd and Zaynab.[46] Once the author had twisted each of these facts almost beyond recognition, he added unmistakable elements of Christian parody: a resurrection promise that backfired and a diabolic vulture in place of the dove that traditionally represented the Holy Spirit.

Despite the fact that these three early Latin characterizations of Islam as a religion—the *Disputatio Felicis,*

Speraindeo's "primer," and the *Istoria de Mahomat*—are, for one reason or another, so obscure, we do know, very roughly speaking, when and where they were written. Two of the three were composed well within Islamic territory, the third, on its shifting northern frontier.[47] And all three were written sometime between the last decade or two of the eighth century and the very middle of the ninth. Though these meager data by no means prove that all or any of the authors qualify as concerned Andalusian ecclesiastics reacting against religious encroachment on the part of Islam, they certainly do not contradict the hypothesis. Far more substantial is the evidence surrounding the work of Eulogius, the first of the early Latin commentators on Islam to provide us with enough information about himself and his world to allow us to place his observations in some sort of meaningful context.

In the late spring of the year 851, a monk named Isaac left his retreat in the mountains above Córdoba and walked the seven or eight miles down to the city. There he approached a Muslim *qadi*, or judge, in front of the emir's palace, and publicly denounced Muhammad and proclaimed the divinity of Christ. On June 3, he was decapitated for blasphemy.[48] Two days later, a Christian soldier serving in the emir's army made the same spontaneous confession and met the same fate.[49] Within yet another forty-eight-hour period, six monks and priests, from a variety of religious institutions in the area, added their names to the growing list of victims.[50] The ensuing so-called "Cordoban martyrs' movement" accounted for the deaths of close to fifty Christians over the course of the decade.[51]

This parade of spontaneous martyrs enjoyed considerable support from the outlying monastic communities that contributed most to their numbers. But within Córdoba itself, opinion was mixed. One hundred forty years of forced coexistence had, as we indicated previously, led to a breakdown of the social barriers that had separated the religious communities in the wake of the conquest. Given the advanced levels of Christian assimilation and acculturation, it is not difficult to imagine why the martyrs were unpopular among Christians in the city. When the Muslim authorities responded to the blasphemers by putting pressure on the community as a whole, the Christians who had the most to lose by being linked in the emir's mind with the Christian dissidents repudiated Isaac and the others. It was in reaction to this split within his community that the Cordoban priest Eulogius produced the works in defense of the martyrs that contain his perceptions of Islam: the *Memoriale sanctorum* and the *Liber apologeticus martyrum*.

In the *Liber apologeticus martyrum*, written sometime between 857 and his death two years later, Eulogius offered a point-by-point rebuttal of the challenges made by the unsympathetic Christians, who were quick to contrast the circumstances surrounding the deaths of Isaac and his imitators with those of their ancient Roman counterparts. The lack of any obvious persecution to compare with the provocative decrees of a Decius or a Diocletian was the main point of criticism, but not the only one. At one point Eulogius was asked to explain how his candidates for martyrdom could be considered legitimate martyrs when they had "suffered at the hands of men who venerated both God and a law."[52]

This is a remarkable, one-sentence window into the minds of the more assimilated Cordoban Christians. As they saw it, the Muslims were monotheists who worshiped the same God as they, though on the basis of a distinct, revealed law. As far as they were concerned, this religious common denominator not only rendered inappropriate the radical actions of the martyrs but also presumably legitimated the cooperative attitudes that governed their own day-to-day relations with the Muslims.[53] Where did the Christians get such an "ecumenical" perspective? From the Muslims. The same Qur'ânic perspective that allowed Muslims to tolerate Christians as monotheists and recipients of a revealed law, provided Christians with a ready-made justification for their participation in Islamic society.

This interpretation of Islam was totally unacceptable to Eulogius, who said,

> Those who assert that these soldiers [that is, the martyrs] of our own times were killed by men who worship God and have a law, are distinguished by no prudence with which they might at least give heed to cautious reflection,

> because if such a cult or law is said to be valid, indeed the
> strength of the Christian religion must necessarily be
> impaired.[54]

Quoting from Paul's letter to the Galatians—"If anyone preach to you a gospel besides that which you have received, let him be anathema"—Eulogius underscored the exclusivity of Christianity, which, as he saw it, had "penetrated every corner of the world and traversed every nation on earth."[55] This left no room, according to Eulogius and Paul, for any new law modifying the one brought by Christ. For a Christian to claim that a more recent revelation had any validity at all was to fail to appreciate the universality of the gospel. Besides, Eulogius asked,

> What is the purpose of believing that a demoniac full of
> lies could speak the truth? that one enveloped in fallacies
> could provide a law? that a perverse grove could produce
> good fruit? In the meantime, that abominable one brings
> forth evil from the terrible treasure of his heart, and offers
> his impious leadership to the foolish crowd, so that both
> he and they incur the pains of the eternal void.[56]

In reaction to what he saw as a dangerous tendency to downplay the differences between the two religions, Eulogius offered his own interpretation, one designed specifically to justify the martyrs' actions. To begin with, Eulogius had to make it very clear that the discrepancies between Islam and Christianity were not as minor as many of his fellow Christians pretended: "He [Muhammad] teaches with his blasphemous mouth that Christ is the Word of God, and the Spirit of God, and indeed a great prophet, but bestowed with none of the power of God."[57] By focusing his readers' attention on the central Christological difference between the two religions, Eulogius not only underscored the carelessness of his opponents, but connected Muhammad's errors to those of a former, particularly infamous enemy of the church: Arius. And this opened the door to a stockpile of readily adaptable polemical ammunition to use against Islam. Just as Hilary of Poitiers, the principal Latin polemicist in the struggle against Arianism, hyperbolized the doctrinal deviance of Arius, transforming him into the most infamous of heresiarchs, so Eulogius placed Muhammad at the apex of error:[58]

> Of all the authors of heresy since the Ascension, this unfortunate one, forming a sect of novel superstition at the instigation of the devil, diverged most widely from the assembly of the holy church, defaming the authority of the ancient law, spurning the visions of the prophets, trampling the truth of the holy gospel, and detesting the doctrine of the apostles.[59]

"Heresiarch" was not the only epithet that Eulogius borrowed from the campaign against Arius. He also applied the label "antichrist" to Muhammad, who, like Arius earned the ignominious title by refusing to accept the divinity of Christ.[60] Eulogius presumably would have made more use of this identification had not his friend and fellow apologist, Paul Alvarus, taken up the task for him.

Alvarus, another student of Abbot Speraindeo, wrote his *Indiculus luminosus* in 854. The first part of this work is a defense of the actions of the martyrs similar to Eulogius's *Memoriale sanctorum* and *Liber apologeticus martyrum*. The second part is a commentary on those passages in Daniel and Job that were traditionally interpreted as references to antichrist. Alvarus interpreted the eleventh horn of the fourth beast in Daniel 7 as a reference to Muhammad.[61] The three kings that he was to "bring down" were identified as the Greeks, the Visigoths, and the Franks. The "words spoken against the Most High" and the fabrication of laws fit what Alvarus knew about Muhammad and his Qur'ân. And the saints that were to be crushed by him corresponded nicely to the Christians executed in Córdoba.[62] Alvarus even calculated the year in which the prescribed "time, times, and half a time" of the antichrist's rule would come to an end: 870, that is, sixteen years from the time he was writing.[63] Alvarus went on to identify the god Moazim of Daniel 11 with the god worshipped by the Muslim muezzins from their "fuming towers."[64] And he used the prophetic reference to the eleventh king's lust for women as an excuse to elaborate his characterization of Muhammad as a libertine worshiped for his sexual prowess and the Qur'ânic vision of the afterlife as a supernatural brothel.[65] Alvarus then moved on to Job 40 and 41, applying the descriptions of the leviathan and the behemoth to the antichrist Muhammad. The former, breathing fire and smoke, and the latter, "wielding his tail like a cedar," symbolized the persecution that the Christians of Córdoba were forced to endure.[66]

For his part, Eulogius dedicated himself to adapting yet another biblical image that had been pressed into service against Arius and therefore was ready to be appropriated for polemical use against Muhammad. This was the false prophet, the coming of which Christ had foretold to the apostles.[67] Three characteristics of the *pseudopropheta* seemed, in Eulogius's opinion, to fit Islam like a glove. First of all, it fit chronologically because Muhammad had experienced his visions some six hundred years after Christ had closed the door behind him to any modification of his message. Second, it fit in terms of the sheer numbers of Muslims that had occupied the eastern, western, and southern shores of the Mediterranean, for Christ had specifically warned his followers that *many* would be led astray by such "ravenous wolves in sheep's clothing."[68] Finally, the "false prophethood" of Muhammad provided an explanation for both the existence of recognizably Christian themes within his doctrinal scheme, and their perverse modification at his hands. It made sense that a false prophet, surfacing in the wake of Christian missionary success, would incorporate twisted versions of the more salient aspects of Christianity to "season his error," making it more attractive to prospective converts. This allowed Eulogius to account for, among other things, the Qur'ânic afterlife: Muhammad had adopted it from Christianity, but had adapted it to meet his own lusty needs until it resembled a brothel.[69]

But if Eulogius selected this model because it made sense out of the readily observable characteristics of Islam in the ninth century, he also realized that it would provide him with a polemically useful way of assessing the character and motives of the movement's founder. By highlighting such episodes as Muhammad's relationship with Zaynab, the repudiated wife of his follower and kinsman, Zayd, Eulogius could easily transform the Muslim prophet into a perfect parody of the ascetic biblical prototype. In this Eulogius was assisted by his chance discovery of the *Istoria de Mahomet* at the monastery of Leyre in 850. He quoted it in its entirety in the *Liber apologeticus martyrum*, presumably with an eye to lending outside authority to his characterization of Muhammad as a false prophet.[70]

All three of the epithets that Eulogius borrowed from the Arian controversy—heresiarch, antichrist, and false prophet— contributed directly to his polemical and apologetic goals. Together they were used to deflate his opponents' claim that Islam was, in some sense, a distinct religion founded upon its own particular revelation. By casting Muhammad in any one of these roles, Eulogius was able to present Islam as the newest in a well-documented series of misguided derivatives of Christianity rather than as an entirely separate and rival system. This in turn allowed him to depict Isaac and other martyrs as heroic defenders of the faith, worthy of the respect of their community.

In concluding, it is worth considering how this hypothesis regarding the emergence of Islam as a religious phenomenon in Andalusian Christian writings can perhaps help us appreciate other early views of Islam whose contexts are not as well known. The *Tultusceptrum de libro domni Metobii*, an explanation of the origins of Islam, is one such example.[71] It survives only as it was recorded in the tenth/eleventh-century codex of Roda, without any indication as to when or by whom it was written.[72] The account begins with a vision experienced by one bishop Osius. In the vision an angel instructed Osius to go and preach "to my satraps who dwell in Erribon," because they had turned from God and thus required correction. Osius accepted the mission before he realized that his failing health would not permit him to carry it out. He thus delegated the task to one of his monks, a boy named Ozim. On his way to Erribon, however, Ozim was stopped by another angel, this time an evil one, who claimed to be the same angel that had initially spoken to his master. The evil angel instructed Ozim to modify the original message entrusted to him by Osius. The angel also changed the boy's name from Ozim to Muhammad and ordered him to repeat the following prayer to the satraps: *"Alla occuber alla occuber sita leila citus est Mohamet razulille."* The author of the *Tultusceptrum* interceded at this point to tell the reader that the boy "did not know that he was invoking demons" everytime he pronounced the prayer and that as a result of the evil angel's intervention, the true revelation was irretrievably lost along with the souls of the satraps and their people who received the corrupted message.

Like the *Istoria de Mahomet*, the *Tultusceptrum* reveals a surprising degree of familiarity with Islam despite its radical distortion of traditional Islamic history. The transliteration of *Allah Akbar* followed by a curious version of the *shahadah* is only the most obvious example. Other crude transliterations of proper names are equally suggestive. "Ozim"—also rendered "Ocim" in the same text—appears to be a derivation of "Hashim," the name of Muhammad's clan. A Latin genealogy of Muhammad dating from the 880s renders the name "Escim," making the phonetic connection clearer.[73] Likewise the place name "Erribon" is most likely a form of "Ethribum" or Yathrib, the pre-Islamic name for Medina.[74]

Beyond the appearance of familiar names, however, the *Tultusceptrum* demonstrates a remarkable appreciation for the fundamental tenet of Islam: that it is based on a direct revelation from God. The story begins, as does the history of Islam, with an angel concerned about the spiritual fate of the Arabs and delegating the task of their correction to a prophet. The account also suggests that the author was aware of the basic Islamic criticism of Christianity: that it amounted to a corruption of an originally pure message brought by the prophet Jesus. Rather ingeniously the author turned the same accusation back on the Muslims, depicting Ozim-Muhammad as a naive boy duped into adulterating an originally pure divine revelation.

These observations help us to place the *Tultusceptrum*, if not in time, at least in function. For if Eulogius found the *Istoria de Mahomat* useful in his efforts to refashion Muhammad into a false prophet, the assimilated Christians against whom Eulogius directed his arguments were more likely to have gravitated toward the *Tultusceptrum* version. By Eulogius's own admission, we know that at least some Cordoban Christians saw the Muslims as "men who venerated both God and a law," and regarded this as justification for their lack of support for the martyrs. As we observed previously, they would have regarded this as a justification for their daily interaction with Cordoban Muslims, a justification adopted and adapted from the Muslim attitude toward other peoples of the book. The *Tultusceptrum* effects a similar "turning of the tables" on Islam, making it appear to be the product of a corrupted revelation, yet acknowledging that its original inspiration, like that of Christianity, was a legitimate, divine one. This is not to claim that the *Tultusceptrum* was written by Eulogius's opponents in mid-ninth-century Córdoba. But the Cordoban situation, which we know generated two opposing views of Islam—one as a dangerous false prophecy and the other as a monotheistic religion based on a distinct revelation—may have been replicated in other Spanish Christian communities under Muslim rule in the period. The *Tultusceptrum*, like the *Istoria de Mahomet*, may have come, in a contextually disembodied way, from just such a community.

NOTES

1. This chapter represents an expanded and updated version of my article, "The Earliest Spanish Christian Views of Islam." My thanks to the editors of *Church History* for their permission to use the article this way.

2. As in the case of Norman Daniel's *Islam and the West*.

3. Both the *Chronicle of 741 (Chronica Byzantina-Arabica)* and the *Chronicle of 754 (Chronica Muzarabica)* can be found in CSM 1:7–14, 14–54. López Pereira has edited and studied the later chronicle: *Crónica mozárabe de 754* (hereafter, CM) and Estudio crítico sobre la *crónica mozárabe de 754*. Another study and an English translation of the *Chronicle of 754* can be found in Wolf, *Conquerors and Chroniclers of Early Medieval Spain*, 28–45, 111–158.

4. Isidore of Seville authored his own universal chronicle that extends as far as 615 (MGH AA 11: 391–497). But his was not so much a continuation as a vastly condensed version of the whole Eusebian project. The chroniclers of 741 and 754 began where Isidore (rather than John of Biclaro) left off, but conceived of their contributions more as Biclaro-like installments designed to bring the universal chronicle up to date.

5. CSM 1:9.

6. Ibid.

7. CM 8; Wolf, *Conquerors*, 113.

8. CM 11; Wolf, *Conquerors*, 115.

9. CM 57; Wolf, *Conquerors*, 133.

10. CM 34; Wolf, *Conquerors*, 124.

11. Despite the author's rhetorical expression of grief at the turn of events in Spain—"Even if every limb were transformed into a tongue, it would be beyond human nature to express the ruin of Spain . . ." (CM 55; Wolf, *Conquerors*, 132; cf. Jerome, *Epistola*, 108.1)—he did not even interpret the invasion as a divine scourge brought to bear against a sinful Christian kingdom. This is particularly remarkable in light of the facts that (1) the author did cast the Muslim conquest of Byzantine territory as a scourge (Wolf, *Conquerors*, 32–37); and (2) Boniface, in a contemporary letter to King Aethelbald of Mercia, described the invasion of Spain as a punishment for sin (*Epistola* 73, MGH *Epistolae selectae* 1, ed. M. Tangi (1955), p. 151). For later, ninth-century Spanish applications of the scourge motif, see Manuel Gómez Moreno, "Las primeras crónicas de la Reconquista," 562–599; and Wolf, *Conquerors*, 46–60.

12. The closest he came to this was when he recounted a Muslim expedition to crush a pocket of Christian resistance in the Pyrenees. CM 81; Wolf, *Conquerors*, 145, 41.

13. On a few occasions, the author did use *christiani* when discussing the periodic tax increases that would have affected only the non-Muslims. This showed a certain level of sophistication on the part of the author who apparently understood the religious basis for the application of the Muslim tax known as the *jizya*. CM 64, 74, 75, 91; Wolf, *Conquerors*, 136, 139, 140, 154.

14. CM 31, 67, 79, 81, 82, 91. Wolf, *Conquerors*, 37–38, 123, 137, 143, 144–146, 154–155.

15. CM 74.1; Wolf, *Conquerors*, 139–140.

16. CM 88.1; Wolf, *Conquerors*, 151–152.

17. CM 93; Wolf, *Conquerors*, 155.

18. CM 82; Wolf, *Conquerors*, 146. Most likely a reference to the Kharijites (a.k.a., al-Haruriya).

19. This is not to mention one report of heresy in Isidore's time (CM 14; Wolf, *Conquerors*, 116) nor the many references to church

councils, mostly confined to the portion of the chronicle covering the preinvasion period.

20. For an overview of eighth-century Spanish heterodoxy, see Rivera Recio, "La iglesia mozárabe."

21. CSM 1:1–6.

22. Ibid., 1:55–58.

23. Ibid., 1:78–112. For a brief overview of the Adoptionist controversy, see Pelikan, *The Growth of Medieval Theology*, 52–59. For Elipandus, see Rivera Recio, *Elipando de Toledo*.

24. CSM 1:68–77.

25. Ibid., 1:114–124. It is worth noting that the famous commentary on the Apocalypse composed by Beatus of Liébana in the 770s is also devoid of information about Islam. Though, as we shall see, the identification of Muhammad and the forces of Antichrist became a theme of anti-Muslim polemic in the next century, Beatus was content to interpret the book of Revelations as if the political climate in the Mediterranean had not significantly changed since imperial times. For more on this, see Williams, "Purpose and Imagery," 227–228.

26. Wolf, *Conquerors*, 43–45.

27. CM 87.1; Wolf, *Conquerors*, 151–152.

28. The Arabic text, with a Castilian translation, can be found in Simonet, *Historia de los mozárabes de España*, 797–798. See also Howell, "Some Notes on Early Treaties between Muslims and the Visigothic Rulers of Al-Andalus.," 3–14.

29. For a recent and succinct overview of the relationship between Muslims and "peoples of the book," see Lewis, *The Jews of Islam*, 3–66. For a more detailed treatment, see Ye'or, *Dhimmi: The Dhimmi Jews and Christians under Islam*. For the situation in Spain, see Glick, *Islamic and Christian Spain in the Early Middle Ages*.

30. Qur'ân 9:29, 2:62, 5:69.

31. Hodgson, *The Venture of Islam* 1:208–209; Collins, *Early Medieval Spain*, 160–161.

32. As Glick (169) has observed, "the intent of the *dhimma* arrangement . . . was to ensure that religious groups were kept separate, distinct and apart from one another, lest the dominant religion suffer contamination from the subordinate ones."

33. For the most up-to-date treatments of this subject, see Ye'or, *Dhimmi*.

34. Those who have considered this autonomy out of its proper context have marveled at the "tolerance" of the Muslims. But, as Glick (174) has observed:

> The communal autonomy of the groups, often represented as the very symbol of tolerance, was in fact the institutional expression of ethnocentric norms which held such groups in abhorrence, as tolerated but alienated citizens who were not to share in social life on the same basis as members of the dominant religion."

Robert Burns (*Islam under the Crusaders*, 186–87) noted the same phenomenon in thirteenth-century Valencia, when the political tables had turned and the Christians were segregating themselves from the Muslim majority: "Tolerance at this extreme is not easily distinguishable from intolerance."

35. The emir al-Hakam I (796–822) created a special bodyguard headed by the Cordoban count Rabi, son of Theodulf. Rabi also served as tax collector and was ultimately executed for alleged misappropriations. Lévi-Provençal, *Histoire de l'Espagne musulmane* 1:164, 196. Samson, who became abbot of Pinna Mellaria (near Córdoba) in 858, composed his *Apologeticus* in response to what he regarded as reprehensible conduct on the parts of Count Servandus of Córdoba and Bishop Hortegesis of Málaga, who were both tax farmers. *Apologeticus* 2 pref., 5 (CSM 2:551). Eulogius of Córdoba, writing in the early 850s, railed against this practice. *Memoriale sanctorum* 3.5 (CSM 2:443). He also referred by name to a Christian soldier in the emir's army, and to a system of military pensions from which certain Christians benefited. Ibid., 2.3 (CSM 2:402); 3.1 (CSM 2:440). We also know of two Cordoban Christians who occupied the office of *katib adh-dhimam* (secretary to the covenant, a liaison between the emir and the Christian community), and a third who served as a translator. Ibid., 2.2 (CSM 2:402); 2.15.2 (CSM 2:435); 3.2 (CSM 2:440); *Apologeticus* 2 pref., 9 (CSM 2:554).

36. Paulus Alvarus (fl. 850s) *Indiculus luminosis* 5 (CSM 1:277–278).

37. Alvarus, *Indiculus luminosis* 35 (CSM 1:314). For more on this, see Coope, "Religious and Cultural Conversion to Islam," 47–68.

38. Glick, 33–35.

39. Geanakoplos, in *Interaction of the "Sibling" Byzantine and Western Cultures in the Middle Ages and the Renaissance*, 18, points out that:

> in times of grave danger to the very fabric of society, particularly when the peril of assimilation to another culture looms, some kind of cultural revival . . . in the

> form of a virtual digging up of the past may break out
> among those alienated from the course of compromise
> or submission being followed by the leaders of that
> society.

Though his particular reference point was a Byzantine Greek culture that felt threatened by Latin domination, the same principle seems to be at the heart of the dilemma faced by culturally sensitive Andalusian Christians.

40. Alcuin, *Epistola* 172. D'Alverny ("La connaissance de l'Islam," 587) stops short of making any connections between his authorship of an *adversus sarracenos* treatise and his involvement in the heresy. But if, as some scholars believe, the Adoptionist Christology was a product of Islamization, someone like Felix may have been especially sensitive to the blurring of the doctrinal lines separating Islam and Christianity. Felix's heretical views were the target of multiple conciliar denunciations from 792 until his deposition in 799.

41. Eulogius, who was a student of Speraindeo at the school associated with the church of St. Zoilus, included an excerpt of one of his own works. The format of the excerpt indicates that the lost treatise was at least in part a point-by-point rebuttal of Islamic doctrine. The portion quoted by Eulogius dealt with the Islamic description of the afterlife, which his master attacked as more of a "lupanar" than a paradise. *Memoriale sanctorum* 1.7 (CSM 2:375–376).

42. For a transcription and translation of the codex of Roda version of this life, see Wolf, "The Earliest Latin Lives of Muhammad," 89–101.

43. Eulogius of Córdoba found it there in 850 when visiting Leyre. Eulogius, *Liber apologeticus martyrum* 16 (CSM 2:483–486); Eulogius, Epistola 3 (CSM 2:497–503). Paul Alvarus referred to its contents in a letter to John of Seville. Alvarus, *Epistola* 6.9 (CSM 1:200–201). For further manuscript information, see CSM 2:483, n. 16.

44. Wolf, "Latin Lives," 90–91.

45. Ibid., 99.

46. Qur'ân 33:37.

47. It is very possible that Urgel, located in the northern extremes of Catalonia, was still controlled by the Muslim governor of Zaragoza when Felix wrote (assuming, of course, that the author of the *Disputatio* was indeed Felix of Urgel). The Franks did not really become a permanent fixture in Spain until the conquest of Gerona in 793. At some point between 793 and the conquest of Barcelona in 801, Urgel became part of the Carolingian Spanish March.

48. *Memoriale sanctorum* 1, pref., 2–3 (CSM 2: 367–368).

49. Ibid., 2.3 (CSM 2:402).

50. Ibid., 2.4 (CSM 2:403–4).

51. For studies of the Cordoban martyrs, see: Wolf, *Christian Martyrs in Muslim Spain*; Edward Colbert, "The Martyrs of Córdoba (850–859): A Study of the Sources"; Franz R. Franke, "Die freiwilligen Märtyrer von Cordova," 1–170.

52. "Dicunt enim quod ab hominibus Deum et legem colentibus passi sunt. . . ." *Liber apologeticus martyrum* 12 (CSM 2:481).

53. This is the earliest reference to Islam as a separate religion. See Daniel, *Islam and the West*, 188–192, for later ones.

54. *Liber apologeticus martyrum* 17–18 (CSM 2:486).

55. Ibid.; Galatians 1.9.

56. *Liber apologeticus martyrum* 17–18 (CSM 2:486).

57. *Liber apologeticus martyrum* 19 (CSM 2:487).

58. The exile of Hilary to Phrygia in 356 exposed him to all of the theological intricacies of the Arian conflict. His writings provided subsequent generations of Latin ecclesiastics with a vocabulary for dealing with later Christological heresies.

59. *Liber apologeticus martyrum* 19 (CSM 2:487).

60. From late antiquity, "antichrist" had two quite distinct meanings. The book of Revelation was the main source for the concept of a specific Antichrist, that would play a key role in ushering in the Last Days. But from at least the time of Tertullian (see, e.g., *Adversus Marcionem* 5:16), Christian leaders also adopted a more general usage of the term based on 1 John 2:22, "He is the Antichrist who denies the Father and the Son" (cf. 1 John 2:18, 4:2–3; 2 John 1:7), and applied it to heretics. It proved an especially popular epithet for those ecclesiastics, such as Arius and Nestor, whose Christological views contradicted the formulae of the ecumenical councils. Hilary wrote of Arius: "When you preach the Father and Son as Creator and Creature, do you think that you can avoid, through disguised names, being regarded as antichrist?" *De trinitate*, 6.42 (PL 10:191). Isidore of Seville included both the specific and general meanings of the term in *Etymologies* 8.11.20–22.

61. Daniel 7:23–25.

62. Alvarus, *Indiculus luminosus* 21 (CSM 1:293–294).

63. Ibid. (CSM 1:294–295). On the basis of Psalm 89, Alvarus substituted seventy years for each of the three and one-half times and came up with 245 years, which he added to 625, the year that he

identified as the beginning of Muhammad's reign, thus coming up with 870.

64. Daniel 11:36, 38. Alvarus, *Indiculus luminosus* 25 (CSM 1:298).

65. Alvarus, *Indiculus luminosus* 23–24 (CSM 1:296–298).

66. Ibid., 26, 30 (CSM 1:301, 307).

67. Matthew 7:15, 24:11, 24:24, etc. Eulogius was not the first Christian author to describe Islam as a heresy, or Muhammad as a false prophet. John of Damascus, whose depiction of the "Ishmaelites" in his treatise on heresies proved paradigmatic for generations of Greek Christians trying to cope with Islam, preceded him by more than a century. But the Damascene never paused to unpack the symbolic baggage that accompanied these identifications. The Cordoban, on the other hand, did. On John of Damascus, see Sahas, *John of Damascus on Islam*.

68. *Memoriale sanctorum* 1.7 (PL 115:744; CSM 2:375), 2.1.2 (PL 115:766–767; CSM 2:398–399).

69. Ibid. (CSM 2:375–76).

70. *Liber apologeticus martyrum* 16 (CSM 2:483–486).

71. For the text and translation, see Wolf, "Earliest Latin Lives," 99–100.

72. For the contents of the codex of Roda (which include one of the versions of the *Istoria de Mahomet*), see Gómez Moreno, "Las primeras crónicas," 562–599.

73. Gómez Moreno, 562–599.

74. According to the Latin version of the seventh-century *Revelation of Pseudo-Methodius*, the Ishmaelites would come forth from the "deserts of Ethribum" and conquer the east. Kedar, *Crusade and Mission*, 29.

CHAPTER 5

"Tathlîth al-waḥdânîyah" and the Twelfth-Century Andalusian-Christian Approach to Islam

Thomas E. Burman

The Spaniard Petrus Alfonsi, a twelfth-century Christian convert from Judaism, once observed that he had "always been nurtured among the Muslims," because he had learned the Arabic language and read Arabic books while growing up.[1] To have "been nurtured among the Muslims" is doubtless an apt description for the life of Petrus, for it is clear from his well-known Latin collection of amusing and edifying tales, the *Disciplina clericalis*, that he was well read in the Arab *adab* literature and had developed a deep fondness for Arab civilization.[2] But to be a Christian "nurtured among the Muslims" was not a condition unique to Petrus Alfonsi in twelfth-century Spain. There was a large number of other Catholics who likewise had been reared on Arabic books. Some, like Alfonsi, were Andalusian Jews who had converted to Christianity; but though they had abandoned the faith of their fathers these converts, or *conversos*, could not possibly erase the deep Arabic imprint on their personalities resulting from their Andalusian upbringing.[3] Most, however, were the descendents of the Romano-Gothic Christians who had lived long under Muslim rule in the centuries since the Arab conquest of Iberia. Over those centuries, these Christians had become Arabicized in language and culture though they maintained their Christian belief and practice. They were known in consequence as

Mozárabes in Spanish and *Mozarabs* in English, both words apparently from the Arabic *musta'rab* or *musta'rib* meaning "one who has become Arabicized."[4]

All these Spanish Christians "nurtured among the Muslims," whether converted Andalusian Jews or Mozarabs, had an intimacy with Islam that no other European Christians could match in the twelfth century. Known best collectively as Andalusian Christians because of their common Christianity and Andalusian cultural background,[5] these Arabic-speaking Catholics had immediate and centuries' long experience of Islam, and as such they provide historians interested in medieval-European perceptions of Islam with the opportunity to examine how Christians who knew Islam in the flesh attempted to understand and confront it intellectually.

There is, moreover, an extant body of largely Andalusian-Christian writings which is particularly well suited to such an investigation. Two short, twelfth-century Christian apologetic and anti-Islamic works in Arabic—an anonymous and titleless tract by a Mozarabic priest from Toledo, and an anonymous treatise known as "Tathlîth al-waḥdânîyah"—have been preserved in the manuscripts of the longer Muslim refutations of them.[6] A longer twelfth-century Andalusian-Christian work of the same type, and originally written in Arabic, exists today in a medieval Latin translation called *The Book of Denuding or Exposing, or The Discloser.*[7] Petrus Alfonsi's fifth *Dialogue*, though appearing in the middle of a longer work against the Jews, is likewise a refutation of Islam similar to the aforementioned three.[8] Complementing these four polemical works are two other works that also shed light directly on the Andalusian Christians and their view of Islam. In his eleventh-century encyclopedia of religions one of the greatest minds of Islamic Spain, Ibn Ḥazm of Córdoba (d. 1064), records religious discussions that he has had with Andalusian Christians;[9] while in the margins of the original manuscript of the first Latin translation of the Qur'ân by Robert of Ketton there is a remarkable, though anonymous, twelfth-century Latin commentary based on Arabic sources and written largely by Andalusian-Christian hands and intended to explain the contents of the first sûrahs to Christian readers.[10]

Taken together these works constitute an invaluable record of how eleventh- and twelfth-century Andalusian Christians approached Islam intellectually. Though this body of literature is naturally interesting for the overall image of Islam which it portrays,[11] these works are also invaluable for what they can tell us about how these Arabicized Christians actually learned about Islam while they developed this image. It is this latter feature that I propose to concentrate on here: What do these works reveal about the concrete steps taken by the Andalusian Christians to gain knowledge of Islam? What do they reveal about the books they had read and about the manner in which they used what they had learned? In this regard, all of these Andalusian-Christian works share certain common features, the most important of which is their authors' remarkable tendency to draw on and interweave material and methods from at least three highly significant bodies of literature: (1) the vast body of Islamic Traditional literature known usually as the Ḥadîth, (2) Middle-Eastern Christian theological and apologetic works written in Arabic; and (3) contemporary Latin theology. In the following pages I propose to demonstrate how the anonymous author of just one of these works, the tract "Tathlîth al-waḥdânîyah," exemplifies this three-strand interweaving. In so doing I hope to sketch a portrait of the educated Andalusian Christian in the process of learning about Islam in order both to refute it and justify his own beliefs in the language of Islamic civilization.

The title "Tathlîth al-waḥdânîyah" might best be translated as "Trinitizing the Unity of God," or "Confessing the Threefold Nature of the Oneness (of the Godhead)."[12] In the form in which it has come down to us, the treatise bearing this title consists of 383 lines quoted in sections of varying length throughout the first half of the much longer Muslim refutation of it. The work's contents, however, are only partially indicated by the title. While the first of the three distinct sections of the work is a fairly rationalistic demonstration of the Trinity,[13] the anonymous author proceeds in the second section to defend the Christian doctrine of the Incarnation,[14] and then argues in the third section that the Old Testament prophecies demonstrate that the Messiah has come.[15] The striking fact that in the final section the author

quotes several passages of the Hebrew scriptures in both
Hebrew and Aramaic suggests quite strongly, as Professor van
Koningsveld has observed, that the work's author is a *converso*
Jew, rather than a Mozarab;[16] other than that, we know nothing
of the author's life. By internal evidence, it is clear that the work
was written before about 1200,[17] while the Latin sources of the
work (to be discussed below) make clear that it must have been
written after about 1120.

Of the three bodies of literature just mentioned, the one to
which the author of "Tathlîth al-waḥdânîyah" most obviously
had recourse in the composition of his treatise was the Ḥadîth.
The use of the Qur'ân in anti-Islamic polemic was a
commonplace among high-medieval European Christians;[18] the
polemical use of the Ḥadîth—that enormous body of traditional
literature that serves as a supplement to the Qur'ân in Islamic
piety, legal thought, and theology—is altogether rarer. Yet like
several of the other Andalusian-Christian authors, the *converso*
author of "Tathlîth al-waḥdânîyah" quotes directly from the
Ḥadîth and does so as if he were fairly familiar with this
literature. Addressing the Islamic audience in general, he
declares that "We do not accept on your behalf [anything] from
the prophecies and tales as attested by Muslim in his book."[19] He
is referring here to Muslim ibn al-Ḥajjâj al-Qushayrî's Ṣaḥîḥ[20]
one of the two most respected Ḥadîth collections. But more
importantly, he then goes on to quote a full ḥadîth with the
isnâd—the chain of successive authorities attesting to its validity
and listed at the outset—intact:

> Sufyân told us on the authority of al-Zuhrî on the
> authority of Qatâdah on the authority of 'A'ishah [that]
> the wife of Rifâ'ah came to the Apostle, and she said to
> him, "I belonged to Rifâ'ah, but he divorced me, so I
> married 'Abd al-Raḥmân ibn al-Zubayr." But the Apostle
> smiled and laughed and said, "Do you want to return to
> Rifâ'ah? [You cannot] until you taste his sweetness
> (*tadhûqî 'asîlatahu*) and 'Abd al-Raḥmân al-Zubayr tastes
> your sweetness."[21]

"To taste someone's sweetness" is a euphemism here for "to
have sexual intercourse with;"[22] the point of the ḥadîth,
therefore, is to illustrate an important aspect of Islamic divorce

law: a divorced woman cannot return to her original husband until she consummates a marriage with another man first and is then divorced from him.[23] This particular ḥadîth can be found in nearly this form with almost the same *isnâd* in the collections of both Ibn Ḥanbal and al-Bukhârî.[24] Our author quotes this ḥadîth in order to show his Christian readers how thoroughly un-Christian the marriage practices of Islam are.

But what is most important for our purposes is to notice that the author gives at least two indications here that he is quite at home with the intricacies of the Ḥadîth literature. First he mentions the famous Ḥadîth scholar, Muslim, by name, knowing that this could not fail to make an impression on his audience. More significantly, however, he also goes out of his way to quote the ḥadîth together with its full *isnâd*, knowing that a hostile Muslim audience would probably attach little credibility to it without this required chain of verifying authorities stretching back to the time of the Prophet—"Sufyân told us on the authority of Qatâdah on the authority of 'Â'ishah. . . ."[25] Both of these facts bespeak considerable familiarity with the Ḥadîth literature, a familiarity that could only have been gained through considerable study of the Ḥadîth itself. "Tathlîth al-waḥdânîyah" quotes at least four ḥadîths in full,[26] but other Andalusian-Christian works, especially *The Book of Denuding*, also draw heavily and explicitly on the Ḥadîth and often quote individual traditions with *isnâd*s similarly attached, demonstrating that intimacy with this important body of literature was not uncommon among Andalusian Christians.[27]

A quotation of a ḥadîth—especially one prefaced by its *isnâd*—is something that stands out in a written text; it is not nearly so easy to recognize the presence of ideas and methods drawn from the other two categories of literature to which these writers had recourse: earlier Middle-Eastern Christian theology written in Arabic, and contemporary Latin theology. In both instances, however, certain telling lexical usages are the first indications of such reliance. For example, the author of "Tathlîth al-waḥdânîyah" describes God as a "substance" using the Arabic word *jawhar*.[28] By so doing he indicates that he has been reading Arab–Christian theological works written in the Middle East, for although Muslims almost never consented to describe God thus, Arabic-speaking Christians had long done so.[29] There is no doubt, moreover, that Arabic works by such Middle-Eastern Christian theologians had made their way to Spain by the High Middle Ages, for the so-called *Apology of al-Kindî*, perhaps the most influential Arab–Christian polemic against Islam,[30] was translated into Latin in Toledo in the early 1140s under the aegis of Peter the Venerable,[31] and a late thirteenth- or early fourteenth-century Andalusian–Christian manuscript extant today in Tunisia contains a version of the late eighth-century disputation between the Nestorian Catholicos Timothy I and the Caliph al-Mahdî.[32] Not surprisingly, both the *Apology of al-Kindî* and Timothy's dialogue with al-Mahdî use the term *jawhar* widely with respect to God.[33]

Although the author of "Tathlîth al-waḥdânîyah" used theological terms that he could only have borrowed directly or indirectly from Middle-Eastern Christians writing in Arabic, he also employed certain Arabic neologisms that indicate that he was influenced by contemporary Latin thought as well. When this Christian author quotes John 1:14, for example, we have *iltaḥamat al-kalimah*, "the Word became flesh."[34] Now Professor Samir has argued that the verb *iltaḥama* which other Andalusian-Christian polemicists also use, is found nowhere else in Arab-Christian literature. Rather, Middle-Eastern Christians use either *tajassada*, "to become a body," or *ta'annasa*, "to become a human being." The word *iltaḥama*, moreover, is an exact translation of the Latin *incarno* (and, for that matter, the periphrastic *caro factum est* as used in the Vulgate in John 1:14), while the two Oriental-Christian words are translations from the Greek. In Samir's view, therefore, *iltaḥama*, is a new Arabic word, formed in accordance with the rules of Arabic morphology but on the model of a Latin word.[35] Here, therefore, is evidence of Latin-Christian influence.

But the reliance of the author of "Tathlîth al-waḥdânîyah" on both earlier Middle-Eastern Christian theology and Latin theology runs much deeper than occasional terminological borrowings. One passage in particular, the author's rather rationalistic argument for the Trinity, draws heavily on both traditions and demonstrates how at least one Andalusian-

Christian was able to weave them together in a rather creative manner.

Briefly this argument runs as follows: After stipulating that his demonstration will be predicated only on what we can know about God as He is known through his actions,[36] the author poses the following question: "Did God's creation [of all that He created] come about by means of power and knowledge and will, or did He create them without these?"[37] Assuming that any Muslim would agree that God created in this manner, the author then asks if these three faculties are names for His essence (*asmâ' li-dhâtihi*) or names for His acts (*asmâ' li-af'âlihi*). One cannot say that they are the former, he argues, without being guilty of anthropomorphism. Hence, they must be the latter, and as such they are the properties on account of which God is called the Powerful, the Knowing, and the Willing, and this, the author contends, is nothing other than the Trinity.[38]

He then observes that if a Muslim should ask why Christians use the terms *Father*, *Son*, and *Holy Spirit* to refer to the Trinity, rather than the terms *the Powerful*, *the Knowing*, and *the Willing*, then one need only respond that Jesus commanded his disciples to baptize in the name of the Father, Son, and Holy Spirit (Matthew 28:19), and these names revealed in Scripture are merely other names for God corresponding respectively to *the Powerful*, *the Knowing*, and *the Willing*—names which we arrive at by reason. Each scriptural name, moreover, suits the particular action of the member of the Trinity to which it is applied.[39]

But it might be objected, the author admits, that we call God many other things besides the Powerful, the Knowing, and the Willing, for He is customarily known as the Mighty (*'azîz*), the Strong (*qawî*), the Victorious (*ghalûb*), the Hearing (*samî'*), and so on. In response, he argues that the three faculties mentioned earlier are the sources (*uṣûl*) of all these other names; more precisely, these other names emanate (*tanbathiqu*) from those three sources and are incorporated (*tandaghimu*) in them. The faculty of power, for example, is the source of names such as *the Mighty, the Strong, the Victorious*, and *the Conquering*; while the faculty of will is the source of such names as *the Forgiving, the Consenting, the Angry*, and *the Punishing*. It might further be objected that God is also called the Living *(ḥayy)* and the Eternal *(qadîm)*, and that these two names cannot be reduced to any member of the triad *Powerful, Knowing,* and *Willing.* Why not believe in a "quintity" *(takhmîs)* therefore? Here the author responds that *Living* and *Eternal* are not names for God's actions, but are rather names of His essence *(asmâ' dhât),* which are only so used by exclusion of their opposites: *Living* by exclusion of *Dead; Eternal* by exclusion of *Temporal.*[40] But as for the names of His actions, these all reduce to three and no more: the Powerful, the Knowing, and the Willing.[41]

The author of "Tathlîth al-waḥdânîyah" then provides an analogy for the relationship and functioning of these three faculties: No act can come into being in the human soul without the same three faculties all working in concert, and if one of them is diminished, the act will not be complete. If one knows and wills, for example, but does not have power, the act remains incomplete. Since we know that God acted outside Himself in creation, we know, therefore, that these three faculties are necessary for God also and must work together in Him. Hence, by the analogy of the functioning of our souls, we can see that God is a Trinity.[42]

Christians do not say, the author observes in conclusion, that three is one and one is three. Rather they say that the one substance *(jawhar)* of God exists in three persons *(khawâṣṣ)*[43] which are undivided, yet distinct. "This is our doctrine of the Trinity of the Unity of the Creator."[44]

Now this Andalusian-Christian author's argument clearly follows an apologetic approach to the Trinity that was developed by earlier Middle-Eastern Christians. Such Christians living within *dâr al-Islâm* could hardly avoid being powerfully influenced by the Islamic scholastic tradition of religious-philosophical thought known as the Kalâm, for by its very nature the Kalâm was an explicative and defensive tool for use in religious disputation.[45] Indeed, educated Christians soon learned that they could turn the Kalâm to their own apologetic purposes quite effectively, for they realized that the elaborate and vehement debate of the doctors of the Kalâm about the nature of God's attributes—a debate that one scholar has recently identified as the central problem of Muslim theology[46]—

provided fertile ground in which to cultivate apologetic arguments for the Trinity. In particular, these Christians were fond of propounding arguments for the Trinity the central thrust of which was to reduce all the attributes of God commonly accepted by all monotheists to three, and then to identify these three with the persons of the Trinity.[47] The *Apology of al-Kindî*, which circulated in Spain, provides a good example of this approach in its long defense of the Trinity.[48]

The Trinitarian argument of the author of "Tathlîth al-waḥdânîyah" clearly follows this general approach thoroughly. Not only are most of the names of God mentioned in the argument drawn from the numerous Islamic lists of the names of God, or from the Qur'ân,[49] but many of them—for example, *'âlim* (Knowing), *qâdir* (Powerful), *baṣîr* (Seeing)—are among the names of God that correspond to the specific attributes that the orthodox Kalâmic scholars believed exist in God but are not identical with Him or other than Him.[50] Like his Middle-Eastern Christian predecessors, again, this Andalusian-Christian author's goal is to demonstrate that all the names of God can be reduced to three in which all the others can be incorporated: *qâdir* (Powerful), *'âlim* (Knowing), *murîd* (Willing). Thereby the attributes of God are automatically likewise reduced to the corresponding three attributes: *qudrah* (power), *'ilm* (knowledge), *irâdah* (will). These, in turn, he equates with the persons of the Trinity: Father, Son, Holy Spirit. The author of "Tathlîth al-waḥdânîyah," therefore, borrowed more than terminology from the theological writings of Arabicized Christians in the Middle East: In this lengthy passage he has clearly borrowed substantially from their apologetic methods as well.[51]

But while in its general features his Trinitarian argument follows this typical Middle-Eastern apologetic approach thoroughly, there is one striking peculiarity here that we must tarry over, and that is the specific triad of divine attributes around which the Andalusian-Christian author constructs his argument. Although Middle-Eastern Christians used several different triads of attributes in their Trinitarian arguments, none of them appears to have used the triad of power, knowledge, and will adopted by our author.[52] This peculiarity suggests that other influences besides Middle-Eastern Christian apologetic

were at work on the development of the "Tathlîth al-
waḥdânîyah"'s Trinitarian argument. Since we know that the
Andalusian Christians were using neologisms based on Latin
words, it makes sense to look for Latin-Christian influences.
Indeed the particular approach to the Trinity taken here, with its
emphasis on psychological analogy, immediately suggests
Augustine as a source. What is more, Professor van Koningsveld
has shown that contemporary Mozarabs were in fact actually
studying the Bishop of Hippo's *De trinitate*.[53] Certainly some
passages in Augustine's works do bear clear similarity to the
Trinitarian argument of "Tathlîth al-waḥdânîyah." Yet the
famous triad of memory, intelligence, and will, which he
frequently used to explain the Trinity, is the closest parallel in
Augustine's works to the Andalusian triad of power, knowledge,
and will.[54] Indeed, Oliver Du Roy prepared an exhaustive list of
the triads that Augustine used to explain the Trinity, and
although this list contains some 115 different triads, that of
power, knowledge, and will is not among them.[55]

Interestingly enough, however, this very triad was current
in the Trinitarian theology of contemporary, twelfth-century
Latin Christendom. Both it and its Trinitarian use appear to have
been the invention of Peter Abelard, who first used it in about
1118 in a treatise called *Theologia 'summi boni'*. Thereafter, in both
Abelard's later works and the works of a number of important
theologians of the twelfth and thirteenth centuries, such as Hugh
of St. Victor, Peter Lombard, Richard of St. Victor, St.
Bonaventure, and even St. Thomas Aquinas, this triad was
prominently used to help explain the mystery of the Trinity.[56]
Now to be precise, this triad traveled in several slightly different
versions. The first member was always *potentia* (power)
corresponding perfectly to the Arabic *qudrah*; the second member
was either *sapientia* (wisdom) or *scientia* (knowledge), the latter
of which corresponds best to the Arabic *'ilm* used by our author;
the third could be any one of several attributes all related to the
notion of God's benevolent will—*bonitas* (goodness), *benignitas*
(benevolence), *amor* (love), *caritas* (love), or simply *voluntas*
(will)—and this last corresponds perfectly to the Arabic *irâdah*
used by the Andalusian-Christian author.[57]

As a result, it is not difficult to find contemporary Latin parallels to much of what the author of "Tathlîth al-waḥdânîyah" says. For example Hugh of St. Victor, who died in 1141, wrote in his *magnum opus, On the Sacraments of the Christian Church,* that

> A certain three things existed [in God] and these three were one, and these three were eternal, and nothing was able to be perfected without these three. . . . If one of these were absent, nothing would be able to be completed. And these three were power, wisdom, will. . . . Will moves, knowledge disposes, power acts.[58]

Hugh ascribes these three attributes to the Father, Son, and Holy Spirit, respectively, just as our Andalusian-Christian author does, and, what is more striking, both authors use the same approach to reducing all the other of God's attributes to these three. "Whatever is said about God and believed truly about Him," Hugh observes,

> is reduced to these three. If you call Him strong and uncorrupt and unchangeable and invincible and other things which are similar, all this belongs to His power; if provident, if inspector, if examiner of things which are hidden, and intelligent, all this belongs to His wisdom; if pious, if mild, if merciful, if patient, all this belongs to [His] good will. And . . . all which is perfect and true is contained in these.[59]

Notice how similar is the following passage from the Andalusian-Christian treatise:

> These [three names] which we have recounted are the origins of all naming [of God], and from [these three the other names] proceed and in them they are incorporated. For the origin of Mighty, and Potent, and Victorious, and Conquering and similar [names] is Power, and from it they proceed and in it they are incorporated. The origin of Forgiving, and Merciful, and Consenting, and Angry, and Punisher is Will; from it they proceed and in it they are incorporated.[60]

These striking parallels between "Tathlîth al-waḥdânîyah" and Hugh's great work indicate that the Andalusian-Christian author discovered this new triad and its Trinitarian use in contemporary Latin-Christian theology,[61] perhaps even in the works of Hugh himself, though since these ideas were so widespread, it is difficult to say which Latin works were the source.[62] Abelard's triad, in short, in the specific form of *potentia, scientia,* and *voluntas*[63] was adopted by this Andalusian-Christian writer, translated into the Arabic triad of *qudrah-'ilm-irâdah,* and adapted for use in a Trinitarian argument constructed in comformity with the older Middle-Eastern Arab-Christian demonstrations of the Trinity.[64] Here, therefore, we have an extraordinary blending of the Latin-Christian and Arab-Christian theological traditions at the hands of an Andalusian Christian. This blending, moreover, is the work of the same author who also showed considerable familiarity with the Ḥadîth by citing individual ḥadîths with *isnâd* attached and by invoking the name of Muslim ibn al-Ḥajjâj in order to make his anti-Islamic arguments more convincing to Muslims. In this Christian author's knowledge of these diverse genres of writing we have, therefore, vivid evidence of the remarkably multi-cultural and multi-lingual nature of the Andalusian-Christian intellectual milieu.[65] In his ability to interweave and adapt information and methods from these diverse sources we have clear evidence of one author's remarkable creativity as well. All this provides very useful insight into the intellectual climate of the Andalusian-Christian community in the eleventh and twelfth centuries, something about which we are still poorly informed.[66] But most important for our purposes, in this Arabic-speaking author's use of Ḥadîth, Middle-Eastern, Arab-Christian apologetic, and twelfth-century Latin theology we see how one of the medieval Christians "nurtured among the Muslims" attempted to come to grips with Islam intellectually.

NOTES

1. He says this in a conversation with his Jewish alter-ego, Moses, in his *Dialogue against the Jews:* Petrus Alfonsi, *Dialogus* 5 of *Dialogi contra Iudaeos,* p. 62; also at PL 157:602a.

2. See Jones and Keller's introduction to their translation of Petrus Alfonsi, *Disciplina clericalis,* 18–20.

3. David Wasserstein has described how similar the culture of these Andalusian Jews was to the dominant Muslim culture of Islamic Spain; see his *The Rise and Fall of the Party Kings,* ch. 7 passim, esp. 215ff.

4. See Dozy, *Glossaire des mots espagnols et portugais dérivés de l'arabe,* 321, though doubt is still expressed about this etymology; see "Mozarab," EI² 7:246–247 [art. Chalmeta]. I have adopted throughout the Library-of-Congress system of Romanizing Arabic as described in the following publications: *Cataloguing Service* 18 (Summer, 1976):15–21; vol. 125 (Spring, 1978):23; *Cataloguing Service Bulletin* 6 (Fall, 1979):44; vol. 46 (Fall, 1989):79–89.

5. The terms *Mozárabe* and *Mozarab* have engendered a great deal of debate in recent decades (see, e.g., Hitchcock, "Quiénes fueron los verdaderos mozárabes?", where the problem is well-stated, though I do not agree with the solution proposed), and I am in agreement with those who believe that these terms have been used far too broadly. For precision's sake I prefer to use the term *Mozarab* to refer only to native-born Christians who, having lived for generations under Islamic/Arabic rule, actually became Arabicized in language and custom. Andalusian Jews who convert to Christianity I prefer to call *conversos* in accordance with the custom of Hispanicists. *Andalusian Christians* is the term I will use to refer to both Arabic-speaking, Christian subgroups together. For a recent overview of Mozarab and Andalusian-Christian studies generally, see M. de Epalza, "Mozarabs."

6. The Mozarabic priest's tract is preserved, apparently intact, in al-Khazrajî, *Maqâmi' al-ṣulbân* sections 2–10, pp. 30–39; "Tathlîth al-waḥdânîyah" is found in Imâm al-Qurṭubî, pages 47, 57, 71, 77, 91, 97, 105–106, 115–117, 163–165, 177, 181–185, 215–217. Hereafter this work will be cited as "al-Qurṭubî," followed by page of the Cairo edition.

7. *Liber denudationis siue ostensionis aut patefaciens.* This work has been mistakenly known in scholarly circles as *Contrarietas alfolica* because a later annotator of the one ms. known to contain it (Paris,

122 Thomas E. Burman

Bibliothèque Nationale, ms. lat. 3394, fols. 237v–263v) added this title to it. I have edited this work in my doctoral dissertation, "Spain's Arab Christians and Islam," 194–346. For bibliography, see my "The Influence of the Apology of al-Kindî and Contrarietas alfolica on Ramon Lull's Late Religious Polemics, 1305–1313," 200, nn. 11–15 and passim.

8. Petrus Alfonsi, *Dialogi*, 62–73; PL 157:594–606.

9. Ibn Ḥazm, *al-Fiṣal fî al-milal wa-al-ahwâ' wa-al-niḥal*, 1:38–52 and 2:19–82. For bibliography on Ibn Ḥazm see "Ibn Ḥazm," EI² 2:790–799, [art. R. Arnaldez].

10. See the margins of Robert of Ketton, trans., *Lex Mahumet pseudo-prophete que arabice Alchoran, id est, collectio preceptorum vocatur*, Paris, Bibliothèque de l'Arsenal, lat. 1162, fols. 26–140, esp. fols. 26–36. Cf. Kritzeck, *Peter the Venerable and Islam*, 57–58, n. 31.

11. This image conforms in general to the typical medieval European view of Islam and its prophet described by Norman Daniel, *Islam and the West*, passim. This is hardly surprising, of course, since, as Daniel argued, this Andalusian-Christian view of Islam was in large part *formative of* the general European view.

12. I believe that *tathlîth*, which of course is often translated simply as "Trinity," must be understood here with the verbal force of its *maṣdar* (i. e., verbal-noun) form intact, just as the much more common *tawḥîd* (a second form *maṣdar* as well) can be translated "unity," although it often means "confessing the unity (of God)."

13. al-Qurṭubî 57, 63, 71, and 77.

14. Ibid., 91, 97, 105–06, 115–117.

15. Ibid., 163–65, 177, 181–85, 215–217.

16. van Koningsveld, "La apología de al-Kindî en la España del siglo XII," 127–129.

17. See ibid., 110, notes 4–5. Van Koningsveld's dating here is based on al-Qurṭubî's own statement about when he wrote it. Devillard and others have wrongly dated it to much later in the thirteenth century. See Devillard, "Thèse sur al-Qurṭubî" [an introduction to, edition of, and French translation of parts one and two of al-Qurṭubî's al-I'lâm, each in separate, unnumbered volumes]), "Introduction," 1–2.

18. See Daniel, *Islam and the West*, 27–77.

19. Al-Qurṭubî 215. "Lâ naqbalu la-ka min al-nubûwât wa-al-riwâyât al-marwîyât 'an Muslim fî kitâbihi."

20. On Muslim and his work see "Muslim b. al-Ḥadjdjâdj," EI² 7:691–692.

21. al-Qurṭubî 215.

22. See E. Lane, *An Arabic-English Lexicon* 5:2046, c. 3 who by coincidence uses this very ḥadîth to explain the meaning of *'asîlah* ("sweetness"), and in proper Victorian fashion observes that the Arab grammarians say that it means "the sweetness or deliciousness of *jimâ'*, *jimâ'*," which he leaves untranslated, means "sexual intercourse."

23. See "Ṭalâk," EI[1] 4:636–640 [art. J. Schact] Ṭalak.

24. See al-Bukhârî, *al-Jâmi' al-ṣaḥîh*, 52. 3. 2 and Ibn Ḥanbal, *Musnad*, 6:37–38. I have not been able to find any version of it in Muslim's collection, however, even though the context would seem to indicate that Muslim's work was its source.

25. On the *isnâd* see "ḥadîth," EI[2] 3:23–28 [art. J. Robson].

26. For the three others see al-Qurṭubî 116–17; cf. al-Bukhârî 97.24.3 (cf. Devillard, "Translation," 110); ibid., 215 in the paragraph before that quoted above; cf. al-Bukhârî 48.6.1–2; and ibid., just after that quoted above, to which this last one is nearly identical.

27. See, for example, *Liber denudationis* 2, Paris, Bibliothèque Nationale, lat. 3394, fol. 239v where the anonymous author of that treatise cites a ḥadîth, with *isnâd* intact, which can be traced to the collections of Abû Dâwûd al-Sijistânî, *Sunan Abî Dâwûd* 34 (*sunnah*) 1, 5:4–6, and Ibn Ḥanbâl, *Musnad* 3:120, 145. Its author quotes at least twenty-five separate ḥadîths in the course of the work.

28. al-Qurṭubî 77: "jawhar qadîm."

29. Normally *jawhar* means either "jewel" or simply "a material substance" (see Reinhart Dozy, *Supplément aux dictionaires arabes* 1:237a). But it was also the Arabic philosophical term for "substance" corresponding to the Latin *substantia* (see "djawhar," EI[2] 2:493–494 [art. S. van den Bergh], and Morewedge, *The Metaphysica of Avicenna*, 30). Muslims normally refused to identify God as a substance or *jawhar*, but Middle-Eastern Christians often did, defining it not as a bodily or material substance, but rather as "a self-subsistent thing" (*al-qâ'im bi-nafsihi*), as the eleventh-century Nestorian bishop Ilîyâ al-Naṣîbî put it. Here see "djawhar," EI[1] 2:1028 [art. B. Carra de Vaux]; Fackenheim, "'Substance' and 'Perseity' in Medieval Arabic Philosophy," 119–125; Graf, *Verzeichnis arabischer kirchlicher Termini*, 36; Haddad, *La Trinité divine chez les théologiens arabes*, 140; and Ilîyâ al-Nasîbî, *Majlis*:75, ll. 89, 92.

30. See Anawati, *Polémique, apologie et dialogue Islamo-chrétiens*, 383; see 380–391 on the *Apology*'s place in Muslim polemic against Christianity and for a summary of its contents. See also Abel, "L'Apologie d'Al-Kindi."

31. See d'Alverny, "Deux traductions latines du Coran au Moyen Age" 87–98; and Kritzeck, *Peter the Venerable*, 101–107. In a later article, d'Alverny observed—rightly it seems to me—that the *Apology* had probably already been in Spain for some time before its translation into Latin; see her "La connaissance de l'Islam en Occident," 593.

32. This ms. was once in the Library of the Mosque of Sīdī 'Uqba in Kairouan but has since been moved to the National Museum of Islamic Art in Reqqada, where, lacking a proper shelfmark, it is known as Tārīkh Yarūnim. The ms. also contains *inter alia* another similar, anonymous Christian-Islamic disputation which has not yet been identified; see G. Levi della Vida, "I Mozarabi tra occidente e Islam," 677, and idem, "Un texte mozarabe d'histoire universelle," 175–176. On the disputation of Timothy and al-Mahdî see Caspar "Les versions arabes du dialogue entre le Catholicos Timothée I et le Calife al-Mahdî."

33. See Pseudo-al-Kindî, *Risâlat al-Kindî* 51–57 passim, e.g., 54: "Fa-âmmâ ṣifât dhât [Allâh]. . . fa-jawhar dhû kalimah wa-rûḥ"; and Tîmâthâwus, *al-Muḥâwarah al-dînîyah* 10 (ed. R. Caspar in art. cited in previous note), 131: "Ka-dhâlika al-ab wa-al-ibn wa-al-rûḥ thalâthat aqânîm jawhar wâḥid."

34. al-Qurṭubî 91. Cf. also his use of the verbal noun or *maṣdar* of the same form of the Arabic root when he writes that "the Word was designated uniquely to become flesh": "fa-ufrida al-kalimah bi-al-iltiḥâm" in al-Qurṭubî 91.

35. Kh. Samir, Review of A. Charfi's edition of al-Khazrajî's *Maqâmi' al-ṣulbân* in *Islamochristiana* 6 (1980):253.

36. ". . . ghayr wâqifîna 'alâ dhâtihi wa-lâ mudrikîna li-shay' min-hu. wa-innamâ naqa'u 'alâ asmâ' af'âlihi fî khalîqatihi wa-tadbîrihi fî rubûbîyatihi" (al-Qurṭubî, *muqaddimah*, 47).

37. al-Qurṭubî 57.

38. Ibid.

39. Ibid., 63.

40. The author's description here of so-called negative attributes is very similar to that proposed by Maimonides in the *Guide for the Perplexed*, as is his implicit insistence that only such negative attributes and actional attributes (*ismâ' lil-af'âlihi*) can properly be used to describe God (see Maimonides, *Dalâlat al-ḥâ'irîn* 1. 58, 71r-v). Maimonides' *Guide* was not written until 1190 in Egypt so it is difficult to see how it could be a source for this view of attributes. More likely the *converso* author learned it from the slightly less similar views of earlier Jewish philosophers such as Judah ha-Levi (see I. Husik, *A History of Mediaeval Jewish Philosophy*, 161–162).

41. al-Qurṭubî 71.

42. Ibid.

43. On this use of the word *khâṣṣah* to mean "person (of the Trinity)" instead of the usual Arabic word, *uqnûm*, see Haddad, *La Trinité divine*, 170, 178–185.

44. al-Qurṭubî 77.

45. Wolfson, *The Philosophy of the Kalam*, 81; see also "kalâm," EI[2] 3:1146 [art. L. Gardet].

46. Caspar, *Traité de théologie musulmane*, 130.

47. Haddad, *La Trinité divine*, 208.

48. See Pseudo-al-Kindî, *Risâlat al-Kindî*, 54–57.

49. See particularly here Gimaret, *Les noms divins en Islam* passim, but esp. his index of the divine names on 431–436.

50. See, e.g., al-Ash'arî's lists of accepted attributes and corresponding names in his *Risâlah ilâ ahl al-thaghr*, 93–94; and Gimaret, *La doctrine d'al-Ash'arî*, 247–322, esp. 259–281. It should be noted that our author does not distinguish adequately between the names of God, e. g., *'âlim* ("the Knowing"), and His attributes, e. g., *'ilm* ("knowledge"): he refers to both as simply *asmâ'* ("names"), though the latter are usually referred to as *ṣifât* ("attributes"); but cf. Gimaret, ibid., 235–245.

51. One could cite many other passages in the apologetic works of the Andalusian Christians that show the same sort of influence. See, e.g., van Koningsveld, "Petrus Alfonsi," in which he demonstrates that the greater part of Petrus Alfonsi's chapter against the Muslims is borrowed from the *Apology of al-Kindî*. See also his "La apología," 114–115, nn. 15 and 18, where he notes that Petrus borrows even "detalles textuales y el orden de la presentación de los mismos" from the *Apology*.

52. Haddad, *La Trinité divine*, discusses the various triads used in ibid., 208–233; see esp. his table on 232–233.

53. Van Koningsveld, *The Latin-Arabic Glossary*, 50. Augustine has in fact been suggested as a source for these Trinitarian speculations, though without substantial proof. See Devillard, "Thèse sur al-Qurṭubî," "Introduction," 75.

54. See e. g., Augustine, *De trinitate* 10. 11. 18, CCSL 50:330, ll. 29–32.

55. Du Roy, *L'Intelligence de la foi en la Trinité selon Saint Augustin*, 537–540.

56. On Abelard see Buytaert, "Abelard's Trinitarian Doctrine," 125–127ff., and J. Châtillon, "Unitas, aequalitas, concordia vel

connexio," 359–364ff., esp. n. 98. On the other thinkers except Bonaventure see Châtillon, ibid., 359–379. For Bonaventure, see his *Commentaria in quartum Sententiarum*, 512.

57. Hugh of St. Victor's *De sacramentis* serves as a good exemplar of the several versions of the triad and their relation to each other since he used most of the possible combinations: "Attribuitur Patri potentia, et Filio sapientia, et Spiritui sancto bonitas sive benignitas" (Hugh of St. Victor, *De sacramentis* 1. 3. 26, PL 176:227c). A few pages later he makes *amor* and *bonitas* equivalent when he describes how this triad in the human soul is a *signum Trinitatis*: "Foris autem potentia non erat, sed signum tantum; neque sapientia sed signum tantum; neque *amor vel bonitas*, sed signum tantum . . ." (Hugh of St. Victor, *De sacramentis* 1. 3. 28, PL 176:230c). While *voluntas* is never expressly made equivalent with the other attributes used as the final member of the triad, this is the clear implication. Just three sentences after writing "Voluntas movet, scientia disponit, potestas operatur," (where, by the way, *scientia* is substituted for *sapientia*) Hugh substitutes *bonitas* for *voluntas* without explanation when he restates his triad: "Quidquid de Deo vere dicitur, aut pie credi potest in Deo, haec tria continent; potestas, sapientia et bonitas" (Hugh of St. Victor, *De sacramentis* 1. 2. 6, PL 176:208b–c). The relationship of *voluntas* to *bonitas*, *benignitas* and the other final attributes is well explained by Hugh's confrere Richard of St. Victor who employed this same triad in his *De trinitate* 6 (PL 196:967–994, esp. 979–980), and who observed in another work that "Bonitatis est autem bene velle. Quid est enim bonitas nisi bona voluntas? (i. e., "To be good will is part of goodness, for what is goodness but good will?)" (Richard of St. Victor, *De tribus appropriatis personis in trinitate*, PL 196:994b).

58. Hugh of St. Victor, *De sacramentis* 1. 2. 6, PL 176:208b–c; cf. a very similar passage in 1. 3. 28, c. 230d–231a.

59. Ibid., 1. 3. 29, PL 176:231a–b.

60. al-Qurṭubî 71. For some reason the author does not state which names are incorporated in knowledge (‘*ilm*).

61. Since we lack any *terminus a quo* for "Tathlîth al-waḥdânîyah" (and for the similar work mentioned in n. 64 just below) it *is* theoretically possible that the influence went in the other direction: that is, that Andalusian–Christian apologists such as the author of "Tathlîth al-waḥdânîyah" invented this triad in, say, the late eleventh century, after which the Trinitarian use of this triad became known to Abelard, who introduced it to Latin Christendom. I view this scenario as extremely unlikely since Latin theologians took no interest in Andalusian-Christian theology, whereas we know from other evidence (see above) that Andalusian-Christians *were* very interested in Latin

theology—Latin theologians, indeed, knew no Arabic in this period while Andalusian-Christian intellectuals did know Latin. Furthermore, Petrus Alfonsi, a possible medium by which such Andalusian–Christian ideas might have passed to the north (and who in a different context used a Trinitarian demonstration in Latin rather similar to those discussed here—see his *Dialogi*, 6–32, 73–80; PL 157:549–561, 606–608; cf. Tolan, *Petrus Alfonsi and His Medieval Readers*, 38–39 and 112–14) is never associated with the use of this triad in Latin even though its use was widespread and he was a very well-known thinker (see Tolan, ibid., 95–103). In fact, some of those who used the triad (e. g., Abelard) were publicly attacked for it (see Buytaert, "Abelard's Trinitarian Doctrine," 128 passim), but Petrus Alfonsi's name is never mentioned in conjunction with this controversy, nor is the name of any other Andalusian Christian. Rather, Abelard appears to have invented the triad in order to have a way of understanding the Trinity in conformity with his nominalist view of universals (see C. Mews, "The Development of the Theologia of Peter Abelard," 184). Finally, the Arabic fragments attributed to a Mozarab named Aghustîn (see n. 64), in which this same Abelardian triad appears in the same kind of hybrid argument, contain fairly clear evidence of the Latin origin of the triad when their author indicates on more than one occasion that the use of this triad is a technical manner of speaking (*al-ta'âruf*) used by foreigners (*al-'ajam*), the latter term nearly always referring to Romance/Latin speakers when used by Arabic writers in Spain (see Aghustîn, "Maṣḥaf al- 'âlam al-kâ'in" in al-Qurṭubî 69 and 83).

62. Not only was the triad itself widespread, but the same methods of using it were employed in many works. E.g., the same technique whereby Hugh and the author of "Tathlîth al-waḥdânîyah" reduced the other of God's names to three is also used by at least one other twelfth-century Latin work, the anonymous *Sententie Parisienses* written between 1139 and 1141:

> In quibus videndum est, si contineatur descriptio summi boni, quia sunt adhuc multa, que de Deo predicantur, ut est eternus, incommutabilis, iustus, pius, misericors. Sed sciendum, quod ista omnia clauduntur sub tribus predictis, scilicet potentia, sapientia, bonitate. . . . Hoc, quod eternus est, attribuitur potentie . . . Ad potentiam quoque pertinet hoc, quod est incommutabilis. Providentia vero sive prescientia sapientie ascribitur . . . Iustitia, pietas, misercordia ad bonitatem pertinent. . . .

(*Sententie Parisienses*, pars 1, ed. A. Landgraff in his *Écrits théologiques de l'école d'Abélard: Textes inédits*, 12, ll. 2–13.). The three passages are similar enough that it is difficult to say which of the two Latin works was the more likely source of the Arabic.

63. It is almost certain, by the way, that this specific version of the triad was chosen, rather than the other possible Latin combinations, because it could most easily be translated into the technical language of the Kalâm in which the Middle-Eastern Christian demonstrations of the Trinity (which are the models for this one) were written. *Qudrah 'ilm*, and *irâdah* are all divine attributes widely recognized by Muslim theologians, while *ihsân* (beneficence) or *jûd* (generosity), for example, terms that would correspond to the Latin *bonitas* or *benignitas*, are not attributes generally applied to God by Muslims. See D. Gimaret, *La doctrine d'al-*Ash'arî, 259–281ff, and the twelfth-century Andalusian-Christian *Glossarium latino-arabicum*, 43.

64. Moreover, "Tathlîth al-wahdânîyah" is not the only Andalusian–Christian author to do this. A fragmentary work called "Mashaf al-'âlam al-kâ'in" ("The Book of the Existing World") attributed to one Aghustîn contains a Trinitarian proof based on the same triad, though with a slightly different approach. These fragments are also extant only in al-Qurtubî's refutation of "Tathlîth al-wahdânîyah. " See al-Qurtubî 81–83, and van Koningsveld, "La apología," 125, n. 38.

65. Remember that this particular author is a *converso* who also knew Aramaic and Hebrew; see above.

66. Although Professor van Koningsveld's groundbreaking studies have filled in many gaps; Levi della Vida's earlier "I Mozarabi" (see n. 32) should be mentioned in this connection as well. My dissertation, cited in n. 7, considers this intellectual climate at some length; see esp. 95–193.

III. Theological Responses to Islam: Fourteenth and Fifteenth Centuries

CHAPTER 6

Antichrist and Islam in Medieval Franciscan Exegesis

David Burr

By the late thirteenth century, as Europe proceeded to narrow its religious and cultural horizons at home through repression of Jews and heretics, European diplomacy was operating in a wide and complex world. A politically resurgent Islam was poised to destroy what remained of the crusader states in Palestine, while Mongol invaders threatened to eliminate Christians and Muslims alike. As Western leaders faced the question of whether to forge an alliance with one non-Christian group against the other, envoys moved across Europe and Asia exploring possibilities. The situation was further complicated by the recovery of the Paleologoi, their marriage ties with the Mongols, and the heavy economic stake of European merchants in the East. Much of the uncertainty surrounding negotiations was eliminated after 1291 when Acre, the last great Latin stronghold in Palestine, fell to the Muslims and the Mongol Ilkhan, who had heretofore campaigned actively for a Mongol-Christian alliance, converted to Islam.

Given this situation, it is hardly surprising that Christian intellectuals found themselves thinking a great deal about non-Christians. Since a number of late thirteenth-century Christians also found themselves thinking about the Antichrist, it is equally unsurprising that they combined these elements. In fact, they did so extensively enough to make the subject too big for a single article. Even if limited to a single order it remains gigantic. The Franciscans said many things about Antichrist in many contexts.

Here I shall pursue the limited goal of looking at a few Franciscan commentaries written between the 1290s and 1330s.[1]

As I have observed elsewhere,[2] Minorite exegetes approached the Apocalypse in two basic ways. The majority followed a course that put them in harmony with their Dominican colleagues—indeed, with the main line of interpretative tradition going back to Bede—by dividing the book into seven visions covering seven periods of church history. Antichrist was identified with the sixth period. While devotees of this approach agreed that each of the first four visions dealt with the seven periods as a whole, they were less sure what occurred after that point. Most of them argued that the last three visions concentrated on the final two periods, offering an emotive close-up of Antichrist and final judgment. In practice, however, they usually followed the logic of the text rather than that of their rather theoretical four/three split, and the text pointed in a slightly different direction. The visions most easily divisible in seven parts were not the first four but the first, second, third, and fifth. Thus, these were most amenable to treatment as tours of church history. The fourth vision, that of the woman, dragon, and two beasts, was notably unsuitable for such treatment but offered excellent material for thoughts on the Antichrist. Thus, commentators were inclined to seek Antichrist in the sixth member of each seven-part vision, in the two beasts of the fourth vision (Revelation 13), and in the beast of the sixth vision (Revelation 17), who could be identified with the beast from the sea in Revelation 13 because both have seven heads.

Those who accepted this approach could avail themselves of exegetical tradition in interpreting specific passages. On the whole, while the Muslims were hardly ignored by this tradition, they were not exactly highlighted by it either. The one exception worth consideration here is Joachim of Fiore, the Calabrian abbot whose commentary was begun around 1183. It is hard to offer any date for its completion, but we are secure in using 1202, the year of Joachim's death, as the moment when all revisions certainly came to an end.[3]

Joachim's thought is complex—one might say kaleidoscopic—and thus defies any brief exposition, but certain preoccupations are evident in his treatment of the present and immediate future, which he identifies with the fifth and sixth periods of church history. These preoccupations include the Byzantine–Latin ecclesiastical rift, the secular-ecclesiastical tensions revealed in the papal-imperial struggles, heresy (particularly the Cathari, referred to by Joachim as Patareni), and Islam. The rise of Islam is introduced by him as a major element of the fourth period, which ran from Justinian to Charlemagne;[4] but Joachim hardly limits its importance to the past. The Muslims return, along with the three other preoccupations just mentioned, in his description of the tribulations plaguing the fifth period,[5] and they are projected into the future in his admittedly tentative suggestions concerning the sixth, the period of Antichrist.

It is of course the latter that interests us. Some of Joachim's most important statements on the matter are in his exegesis of chapters 13 and 17. He identifies the seven heads of the beast from the sea (Rev. 13:1) with the four beasts in Daniel 7 and interprets them as seven kingdoms: the synagogue, the pagans, the Arians (who are conveniently subdivided into four groups), and the Muslims.[6] Thus, as he explicitly observes,[7] they do not correspond to the seven periods. The seventh kingdom, the Muslims, is introduced in the fourth period and still remains. Nevertheless, the seven kings in 17:9 *are* identified with the seven periods. The first five are Herod and his successors; Nero and his successors; Constantius the Arian and his successors; "Muhammad or rather Cosroes, king of the Persians, and his successors"; and "the first one in the West who began to wear down the church concerning investitures, from which many schisms and tribulations have arisen." The sixth, of whom it is said "one is" (17:10), is the eleventh king in Daniel 7,[8] in whose time the new Babylon will be stricken. Afterward, the seventh head will be mortally wounded and the church will have tranquility for a while.[9]

This is, to say the least, vague; yet Joachim fleshes the scenario out in a number of places. In one place he identifies the eleventh king with Antichrist,[10] while in another he seems to identify him of whom it is said "one is" with "Saladin, that famous king of the Turks by whom was captured that city in which Christ suffered, and he of whom it is said 'another will arise after him, more powerful than those who preceded'";[11] yet these passages are less important than Joachim's regular tendency to predict a coming desolation of Christendom through an alliance of corrupt Christians and pagan forces. This is expressed in various ways. The beasts from sea and land in Revelation 13 could be made to stand for a world emperor and a great prelate on the model of Nero and Simon Magus;[12] yet Joachim, while willing to see corruption in the church, is not comfortable with the idea of a bad pope leading the persecution of Antichrist. On the whole he tends to favor the Muslims for the role of Nero and the Cathari for that of Simon Magus. In fact, he announces that a trustworthy man recently imprisoned in the Alexandria area heard from a Muslim that the Cathari had sent legates seeking (and receiving) an agreement of unity. Joachim heard this news in 1195 from the man himself.[13] Shortly thereafter, he suggests that the attack will be launched, not only by three different varieties of Muslim (Turks, Ethiopians, and Moors), but by the northern pagans against whom the Germans had fought.[14]

Thus, two of the four preoccupations mentioned earlier will combine in the attack. The other two will also be instrumental, but in a passive sense. Joachim seems to assume that the desolation of Christian nations caused by this assault will be made possible by Christian weakness caused in turn by internal strife.[15]

An additional complication to the scenario is contributed by the prediction in Revelation 17:8 that the beast will rise again from the abyss. Joachim takes this to mean that Islam will be temporarily defeated, then rise again. This will scandalize weaker Christians, who will say, "If Jesus were really the son of God this would not have been allowed to happen."[16] Joachim offers two possibilities. Either this passage refers to Islamic resurgence after the first crusade, in which case his era already has witnessed the death and resurrection of Islam; or it refers to a future weakening of Islam through conversion, followed by its recovery. Surprisingly enough, he expresses a preference for the second option.[17]

While Joachim's commentary was available to Franciscan exegetes before the 1290s and most of the latter shared his view of the Apocalypse as seven visions concerning seven periods, they generally ignored his thoughts on Islam.[18] The only Minorite commentary that gave the Muslims a major role in the apocalyptic drama was also the only one to reject the accepted seven-vision, seven-period model, proceeding instead on the assumption that the Apocalypse should be read as a progressive history of the church from the apostles in chapter 1 to the eschaton in chapter 22. Its author, Alexander Minorita, was largely ignored in his own time but rehabilitated in the fourteenth century and copied so closely at that time that consideration of his exegesis will be deferred until later.

Once we proceed into the 1290s and beyond, we find at least three commentaries that display significant Joachite influence concerning the Muslims. The first is probably by Vital du Four[19] and, if so, was written in the 1290s or the following decade. Vital's allusions to Joachim are scant and seldom by name; yet in his exegesis of Revelation 13 and 17 he echoes Joachim on the seven heads as seven persecuting kings.[20] More important for our purposes, he follows Joachim in offering an interpretation of the ten horns in 13:1 based partly on the four beasts of Daniel 7. Thus Vital, too, introduces the Muslims as the last of four major challenges to the church.

In neither of these cases does Vital explicitly cite Joachim; yet he does invoke him in an equally significant context, his exegesis of Revelation 17:18, "and the woman you see is a great city." He identifies this city as "all the reprobate, or the city of Rome, which has kingship over all the kings of the earth." Vital observes that John "speaks for that time in which Roman idolatry was strong, or for a future time when heresies and perhaps all perfidy will reign." He refers at this point to Joachim, then seems to identify that time as one under the leadership of the king of whom it is said, "one is." In that time, however,

> kings will be gathered to fight with him and to strike a blow at the sons of Babylon who call themselves sons of Christ and are not, but are rather the synagogue of Satan. Their intention, indeed, will be evil for all and in all things, but nevertheless they will unknowingly do God's will both in killing the just, who must be crowned with martyrdom, and in bringing to judgment the impious by

whom the earth was stained with blood. After this
affliction, which has now partly begun, there will be
victory for the Christians and joy for those who fear the
true God.[21]

Vital's reference to Joachim ensures that, although the
Muslims are never mentioned here, their shadow hangs over the
passage, giving it a special interest in the light of what we find in
Peter Olivi and Henry of Cossey.

When we turn to Olivi's commentary, composed just
before his death in 1297, we enter another world.[22] Like Vital, he
thinks of the Apocalypse as having seven visions which are
mostly recapitulative,[23] sees church history as divided into seven
periods, sees the fifth as a period of decline preparing the way
for Antichrist, and places Antichrist in the sixth. In diagnosing
the ills of the fifth period, both men speak of heretics, philosophers, secular rulers, and corrupt *praelati*.

There the resemblance ends, however. Whereas Vital
thinks he stands at the beginning of the fifth period, Olivi places
himself in the overlapping time between the fifth and sixth
periods. While Vital sees the sixth period in negative terms as the
time of Antichrist, Olivi also depicts it in positive terms as a
period of renewal, the dawning of a new age, and gives his own
order a major role in that renewal. Whereas Vital expects a single
Antichrist, Olivi awaits two, the mystical and the great, and hints
that one or both might be wearing the triple tiara.[24] These are
hardly minor variations, but they are less significant for the
moment than another: Olivi's increased interest in allowing
Islam a major role in the coming temptation.

His interest in doing so emerges clearly in his handling of
the two beasts in Revelation 13. The beast from the sea, he says,
is from an infidel nation.[25] Since it is the custom of prophetic
scripture to speak of one special case but generalize from it, the
beast stands particularly for the Saracens but more generally for
the whole beastly crowd of reprobate fighting against the elect
from the beginning of the world to its end. Its ascent signifies
Muslim conquests.[26]

Like Vital, Olivi tries his hand at identifying the seven
heads with seven groups that have opposed the church since
Christ. He identifies the seventh head with Islam. Nevertheless,

he soon approaches the problem in a much different way, suggesting that, while what is said of the beast applies in general to the reprobate as a whole, it can be referred particularly to the beast arising "from the fourth period through the end of the church."[27] The seven heads stand for the seven centuries between the rise of Islam and the coming of Antichrist. The head that is wounded and recovers signifies a future death and recovery of Islam. Elsewhere Olivi makes it plain that he conceives this process, not in terms of military events from the first crusade on, but in terms of a mass conversion of Muslims to Christianity in the near future, followed by an Islamic resurgence.[28]

When he turns to the beast from the land, Olivi describes it as a group of pseudoprophets arising from Christianity itself and supporting the (Muslim) beast from the sea.[29] Thus he envisages a future alliance between Islam and carnal apostate Christians in the time of Antichrist. The two will be conflated into one ungodly sect. Who, then, will be Antichrist in this scenario? Olivi grants that he could be either the pseudopope (the apostate Christian who heads the sect) or the king in league with him; yet shortly thereafter he seems to come down on the side of the pseudopope.[30]

Olivi's interpretation of 666, the number of the beast, inspires still another consideration of the Muslims. After citing several possible approaches to the passage, he notes that "certain people" identify it with the 666 years between the year A.D. 635, when the Saracens defeated the Persians, and the year A.D. 1300. There are also 666 years from the year A.D. 648, when they took Africa, to the year A.D. 1323, which is 1,290 years from the death of Christ. If the number 1,290 (found in Daniel 12:11) represents the number of years between the time the yoke of sacrifice was lifted from the Jews and the appearance of Antichrist, then there should be 666 years between the time the Saracen kingdom was spread out over Asia and Africa and the arrival of Antichrist. There are, then, twenty-three years left before the persecution of Antichrist begins, and only twenty if the 1,290 years include the entire reign of Antichrist. "I don't know what will happen next," Olivi remarks. "God knows."[31]

At this point, Olivi has not yet told us which Antichrist he is talking about, the mystical or the great. We eventually discover that he has been projecting his investigation into the period after the decline and revival of Islam and speaking of the great Antichrist. Nevertheless, he goes on to remark that "wherever in this book the great Antichrist is discussed, the time of the mystical Antichrist preceding the great is implied *more prophetico*." Olivi adds that

> according to this reasoning, through the beast ascending from the sea is signified the bestial life and people of the carnal and secular Christians which, since the end of the fourth period, has had many heads in the form of carnal princes and prelates, and this has been going on for six hundred years now.

He identifies the beast from the land with yet another pseudopope—in fact, with a decadent Franciscan—who will corrupt Christian doctrine and will be supported by the beast from the sea, a king within Christendom. Here again he is not willing to state definitively which of the two will be the mystical Antichrist, but he quotes with obvious approval the opinion of "some people" that it will be the pseudopope.[32] Thus wretchedly led, the institutional church will continue to decay until it is destroyed by an Islamic army, clearing the way for the temptation of the great Antichrist.

In other words, Olivi sees a parallel between the mystical and great Antichrists. The same biblical passages refer to each. In each case, there will be a pseudopope supported by a ruler. In the case of the mystical Antichrist, both will come from within Christendom and the result will be a perversion of the faith promulgated in the name of Christianity. In the case of the great Antichrist, a renegade Christian leader will be in league with a Muslim ruler and the result will be an ungodly amalgam of faiths. Olivi tends to identify Antichrist with the pseudopope in both cases; yet one gets the impression that the identification may be less interesting to him than it is to us. In the long run, it is the king–pseudopope combination that fascinates him, not a single malign leader called "Antichrist." What he finds in the Apocalypse is a chain of events, a scenario that he thinks is already unfolding around him. The evangelical renewal signaled by the Franciscan rule and approved by Innocent III a century earlier must contend with an increasingly corrupt institutional church which, supported by secular authority, will eventually turn against that rule. A Muslim invasion will get rid of the church and presumably the secular authority as well, but the elect will then be open to persecution by a ghastly alliance of Muslim ruler and apostate pseudopope. They, too, will eventually be destroyed, and the era of evangelical perfection will be established.

Olivi's Apocalypse commentary was not well received in higher ecclesiastical circles. It was, in fact, condemned by his own order in 1319 and by the pope in 1326. The fate of his work may be related to the fact that Apocalypse commentaries by two eminent Parisian scholars, Pierre Auriol (1319) and Nicholas of Lyra (1326), departed from the seven-vision, seven-period, recapitulative model followed by Olivi and by most preceding Franciscan exegetes, opting instead for the radically different progressive approach employed earlier by Alexander Minorita.[33] We can now finally turn to that approach.

Alexander, Pierre, and Nicholas all proceed on the assumption that the book of Revelation should be read as a progressive history of the church from the apostles in chapter 1 to the eschaton in chapter 22. Obviously this way of reading the Apocalypse limits the number of places where one might expect to find Antichrist. Since he is to come in the future, one can hope to locate him only in those passages that refer to the future, and those who read the book as a progressive history place most of it in the past. Alexander does not manage to work Francis of Assisi in until Revelation 20:6. He discerns the expiration of the millenium in 20:7 and is thus free to confront Antichrist at that point, but has him consigned to the everlasting fire by 20:10. Pierre follows roughly the same schedule. Only Nicholas departs from it, as we will see.

It is equally obvious that this approach limits the use one can make of the two beasts in chapter 13, because by the time they reach that point our three commentators are just heading into the seventh century. That allows them to identify the dragon and beast from the sea with Chosroes and his son and the beast from the land with Muhammad, but none of these people can then be identified with Antichrist, who is still far in the future. Nevertheless, it offers some interesting possibilities for the number 666. Alexander, living in the early thirteenth century, can see it as a prediction of how long Islam will last, but Pierre, writing in 1319, has to acknowledge that the period has expired. He observes that some Muslims feel they have exceeded the time predicted by their prophets and are now living on borrowed time (*de gratia*), but others feel the 666 years should be begun from the reorganization of the faith and correction of the Koran which occurred after Muhammad's death, in which case they are still unfolding. Pierre announces that he himself does not know what to think.[34]

Nicholas of Lyra does. He accepts the idea that the beast from the land is Muhammad, but rejects as improbable any effort to see the number as leading to the end of Islam, even if one begins from the reorganization after Muhammad's death. Far from fading, Islam seems to be prospering, as the extensive Mongol conversions to it suggest. Nicholas offers the alternative of counting backward instead, making 666 represent the time between Christ and Muhammad.

From that point on in their commentaries, Pierre and Nicholas differ notably on the Muslims. Pierre, following Alexander, concentrates on Western affairs until 16:13, but at that point returns in force to the Holy Land. He picks up the interpretation of dragon and beast already developed in chapter 13, and everything from there to the end of chapter 19 becomes a continuous narrative of Outremer. Chapter 20 turns briefly to the investiture controversy, and the dragon of 20:2 obligingly becomes the emperor for a moment, just long enough for the thousand-year imprisonment of the dragon to refer, not to Islam, but to the millenium after Pope Sylvester;[35] but by 20:4 we are back in the holy land for Saladin's conquest of Jerusalem and the next four crusades, followed by Frederick II, Francis, and Dominic in verse 5. Obviously time is flying by for Pierre, since the dragon must be released and Antichrist arrive in verse seven, when the thousand years elapse. Since, following Alexander, Pierre dates this period from the time of Pope Sylvester and places his election in A.D. 316, he seems to have a more or less solid date for the arrival of Antichrist, 1316. That gave Alexander close to three-fourths of a century between himself and Antichrist, but Pierre is less fortunate. He remarks that, since Silvester became pope in 316 and it is now 1319, the Antichrist must already be three years old. Recoiling from his own mathematics, Peter suggests that "certitude concerning this number should be left up to the Holy Spirit."[36]

Placing Antichrist at Revelation 20:7 gives him some interesting company, Gog and Magog. Pierre observes that many identify them with the Mongols. The latter were enclosed beyond the Caspian Mountains by Alexander the Great, but in 1240 they broke out and have been running amok ever since. Pierre is obviously taken with this theory, but eventually feels compelled to bow to Augustine's insistence that Gog and Magog refer to the entire body of those following the devil, not a specific people.[37]

Nicholas of Lyra's commentary on the same chapters works from the same basic presupposition that the book is a successive narrative of church history, yet breaks with the chronological framework established by Alexander and adopted by Pierre. He applies chapter 16 to the first crusade as they do, but begins the next chapter with the announcement that he will exposit 17:1 through 20:6 on the assumption that it refers entirely to past events, then say what he thinks of that assumption. This sets the stage for a double critique of Alexander and Pierre. On the one hand, he is judging their interpretation and offering an alternate one on the assumption that 17:1 to 20:6 refers to past events. On the other hand, he is judging the assumption itself.

What follows will not have been pleasant reading for Alexander and Pierre. Nicholas finds three basic difficulties in the received interpretation. First, consistent application of the text to the Muslims forces the reader into interpretive inconsistencies. At one point, the beast with seven heads is the king of Egypt, yet at another point, one of the seven heads turns out to be the king of the Turks. Second, it involves a simplistic and thereby distorted reading of history. Nicholas, a much better historian than Pierre, finds himself noting that the Turkish head on the Egyptian beast is not only exegetically inconsistent but historically ironic, considering the actual relations between the two powers. Earlier he gently corrects Pierre's notion of a great

Islamic Anti-Christian alliance in the 1090s, observing that the Muslims were split until the time of Saladin.

These two objections can be met at least partly by reinterpreting a few passages, and Nicholas provides such a reinterpretation as he proceeds. In the process, the exegesis broadens out to include the Mongols, who make a cameo appearence at 20:4. Nevertheless, such cosmetic surgery does little to meet Nicholas' third objection, which is that seeing everything to 20:7 as past history leaves nothing said about events between the present and the arrival of Antichrist. Pierre, of course, raises the possibility that there could be no such events, since the Antichrist already has appeared; yet he then suggests that this very implication should cause us to reserve judgment on the meaning of the thousand years. Nicholas is more resolute. He affirms that "the arrival of Antichrist still is not near."

Thus Nicholas thinks it wiser to assume that the events described from chapter seventeen on have not yet been completed. Having said so much, he deftly and somewhat ironically excuses himself from saying much about them. "Since I am neither a prophet nor the son of a prophet," he says, "I wish to say nothing about future events except what can be elicited from holy scripture, the saints, or the authentic doctors. Thus I leave exposition of this text to wiser men." Nevertheless, Nicholas promises to get in touch with us should God provide him with any additional insight.

The rest of his commentary on Revelation 20 is cursory and unexciting. The thousand years simply represent church history to the time of Antichrist, while God and Magog represent all those adhering to Antichrist.

While it is tempting to posit a connection between condemnation of Olivi's Apocalypse commentary and the surprising shift at Paris from the standard recapitulative pattern to Alexander's hitherto-rejected progressive pattern, the limited number of extant Franciscan commentaries makes it risky to move beyond Pierre and Nicholas to any generalization about Parisian exegesis.[38] We have even less to examine from England—a single commentator, Henry of Cossey—but Henry's commentary shows that the recapitulative pattern was far from discredited in his country.[39]

It is at least arguable that Olivi's unfortunate *Nachleben*, linked as it was to spiritual Franciscan defiance of the papacy after 1318,[40] affected subsequent exegesis in a slightly different way. It encouraged those dealing with the persecution of Antichrist to concentrate on enemies outside the church rather than on corruption within it. Reference to internal difficulties was hardly forbidden, but the sort of assault on *praelati* offered by Olivi, Vital, and others in the thirteenth century seemed vaguely subversive in the early fourteenth century. This theory is hardly unquestionable, but it does accord well with the approach found in Pierre, Nicholas, and to a lesser extent, Henry of Cossey, to whom we must now turn.

Henry sees all four sevenfold visions as miniature histories of the church. The fourth period—running, according to Henry, from Justinian to Charlemagne—was that of the hermits and virgins. Here most preceding commentators saw the enemy as hypocrisy or laxity, and so does Henry; yet he also speaks constantly of the Saracens. In reality, these elements fit together nicely for him. He refers to the fact that the seventh-century Saracen invasion overran monastic establishments in the Thebaid,[41] and describes the fourth persecution as caused by "the hypocrisy and power of the Muslims . . . from the time of Justinian through that of Charlemagne."[42] The white horse of Revelation 6:8 is seen as a symbol of Muslim hypocrisy, a subject upon which Henry expatiates with gusto.[43]

His view of the fifth period is in some ways typical of Franciscan exegesis. Like others, he speaks of heresy, ecclesiastical corruption and church-state conflict as major problems; yet, like Olivi, he also refers to the Muslims in connection with the fifth period, albeit only once.[44] Moreover, whereas most Franciscan exegetes seem to place themselves in the early fifth period at the latest, Henry, like Olivi, seems to think he is near the end of it. He actually leaves the end of the period open, but in such a way as to make it unclear on which side of his own time the boundary might lie. At one point he cites Joachim to the effect that the fifth period runs from Charlemagne to Antichrist,[45] yet at another he describes it as running from Charlemagne to Joachim. In this latter case he goes on to note that the period actually extended beyond Joachim, but we do not know how long.[46] The lack of any clearcut answer to this question is rendered somewhat less important by the fact that Henry agrees with Joachim, Olivi, and others in linking the fifth and sixth periods in a single battle beginning in the fifth period and climaxing in the sixth.[47]

In discussing this battle, Henry portrays a double threat: continuing conflict with nonbelievers outside the church, laxity and heresy within it. Antichrist's following is composed of all these elements. He will be supported by an odd assortment of evildoers including Jews, Moslems, heretics, pagans, and false Christians.[48] The result would be a temporary victory for Antichrist, the mechanics of which are most clearly stated by Henry in his interpretation of the dragon and the beasts from land and sea (Revelation 13), the pouring of the sixth vial (Revelation 16:12–16), and the beast on which the whore rides (Revelation 17).[49] His exegesis of these three passages reveals a scenario in which the political force that has guarded Christendom from external threat is gradually weakened by sin and eventually finds itself unable to withstand attack. In dealing with the sixth vial Henry simply refers to an attack "from the east," but in his examination of the beast from the sea he envisages the same fourfold attack by Turks, Ethiopians, Moors, and "those who frequently war with the Germans" already suggested by Joachim.[50]

Nevertheless, however many groups Henry chooses to include, he sees the Muslims as a central element in the assault. Their centrality is seen in his examination of the beast from the sea. Henry does not identify the beast with Islam, but rather with the entire mass of infidels and false Christians throughout history. Nevertheless, like Joachim he interprets this passage in the light of the four beasts in Daniel 7, thus making Islam the last great power to threaten Christianity; he moves neatly from this interpretation to the (equally Joachite) notion that the slain and recovered head of Revelation 13:3 is Islam; and, like Joachim, he identifies its apparent destruction with Christian victories in the eleventh century.[51] Moreover, in dealing with the rest of the verse ("and people followed after the beast in wonder") Henry comments that

> many Christians, seeing so many people follow the Islamic sect, will say that God could never have wished so many people to be lost and so many of his faithful to be so hard pressed. Thus deceived, they will follow the beast.[52]

In dealing with the number 666, Henry cites various ways in which some have linked it with Islam. Among these is the notion that it represents the number of years Islam will last, a view he associates with Innocent III. He cites as confirmation an astrological prediction by Abū Ma'shar that Islam cannot last longer than 693 years. Unfortunately, he observes, it is now 1333 and Islam has endured for 731 years. Some impious Muslims explain this discrepancy by claiming that their religion has continued to exist through grace, while others say that the counting should begin, not from its origin under Muhammad, but rather from its rebirth under "a certain successor." Since all of this seems uncertain, however, Henry suggests that one will be better off relying more on the standard interpretation, which attempts to view the numbers as letters spelling Antichrist's name rather than as a specific number of years.[53]

Henry's interest in an apocalyptic role for Islam is also seen in his consideration of the beast in Revelation 17. He describes it as the multitude of reprobate and infidel peoples, yet becomes substantially more specific in dealing with its seven heads. When he comes to the announcement that "the seven heads are seven hills" (17:9) he observes that, historically interpreted, these represent the seven infidel peoples who have opposed the church. Six of the seven have passed, leaving only the Saracens.[54] So far Henry seems to be making sense, but he then complicates the matter by announcing that he of whom it is said "one is" can be identified as a precursor of Antichrist under whom the destruction of the Roman Empire will be completed. After that, the seventh head of the beast, the Saracens, will be destroyed and the elect will have a brief respite, since both of their major problems (a persecuting Christian Roman Empire and a threatening non-Christian one) will be gone; yet the beast will rise once more from the abyss of paganism for a final persecution.

So Henry seems to say. On closer examination, however, this scenario makes little sense, since it omits Antichrist. Perhaps Henry himself seems to think he has been imprecise, for in dealing with verse 11 ("the beast which was, and is not, is an eighth but belongs to the seven") he offers an important clarification. This beast can be identified with Islam, since it is powerful, then destroyed, then powerful before being destroyed again.[55] It is eighth because it comprises an eighth persecution, yet is one of the seven as well. One might expect Henry to say that it is the latter because it was a menace earlier, but he does not. Instead he says that it is of the seven because when the Muslims arise and conquer they will join to themselves all the survivors of the preceding heads—the remaining Jews, pagans, and heretics—and attack Christianity with a collection of all the errors ever perpetrated. This persecution will be carried out during the reign of the seventh king, Antichrist himself.[56]

One may feel as if the ground has shifted under one's feet several times during the exegesis of this passage; yet Henry's interpretation makes sense if we assume that, like Olivi, he is following Joachim but, unlike Olivi, he has chosen the other alternative offered by Joachim. He identifies the death of Islam with the first crusade and its subsequent resuscitation with a successful attack on Rome and the persecution of Antichrist. Both of the latter will be parts of a single event involving the revitalized Muslims.

Henry's commentary strengthens what may be taken as the basic conclusion of this article: There were two basic ways of approaching the Apocalypse, and each allowed the ingenious commentator to construct a relatively specific scenario involving non-Christian peoples. In view of the medieval legend concerning Antichrist's parentage and the general Christian anti-Jewish feeling of the period, it would have been amazing had the Jews not been worked into the resultant scenario in some way. Moreover, those who saw the early periods of church history as a series of persecutions by Jews, pagans, heretics, and hypocrites followed by a grand finale of sorts in which all preceding temptations were reintroduced in combination—a view explictly stated by exegetes both inside and outside the order—would almost be required to give the Jews some place in the temptation of Antichrist. Again, given the profound effect exercised on the European imagination by the Mongol attacks, it was almost inevitable that they too would receive some mention, and the shadowy figures of Gog and Magog offered an ideal context for it, although exegetes, swayed by Augustine's insistence that Gog and Magog represent all persecutors of the church, could offer the Mongols only a minor apocalyptic role at best.

In the final analysis, it was not the Jews or Mongols but the Muslims who attracted the lion's share of attention. Their appeal to exegetes rested at least partly upon Joachim's continuing influence; yet Franciscan exegetes who sought to make the beast from the sea relevant to contemporary concerns hardly needed Joachim to remind them of Islam. A special concern with it is detectable even in the Franciscan *legenda* and rule. Francis preached to the sultan, and the rule closes with a chapter on preaching to the Muslims. Again, Franciscan anxiety over the impact of an Islamicized Aristotelianism on contemporary philosophy, a concern that Bonaventure already had woven into his apocalyptic program over three decades earlier,[57] may also have contributed. Furthermore, the very duration of Islam constituted a theological problem. Exegetes like Olivi and Cossey could see why God might have thought it wise to launch the Muslims as a punishment for his people, much as he once used the Assyrians and Babylonians; but they found it harder to understand why he had then kept them around for another six hundred years. Their remarkable staying power seemed to suggest that they were destined to play a major apocalyptic role. Moreover, their endurance was rendered all the more significant by their increasing menace. As exegetes saw the crusader kingdoms disappear and the Mongols converting to Islam, they could hardly help thinking that the head of the beast, once nearly slain, had somehow been healed and menaced them more than ever.

NOTES

1. In seeking news of Antichrist, the medieval exegete also went to other books, especially Daniel, I Thessalonians, I and II John, and the synoptic gospels. Moreover, they discussed the matter extensively in other literary genres besides Bible commentaries. For a survey of thought on Antichrist, see Emmerson, *Antichrist in the Middle Ages*. A good general summary of medieval apocalypticism, together with key primary sources in translation, is found in McGinn, *Visions of the End*. For recent bibliography see McGinn, "Awaiting an End," 263–289.

2. Burr, "Mendicant Readings of the Apocalypse," in *The Apocalypse in the Middle Ages*. As I indicate there, the topic is dramatically underexamined. Problems of attribution alone will provide material for several dissertations.

3. There is as yet no critical edition of Joachim's commentary. References here will be to Joachim's *Expositio in apocalypsim*. On Joachim see most recently McGinn, *The Calabrian Abbott*.

4. Joachim, *Expositio*, 9vb.

5. Ibid., 117ra–va.

6. Ibid., 163ra.

7. Ibid., 196va.

8. Daniel 7:8, 7:24.

9. Joachim, 196va–vb.

10. Ibid., 168rb. At 133ra he states his suspicion that the Antichrist is already present in the world, though he has not yet been revealed.

11. Ibid., 197ra.

12. Ibid., 167va–168rb.

13. Ibid., 134rb.

14. Ibid., 134va.

15. E.g., ibid., 197va. This passage and 190va make it clear that the destruction will represent divine judgment on a sinful Christian community, although the agents will not recognize it as such.

16. Ibid., 196rb.

17. Ibid., 164vb–165ra.

18. They often cite Joachim, but not in this context. See Burr, "Mendicant Readings." One exception is a commentary published as Alexander Halensis, *Commentarii in apocalypsim* (Paris, 1647), then as

Bonaventure's in Bonaventura, *Sancti Bonaventure . . . Operum . . . Supplementum* (Trent, 1773), vol. 2. The date and authorship are as yet unsettled. This commentator echoes Joachim on the seven heads in Revelation 13:1 as seven evil princes since Christ.

19. Vitalis de Furno, *Expositio super apocalypsim*, MSS Assisi 46, 66, 71, 358 and elsewhere. Published in large part (but with passages from other commentaries interspersed) in Bernardinus Senensis, *Commentarii in apocalypsim*, in *Opera* (Paris, 1635), vol. 3. On the evidence for this attribution see Burr, "Mendicant Readings." I shall cite Assisi 66 here, but refer to the edition when correction is necessary.

20. In dealing with Revelation 13:1, the 1635 edition, 110f. provides a list of names very close to Joachim's, but says that the fifth is "the king of the new Babylon, Henry the king of the Germans," who, wishing to be like God, launched many persecutions against the church. The sixth is:

> a certain unnamed king of whom it is said in Dan. 6, 'And another will arise after them, more powerful than the earlier ones, and he will humiliate three kings.' This one, whoever he may be, will wreak many evils upon the church of his time, but his identity is not for us to decide.

Assisi 66, 99r says the fifth king is Hirtacus. In dealing with Revelation 17:9, the 1635 edition, 144 describes the fifth head as *Diocletianus et quod dicitur in textu*, while Assisi 66, 129rb calls it *Henricus Alamanus et Federicus*. Thus it seems likely that the author mentioned Henry in both places but, somewhere along the line, Hirtacus and Diocletian were substituted.

21. Assisi 66, 130ra–rb:

> *Et mulier quam vidisti est civitas magna*, idest reproborum universitas, vel romana civitas, que habet regnum super reges terre. In quo dominium est imperii universalis et loquitur pro tempore illo in quo vigebat romana ydolatria, vel pro tempore futuro, quando forte ita regnabunt hereses et omnis perfidia, secundum Ioachim, ex omnibus datur intelligi, quod per istum primum quidem regem intelligimus sextum de quo dictum est, *unus est*, sollum illo tempore, oportet congregari reges ad pugnandum cum illo, et ad percutiendum fillios babilonis, qui dicunt se fillios christi et non sunt, sed sunt sinagoga sathane, et quidem illorum intentio, per omnia et in omnibus

prava erit, sed tamen inscii et nescientes, facient in
utroque volluntatem dei sive occidendo iustos quos
oportet coronari martirio, sive iudiciis impiis, a
quibus corrupta in sanguibus est terra. Post plagam
igitur istam, que iam ex parte inchoata est, erit
victoria christianis, et gaudium timentibus verum
deum, prostrato capite isto super quo regnat unus rex,
et usque ad consumationem de draco.

Compare Joachim, 197ra–rb (re. Rev. 17), which contains no suggestion
that the church will be swamped by heresy and perfidy in the future.

22. Olivi, *Lectura super apocalypsim*. On this commentary see
Manselli, *La "Lectura super apocalypsim" di Pietro di Giovanni Olivi*.
Another edition is currently being prepared by Paolo Vian. I cite the
Lewis edition.

23. There is some difference in their approaches to the last three
visions, since Olivi tends to see all seven (with the possible exception of
the last) as recapitulative, whereas Vital theoretically adheres to the
more traditional four/three pattern; yet in practice they are
substantially similar in handling these visions.

24. See Burr, "Olivi, the *Lectura super apocalypsim*, and Franciscan
Exegetical Tradition," 115–135.

25. Olivi, *Lectura*, 694.

26. Ibid., 698f.

27. Ibid., 706.

28. Ibid., 708f. Thus he chooses the alternative favored by Joachim,
165ra.

29. Ibid., 718.

30. Ibid., 720.

31. Ibid., 733f. Burr, "Olivi's Apocalyptic Timetable," 237–260,
notes that the mathematics of this passage seem scrambled.

32. Olivi, 734.

33. Pierre Auriol, *Compendium sensus literalis totius divinae
scripturae*, pp. 438–555 (hereafter "Pierre"); Nicholas of Lyra, *Postilla
super totam bibliam*. The pages of the Nicholas edition are unnumbered.
Nicholas, Pierre, and Alexander are also discussed in Philip Krey's
chapter in this volume.

34. Pierre, 505.

35. Ibid., 543. During this time "priests began to reign and were
honored as kings."

36. Pierre, 548: Propter quod certitudo istius numeri magis debet sancto Spiritui reservari.

37. Ibid., 549.

38. I know of only one other commentary besides those discussed here, that authored by Poncio Carbonnel, MS Toledo, Biblioteca Publica de Toledo, Provincial 450. The commentary is at 94–139ff., and is followed at 139–141ff. by a defense of his methodology in the commentary entitled *Expositio brevis vel divisio libri apocalypsis*. On this commentary see Reinhardt, "Das Werk des Nikolaus von Lyra im mittelalterlichen Spanien," 321–358; and Krey, "Nicholas of Lyra: Apocalypse Commentary as Historiography," 122–125. I have seen only the *Expositio brevis*, which seems to imply that Poncio endorses the recapitulative pattern as found in pre-Franciscan commentators like Richard of St. Victor. I must reserve judgment until I see the whole commentary, however.

39. Hereafter cited as "Henry." I will cite from MS Oxford Bodl. Laud. misc. 85, occasionally correcting it on the basis of MS Holy Name College 69, now at the Franciscan Institute, St. Bonaventure University. Folio numbers alone will refer to the former MS, folio numbers preceded by a "St.B" to the latter.

40. See especially Manselli, *Spirituali e Beghini in Provenza*.

41. Henry, 80ra.

42. Ibid., 96rb.

43. Ibid., 96va. See also 96rb.

44. Ibid., 97va.

45. Ibid.

46. Ibid., 75rb. In this manuscript he says that it lasted until the year 1200 and longer, which will be the equivalent of his previous remark that it extended to the time of Joachim; yet in MS St.B, 47v, the date is 1300, which will mean that it extended at least into Henry's own lifetime.

47. Ibid., 108rb.

48. Olivi sees the various elements as united by a common commitment to carnality. Henry ascribes much the same function to luxury, e.g, *Lectura*, 109rb.

49. Henry, 120vb–123va, 135vb–136ra, 141va–143ra.

50. Ibid., 108va. The idea of an attack from the east reflects, not only Joachim's, but Henry's acceptance of elements within the Antichrist legend, such as the fact that Antichrist will be from the tribe

of Dan and born in the East. See 136ra, 141va. These are relatively unimportant factors, though. Far from playing any central role through a special relation to Antichrist, the Jews are simply one more group in the great Antichristian coalition.

51. Ibid., 121rb–va. He notes that, of the four groups predicted in Daniel 7, only Islam remains, since most adherents of the first four either have been destroyed or converted. Note, too, the final position of Islam in Henry's world-historical interpretation of the seven heads at 118ra, where the seven are identified as Lucifer, Cain, Herod, Judas, Pilate, Simon Magus, and Muhammad.

52. Ibid., 121va–vb. The beast from the land is viewed as a great preacher who will seduce people from Christianity, but little is said about him. See MS St.B 74v (page missing from MS Bodl Laud. misc. 85).

53. Henry, 123ra–va.

54. Ibid., 141vb. The first six are the Jews, Romans, Greeks, Vandals, Goths, and Lombards. Thus, the seven are identical with the groups normally cited when interpreting the seven heads in the light of the four beasts in Daniel 7; yet in dealing with the next verse he offers a slightly different pattern. The five defunct heads become Herod, Constantine, Chosroes, Arius, and "one other who vexed the church on the matter of investiture." A long historical aside traces the debate and tentatively identifies the person in question as Henry IV.

55. Ibid., 112va–vb.

56. Ibid., 142ra.

57. See Burr, "The Apocalyptic Element in Olivi's Critique of Aristotle," 15–29. One finds a mild anticipation of the preoccupation with pagan philosophy even in premendicant exegesis. Thus Richard of St. Victor, *In apocalypsim Ioannis*, PL 196:804 remarks that the first beast resembles a leopard *per variam assertionem philosophorum*. Richard was one of the two commentators Olivi constantly consulted on the Apocalypse, the other being Joachim.

CHAPTER 7

Nicholas of Lyra and Paul of Burgos on Islam

Philip Krey

When late-medieval theologians commented on a particular book of the Bible, like their modern counterparts, they frequently had the books of predecessors and contemporaries on their writing desks. The late-medieval commentary was not only the culmination of years of study and classroom lectures, but also a continuing conversation among scholars both living and dead. The commentary was intended, therefore, not only for preachers and interested laypersons, but also as a proposal to the continuing academic discussion.

Because historical circumstances change and historical contexts affect the bookish conversations among scholars, there was no end to the writing of biblical commentaries. The meaning of the biblical text was affected by the context of the interpreter. This was especially true of the only prophetic book of the New Testament, the Book of Revelation, which lends itself to the interpretation of historical events. In particular, exegetes sought to identify its bizarre figures, including the Beasts and the Antichrist. The rise and successes of Islam provided grist for the mills of countless exegetes on the Apocalypse.

Nicholas of Lyra

When Nicholas of Lyra OFM (1270–1349) wrote his literal commentary on the Apocalypse in 1329, he had on his desk the *Exposition of the Apocalypse* of Alexander Minorita OFM (d.1271) and the *Literal Compendium of the Whole of Sacred Scripture* of Lyra's younger contemporary, Pierre Auriol OFM (1280–1322).[1]

The historical-linear genre initiated by Alexander characteristically cites an image, symbol, or phrase from the Apocalypse and finds the appropriate fulfillment of its implications in an historical character or event. The pattern of the Apocalypse serving as a blueprint, its visions are fulfilled according to the order of history.[2]

Lyra's younger contemporary, Peter Auriol, who became an important theologian in his own right, adopted Alexander's method. Alexander and Peter had both written interpretive accounts of Church history which were propapal and triumphalist about the crusades. Nicholas's edition (1329) in the *Literal Postil* represents an historiographical critique of these commentaries by Alexander (1235–1249) and by the more proximate model, Peter (1319). Lyra criticizes the conclusions of his models by comparing them to the standard histories of his day and by employing his own set of hermeneutical rules.[3]

All three Franciscans have a crusading tone, although to varying degrees. Lyra's modified Augustinian understanding of history ultimately makes him suspicious of glorifying human achievements. The holy war between Heraclius and the Persian Emperor Chosroes, the victories of the Carolingians over the Muslims, and the Crusades are given pride of place in their histories that the Apocalypse outlines. All three interpret Revelation 13 in the light of Islam. The Beast from the Land is Muhammad (Revelation 13:11). In one way or another, the number 666 (Revelation 13:18) is associated with Muhammad— for Alexander as the length of Islam's dominion; for Peter, Alexander's interpretation could be right, or the number could refer to the period after the death of Muhammad, he is not quite sure; for Nicholas, as the number of years from the Incarnation to Muhammad's death.[4]

Contrary to his models, however, Lyra perceives the strength of Islam to be waxing and not waning. All three considered Islam a formidable historical challenge to

Christendom. Alexander and Peter are confident that Islam will soon be defeated. In spite of the Fall of Acre to Sultan al-Ashraf in 1291 as the Mameluk Empire gradually took back Crusader strongholds, and despite the fact that in 1316 all hope of a Mongol/Christian alliance had faded, Peter's hopes still persist.[5]

Lyra's historical consciousness and awareness of current events, on the other hand, make him less hopeful and compel him to accept the forces of Islam as a real and inscrutable mystery that will not easily be resolved.

Lyra's fifteenth-century critic, Paul of Burgos (1351–1435), joined the continuing exegetical discussion by addressing Lyra's unspoken question and arguing that Lyra was wrong in being perplexed about Islam's endurance.[6]

Although critical of Islam as a religion, Paul argued that if one were to look at its positive aspects, one could understand God's ways. Although Islam could be found in the images of Revelation 13, it was not like other pagan religions: the Saracens were not idolatrous; they did not force Christians to apostatize, but only to pay taxes; there were many Christians in Islamic territories; and Islam considered Jesus to be the most excellent of all creatures.

Strongly biased toward the papacy in its controversies with the Holy Roman Empire, Lyra's sources, Alexander and Peter Auriol, saw the Crusades, the foreign policy of the papacy against the forces of Antichrist (in the form of Islam), as a triumph for the Church. For them the Church stood in the center of historical progress, and they took heart in its endurance in spite of tribulations. This crusading zeal did not apply only to the movements that began in Clermont in 1095. For Lyra, as well as his models, the struggle between the Persian, Chosroes, and Heraclius, who defeated him, attracted considerable attention.[7]

Chosroes was interpreted as none other than the dragon of Revelation 13.[8] Due in part to heresy, the Empire was then translated from the East to the West under Charlemagne; he continued the crusades against the infidels. A Francophile, Lyra was particularly fond of noting the legendary crusading accomplishments of Charlemagne in Spain, and his famed crusade to the Holy Land.[9] Although he admitted that the Carolingian successes against the Saracens were short lived, he spent an inordinate amount of space highlighting them.

Chapter 16 of the Apocalypse serves as a good example on which to pause to illustrate Lyra's interpretation of the role of Islam in Church History. This chapter, which describes the pouring of the bowls, is the last chapter that Lyra ventures to interpret as completed history in the commentary. Here he distances himself from his models, and his exegetical consistency, his historical sensitivities, and his biases begin to reveal themselves. Verse 16:11 marks the end of a passage in which Lyra sees the interpolation of other important issues between the two phases of Islamic attacks. In 16:12 Lyra turns his attention back to the Saracens. Peter had identified the pouring of the fifth bowl with Otto III's intervention in the papal election, in which John was expelled and Gregory V was reinstated. Lyra rejects Peter's interpretation and substitutes the legend that Charlemagne went on a crusade to the Holy Land and drove back the Saracens for a time.[10] He then rejects Peter's correlation of the sixth bowl with the Investiture Controversy between Pope Gregory VII and Emperor Henry IV. Lyra proposes instead another legend about Charlemagne, his liberation of the way to the tomb of St. James at Santiago de Compestella.[11] Charlemagne was Lyra's ideal ruler; no one in Lyra's account receives as many accolades as Charlemagne.[12]

Lyra considers verses 13–16 of chapter 16 to be an introduction to the pouring of the seventh bowl, which represents the First Crusade. His discussion of the motivation for the Crusade in light of the biblical text and its results is closely argued with frequent appeals to the chronicles of William of Tyre and James of Vitry. He points out that, according to William of Tyre, from the time of Chosroes to its liberation at the time of Godfrey of Bouillon, the Holy Land was for the most part under the subjugation of the Saracens; the liberations under Heraclius and Charlemagne were only temporary. In fact, the Holy Land changed hands even among the Saracens.[13]

For Alexander and Peter, there were other challenges that the church had to survive, especially the Investiture struggles with the Holy Roman Emperors.[14] However, no challenge to the Christian mission was more critical than that of Islam (Muhammad was the beast from the earth, Revelation 13:11), and no triumph was sweeter than the First Crusade, when saints from so many countries responded to the call and established the Latin Kingdom in the Holy Land. Alexius, Godfrey, Ademar, and Baldwin were all protagonists for them. The Islamic rulers of the Turks and Egypt are represented by negative images in the Apocalypse, as is Frederick II. The victories of the First Crusade and subsequent crusading were given eschatological significance.

While rejecting the emperors as antagonists to the will of God, Lyra accepted the First Crusade as significant to a limited extent; nevertheless, he could not provide the movement as a whole with the ultimacy assigned by his predecessors. The total effect leaves one with an Augustinian sense of ambivalence about history.[15] As far as he could determine from reading the histories, the First Crusade was successful because the Saracens were divided.[16]

Furthermore, the land gains acquired by Baldwin and others were partial and temporary, much like the Carolingian achievements. The Saracens remained in control of Egypt and Asia Minor, and what was conquered was lost again to Saladin. Even those places like Acre and Tripoli which remained under Christian control, were later recaptured by the Saracens.

Lyra did not seem to be motivated by the Franciscan/ Joachite critique of the Crusades, which argued for a combination of persuasion over violence and a hope that the Muslims and the Jews would be converted in the Third Status.[17] There is no expression of hope in his commentary that the Jews would convert, and he does not even mention the possibility for Islam, as does Alexander.[18] Nor is Lyra in the least favorably disposed to the historical role of Judaism or Islam as world religions. Lyra chose realism and practicality over apocalyptic hopes. To the continuing late-medieval academic discussion over the role of Islam in the Apocalypse, Lyra proposes that historical facts take precedence over ideology and wishful thinking.[19]

Nicholas also relativizes and debunks the nature of the crusading propaganda he has inherited. As noted earlier, Alexander and Peter for all practical purposes associated the number 666 with the length of Islam's dominion. This, of course, would have meant that Islam's expansion was nearing an end.

Nicholas rejected this explanation for the number 666 because, as he had learned from an anonymous Franciscan bishop who lived among the Tartars, a majority of this people had only recently accepted the Islamic law.[20] Lyra understands this to evidence Islam's vitality, not its decline. That the Tartars chose Islam over Christianity, of course, was a blow to the Western Christian psyche.[21]

Most of Lyra's knowledge of Islam is from standard encyclopedic works like Vincent of Beauvais's (ca. 1190–ca. 1264) *Speculum Historiale.* Lyra cites anecdotes that are to be found elsewhere, such as his claim that he is narrating a report delivered to him personally by a traveling friar.[22]

However, there is one example in which he demonstrates an intent to relativize any crusading zeal. The frogs that proceed from the mouth of the false prophet in 16:13 he identifies as the Saracen preachers, who preached against the Christians in the same way that Christians preached against the Saracens.[23]

Although Peter Auriol had also included this idea, in Lyra's hands crusading is relativized—the Christian conquest is merely part of a series of temporary occupations of the Holy Land, even as religious authorities of both sides pump up their peoples against one another.

In summary, then, Lyra was convinced that Islam was identified with the forces of Antichrist in the world, but he had little hope that the Muslim world would soon experience a decline, that a mass conversion to Christianity was in the future, or that some apocalyptic confrontation was on the horizon. He saw that the Islamic world was expanding, that the Tartars had become Muslim and not Christian, and that all Western attempts since Charlemagne to contain them had been ephemeral victories at best. Lyra was consequently agnostic about the future of Islam and about Antichrist's arrival. Similar to his models, he trusted, however, that the Church of Christ would ultimately prevail.

Paul of Burgos

Pablo de Santa María (1351–1435) noted in his prologue to the *Additions to the Postillae of Nicholas of Lyra on the Bible* that no other biblical commentary except the *Glossa Ordinaria* was more widely used in Spain and probably in France.[24]

This converted Jewish Rabbi, Solomon ha-Levi, who became Pablo de Santa Maria in 1390, wrote the *Additions* from 1429–1431. Paul became Bishop of Cartagena on the Mediterranean coast (ca. 1405) and ultimately became lord chancellor of Castile and Archbishop of Burgos in 1415.[25] He was no friend of the Jews after his conversion; as lord chancellor he drafted a decree in 1412 designed to separate the Jews who did not convert from the Christians and to hinder their commerce. Having read the Qur'ân, he was better informed than Lyra about Islam, but endorsed the role of the crusades in history and particularly the campaign against Granada led by Alvaro de Luna. Proximity to Muslims and better knowledge about them did not necessarily contribute to charitable relations. Paul's *Additions* to Lyra's commentaries are included in almost every edition of the *Postillae*.[26]

The *Additions* are made up of eleven hundred glosses on passages in the Bible, most of which concern the Old Testament. They both criticize and affirm Lyra's interpretations. There are only three glosses that address Lyra's commentary on the Apocalypse.[27] Only the lengthy gloss added to chapter 13, which addresses Lyra's image of Islam, is discussed here.[28]

Concerning the *Literal Postill* on the Old Testament, Paul criticized Lyra for his inadequate knowledge of Hebrew and his resultant undue reliance upon Rashi's commentaries.[29] In the one major addition to the *Apocalypse*, he scolds the postillator (Lyra) for his inadequate knowledge of Islam. Spanish biblical commentators, especially the Bishop of Burgos, rightly felt superior in their knowledge of Hebrew to their northern colleagues.[30]

Paul also demonstrates a more complex and intimate understanding of Islam, its theology, and its relationship to Christians living among its adherents. Paul's comments are certainly not new, and his is certainly not an enlightened view of Islam.[31]

Lyra took pains to search the notable histories and oral evidence available to him to show that Islam was a more formidable force than his sources had assumed or hoped.

Approximately one hundred years after Lyra wrote his commentary on the Apocalypse, Paul made a greater effort to inform himself about Islam and the historical situation of Christians in Islamic territories.

In his lengthy addition to chapter 13, which Lyra and his models had used to associate Muhammad with the beast of the Apocalypse, Paul expands on Lyra's relativization. While insisting that the Islamic sect was an evil force in the world, he proposes that Islam rose due to the tyranny of the late-Roman Empire under Heraclius.[32] Furthermore, the people of God had always been persecuted by forces in the past, and by comparison, Islam had not been as oppressive. Consequently, God permitted them to rule much longer than expected.[33] Thus, he eliminates the need to use the symbols of chapter 13 to calculate a date for the demise of Islam, as his predecessors had done.[34]

If one were to look at the positive side of Islam, he argues, one could understand God's ways. First, Islam was not like other religions; Muslims are not idolatrous. This was the chief sin of all the other persecuting religions from the Assyrians to the time of Chosroes, and idolatry is a sin intolerable to God. Since the Muslims are not idolatrous, God has tolerated them longer than other previous oppressors.[35]

Second, Paul argues that whereas all other oppressive forces coerced the faithful to pray to or to burn incense to idols, the Muslims do not coerce the faithful into apostasy. For it is written in the Qur'ân, he notes, that all who do not accept the law must be killed unless they pay tribute. Paul substantiates this by cataloging the various territories controlled by Muslims in which Christians still reside, namely, Egypt, Palestine, and Asia Minor. He notes the number of monasteries still in existence in the East.[36] Spain historically had experienced the tolerance and high culture of the Muslims and this seems to have had its effect upon Paul.

Third, Islam considers Christ to be the most excellent of all creatures. Paul is clear on the fact that Islam's theology, and especially its christology, is not acceptable—he borrows substantially from Book One of Thomas Aquinas's *Summa Contra Gentiles* to contend that Islam's theology is only a natural and human simplification of the subtleties of Nicea and Chalcedon.[37] Nevertheless, whereas other oppressors of the faithful forced them to deny not only Christ's deity but also his human virtue, this sect concedes that Christ was the most excellent creature of all creation.[38] Paul concludes that, consequently, God has been more tolerant with Islam than any other opponent.[39]

Because of these mitigating qualities of Islam's persecution, Paul is also careful not to identify Muhammad with the Antichrist. He is an antiapostle and an antiprophet, but not the Antichrist.[40] Antichrist will come in the future. Furthermore, Paul is careful to note that Antichrist's reign will be very brief because it will be so severe, and this is not true of the reign of Islam.[41]

Nevertheless, as noted previously, these views do not make Paul of Burgos any less harsh on Muhammad or his followers; nor does his having read the Qu'rân favorably dispose him towards Islam.[42] He agrees that John foresaw Muhammad when he saw the beast from the land in Revelation 13.[43] He affirms the crusades much as Lyra's predecessors had done and identifies the crusading kings with the holy martyrs who triumphed over previous tyrannies.[44] In particular, for his own context, he celebrates the campaign of Alvaro de Luna against the Muslims in Granada.[45]

Paul wrote the additions to Revelation after July 1431, the date of a significant Castilian victory over the Moors near Granada. Although the reconquest of Spain was almost complete, and the Muslims posed no threat to Spain, his informed image of Islam and theological critique is distorted by crusading propaganda and his own zeal for the court of Castile.

Nicholas of Lyra, writing in Paris, knew less about Islam than Paul but was more skeptical of the never-ending warfare between the religions. The loss of Acre and the expansion of the Mameluke Empire posed serious questions for his understanding of God's providence. He is fully convinced that Islam was identified with the forces of Antichrist and that they were a rising and inscrutable threat to the Church greater than any internal strife. Nevertheless, neither crusading nor conversion was a possible option for him.

Approximately one hundred years later, Paul of Burgos, writing in Castile, knew more about Islam, but "his familiarity did not facilitate understanding or willingness to understand in an atmosphere of tolerance."[46] Although he was willing to give Islam a place in God's providential plan beyond a mere punishment of wayward Christians, he used his knowledge of Islam largely to show its inadequacy and its role as a force of evil in the world.

Juan de Segovia

It would take many centuries before the style of a contemporary of Paul of Burgos, Juan de Segovia (ca. 1400–1458), would be considered. This professor of theology at the University of Salamanca and representative of King Juan II of Castile to the Council of Basel (1432) organized peaceful discussions with a soldier and the ambassador of Granada in Medina del Campo, although these discussions with Muslims were held in the aftermath of the Christian victory at Higueruela in 1431.[47] Like Paul, Juan de Segovia was also affiliated with the chancellory of King Juan II, and he began his dialogues in 1431 with the soldier and the ambassador in July and October, respectively.

Juan de Segovia, who later supervised an accurate translation of the Qur'ân in both Castilian and Latin, was convinced that Christianity would triumph, given the opportunity for peaceful dialogue. He lamented that the Qur'ân was little known among Christians of his time; in fact, it was difficult to find a copy.[48] Consequently, according to Juan, an intellectual challenge to Islam was never really attempted. He argued for peaceful coexistence in order that the truth would eventually prevail through reasonable dialogue.

Although Juan de Segovia by no means held Enlightenment views of Islam, his peaceful overtures and initiatives in the chancellory in 1431 could well have served as the catalyst and context for Paul's unusually long addition to Nicholas's commentary on the thirteenth chapter of Revelation in the latter half of the same year.[49]

Like Nicholas and Paul, Juan de Segovia was concerned with Islam's rapid growth and endurance at the expense of Christianity. There is little doubt that he was aware of Lyra's *Commentary on the Apocalypse* since he noted that he had read many commentators on the issue and used Lyra's arguments to critique the Crusades in his *Prologue to the Qur'ân*.[50] Both Paul of Burgos and Juan de Segovia to a greater or lesser degree responded to Lyra's Apocalypse commentary, although each chose a different vantage point.

Juan and Paul had an opportunity of which Lyra was deprived, namely some experience of peaceful coexistence with Muslims. Paul was intolerant, but was at least able to find common ground between the traditions. For Lyra in Paris, Islam was a distant threat and a speculative problem for his theology of history. Given God's providence and the perceived biblical promises that the Christian Church would prevail, Islam's successes were a mystery to him. Paul responded to Lyra's commentary with a theodicy to explain God's providence despite the growth of Islam. Juan's concern was more practical. Like Lyra he believed that the Crusades were ineffectual, and he proposed that Christians inform themselves about the Islamic faith and, beginning with the common beliefs, discuss the differences.

NOTES

1. The following sources are of primary importance for biographical information about Lyra: the various articles by Henri Labrosse (see Bibliography); Langlois, "Nicolas de Lyre, Frère Mineur," 355–400; Hailperin, *Rashi and the Christian Scholars*; Gosselin, "Bibliographical Survey: A Listing of the Printed Editions of Nicolaus de Lyra," 399–456 (see esp. his lengthy bibliographical note on p. 399). See also, Klaus Reinhardt, "Das Werk des Nikolaus von Lyra im Mittelalterlichen Spanien," 321–358. The 1634 Antwerp edition used for this study includes two additional authentic works by Lyra, *Quaestiones judaicam perfidiam improbantes* and *Responsio ad quemdam judaeum*, and

one pseudonymous work, *Praeceptorium decalogi*; the *Interlinear Gloss* is also included. The Antwerp edition is used in this chapter for all Apocalypse citations. For Alexander Minorita see Schmolinski, *Der Apokalypsenkommentar des Alexander Minorita.*

2. Although such correlations were not new in the Apocalypse-commentary tradition, it was an innovation to read so much of Church history into the commentary and to interpret the images in the Apocalypse consecutively rather than recapitulatively. Peter was a young Franciscan master at the University of Paris, a Conventual and a favorite of John XXII. His *Literal Compendium of the Whole of Sacred Scripture* became a standard textbook in the later Middle Ages. Pierre Auriol's commentary on the Apocalypse comprises more than one third of his *Compendium sensus litteralis totius sacrae Scripturae.* For a discussion of Auriol's Apocalypse commentary see Ernst Benz, *Ecclesia Spiritualis* (Stuttgart: Kohlhammer, 1934), 432–472. See also Burr, "Mendicant Readings of the Apocalypse," 89–102, as well as his chapter in this volume. See also Valois, "Pierre d'Aureoli," 479–528. For Auriol's importance for the latter Middle Ages see Tachau, *Vision and Certitude in the Age of Ockham.*

3. See my dissertation "Nicholas of Lyra: Apocalypse Commentary as Historiography," and my forthcoming article in *Franciscan Studies*, "Nicholas of Lyra, Apocalypse Commentator, Historian, and Critic."

4. For a more complete discussion, see the chapter in this volume by David Burr. This view of Alexander and Peter was a commonplace in the thirteenth century. See Roger Bacon (ca. 1214–1292), *The Longer Work,* translated in McGinn, *Visions of the End,* 155. In the later Middle Ages there were numerous prophecies concerning the end of Islam. See McGinn "Moslems, Mongols, and the Last Days," in *Visions of the End, 149–157.* Nicholas rejects Peter's solution to the number 666 because he understands Islam to be expanding and not in decline. It is important to note that for Lyra and his models, the forces identified with Antichrist (i.e., Muhammad and the Saracens), are included with heretics and enemies who are outside the *corpus christianum*: pagans, schismatics, and other infidels. The radical Franciscan apocalyptic tradition tended to locate the forces of Antichrist within, that is, in the Empire or the Papacy. This, of course, was not acceptable to the Church and proved not to be an option for Auriol and Lyra, perhaps, but not exclusively, because Peter Olivi's *Apocalypse* commentary was in the process of being condemned as they were writing.

5. Runciman, *A History of the Crusades* 3:440.

6. For futher information on Paul of Burgos, see Reinhardt, 346,347.

7. For a discussion of this conflict as the first Christian holy war, see Ostrogorsky, *History of the Byzantine State*, 104.

8. The angel, Michael, is none other than the Emperor Heraclius (610–41), who saved the Empire. The beast from the sea in Revelation 13:1–10 is the son of Chosroes, whom Heraclius ultimately defeated, ending the Persian Empire. Lyra:

> *Et peperit filium*: Hic consequenter describitur ecclesiae liberatio. . . . *Michael et angeli eius*: . . . Sed quia per draconem et Angelos eius intelligitur Cosdroe et suus exercitus secundum omnes expositores, convenientius est ut similiter per Michaelem et Angelos eius intelligatur Eraclius et bellatores eius. Michael enim interpretatur *quis ut Deus* Eraclius; enim in hoc bello pro ecclesia erat Dei vicarius. Et supradictis etiam patet, quod in hoc libro boni et mali homines frequenter nominantur angeli. (Revelation 12:5–7, cols. 1579–1580)

9. See Krey, "Nicholas of Lyra, Apocalypse Commentator, Historian, and Critic," and Runciman, "Charlemagne and Palestine," 609–616.

10. See n. 9.

11. Revelation 16:12, col. 1627. "Aliter tamen potest exponi et magis proprie ad litteram (ut videtur) de Carlo magno, qui invitatus a beato Jacobo purgavit viam ad eius sepulchrum prius ignotum, eo quod tota Hispania erat a Saracenis occupata . . . "

12. Ibid., 16:8, col. 1625.

> Dicitur autem Carolus Imperator sol: quia sicut sol praecellit planetas alios, sic Carolus fide et magnanimitate refulgens praecellebat cunctos reges terrenos. . . . Quia data sibi a Deo virtute Romam adiit causas examinavit, et Deo rebelles et ecclesiae graviter afflixit et punivit, et Leonem papam in sedem sua iterum collocavit, ut habetur in *Chronica* Sigisberti.

Lyra was a francophile and very fond of the Valois family, who returned the affection. See Buc, "Pouvoir Royal et Commentaires de la Bible (1150–1350)," 691–709.

13. Revelation 16:13, col. 1628.

Et vidi: Hic ponitur septima plaga, cuius primo
ponitur motiva ratio, secundo eius executio, ibi: *Et
septimus angelus*. Circa primum sciendum quod a
tempore Cosdroe regis Persarum pro majori parte
populus catholicus in terra promissionis habitans et
circa, fuit in afflictione et servitute dura usque ad eius
liberationem per principes occidentales Christianorum, et tempore Gotfredi de Buillon ducis
Lotharingiae; nam aliae liberationes dicti populi per
Eraclium et Carolum magnum de quibus supradictum
est, fuerunt momentaneae, quia cito transierunt. Nam
recedente Eraclio de Jerusalem post Cosdroe interfec-
tionem et sanctae crucis reportationem, Arabes
Homaro duce terram sanctam et plures alius sibi
subjugaverunt, et similiter post recessum Caroli
magni de terra sancta Saraceni dominantes in
Aegypto Judaeam sibi subjugaverunt, et postea Turci
eam de manu Caliphae Aegyptii auferentes eam
tenuerunt, usque quo debellati fuerunt per principes
praedictos in partibus Antiochenis, tunc enim
debilitata Turcorum virtute Aegyptii abstulerunt
Jerusalem et Judaeam de manibus eorum, ut dicit
episcopus Tyrensis lib.7 cap. 12. Sed infra annum vel
circiter Christiani de manibus Aegyptiorum eam
abstulerunt vi armorum.

14.   This is not true for Lyra; he refuses to associate the emperors
with the evil symbols of the Apocalypse.

15.   Lyra's Augustinian themes, however, have to be viewed as
modified. St. Augustine would never have agreed that the Bible could
serve as a blueprint for church history. Lyra's interpretation of chapters
1 to 16 could not have been construed as Augustinian. He adopts an
Augustinian perspective in chapter 17 when he becomes profoundly
agnostic about the future course of history and the ability to deduce the
future from the symbols of the Apocalypse.

16.   Peter had described the symbol of Armageddon as the place
where the Muslims would assemble as a unified front against the
Christians before the First Crusade. Having read the accounts of
William of Tyre and of James of Vitry, Lyra cannot accept this. The
historians point out, he argues, that shortly after the death of
Muhammad, there were already two sects among the Saracens, one in
Egypt and one in Persia, each having different laws and each calling the
others schismatics. Consequently, there was contention among them

until the time of Saladin, who did not rule until 1180, long after the First Crusade. Any good history book would say, he points out, that neither before nor after Saladin did the Muslims confront the Christians as a unified army. Lyra takes the triumphalism out of his sources' accounts. He also provides a lesson in historical understanding—if one intends to make an historical argument, one must pay attention to the order of things (successive) and not assume that everything one considers relevant to an issue can be applied to the same time or event (simul quantum ad omnes) (Revelation 16:16, col.1629).

17. See Daniel, "Apocalyptic Conversion: The Joachite Alternative to the Crusades," 127–154, and for a history of Christian mission among the Muslims and Muslim conversions, see Kedar, *Crusade and Mission*.

18. See Alexander Minorita, *Expositio in Apocalysim*, 288–289, esp. n. 1.

19. Given that Auriol and Nicholas were writing in the fourteenth century, long after the failures of the Crusades to regain the Holy Land, it may be fruitful to ask why Auriol uncritically adopted Alexander's crusading account. The answer may lie in Peter's propapal perspective and his close association with John XXII, who was still, perhaps cynically, attempting to raise money for a crusade from Marseilles in 1319. Lyra's less than enthusiastic approach to the foreign policies of the papacy allowed him to be more critical about the limited achievements of the movement. There were other plans for crusades made in the fourteenth century. See Kedar, 199–203.

20. Revelation 13:18, col 1596.

> Tamen lex Mahumeti non videtur hic propinqua cessationi: nam a paucis annis multum invaluit. Tartari enim qui sunt in maximo numero, legem receperunt pro majori parte illius populi, sicut audivi assertive a quodam episcopo ordinis nostri, qui per plures annos inter Tartaros habitavit.

Another example of this relativization occurs in chapter 15: According to Lyra, chapter 15 of Revelation describes the celebration of the saints in heaven of the Church's triumph over its enemies, and a new division of history begins. In verse 5 and following, the seven angels with the plagues are introduced, even though the pouring of their bowls occurs in the next chapter. Verse 8 of this chapter, describing how no one could enter the temple until the seven plagues of the seven angels were ended, permits Nicholas one more historical quarrel with his sources. Others had argued that this verse predicts the fact that no Christians could enter Jerusalem until the time of the First Crusade, when Godfrey captured Jerusalem (in this interpretation the passage would foreshadow what happens later in the Apocalypse). Peter, for instance, assigns this passage to the First Crusade without mentioning Godfrey, although Alexander uses it as an opportunity to criticize lay investiture. Lyra argues that the historical context is wrong because Christians were in Jerusalem all along. He objects to the interpretation given by Peter and possibly others, but not that of Alexander. Lyra here serves notice that the Crusades are not one of the climaxes of Church history for him (Revelation 15:8, col. 1620).

21. See McGinn, *Visons of the End*, 150, 151.

22. The story of the sale to the Sultan of poor Christian boys who would later fight as Muslims against the Christians was a convention.

>"Unde et ego audivi a fratre fide digno, quod viderat naves impleri de pueris Christianis quos mercatores emerant a parentibus eorum pauperibus, ut venderent eos Soldano pro magno precio, qui eos faciebat informari in lege Mahumeti, quia de Christiana nihil adhuc sciebant, ut adulti facti contra Christianos pugnarent. (Revelation 18:3, col 1643)

23. Ibid., 16:13, col. 1628.

>Notandum etiam, quod sicut inter Christianos sunt praedicatores eos excitantes ad impugnandum Saracenos, sic inter Saracenos sunt qui aliqui litterati excitantes alios contra Christianos . . .

That propaganda was used by both sides has been shown recently by Al-Azmeh, "Barbarians in Arab Eyes," 3–18.

24. "Haec enim Postilla, saltem in his partibus Hispaniae, et, ut credo, Galliae, communior est caeteris, circa Glossam ordinarum. Ad istam enim recurrunt non solum theologi, sed etiam juristae et alii intellectum sacrae Scripturae planum habere desiderantes." Paulus Burgensis, *Additio super utrumque prologum magistri Nicolai de Lyra* (PL 113:46). For more information on The *Additiones ad Postillam Nicolai de Lira super Biblia* see n. 28.

25. Henry III (1390–1406) named Paul to be tutor of his son John II in his will. The infant king's reign (1406–1454) was first administered by his uncle Don Fernando and then dominated by Alvaro de Luna. Alavaro de Luna launched a campaign against the Moorish kingdom of Granada. The Moors were defeated at Higueruela in 1431, a date which Paul notes in the text.

26. See Gosselin.

27. The other very brief additions are in chapters 7 and 9.

28. This gloss occupies eight full columns in the 1634 Antwerp edition of Lyra's *Postillae Super Bibliam.*

29. See Reinhardt, 348, 349.

30. Ibid., 348.

31. See Southern, *Western Views of Islam in the Middle Ages,* for a range of medieval Western views of Islam.

32. Antwerp, 1634, col. 1597–1598.

> Videtur tamen quod hoc traditur sufficienter in quadam historia brevi fratris Ptolemaei de luca qui de historiis Isidori et Richardi et Martini multa colligit ad hoc pertinentia, in qua quidem historia habetur, quod causa seu occasio ex qua huiusmodi error sumpsit principium, fuit magna tyrannis Eraclii imperatoris, qui post victoriam de Persis habitam, in superbia elevatus et nimia cupiditate accensus, nimis premebat Persas et Arabes et Chaldaeos et alios confines in tributis et aliis exactionibus gravibus et inordinatis, ex quo populi illarum regionum inclinati fuerunt ad resistendum exactoribus imperatoris: quod tamen non audebant committere, timentes eius tyrannidem et magnam potestatem. Sed Mahumetus qui maxime audacie et versutiae erat, et etiam magnis artibus eruditus se eis adiunxit, qui inveniens dispositionem gentium praedictarum, ad rebellandum Romano imperio, eos incitavit ad committendam praedictam rebellionem, specialiter inde negandis tributis sub colore liberandi illas gentes a praedictis exactionibus. Unde gentes ille acceperunt eum in ducem et caput sub quo saepe debellaverunt collectores, et gentes imperii de quibus praedictus Mahumetus obtinuit multas victorias.

33. Ibid., col. 1604. "Et sic patet ratio quare ista diu duret, licet mala et pernitiosa, non tamen fidelibus nociva nec periculosa sicut aliae sectae praecedentes, quae conabantur cogere Christianos ad apostatandum de fide et negando Christum. Unde non est mirum, si diutius toleretur quam secta erroneae praecedentes." Contrary to Nicholas, Paul also sees the pre-Constantinian Church as spiritually superior to the Church after the establishment of Christianity as the official religion of the Empire.

Ex quo patet manifeste, quod veritas ecclesiasticae
dignitatis non consistit in prosperitatibus mundanis
... sed potius in adversitatibus mundanis pro
nomine Christi tolerandis. Quod etiam ex processu
primitivae ecclesiae in bonis spiritualibus potest
haberi. Manifestum est enim, quod in ecclesia
primitiva a tempore Apostolorum usque ad tempus
Silvestri Papae, quanda nulla potestas mundana erat
apud fideles, tunc ecclesia maxime prosperabatur in
spiritualibus. . . .

34. Ibid., col. 1602.

Circa quintum de duratione illius sectae attendum,
quod nonnulli mirantur de hoc quod secta ista tam
erronea et vitiosa, ut dictum est, tam diuturne durat,
cum ex decursu veteris ac novi Testamenti usque ad
ipsam exclusive nulla secta falsa seu ritus erroneus
tantae fuit durationis. . . . Nam Deus videtur tacere
permittendo quod populus tantis erroribus et vitiis
implicatus populum iustiorem se devorat, scilicet
Christianum: et hoc per tam insuetam durationis
diuturnitatem. Nam ut dici postillator infra eodem
capi. iam transiuerant plusquam septingenti triginta
anni ab initio huius secta usque ad tempus in quo
hanc postillam scripserat, et hodie, scilicet anno
domini Millesimo quadringentesimo trigesimo primo
iam transierunt octigenti et quatuor fere anni ab initio
huius sectae usque nunc, nec tamen adhuc apparent
signa consummationis ipsius, de quo non solum multi
mirantur tanta durationis causam non invenientes sed
etiam quidam alii claudicant murmurantes de Dei
providentia et eius aequissima iustitia.

35. Ibid., col. 1602–1603.

Quorum primum est, quod haec secta licet mala et
pessima, ut dictum est, non tamen est idololatricia nec
cultum idolorum publice in suo domino permittit
sicut aliae sectae praecedentes communiter faciebant
ut est manifestum. Nam a tempore Assyriorum et
Chaldeorum usque ad tempus Cosdroe inclusive,
cuius dominium propinquum fuit ipsi Mahumeto
semper viguit cultus idolorum inter Gentes qui
populum Dei vexabant, ut patet in veteri Tetstament
et in historiis ecclesiasticis et in legendis sanctorum.

Constat autem quod inter omnia peccata quibus Deus offenditur, peccatum idololatriae est potissimum, intantum, quod deus se ostendit ferventius seu ardentius illud punire quam alia peccata. . . . Et quia ista secta non incurrit peccatum idololatriae, committendo nec permittendo; ideo Deus cum longiori tempore tolerat quam alias sectas praecedentes, quarum quaelibet publice idololatrabat.

36. Ibid., col. 1603.

Secundum vero in quo differt ista secta ab aliis praecedentibus, est, quod praecedentes communiter cogebant fideles ad orandum seu thurificandum idolis . . . Tenentes vero istam sectam Saracenicam communiter, ut in pluribus, non cogunt fideles ad apostantandum. Nam in Alchorano praecipitur, prout habetur in praedicto tractatu, quod omnes homines non recipientes legem suam occidantur, nisi soluant tributum. . . . Quod autem Saraceni non cogunt fideles ad apostatandum in fide est manifestum per experientam nam in partibus Aegypti et Judae [etc.] . . . permittuntur fideles Christi non solum ad habitandum, sed etiam ad habendum parva monasteria et aliqua oratoria.

37. Ibid., col. 1601.

Ad quod dicendum, quod prout potest haberi a sancto Thoma in *Summa Contra Gentiles* libro 1, cap. vi, Mahumetus introducendo errorem suum processit via contraria illius viae qua veritas evangelica per Christum et eius discipulos fuit in orbe introducta. Veritas enim evangelica non humano modo seu mundano, sed solum divino fuit in mundo introducta, secta vero huius Mahumeti modo totaliter opposito: quod sic patet. Nam in veritate evangelica omnem humanem intellectum excedentia praedicantur, ut trinitas personarum cum unitate essentiae in divinis, et natura divina et humana in Christo coniunctae in unitate personae, et huismodi quae cognitionem naturalis intellectus humani excedunt. In secta vero praedicta nihil traditur credendum, nisi quod de facili a quolibet mediocriter intelligente naturali ingenio cognosci possit , ut unitas Dei, et excellentia Christi hominis.

See *The Summa Contra Gentiles of Saint Thomas Aquinas*, Book I: *God*, chap. 6, art. 4, p. 73.

38. Paul like Thomas uses the term sect to describe Islam, as if it was a Christian heresy. This, of course, is not new in the tradition.

39. _____, col. 1605.

> Tertium vero, in quo differt ista secta a praecedentibus est, quod praecedentes sectae idolatrarum dignitatem Christi in omnibus et per omnia denigrabant, negantes non solum eius veram deitatem sed etiam eius bonitatem seu virtuositatem humanam, asserentes ipsum fuisse seductorem et maleficum et huismodi . . . Secta vero ista hoc non fecit. . . . Licet deitatem Christi neget, quae est summa et ineffabilis excellentia divinae personae concedit tamen ipsum fuisse excellentissimum super omnes creaturas mundi, ut dictum est, unde non mirum si contra istam sectam tolerabilius se habeat divina iustitia, diutius eam sustinendo quam alias praecedentes Christum hominem vituperantes.

40. Ibid., col. 165.

> Et attendum, quod circa finem mundi Antichristus surget, prout II Thes. habetur II ca. qui omnes persecutiones omnium sectarum praedictarum excedet. Nam fideles non solum coget ad recedendum a cultu Christi, sed etiam ad adorandum ipsum Antichristum tanquem Deum, ut ibidem, et ideo non solum dicitur Antiapostolus et Antipropheta, sicut Mahumetus, ut dictum est, sed etiam Antichristus tanquam caeteris magis Christo contrarius.

41. Ibid., col. 1606. "Nam quia persecutio Antichristi erit maxima, ideo erit brevissima, iuxta illud Marci xiii, c."

42. Although he remained in constant dialogue with Jews after his conversion to Christianity (e.g., Joseph Orabuena, chief rabbi of Navarre, and Joshua ibn Vives), Paul became a bitter enemy of Jews in Spain, as well. He drafted an edict as chancellor of the kingdom of Castile in 1412 designed to separate Jews from Christians, hinder their commerce, and to convert them. He is also well known for his *Dialogus Pauli et Sauli Contra Judaeos, sive Scrutinium Scripturarum*.

43. Antwerp, 1634, col. 1601. "Alchoranum est plenum erroribus et vitiis, unde et proprie figuratum fuit in revelatione beati Ioannis per

bestiam et meretricem, ut per bestiam intelligantur errores in cognitione quia sicut bestia caret cognitione ratione. . . . "

44. Ibid., col. 1606. Citing I John 5:4,5 he writes:

> Sic contra persecutionem Saracenorum disposuit reges qui licet in fidei firmitate non tantum gradum attingeret sicut martyres sancti, fuerunt tamen in fide stabiles, et in armorum potentia Deo strenue militantes, in tantum quod de ipsi potest dici, quod per fidem vicerunt regna, licet non mundum, . . . et haec fuit sufficiens provisio ad Saracenorum malitiam refrenandam.

45. Ibid., col. 1604.

> Unde et hodiernis temporibus, scilicet, in prima Iulii, anno domini Mccccxli [sic, it should be 1431] anni praesentis suprascripti, illustrissimus rex noster Ioannes cum magna potestate regni sui, licet non totam, intravit terram Saracenorum usque ad civitatem metropolim, scilicet, Granata, ubi rex eorum residebat: ubi prope illam bellum inivit cum magna multitudine Saracenorum: in quo bello suffragante divina clementia et beata virgine intercedente cum beato Iacobo patrono nostro, totam illam multitudinem devicit, et usque ad portas civitatis fugavit. Occisis de inimicis crucis Christi plusquam quinque milibus, et nisi solis occasus supervenisset multo maior fuisset eorum ruina. Ex quo magna Deo laudes referendae sunt, et gratiarum actiones sperantes Dei clementia circa hoc maiora et viciniora saluti per serenissimum regem nostrum praefatum fienda.

46. This is the conclusion regarding Raymond Lull by Anwar G. Chejne, *Islam and the West: The Moriscos*, 93.

47. See Cabanelas, *Juan de Segovia y el Problema Islámico*, 44–45, 100–107, and 155ff. The second discussion in October, 1431, was described by Juan de Segovia in a letter to Nicholas of Cusa. See Chejne, 93.

48. See Cabenelas, 286. See also Fromherz, *Johannes von Segovia*, esp. 20, 42–56.

49. Whether there was a direct connection cannot be determined at this time. For Juan's traditional views of Islam, see Cabanelas, 265ff., esp. 283.

50. See Cabanelas, 283. Juan's major work on peaceful dialogue with Islam was written two decades after Paul's response to Lyra; *De gladio divini spiritus mittendo in corda Saracenorum* was written in 1453. A summary of the work can be found in the appendix of Cabanelas, 265–276. In addition, the *Prologue to the Qur'ân* and his correspondence with Nicholas of Cusa in Cabanelas' appendices are rich sources for his views of Islam.

CHAPTER 8

Frederick II, His Saracens, and the Papacy

John Phillip Lomax

Although it is often difficult to extract much meaning from the specific charges that Pope Gregory IX made against Emperor Frederick II in the bull of excommunication of March 1239, at least one of them is so obscure as to be almost opaque. The fifth item of the bull states, "We excommunicate and anathematize him because in the Kingdom churches consecrated to the Lord are destroyed and profaned."[1]

The kingdom to which the pope referred was the kingdom of Sicily, which Frederick's maternal ancestors, the Normans, had created in the eleventh and twelfth centuries. It was comprised of the island of Sicily and nearly the whole of peninsular Italy south of the papal states. The churches at issue were in and around the city of Lucera in northern Apulia. The alleged perpetrators of these sacrileges were the Saracen colonists whom Frederick himself had settled in Lucera and its vicinity. Gregory at this point excommunicates Frederick on the grounds that the emperor did not prevent the Saracens under his jurisdiction from destroying and profaning certain churches, punish them after they had, or repair the damaged churches and restore them to Christian worship.

Gregory held Frederick responsible for the physical security of Christian churches in the kingdom. The right of the pope to sanction the emperor for failing to protect churches rested on the numerous oaths Frederick had sworn to the papacy to defend the church and its liberties. Gregory's charge also evokes a body of jurisprudence that expounded upon one of the principal liberties of the church, the inviolability of the *res spiritualia*—the clergy, property, and privileges of the church— which canon law required a Christian ruler to defend. Frederick also worked under the added liability that canon law placed on those rulers who had infidel subjects. As such, he had a particular obligation to shield the faith and the faithful from the influence of infidels, especially Jews and Saracens, and to assist in their conversion.

Is it significant that Gregory omits explicit mention of the Saracens of Lucera in the charge? Perhaps not; by 1239 the pope had stripped his case against Frederick down to basics, and nothing was more basic than papal concern for ecclesiastical liberty. In fairness to Gregory, it is probably accurate enough to say that most of the lawyer-popes of the high Middle Ages did not, or perhaps could not, distinguish between the need to preserve liberties of the church, especially those of the papacy, and the need to safeguard the spiritual welfare of the *congregatio fidelium*. Nonetheless, Gregory truly feared Frederick's Muslim subjects, who represented a special kind of threat to the well-being of papacy. When Frederick created the Saracen colony at Lucera in 1224, Islam moved from the periphery of Christendom to its center. The existence of this community of Muslims— appallingly close to Rome, entirely loyal to Frederick, and utterly impervious to ecclesiastical fulminations—intensified the chronic papal fear of imperial domination, a fear that escalated into open hostility during the 1230s, especially after Frederick moved once again to subdue the recalcitrant cities of the Lombard League in 1236.

To Gregory IX, the Saracens of Lucera seemed to threaten the church in Apulia much the same as Frederick and his imperialist policies seemed to threaten the papacy and the entire church. Furthermore, Muslim Lucera served as a metaphor for Frederick's rejection of the papal ideal of the crusade, most fully expressed in *Ad liberandum terram sanctam*, the great crusading bull issued by Pope Innocent III at the Fourth Lateran Council.[2] Rather than accept papal headship and supervision of the movement to drive the Saracens from the margins of Christendom, Frederick had conducted an unauthorized and virtually nonviolent (albeit successful) crusade to the Holy Land in 1228–1229. That Frederick had also created a Muslim settlement at Lucera turned the papal ideal of the crusade on its head: Rather than engage the Muslims at the periphery, Frederick nurtured them at the center; rather than force his Saracens to choose between death and conversion, he employed them in his wars against Christian powers, including the papacy's most reliable client, the Lombard League.

In the eyes of the pope, Frederick II had adulterated the Christian commonwealth, the community of the baptized, by establishing a Muslim colony at Lucera; he had, furthermore, diminished the moral authority and political independence of the papacy.[3] This chapter examines how Gregory IX employed the canonical jurisprudence relating to ecclesiastical liberty and the control and conversion of infidels—and, at one key point, the rhetoric of papal supremacy—to justify and further the termination of what was, for the pope, nothing less than an affront to the right order of Christendom.

The Saracens of Lucera came from western Sicily. At the onset of the Norman conquest of Sicily in the late eleventh century, the island had a population of perhaps 250 thousand Muslims and about as many Greeks. However, Norman royal policy favored Latin culture at the expense of the Saracens and the Greeks. By 1200, conversion, persecution, and emigration had reduced the Muslim population by about 90 percent. The remnant was forced into western Sicily by aggressive Latin settlement at the eastern end of the island. Continued Latin pressure on these Muslims brought on a full-scale rebellion in the mountains and hills south and west of Palermo and Monreale in 1220, but Frederick was unable to respond to it until 1222. His forces subdued the rebels after two years of bitter fighting. Frederick then decided that only by resettling the Saracens in a more secure area, one totally isolated from the Muslims of North Africa, could he prevent further uprisings. Although the depopulation of much of western Sicily substantially decreased the productivity, versatility, and profitability of its agriculture, Frederick placed firm control of his dominions ahead of nearly every other consideration, even if to do so occasionally exacerbated his chronic shortage of revenues.[4]

Frederick transported the Sicilian Muslims to royal properties in and around Lucera, which is located in the part of northern Apulia then known as Capitanea. The population of that area was well below the carrying capacity of the land. But David Abulafia has argued that the forced resettlement of Sicilian Muslims was "not . . . simply a question of improving revenues from the region of Lucera; there were important political motives at work, too."[5] Removing the Saracens to Capitanea did indeed increase the productivity and security of near-vacant royal estates, but it also separated these insurgents from their homeland and isolated them from other Muslims. They were wholly dependent on Frederick for their livelihood and their safety. To render them reasonably happy and productive subjects, Frederick seems to have exempted them from all the royal taxes levied on his subjects in the peninsular portion of his kingdom. He also granted them religious freedom and a significant degree of self-government. In return he expected and received labor and military service from them. Thus, the pacification and relocation of these Muslims yielded Frederick labor, revenue, and political leverage.

As the ruler of a population of infidels, Frederick had a canonical obligation to guard the church, the clergy, and the Christian community from them, both physically and spiritually. At issue were miscegenation and the political or economic domination of Christians by infidels.[6] Frederick also had an obligation to assist in their conversion to Christianity, although he could not actually compel them to accept baptism. However, canon law and contemporary canonistic opinion were hardening on this issue, and at least one canonist recommended a strategy that differed little from forced conversion. Moreover, some contemporary canonists had begun to number conversion of the infidels among the purposes of the crusade.[7]

The papacy also claimed legal rights and obligations with respect to infidel populations, both within and without Christendom. The canonical underpinnings of papal policy toward Jews, Saracens, and other infidels began to take shape in canonical legislation of the latter half of the twelfth and first half of the thirteenth century.[8] This development reached something of a culmination in the mid-thirteenth century canonistic commentaries of Pope Innocent IV and Henry of Segusio, Cardinal Hostiensis, who collected and rationalized the papal claims. Innocent claimed for the papacy a *de iure* jurisdiction over infidels, based on the Donation of Constantine and an adaptation of the doctrine of the just war, which permitted a pope to "send missionaries into their lands to instruct nonbelievers in the proper way of worshipping God," especially if a *de facto* Christian ruler had failed in his obligation to evangelize the infidels.[9]

Gregory IX yearned to Christianize the Muslim community in Lucera, which was so distressingly close to Rome. James Powell has argued that "concern for the faith of the nearby Christian population [of Capitanea] provided the chief impetus for efforts to promote the conversion of the Muslims." It is more likely that, in the case of Lucera, the pope was moved as much, or more, by fear for the security of the papacy as by the fear of spiritual contamination. Powell correctly asserts that Frederick did not settle his Saracens in Capitanea in order to threaten or provoke the papacy; the emperor had other and better reasons. Indeed, the pope under whom Frederick initiated the policy of resettlement, Honorius III, seems not to have objected to the colony.[10] However, Honorius was never at war with the emperor. Nearly every succeeding pope, from Gregory IX through Boniface VIII, made war on Frederick and the Hohenstaufen or their Angevin successors. The existence of a population of Saracens in central Italy under the firm control of the king of Sicily became a factor of the cruel calculus of those tragic struggles. The bitter and inflammatory rhetoric with which the popes consistently assailed the Muslims of Lucera, and often their royal masters, reveals the depth and character of papal animosity.

The strategy Gregory promoted, the isolation and virtual forced conversion of the Muslims, was canonical, practical, and reasonably well established. If successful, it would have served both the political and spiritual aims of the papacy. However, Gregory needed the active cooperation of the emperor to contain or convert the Muslims of Lucera, for they were decidedly

Frederick's subjects, notwithstanding papal theorizing with respect to infidel populations.[11]

The pope seems at first to have been more intent on containing the Muslims than converting them. Safeguarding the liberties of the church was always at the top of the papal agenda, especially in its quarrels with Frederick. The fiery Gregory was perfectly in character in *Ubi nobis impietates,* a letter that he sent to the emperor in December 1232. In it he took a hard line on the alleged Saracen depredations that underlay the charge later found in the 1239 excommunication. Gregory harped stridently on the lax royal response to the "damnable presumption" of the Muslims. He charged that those "sons of perdition," the Saracens of Lucera, had, with Frederick's apparent consent, torn the church of St. Peter in Foiano down to its very foundations to obtain stone and lumber, "transforming into a place of degradation what was once the dwelling-place of angels." Because such "wicked presumption" insulted the Creator, injured the apostolic see, and disgraced all who were involved, Gregory admonished Frederick to heed his duty to protect Christian churches, especially those in his kingdom. For God had designated Frederick the defender of churches, and they ought to enjoy his protection. If any church were "demolished by the sacrilegious hands of infidels," Frederick was to order it rebuilt and its goods restored.[12]

Gregory then asserted that Frederick had granted the Muslims of Lucera an excess of privileges (*nimietas libertatis*), which harmed neighboring Christians and horrified all who heard about it. The pope urged Frederick to "shatter" the "presumptions" of these Muslims so that they would dare not disturb the hearts of God's faithful even a little, "especially since particular injury will seem to be done to our Redeemer if the sons of Belial, who are bound by the shackle of perpetual servitude, assail the sons of light within our borders or damnably imagine themselves to be equal to them in privileges."[13]

Gregory explicitly instructed the emperor to deal with these problems, which, of course, could not be resolved to the pope's satisfaction if Frederick would not act. We possess no direct response to *Ubi nobis impietates,* although Frederick later characterized similar charges as "persistent fables."[14] Nonetheless, this harsh missive brought two things to Frederick's attention. First, he had a statutory and contractual duty to defend *res spiritualia* from harm. Indeed, Gregory clearly meant his remark about "our borders" to remind Frederick that he held the kingdom of Sicily in fief from the papacy, subject to all the obligations expressed in his oaths of fealty to the popes. Second, Frederick had a duty to reduce his Saracens to a greater state of subjugation. The privileges that he had granted to them had to be curtailed so that they could in no way imperil the church or their Christian neighbors. As noted previously, this aspect of the papal critique was very much in line with recently enacted restrictions that church law had placed on Jews and Saracens who lived among Christians.[15]

Thus, the pope's first attack on the Muslim colony in Lucera turned on the defense of *res spiritualia*, especially churches, and on the containment of Muslims who lived among Christians. But between the initial charges and the final sanction, both of which focused on the issue of ecclesiastical liberty, Gregory introduced other, more sublime themes into his campaign against Frederick's Saracens.

In August 1233, Gregory signaled his determination to dissolve the infidel stronghold in Lucera through conversion. This was a much more ambitious goal than the isolation and containment of the Saracens, and it, too, required the active cooperation of Frederick. At this point Gregory unpacked the rhetoric of papal superiority. While doing so, he indirectly made the case for the intolerability of Muslim communities within the body of Christendom.

In *Post vicarium Iesu Christi* Gregory temporarily abandons the parlance of spiritual contamination. Instead he deploys two potent metaphors to justify what would have been, effectively, forced conversion of the Muslims. The term "vicar of Christ," seen in the *incipit* of this letter, was fundamental to the thirteenth-century doctrine of papal monarchy. The popes claimed that, as the sole vicars of Christ, they were the fully empowered agents of Christ on earth (possessing what was termed *plenitudo potestatis*) and, hence, entitled to do all that which Christ could (and would) do if he were present.[16] Gregory also used the image of the two swords, a more specific claim of papal superiority over secular rulers and of the authority that this superiority was said to confer. From the time of the Investiture Conflict—the crucible in which modern Western ideas of hierarchy, of right order, were first formed—every version of this metaphor had Jesus giving two swords to his followers, the spiritual sword and the material sword, to govern and safeguard the community of the faithful in His absence. But a key question continued to vex Western Christendom for centuries: just how had Christ distributed responsibility for the welfare of the baptized? Had He designated two vicars, equal in power, to act on His behalf, or one all-powerful vicar? Did he give the spiritual sword directly to the spiritual magistrate and the material sword directly to the temporal magistrate; or did he give both swords to the spiritual magistrate, the pope, who in turn conferred the material sword on the temporal magistrate? The correct ordering of Christendom turned on the answer. Emperors, kings, and other secular rulers adhered to the first position, which modern scholars call dualist. The Gregorian reformers of the eleventh and twelfth centuries, who were the first to formulate the question in just this way, adhered to the latter, monarchical position. Canon law could be made to support either position.[17]

From the very start of *Post vicarium Iesu Christi*, Gregory argued at length that, as the vicar of Jesus Christ, he had an obligation to evangelize the infidels both near and far and that the secular prince was not only authorized, but also compelled to employ the material sword, which his spiritual superior had conferred on him, to aid God's work of conversion. To that end the pope announced that he was directing Dominican friars to evangelize those Saracens in Capitanea who could understand Italian. Gregory exhorted Frederick to instruct the Saracens to receive these missionaries in peace and listen to them carefully. However, the pope also invoked the example of Jonah, who had terrorized the people of Nineveh into repentance, to justify something very much like forced conversion. Gregory urged Frederick to support the Dominicans with the "material sword," without which their mission might fail; indeed, to "drag this people, who are openly deceived by the error of perdition, to the font of regeneration and renewal by means of terror, because then their servitude will be more fruitful, since the one God shall have come to you and to them."[18]

We can see that Gregory just barely adhered to the canonical prohibition against forcing infidels to convert; indeed, he seems to have all but insisted that Frederick compel the Saracens of Lucera to accept baptism. Gregory put Frederick in the position of thwarting a lawful prerogative of the papacy and of neglecting his obligation as a Christian prince if he did not sincerely assist the Dominicans in their mission. Abulafia notes that Frederick "probably knew canon law well enough to resist the temptation to convert by force."[19] This is an understatement: Frederick was fully aware of what the canons required, and his response to Gregory shows it.

In December 1233 Frederick replied that, since it pleased the pope to send Dominican friars to convert those among the Saracens of Lucera who spoke Italian, he welcomed their mission to preach the name of the Lord. He added that he would soon be able to assist the friars in person, for he was about to travel through that very district.[20] This was the correct response. Even though conversion of these Muslims was far more a priority for the pope than for the emperor, Frederick professed to welcome and even assist in their conversion. At the same time he neatly avoided committing himself to the compulsory conversion that the pope had urged on him. And, at no point did he acknowledge that the Muslims of Lucera represented any kind of threat to the church or to their Christian neighbors.[21]

Perhaps Frederick was in fact eager to convert the Muslims, or at least not opposed to it. Neither he nor his Norman ancestors were all that kind to their Muslim subjects. Frederick waged war against them in 1222–1223 and again in 1246, forced them to resettle far from their homes, and kept them under his strict dominion. He granted them certain privileges, but only to assure their productivity and service. Frederick accorded them a number of legal protections, but his commitment to the security of his Saracen subjects seems to have been anything but wholehearted.[22] Abulafia maintains that Frederick probably expected the Luceran Muslims "to become fully assimilated into the surrounding Christian society," although, like most of his contemporaries who controlled useful populations of subject infidels, he seems not to have put much effort into incorporating them into the community of the baptized.[23]

It is essentially incorrect to assert that Gregory had "concern but no direct objection to the existence of the [Muslim] colony" at Lucera,[24] given that from 1232 forward he agitated relentlessly against it. As we can see here, in 1233, not ten years after the Sicilian Muslims were resettled in Capitanea, the pope plainly directed Frederick to terrorize his Saracens into conversion. Muslim Lucera was of special interest to the pope. Gregory did not don the full panoply of papal supremacy in *Post vicarium Iesu Christi* merely to lend weight to a request for routine assistance to some Dominican missionaries. Rather, he was explaining to Frederick, in some considerable detail, that, as Christ's sole vicar, the pope had the right and the obligation to instruct the emperor, on whom the papacy had conferred the temporal sword, to deal firmly with the problem that Frederick himself had created for the church by introducing Muslims into the heart of Christendom. *Post vicarium Iesu Christi* evinces real dread of the infidel at the door. More than that, the Saracens of Lucera vividly reminded Gregory of what a menace Frederick himself could be, to papal independence every bit as much as to the souls and churches of Christendom.

The plan to evangelize the Muslims of Lucera that Gregory laid out in *Post vicarium Iesu Christi* appears to have gone nowhere, and the popes seem never again to have launched a similar initiative. Although Powell suggests that "the chief impetus" behind the proposed Dominican mission was an ongoing papal "concern for the faith of nearby Christians," neither Gregory nor his successors seem to have mounted a "sustained effort" to convert these Saracens.[25] Although thirteenth-century popes repeatedly urged the containment and dismemberment of the colony, B. Z. Kedar reports that no missionaries are ever known to have been active among the Muslims of Lucera.[26]

The issue of the Saracens of Lucera lapsed through 1234–1235, a period of relative cooperation between Frederick and the pope. The full exercise of the liberties of the church within the city of Rome seems to have been at the very top of Gregory's personal list of vital interests, and Frederick had agreed to suppress a rebellion of the Roman barons. But papal-imperial tensions were again running high in early 1236. The pope had temporarily regained control of Rome in mid-1235. At about the same time Frederick began to mount a campaign against the rebellious cities of the Lombard League, which were the papacy's natural allies in its ongoing struggle to prevent imperial domination of central Italy. To halt the planned imperial invasion of northern Italy, Gregory hurled an excommunication warning at Frederick at the end of February 1236. One of its many specifications alleged the destruction of churches by the Saracens of Lucera.

Remember that excommunication is a juridical sentence, and, as such, it requires due process. In medieval jurisprudence this could be supplied by a sequence of legal procedures known as *ordo iuris*.[27] The Romano-canonical accusatorial *ordo* that still prevailed in the early thirteenth century required that the accused be summoned three times to answer specific charges, which gave the accused the opportunity to respond effectively to the allegations in open court. If the alleged crimes were somehow deemed *manifesta*, so obvious that a trial was rendered superfluous, the *ordo* required that the accused be provided three warnings, which would give him ample opportunity to repent and to mend his ways before sentence could be passed.[28] As one might expect, this latter exercise of *ordo iuris* was very difficult to apply in actual criminal cases, but it was perfectly suited to the high-stakes political game that Gregory was playing with Frederick.

In February 1236, Gregory charged Frederick with numerous *crimina manifesta* in a letter entitled *Dum preteritorum consideratione*. In it the pope served notice to Frederick that he would be excommunicated if he did not turn from the crimes that it specified. At one point Gregory recurred to the bitter rhetoric of his 1232 letter:

> Behold the ramparts of Babylon are built from the ruins of Jerusalem and schools for the sons of Hagar from the stones of Zion. Buildings in which the divine name is honored are forced to become places where the damnable

Muhammad is adored. And a more cruel and lamentable
sword cuts us as well. The uncircumcised, placed almost
in the middle of the Kingdom, can more easily corrupt the
Catholic faith by the venom of their infidelity. Thence
greater dangers take hold, for Christians are mixed in with
them. Through companionship with pagans the flocks of
the faithful depart from the Lord's fold, and the Hebrews
are so oppressed by the Egyptians that it is as though they
are subject to their rule.[29]

This diatribe vividly reiterates the pope's earlier charges and
again expresses his fear of a dangerous and widening spiritual
contamination taking place at the very center of Christendom. It
also repeats the rationale of those canons noted previously that
mandated action to prevent violations of ecclesiastical liberty,
miscegenation, and the dominion of infidels over Christians.[30]
References to conversion, by whatever means, henceforth
disappear from Gregory's letters. *Dum preteritorum consideratione*
was a legal and political instrument. Among other things, the
pope held Frederick criminally liable for churches allegedly
destroyed by infidels for whom the emperor was directly
responsible, infidels whom contemporary canonistic thinking
largely presumed to be a dangerous threat to the faith and the
faithful. But, whatever the spiritual or canonical foundations of
these and the many other charges in *Dum preteritorum
consideratione*, this letter of warning was the direct result of rising
political tensions: Gregory was using the threat of
excommunication, with its many political consequences, to force
Frederick to back down.

Frederick responded carefully to the allegations, including
those relating to Lucera, in April 1236. He asserted that the
"persistent fable [*inveterata . . . fabula*]" that the Saracens on his
estates in Apulia had razed churches ought to be laid to rest. As
far as he knew, nothing of the sort had occurred. Frederick
expressed disappointment that Gregory would even mention
these rumors, since he had, at great expense and effort, removed
the Saracens from their mountain fastness, halted their iniquities,
and placed them in the midst of Christians who daily served as
an example to them. Frederick noted that a third of the Saracens,
envious of the liberties enjoyed by the baptized, had already
converted to Christianity, to the evident distress of the Muslim

leaders of Lucera. The emperor conjectured that, if the past indicated anything about the future, the rest of them would soon convert.[31]

Frederick's point was that his resettlement of Saracens in Lucera did not contaminate the company of the baptized; on the contrary, it had and would continue to increase, not diminish, the body of Christ. Note that Frederick was accomplishing this without the "harsh measures" (*asperitates*) that compulsion necessarily requires; rather, he used "allurements" (*blandimenta*), "reason" (*ratio*), and "mildness" (*mansuetudo*), inducements that Pope Gregory I plainly specified in *Qui sincera intentione*, the classic proof text for canonistic arguments against forced conversion.[32]

The responses that Frederick made to this and the other allegations in *Dum preteritorum consideratione* were unlikely to have satisfied Gregory. What really mattered early in 1236 was that the pope and the emperor could not come to terms over the status of the Lombard cities. For the pope, the freedom of those cities from imperial control remained and would continue to remain critical to the independence of the papacy from imperial domination. When imperial forces actually invaded northern Italy in summer 1236, Gregory appears to have sent Frederick a second excommunication warning. The pope again alleged that "schools for the sons of Hagar are built from the stones of churches" and that "many churches have been torn from their foundations." He also charged that "Christians are subjected to the rule of pagans."[33] Frederick politely denied all of the charges, one by one, and requested specific examples of the alleged crimes.[34]

During a lull in hostilities that lasted through much of 1237 the papacy attempted unsuccessfully to negotiate a settlement between Frederick and the Lombard League. The emperor again took the offensive in the fall. His army won a seemingly decisive victory over the Lombards at Cortenuova in November 1237. A dull peace prevailed through the first half of 1238. Frederick's great victory made him more truculent than necessary. He refused to negotiate seriously with the League. After the emperor laid siege to the city of Brescia in summer 1238, Gregory decided to throw his lot in with the Lombard cities, the traditional guarantors of papal independence from imperial domination.

In October 1238, Gregory sent to the emperor a third and final excommunication warning, which consisted of a severely abridged list of the allegations the pope had made in his previous warnings to Frederick. The bull of excommunication that Gregory promulgated in 1239 reiterated, nearly word for word, the allegations made in this final warning. Included among them was the charge that "churches consecrated to the Lord are profaned and destroyed."[35] In his response, Frederick flatly denied that he knew of any such case. He did suggest, however, that the pope might be thinking about the church of Lucera itself, which was said to be collapsing under its own weight due to extreme age. Frederick assured the pope that he would not only permit it to be rebuilt, he would render honor to God by helping the bishop to do so.[36] Both parties were merely going through the motions: *ordo iuris* required it. The sentence of excommunication followed on March 20, 1239. The rhetoric of the conflict soon intensified to the point that the juridical foundations of both the papal and the imperial cases were sometimes obscured by more colorful arguments.

Papal ire over the existence of the Muslim enclave at Lucera, and the legal arguments with which Gregory IX supported his attacks on it and its imperial patron, persisted long after Gregory's death in 1241 and that of Frederick in 1250. The canonical jurisprudence pertaining to Muslims helped to justify not only the sentence of excommunication in 1239, but also the sentence of deposition laid on Frederick by Innocent IV at the Council of Lyons in 1245. The canonistic commentaries of Innocent IV and Hostiensis enlarged and rationalized this body of law and thus confirmed the leading role of the pope in the ongoing clash between Christians and infidels.[37]

The Saracens of Lucera were hapless pawns in the papal-imperial struggles of the mid-thirteenth century. They remained so through the papal wars and crusades that plagued southern Italy to the end of the century. The colony at Lucera remained steadfastly Muslim, and a thorn in the side of the papacy, until its dissolution by Charles II, the Angevin king of Naples, in 1300. Frederick and his son Manfred, and indeed the Angevins who defeated Manfred in 1266, regularly employed Saracen archers from the colony in their wars against the Lombard League and others. It enraged the popes that the emperor and his successors did not force their Saracens to accept baptism and, perhaps worse, that they actually used Muslims to attack Christians. Indeed, it must have seemed to them to be the very inversion of the crusade, the principal mechanism by which Christendom did battle with Islam and which, by this time, was widely justified as a means of converting Muslims.

Popes from Gregory IX to Boniface VIII hounded the successive lords of Lucera about their Muslim subjects. Frequently they listed the mere existence of the colony among the *casus belli* for the series of crusades that Pope Innocent IV and his successors launched against the Hohenstaufen and subsequent enemies of the papacy in southern Italy.[38] Frederick may not have meant to frighten the papacy with the Muslim community he had established, but the popes nevertheless dreaded the Saracens of Lucera. They considered their close proximity to the very heart of Christendom a dangerous anomaly that could not be tolerated. Norman Housley characterizes the deep papal animosity toward these Muslims and their protectors in a passage that bears lengthy quotation.

> The outstanding example of *impium foedus* [an ungodly covenant] was the Staufen tolerance of and active employment of the Muslim colony of Lucera. Useful as the Curia found the colony in propaganda terms, the existence of such an outpost of Islam, less than 200 miles from Rome, and the tolerance with which the Staufen permitted it to observe all the laws and customs of that faith, even to the daily call of the muezzin, seems to have genuinely appalled the popes; Boniface VIII was delighted at its final destruction in 1300.[39]

It is typical of the times that for nearly the entire history of the Muslim community at Lucera the popes expressed their consternation at its existence in terms that were fundamentally juridical. The canons regarding ecclesiastical liberty and the isolation and conversion of infidels provided the popes a rationale, a strategy, and a pretext for eliminating what they considered to be a clear and present danger to the papacy, which to them was all but indistinguishable from Christendom as a whole. That medieval society was legalistic and litigious to a fault meant that the parties to these hostilities could expect readers to respond readily to juridical arguments. Gregory IX and Innocent IV characterized Frederick and his Saracens as unlawful and intolerable threats to the papacy, the church, and the faithful. And, on a higher level, these popes viewed Muslim Lucera, like Frederick, as an obstacle that stubbornly and recklessly blocked realization of the papal vision of the right order of Christendom: a community of the baptized, wholly subject to the jurisdiction of the papacy. It is only to be expected that the popes used legal arguments to justify the liquidation of Frederick II, his successors, and his Saracens, and that Frederick defended himself in kind.

NOTES

1. *Excommunicamus* (March 20, 1239) in Matthew Paris, *Cronica maiora*, 149.

2. COD³, 267–271.

3. I wish to thank Professor Marci Sortor of Grinnell College for focusing my attention on the place that "right order" held in this episode of the often-troubled relationship between Frederick and the papacy. Pakter makes a curiously parallel, but apt, observation about the papacy, the empire, and the Jews: "Papal intervention in internal Jewish affairs coincided with the final struggle between the Holy See and the Holy Roman Empire. Jews and the Empire had one thing in common; both represented a challenge to papal assertions of universal authority." *Medieval Canon Law and the Jews*, 67. For a lengthy and detailed analysis of the scholarly literature on the medieval idea of Christendom, see Van Engen, "The Christian Middle Ages as an Historiographical Problem," 519–522. For Van Engen's views on Christendom as fundamentally a community of the baptized, see his "Faith as a Concept of Order in Medieval Christendom," chap. 1 in *Belief in History: Innovative Approaches to European and American Religion*, 19–67.

4. On the Latinization of Norman Sicily, see Abulafia, "The End of Muslim Sicily," 103–133. On the balance that Frederick struck between political and fiscal demands, see idem, "The State and Economic Life in the Kingdom of Sicily under Frederick II," 4, 9–10, 14 (Correspondence concerning this paper may be sent to Dr. David Abulafia, Gonville and Caius College, Cambridge CB2 1TA, England). Powell also discusses the political, military, and economic considerations that induced Frederick to relocate his Sicilian Muslims in Apulia in "The Papacy and the Muslim Frontier."

5. Abulafia, "The State and Economic Life," 9.

6. In referring to the *Decretum Gratiani*, I will use the following standard abbreviations: D. for Distincto, C. for Causa, q. for quaestio, c. for canon (with cc. as plural for canons). De con. refers to De consecratione, the third part of the *Decretum*.

On the protection of Christians from infidels, see, in particular, book 5, title 6 of the *Decretales Gregory ii IX*, "De iudaeis, sarracenis, et eorum servis" (X 5.6). Under this title are several canons, most of them from the late twelfth and early thirteenth centuries, that set terms for the manumission of a slave who belongs to a Jew and is a Christian or wishes to become a Christian (cc. 1, 19); forbid Christians from taking service with Jews or Saracens (cc. 2, 5 [Third Lateran Council (1179), c. 26]; and cc. 8, 13), "quoniam Iudaeorum mores et nostri in nullo concordant, et ipsi de facili ob continuam conversationem et assiduam familiaritatem ad suam superstitionem et perfidiam simplicium animos inclinarent" (c. 8); prescribe distinctive clothing for Jews and Saracens to inhibit miscegenation (15 [Fourth Lateran Council (1215), 68]; and prohibit placing Jews or Saracens in positions of authority over Christians (c. 16 [Fourth Lateran Council (1215), c. 69]; and c. 18). For a lengthy analysis of the rationale for isolating Jewish and Muslim populations in Christian lands, see Powell, "The Papacy and the Muslim Frontier," 175–203, esp. 186–198; for his treatment of papal policy toward the Saracens of Lucera, see ibid., 193–197. Powell reviews the increasing linkage of Jews and Saracens that occurred in canon law during this period, ibid., 189–193. On this linkage, see *Decretales Gregorii* X 5.6.5,18 and the *Glossa ordinaria* to chap. 5, s.vv. ("at the words") Iudaei sive Saraceni.

7. As a general principle of canon law, no one could be forced to accept baptism, the rationale for which is clearly expressed in canon of St. Augustine, which states: "Verus baptismus constat non tam ablutione corporis quam fide cordis." (De con. D.4 c. 150); cf. De con. D.4 c. 34 (with *Gl. ord.*, s.v. Corde); De con. D.4 c.156 (with *Gl. ord.*, s.v. Gratiam); De con. D.4 c. 97; D.45 c. 3 (with *Gl. ord.*, s.v. Licentiam); D.45 c.5; and C. 23 q.5 c.33 (with *Gl. ord.*, s.vv. Nisi elegerit). A decretal of Pope Clement III, *Sicut iudaei* (X 5.6.9, with *Gl. ord.*, s.vv. Christi fidem habere), forbids compulsory baptism. However, the *Gl. ord.* to *Sicut iudaei*, s.v. Invitos, distinguishes between "absolute" and "conditional"

compulsion, on an analogy with matrimony, and this allowed a great
deal of lawful pressure to be put on an infidel to convert; cf. *Gl. ord.* to
D.45 c. 5, s.vv. Coacti sunt, which stresses the analogy between baptism
and matrimony. How canon law and canonists answered some of the
major questions relating to the conversion of Muslims is treated in some
detail by Kedar in "Muslim Conversion in Canon Law," 321–332; see, in
particular pp. 328–330, where he examines forced conversion. Kedar
maintains that the "consensus of canonist thought branded forced
christianization of Saracens unlawful." Ibid., 328. But recourse to the
"harsh measures" that Pope Gregory I prohibited in *Qui sincera
intentione* (D.45 c. 3) was not ruled out by some canonists, especially
Alanus Anglicus, who endorsed compulsion "just short of death [*citra
mortem*]." Ibid., 328, and n. 32, which gives Alanus' gloss of C. 23 q.4
d.p.c.36, s.v. Rationibiliter. However much canonist opinion hardened
on the topic of forced conversion, Alanus' harsh prescription did not
become the standard approach. But by the thirteenth century there was
wider acceptance among canonists of the use of "conditional"
compulsion, which could be very harsh indeed. Ibid., 328–330; see also
Kedar, *Crusade and Mission*, 72–74, 185–189, which includes a passage
from the *Summa Parisiensis* that vividly depicts the perceived connection
between Saracens and Jews; ibid., 72–73, n. 88. The parallels between
forced conversion of Saracens and forced conversion of Jews were
necessarily close. See Pakter, *Medieval Canon Law and the Jews*, 317–330,
which examines canonist doctrine on the involuntary baptism of Jewish
children. The high medieval church was shot through with ambivalence
on the Saracen menace: what *was* the best solution, conversion or
crusade? See Kedar, *Crusade and Mission*, passim.

8. See Powell, "The Papacy and the Muslim Frontier," 198–203.
For the development of canonical jurisdiction over Jews, see chap. 1,
"Jurisdiction," in Pakter, *Medieval Canon Law and the Jews*, 40–83.

9. Muldoon, *Popes, Lawyers, and Infidels*, 9–15; passage quoted
from p. 11. Cf. Pakter, *Medieval Canon Law and the Jews*, 73–83.

10. Powell, "The Papacy and the Muslim Frontier," 193–198;
passage quoted from p. 197.

11. Ibid., 185. Powell reinforces the point that isolation or
conversion of infidel populations required the active cooperation of the
secular authorities, ibid., 185.

12. MGH Epist. saec. XIII, 1:398, no. 494. On the general immunity
from harm that canon law accorded *res spiritualia*, a privilege that the
canons included among the liberties of the church, see C.17 q.4
cc.8,10,12,18; X 3.13,2,5,11–12; X 5.17.1–2; and X 5.39.22. Violations of
this immunity usually entailed excommunication *latae sententiae*, i.e., an

automatic sentence of excommunication. See, for example, the *Gl. ord.* to X 3.13.12 [Fourth Lateran Council (1214), c. 44], s.v. Compellendis: "Immo sunt ipso iure excommunicati." This gloss cites X 5.39.49 (*Noverit fraternitas tua*), which automatically excommunicates heretics and violators of ecclesiastical liberty. On excommunication *latae sententiae*, which applied almost exclusively to cases of heresy and the violation of ecclesiastical liberty, see Vodola, *Excommunication in the Middle Ages*, 28–35. For the specific immunity from harm enjoyed by churches, see X 3.49.9 and X 5.17.2.

13. MGH Epist. saec. XIII 1:398–399, no. 494.

14. See discussion that follows in text. See also n. 31.

15. See n. 6.

16. On the development of the term *vicarius Christi*, see Maccarrone, *Vicarius Christi: Storia del titolo papale*, 1–4. For another analysis of this term's development before and during the pontificate of Innocent III and of its twelfth-century fusion with the related concept of *plenitudo potestatis*, see Kay, *Dante's Swift and Strong*, 124–141. The most thorough treatment of the canonistic foundations of the language of papal sovereignty, especially *plenitudo potestatis*, remains Watt, "The Theory of Papal Monarchy in the Thirteenth Century: The Contribution of the Canonists," 179–317. See also Ladner, "The Concepts of 'Ecclesia' and 'Christianitas.'"

17. On medieval concepts of the relationship between church and state, and the doctrine of the two swords in particular, see the series of articles by Alfons Stickler listed in the bibliography. See also Ladner, "The Concepts of 'Ecclesia' and 'Christianitas'," 495–498; and Chodorow, *Christian Political Theory and Church Politics in the Mid-Twelfth Century*, 54–60, 211–246. See, in particular, pp. 223–246 on the use of force by the church.

18. MGH Epist. saec. XIII 1:447–448, no. 553. Gregory may have intended his reference to "their servitude [*eorum . . . servitus*]" to allay any concern that Frederick might have had that the conversion of his Muslims to Christianity might bestow free status on them. Kedar has noted in "Muslim Conversion in Canon Law," 327–328, that the canonist Raymond of Penyaforte argued in favor of the manumission of Muslim converts to Christianity, if it were conferred on those converts by local custom. But in two letters sent to the Kingdom of Jerusalem, Gregory IX "knowingly sacrifices the amelioration of their [the converts'] temporal status promised by local custom to overcome the crusader masters' opposition to the amelioration he considers paramount, namely baptism." That Gregory limited the proposed Dominican mission to

those Saracens "qui . . . Italicum ydioma non mediocriter . . . intelligunt" does not necessarily imply that the presence of Saracens who had learned the local tongue was a special threat to local Christians and, thus, provided perhaps the prime impetus for the proposed mission, as Powell maintains in "The Papacy and the Muslim Frontier," 195. This reference could also represent implied recognition of the canonical precept, found at C. 8 q.1 c.12, that required preachers to use language that their listeners could understand. Some Spanish Dominicans must have known Arabic in 1233, but how many of them would have been available for this mission? Likewise, the text of *Post vicarium Iesu Christi* (MGH Epist. Saec. XIII 1:447–448, no. 553; see n. 18) in no way connects the presence of Italian-speaking Muslims to the overall purpose of the Dominican mission, which in this letter Gregory identifies solely to be that of conversion; nowhere does the pope refer to spiritual contamination or the destruction of churches. Powell is probably correct when he states that the Dominicans were "called on," (p. 195), but in all likelihood by Gregory himself. No evidence exists to suggest that the proposal to evangelize the Muslims of Lucera was anything but a papal initiative, which was in itself unusual. Powell asserts that in Spain, where, of course, there were many more Muslims to convert, there were no such papal initiatives, ibid., 187.

19.   Abulafia, "The End of Muslim Sicily," 129, n. 74.

20.   *Apostolici culminis littere,* in HB, 4,1:457–458.

21.   Frederick would later maintain that the proximity of Christians and Muslims had produced more Muslim converts to Christianity rather than the reverse, as Gregory was arguing. See discussion that follows in text. See also nn. 31 and 32.

22.   See Frederick II, *Liber augustalis* (also known as the Constitutions of Melfi), 1.18[21] and 1.28[32], 22, 30. The latter law places Jews and Saracens under the protection of the crown in cases of "secret murders and injuries whose authors cannot be found," but seemingly only because Frederick felt Christian persecution of Jews and Saracens to be "too great at present." He certainly did not foreswear persecution of his religious minorities. Powell repeats this point in "The Papacy and the Muslim Frontier," 194–195. Cf. Abulafia, "The End of Muslim Sicily," which lays out in detail the pressures that Frederick and his predecessors placed, and allowed to be placed, on their Muslim subjects, but esp. 120–121, passim 128–130.

23.   Abulafia, 128. On the strictly utilitarian attitude of Frederick toward his Muslim subjects, see Abulafia, "The State and Economic Life," 9. Cf. Powell, "The Papacy and the Muslim Frontier," 203, where he asserts that "*Utilitas* provided the real basis for the continued

existence of these communities [of Muslims and Jews]. In the case of the Muslims, once their utility to their secular masters declined, the only alternatives were expulsion or assimilation." Certainly the utility of the Muslims of Lucera was great enough under Frederick II to forestall any such measures, but, as noted in text that follows, Charles II, king of Naples, dispersed the community in 1300 under papal pressure.

24. Powell, "The Papacy and the Muslim Frontier," 197.

25. Ibid., 197–198.

26. Kedar, *Crusade and Mission*, 145. He makes this observation in the course of a chapter (pp. 136–158) on the role played by the Mendicant orders in the evangelization of Saracens and, ultimately, in the promotion of the crusade, after their attempts at conversion proved virtually fruitless.

27. On the nature of accusatorial process in canon law, see Fraher, "Conviction according to Conscience," esp. p. 60 and n. 311. See also Lomax, *"Ingratus* or *Indignus,"* 18–19 and nn. 48–51 in chapter 1.

28. Fraher," 41–44, 48–50, 54. See also Lomax, 19–21 and nn. 52–53 in chapter 1; and Vodola, *Excommunication*, 166. Vodola, 33–34, and Fraher, especially 33–40 passim, chart the progress of inquisitorial process at the expense of the more cumbersome accusatorial process in the late twelfth and early thirteenth centuries. However, this transition did not affect the highly politicized legal dialogue in which Frederick and Gregory were engaged.

29. MGH Epist. saec. XIII 1:574–575, no. 676.

30. See above nn. 6, 12.

31. *Preterita nostre sinceritatis*, HB, 4,2:831.

32. D.45 c.3. The *Glossa ordinaria* to this canon includes "muneribus" among the inducements that may be employed, s.v. Blandimentis. Later, the gloss argues, s.v. Licentiam, that permitting the Jews to celebrate their festivals without interference does not constitute a "licentiam peccandi: sed liberationem a poena." Indeed, the gloss continues, if the Jews are prohibited from celebrating their festivals, "ergo iam cogerentur ad fidem."

33. MGH Epist. saec. XIII 1:597–598, no. 700. These passages are taken from a list of complaints found in the Registers of Gregory IX (5.1). It appears to be an abbreviated version of a fuller text that was sent to the papal legate, Jacobus de Pecoraria, cardinal bishop of Palestrina, sometime in August 1236 and probably to Frederick himself at about the same time. Frederick replied to each of these charges in *Nuper ad iustum* (cited in n. 34) which is dated September 20, 1236.

34. *Nuper ad iustum*, HB, 4,2:906.

35. *Cum omni reverencia*, MGH SS 28:156. This is an imperial letter in which Frederick repeated and responded to the papal allegations *seriatim*. Profanation was a new note. Burial of an excommunicate or a pagan in a church profaned it, as did bloodshed, sexual intercourse, fire, and vandalism. I cannot locate a canon or gloss that specifically states that Islamic or pagan worship profaned a church, but Gregory certainly implied that such was the case. On the profanation of churches, see C.23 q.8 c.32; De con. D.1 cc.19–24; X 3.40.7,9–10; and X 5.39.19,22.

36. *Cum omni reverencia*, MGH SS 28:156.

37. For a discussion of these canonistic commentaries, see Muldoon, *Popes, Lawyers, and Infidels*, 3–28. The imperial legate, Thaddeus of Suessa, defended Frederick at the First Council of Lyons. Matthew Paris describes Thaddeus' defense in the *Cronica maiora*, MGH SS 28:258–261, at the beginning of his account of the council. During the debate that preceded promulgation of the bull of deposition, Innocent IV listed among the "enormitates imperatoris" that "civitatem quandam [Lucera] in christianitate construxerat novam, fortem et magnam, quam Sarracenis populaverat communitam, ipsorum utens, sed pocius abutens ritibus et supersticione, spreto christianorum consilio et religione." Ibid., 259. This passage expresses as clearly as any the nature of papal objections to Muslim Lucera. Note, in particular, that this "new city, strong and great" was built "within Christendom," which would render it both dangerous and out of place. Thaddeus responded that Frederick had prudently done this "ad rebellionem scilicet quorundam et insolentiam reprimendam sibi iure subditorum et sedicionem expurgandam." The bull of deposition itself does not refer quite so directly to Lucera, although it does allege that Frederick maintained a close and, in some cases, perverse relationship with the Muslims in the Holy Land and in Sicily. See COD3, 282.

38. Housley, *The Italian Crusades*, 40, 62, 64–65. Powell asserts in "The Papacy and Muslim Frontier," 196–197. that "the second half of the thirteenth century witnessed a hardening of the attitude toward the [Muslim] colony [at Lucera] on the part of the popes." He attributes this "increased concern" to the "failure of the effort to convert" the Saracens and the Angevins' continued employment of Saracens in the wars of the late thirteenth century. However, it is clear that the attitude of the papacy was already quite hard as early as the 1232, and papal agitation against the Saracens of Lucera continued virtually unabated to the end of the century and a little beyond. Apart from the lack of evidence that there was any "effort to convert," this perceived "hardening" could signify a different sort of papal frustration. Extermination of the

Hohenstaufen did not produce the political and military relief that the popes had expected. The Angevins were nearly as troublesome as the Hohenstaufen. The Angevins' continued recourse to Saracen arms simply heightened papal exasperation at this distasteful reality.

39. Housley, 65.

CHAPTER 9

John-Jerome of Prague and the Religion of the Saracens

William Patrick Hyland

Introduction

A curious opusculum concerning medieval Christian views of Islam can be found among the unedited writings of a Camaldolese monk known as John-Jerome of Prague. John-Jerome claims to have found the work, known as *Miraculum noviter factum*, while traveling in the Holy Land in 1430. It recounts a miraculous story in which Christian merchants of Arabia are accused unjustly of murdering a rich Saracen merchant, and are threatened with either forced conversion to Islam or horrible execution. In answer to the desperate prayers of the Christians, the cadaver returns to life and vindicates the Christians, and also warns the Muslim king that he must embrace the Christian faith or be forever damned. The king then accepts baptism together with his people, and the story ends with the promise that these Christian neophytes would wait in the mountains of Galilee to aid any Christian army willing to come to conquer the Holy Land.

The main purpose of this chapter is to present the Latin text of this interesting opusculum along with an English translation.[1] However, I would first like to briefly give some background on the life of John-Jerome of Prague, and the place this text has within the body of his work.[2] Originally known simply as John of Prague, he was born c. 1370 in Prague and attended the local Caroline university where he studied canon law. He became a Premonstratensian canon at Strahov in Prague, and eventually in the mid-1390s traveled to Poland and became a chaplain at the court of Wladislaus-Jagiello in Cracow. From Poland he launched a missionary campaign into Lithuania, and in 1410 became the abbot of a new Premonstratensian foundation south of Cracow at Nowy Sacz. In 1413 he moved to Tuscany and embraced the eremitical life at Camaldoli, assuming the name of Jerome. As a Camaldolese he participated in the reform efforts within his own order, and in the reform councils held at Siena and Basel. He was an active opponent of the Hussites, and composed tracts against them as well as many sermons on various subjects. He died in the Camaldolese house of San Michele in Murano outside of Venice in 1440.

From 1430 to 1432 John-Jerome visited the Holy Land and eastern Mediterranean islands, and claims to have found this opusculum written in Greek in Nazareth. In all of his other writings John-Jerome never displays any knowledge of Greek, and it is unlikely that he was able to evaluate this text personally from a Greek original. This leaves several possibilities. One of the neophytes mentioned in the story could have prepared this translation, or else one of the many Greeks John-Jerome met on his return trip to Italy. Another possibility is that John-Jerome himself put this text together from a story he heard during his travels, and that the purported discovery of a written text in Greek is a literary device. This last theory is unlikely, however. John-Jerome asserts both at the beginning and end of the opusculum that he had discovered the story in written form, and never claims to have translated it himself. The story contained in the *Miraculum noviter factum* may well represent an authentic eastern Christian tradition, which John-Jerome discovered in Nazareth and brought home for the edification of a monastic audience in Italy.

The story is obviously intended for a Christian audience, with the simple message being the unique truth of the Christian religion. John-Jerome acknowledges at the end of paragraph 10 that he intends it to be read by a "neophyte." The truth of Christianity is proved by a simple yet profound direct divine intervention. Several typical elements of medieval polemics against Islam are present in the narrative. Muhammad is the focus of the resuscitated cadaver's criticisms of Islam. Islam is referred to as a fable and not a true religion at all. Muhammad is described as a necromancer and a magician, who was able to seduce the Arabians into following him.[3] All Muslims are considered to be damned. The resuscitated cadaver speaks with supernatural knowledge, and from his vantage point there is no true religion except Christianity.

Despite the marvelous events and the criticism of Muhammad's character, it must be said that the author is relatively judicious in his treatment of Islam. He correctly notes that Muhammad is regarded by Muslims as the *nuncius dei*, and there is no suggestion that they regard him as a god or an angel or anything of the sort found in the more popular Christian folklore. There are also none of the typical suggestions of sexual immorality or secular ambition on Muhammad's part.[4] The king of the Saracens is certainly portrayed as blustering and cruel at first, but he also is sincere in his desire to know the truth about religion. He acknowledges the secular prosperity of the Christian kingdoms, and is unhesitating in his punishment of the real murderers once they have been uncovered.

Whether or not he was the author of the story itself, John-Jerome probably found the relatively calm attitude toward Islam in this opusculum congenial. In his own writings he displayed little rancor toward the Muslims. While listing various heresies in a sermon given at the Council of Siena in February 1424, he mentioned the Muslim belief that Christ did not truly suffer or die.[5] In his tract against the Hussites written in 1433, John-Jerome compares the morality of the Muslims favorably with that of the Hussites:

> How truly just and innocent are all the pagans and Saracens, with respect to the morals of the Bohemians. For this reason the Saracens will stand up at the judgment with the wicked generation of the Bohemians, and will condemn it, because the Saracens, being ignorant of the faith of Christ, nevertheless with regard to morals are innocent and just.[6]

This technique of using the morality of Muslims to criticize fellow Christians had been employed by Bonaventure and other moralists before.[7] Although John-Jerome's statement is more of a polemical slur against the Hussites than anything else, it is clear that John-Jerome did admire the personal morality of some of the Muslims he encountered in his travels.

The lingering fascination for a crusade finds expression in this tract, and John-Jerome seems to believe that there really is a large armed Christian force in Galilee waiting to aid a crusading army. Indeed, in the very last line of the opusculum he claims to have seen it. From his other writings we know that he supported the idea of a military conquest of Constantinople and giving the city into the possession of the Knights of St. John of Rhodes,[8] and it is possible that the last part of this tract is intended to rekindle an interest in Italy to support the precarious military position of the Latin Christian states in the eastern Mediterranean islands he had visited.

The manuscript is a bound codex found in the Biblioteca Nazionale Centrale in Florence. Although the manuscript itself has been referred to by certain recent scholars, this particular unedited opusculum has not.[9] The codex is originally from the hermitage of Camaldoli, and is dated to 1435. It contains many of John-Jerome's own writings in 227 folios. The opusculum is written in a current hybrid Gothic script in brown ink, with some highlighted passages and capitals in bright red ink. Each page is 20 cm long and 14 cm wide, with 1 cm right margins. Each page has two columns, and a full column of text is approximately 17 cm long, with a 0.5–1 cm space between the columns. The opusculum is three and one-half columns long.

The following is a diplomatic transcription, although I have provided paragraph and punctuation structure, and have regularized the capitalization of proper names.

Latin Text

Florence, Biblioteca Nazionale Centrale C.S.D. 7 886[10] [Fol. 191r]
1. *Incipit miraculum noviter factum.* Omnibus patent Christi miracula que ipse dominus exemplo patris usque modo operari non cessat, presertim hoc novissimo tempore, quo totus mundus in maligno positus est, sicut greca lingua scriptum reperimus in

partibus orientalibus tale fertur contigisse miraculum et anno ab incarnacione domini m°cccc°xxx°.

2. In civitate Allexandria erat quidam Saracenus mercator ditissimus qui profectus ad negociandum venit in Arabiam cumque illuc mercaretur et lucra quereret. Servi regis Arabum considerantes locupletem virum inito secreto concilio sub nocturno silencio prefatum Saracenum occiderunt et ablatis omnibus posuerunt cadaver mortuum ante fundicum hoc est ante domum Christianorum in qua omnes mercatores Christiani simul cum uxoribus et parvulis habitabant. Mane facto clamor populi atollitur, Christiani tamquam homicide acusantur, capiuntur, ligantur et simul cum parvulis ante regem Arabum aducuntur.

3. Quos ut vidit rex, inflatus potencia turbatusque cum ira maxima pomposis verbis cum furore nimio talem protulit sentenciam, ut omnes Christiani qui in regno suo inventi fuissent simul cum uxoribus et parvulis, aut negarent fidem Christi et susciperent fidem Machomethi aut omnes proiecti in ignem flammis atrocibus comburantur. Ad hec Christiani confisi in Christo petunt trium dierum inducias simulque ut cadaver Saraceni mortui triduo inhumatum remaneret. Quibus obtentis, reversi ad domum propriam de comuni concilio hoc inter se statuerunt ut nullus cibum aut potum triduo sumeret simulque parvulis et sugentibus ubera cibum ac potum negarent.

4. Mira res! Saracenus qui occisus fuerat die tercio vivus surexit et ad regem properavit. Quem videns rex stupore et amiracione territus voce tremula an vere viveret requisivit. Ad quem Saracenus, qui mortuus fuerat, "Vivo", inquit, "Christianorum precibus et huc ad te veni, ut tibi eos qui me occiderunt demonstrarem. Jube ergo omnes servos tuos huc venire ut tibi homicidas meos digito ostendam."

5. Citantur igitur ex iussu regis omnes servi et familia. Sed interim rex interrogat Saracenum defunctum in hec verba: "Dic michi, amice carissime, que fides in hoc mundo est melior? Scimus enim quod Iudei habent fidem satis bonam et per patriarchas et prophetas ac per Moysen aprobatam. Christiani eciam habent fidem licet non aprobatam, tamen est satis magna, quia multe civitates, comitatus, ducatus, et regna sunt de fide Christiana. Nostra autem sancta fides Machomethi est a deo

probata, quia Deus locutus fuit cum Machometo qui fuit ultimus et inmediatus nunccius Dei."

6. Ad hec Saracenus qui mortuus fuerat respondit: "Crede michi, O rex, quod fides Iudeorum erat bona quousque veniret messias qui in lege eorum promisus erat. Quem quia non cognoverunt sed dominum glorie crucifixerunt; ab illo tempore omnes Iudei dampnati sunt. Nostra autem fides [191v] Machometi quam tu dicis sanctam non est fides sed est fabula, quia Machomet non fuit ultimus nunccius Dei, sed fuit de Arabia nigromanticus et per artes magicas seduxit Saracenos. Ideo omnes Saraceni, Arabes, Syri, Thurci, Thartari, Assirii, Barbari et omnes de secta Machomethi sunt dampnati. Et ego dampnatus sum, sed ad preces Christianorum Deus voluit me ad tempus vivere ut tibi veritatem ostenderem et a pena incendii Christianos liberarem. Una ergo vera et sancta fides est Christiana, quia sicut unus est deus, ita una est fides et unum babtisma Christianorum. Ve michi, quia mortuus sum absque babtismo."

7. Cumque hec diceret, supervenerunt servi regis. Tunc rex ait: "Quis horum est qui te interfecit?" Saracenus autem qui mortuus fuerat, extendens manum, quattuor servos digito ostendit et statim mortuus et fetens ad pedes regis cecidit. Tunc rex iussit cadaver eferri et speliri. Illos autem quattuor homicidas iubet suspendi. Et mitens vocat ad se omnes Christianos quos benigne suscipiens a sentencia quam male dictaverat absolvit. Rogatque omnes ut sacerdotem catholicum sibi velint dirigere. Quo veniente, rex flexo utroque poplice petit babtizari. Baptisatique sunt in illo die rex cum filio parvulo et Arabum utriusque sexus maxima multitudo ex quibus XL^a milia Arabes neophiti hucusque habitant in montanis Galilee.

8. Et omnes Saracenos venientes capiunt et occidunt. Christianis autem venientibus omnem humanitatem exhibent et honorem, hortantes omnes Christicolas ut venirent ad aquirendam terram sanctam et Ierusalem, et ipsi Arabes neophiti promitunt quod XL^a milia armati precedent exercitum Christianorum dabuntque eis totam terram sanctam et zoldanum.

9. Sed quo fine hoc miraculum claudendum sit? Ille novit in cuius conspectu luna non splendet et stelle non sunt munde,

cui nichil est dificille, et sine quo nichil est posibile posideri, Ihesus Christus Dei filius, qui cum patre et sancto spiritu super omnia est Deus benedictus in secula. Amen.

10. Ego frater Jeronimus de Praga sacre heremi Camalduli reclusus heremita, dum anno preterito venissem in civitatem Galilee cui nomen Nazareth, reperii hoc miraculum Greca lingua scriptum. Et vidi prefatos Arabes, neophito ideo cum securitate hec scripsi.

Translation

1. *Here begins a miracle recently performed.* Evident to all are the miracles of Christ, which the Lord himself by the example of the Father does not cease to work up to the present, especially in these last days in which the whole world is steeped in wickedness; such a miracle is said to have taken place in the year from the Incarnation of the Lord 1430, as we found written in the Greek language in the East.

2. In the city of Alexandria there was a certain very wealthy Saracen merchant who for the purpose of making a profit came into Arabia, and while there traded and acquired much wealth. The servants of the King of the Arabs, sizing up this wealthy man, formed a secret plot, and in the silence of the night killed the previously mentioned Saracen. Having taken from him all of his possessions, they placed the dead body in front of the trading post which is in front of the Christians' dwelling place, where all of the Christian merchants live together with their wives and children. In the morning a great clamor arose among the people. The Christians were accused, seized, and bound as if they were the murderers, and together with their children were led before the king of the Arabs.

3. When the king saw them, puffed up with power and disturbed by the greatest anger, in pompous words and with excessive furor pronounced this sentence, that all Christians who had been found in his kingdom, together with their wives and children, were either to deny the Christian faith and accept the faith of Muhammad, or else all were to be thrown into the fire to be consumed by horrible flames. In response the Christians,

trusting in Christ, requested a delay of three days, and asked that the body of the dead Saracen remain unburied for three days. These two requests having been granted, they returned to their own home. The Christians took common counsel among themselves, and decided that no one should consume food or drink for three days, and they should even deny food and drink to suckling infants.

4. Behold what happened! The Saracen who had been killed came back to life on the third day, and went to the king. Upon seeing him the king was terrified with astonishment and wonder, and in a tremulous voice asked him whether he was truly alive. The Saracen who had been dead responded: "I live because of the prayers of the Christians, and I have come here to you so that I might point out to you those who killed me. Therefore command all your servants to come here, so that I might point out my murderers to you."

5. Therefore by command of the king all of the servants and royal family are summoned. But in the meantime the king questions the dead Saracen in the following words: "Tell me, dear friend, which faith in this world is better? For we know that the Jews have a good enough faith, and one that has been approved by the patriarchs and prophets and Moses. The Christians also have faith, and although it is not approved, nevertheless it is great enough, because there are many Christian cities, counties, duchies and kingdoms. Moreover our own holy faith of Muhammad is approved by God, because God spoke with Muhammad, who was the last and immediate messenger of God."

6. To these words the Saracen who had died responded: "Believe me, O king, that the faith of the Jews was good until the Messiah came who had been promised in their Law. Because they did not recognize him but rather crucified the Lord of glory, from that time all Jews have been damned. Our Mohammedan faith which you call holy is not a faith at all, but a fable. For Muhammad was not the final messenger of God, but rather a necromancer from Arabia who seduced the Saracens through magical arts. Therefore all the Saracens, Arabs, Syrians, Turks, Tartars, Assyrians, Berbers and all Mohammedans are damned. I too am damned, but due to the prayers of the Christians God

desired that I live for a time so that I might point out to you the truth, and free the Christians from the penalty of fire. Therefore the one true and holy faith is the Christian, because as God is one so is there one faith and one baptism of the Christians. Woe to me because I died without baptism!"

7. When he had said these things the servants of the king approached, and the king said: "Which of these is the one who killed you?" The Saracen who had been dead, stretching out his hand, indicated with his finger four of the servants, and immediately fell dead and rotting at the feet of the king. Then the king commanded the cadaver to be borne away and buried. Those four murderers, however, he ordered to be hanged. He then summoned[11] all of the Christians, and receiving them benignly absolved them from the sentence he had maliciously pronounced. He begged[12] them to send to him a Catholic priest. When the priest came the king went down on both knees and asked to be baptized. There were baptized on that day the king with his little son, and a vast multitude of Arabs of both sexes, from which forty-thousand Arab neophytes live to this day in the mountains of Galilee.

8. These men capture and kill all the Saracens who come, and exhibit every human kindness and honor to those Christians who come. And they urge all worshipers of Christ to come for the purpose of acquiring the Holy Land and Jerusalem, and these Arab neophytes promise that forty-thousand armed men will precede the Christian army, and hand over to them the sultan and the entire Holy Land.

9. But with what end should this miracle be concluded? He knows in whose presence the moon does not shine and the stars are not pure, for whom nothing is difficult and without whom nothing can be possessed: Jesus Christ the Son of God, who with the Father and the Holy Spirit is God over all things, Blessed forever, amen.

10. I, brother Jerome of Prague, a recluse and hermit of the holy hermitage of Camaldoli, when in the previous year I came into the town of Galilee called Nazareth, found this miracle written in the Greek language. And I saw the previously mentioned Arabs. To a neophyte, therefore, have I written these things with confidence.

NOTES

1. I would like to express my thanks to Professor James J. John of Cornell University for all of his help and invaluable suggestions regarding the edition and translation of this text.

2. For a complete discussion of John-Jerome's life and work, see my "John-Jerome of Prague."

3. For a history of these motifs, see Daniel, *Islam and the West,* 87ff.

4. Ibid., 91 passim.

5. *Sermo Modernus ad Clerum Factus in concilio Universali in Civitate Sena,* in John-Jerome of Prague, Opera, 735.

6. *Tractatus contra Haereticos Bohemos,* in *John-Jerome of Prague, Opera,* 796.

7. Daniel, *Islam and the West,* 195–199.

8. *De Erroribus Graecorum,* in John-Jerome of Prague, *Opera,* 918–919.

9 For mention of this manuscript, see Kristeller, *Iter Italicum* 1:158; and Magheri-Cataluccio, *Biblioteca et Cultura a Camaldoli,* 232, 248. Neither author mentions the *Miraculum noviter factum* in their respective references to the manuscript.

10. I would like to thank the Biblioteca Nazionale Centrale of Florence for its gracious permission to edit and publish this text.

11. At this point the narration inexplicably switches to the present tense. I have regularized the tense structure by translating *vocat* as "summoned."

12. As in n. 11 above, I have regularized the tense structure by translating *rogat* as "begged."

IV. Islam in Western
Vernacular Literature

CHAPTER 10

Jacob van Maerlant on Muhammad and Islam

Geert H. M. Claassens[1]

Introduction

When the thirteenth-century Flemish poet Jacob van Maerlant tells us in his *Scolastica* how Abraham begets a son by Hagar, called Ishmael, he adds the following verses:

> His [= Ishmael's] lineage will come—as some have written—and subdue the world harshly with cruel deeds. They will hack priests to pieces and also rape the women. Their horses and their cattle too they will house in holy places. Thus they will avenge the sins of the foul Christian dogs.[2]

In these ten verses Maerlant presents succinctly a number of opinions on Islam that were current in medieval *christianitas*. First, he implies that the Muslims are descended from Ishmael, son of Abraham and his Egyptian concubine Hagar. Moreover, he mentions the violent nature of the Muslims. They will conquer the world, kill priests, violate women, and turn churches into stables. Finally, Maerlant indicates the historical position of Islam. It prospers as a divine punishment for the sinfulness of the Christians. Thus these verses—rooted in Genesis 16— reflect *in nuce* the medieval concept of the "divided world": the Christians, as the legitimate offspring of Abraham and Sarah, oppose the illegitimate offspring of Abraham and Hagar, the Muslims.

This concept of a "divided world" found a very tangible expression in the crusades.[3] But this conflict, prefigured in Genesis 16:12, was fought not only on the battlefield. Maerlant's statements stand in a widespread tradition of written polemic with Islam. (Written polemic does not imply that these texts were meant to be read by Muslims). In this controversy two main and a smaller tradition, interconnected on many points, can be distinguished. The first, surveyed by William W. Comfort and C. Meredith-Jones, and interpreted by Norman Daniel, includes the presentation of Islam in vernacular texts such as the *chansons de geste*.[4] General features of this tradition—which I shall call the "literary"—are the following: (1) The presentation of Islam as a fictitious counterpart of Christianity, describing the Saracens in terms of christian feudality; (2) The presented image of Islam is almost exclusively negative, based on prejudice instead of accurate and available information (The topos of the "good Saracen" is one of the few exceptions, but note that the good Saracen—of which Saladin [d. 1193] is a striking example—in vernacular literature is usually provided with an innate inclination towards Christianity.); (3) A complete lack of argumentation; (4) The imagery is totally subordinated to the story, the narrative being more important than the information; (5) The use of the vernacular as a medium, which strongly suggests that the intended audience is predominantly the nobility, cultivated, but *illiteratus*.

The second tradition, exemplarily described by—again—Norman Daniel, contains the learned polemic with Islam.[5] Propagated in discursive texts, usually—though not exclusively—written in Latin, I have called this tradition "clerical". At the formal level it is characterized by the predominant use of Latin and the application of a scholastic, theological argumentation in presenting the image of Islam. At the level of content we find a selective processing of the reliable information available on Islam (the polemic purpose determinating the choice and presentation of it), besides a processing of some prejudices known from the literary tradition.

The third tradition includes some pseudotheological "tracts," descriptions of the life of Muhammad. These poems (in Latin, one in French) draw on whatever information is available, good and bad. The pseudoclerical tradition shares features with both the clerical and the literary tradition, being a blend of narrative and argument (in Latin).[6]

This antithesis between the literary and clerical tradition —in reality less absolute than in my simplified representation— is clearly apparent from the way both traditions treat the question of the trinity. Ideas on the nature of God were (and still are!) an important bone of contention between Christianity and Islam. In the literary tradition, the Muslim denial of the Holy Trinity is ridiculed by attributing to Islam three gods: Muhammad is represented as an idol, accompanied by others such as Apollo, Baraton, Jupiter, Cahoun and so on. They usually appear in combinations of three: a negative reflection of the Christian trinity. Within the clerical tradition there is a clear awareness of Islam as a monotheistic religion: The learned Christian authors were well acquainted with the Muslim denial of the Holy Trinity; after all, this is one of the most difficult doctrines of Christianity.[7] The admitted correspondences between Christianity and Islam forced the learned authors to replace—at least partly—the undifferentiated invectives of the literary tradition with a scholastic argumentation. Persuading the opponent was as important an aim as painting a negative portrait.

What I want to demonstrate in this chapter is how in his work Jacob van Maerlant tries—at least to some extent—to bridge the gap between the literary and clerical traditions. It goes without saying that he has an unfavorable view of Islam. His position as a Christian author leaves him little scope for a nuanced approach, let alone a positive one.[8] Yet it can be established that Maerlant aims at a discourse on Islam and its founder that rises above the literary prejudices. Maerlant uses— at a remarkably early stage—the language (vernacular) and form (verses) of the literary tradition, but he uses it to depict an image of Islam that according to his own understanding is "scientific" and "truthful." The quotation from his *Scolastica* shows but a fragment of Maerlant's view of Islam. For a coherent and more comprehensive discourse we must turn to his *Spiegel Historiael*.[9] My main question is this: How are we to understand his view of Islam in its historical context? But before starting this discussion, it seems appropriate and necessary to introduce part of this historical context, that is, the life and works of Jacob van Maerlant.

Life and Works of Jacob van Maerlant

Little is known about the life of Jacob van Maerlant. And what we do know is to a large extent contested. Because this is not the place for a detailed discussion of all the opinions about his biography, I will confine myself to an elementary sketch.[10] Neither his year of birth, nor his year of death can be established with certainty. Yet a reasonable case can be made for his passing away in 1288 or shortly afterward. It is now generally assumed that he was born circa 1230. As far as we know he was Flemish by birth, originating from Bruxambacht, that is to say: the "Freedom of Bruges" ("het Brugse Vrije"). His oeuvre clearly indicates that he was well educated, even though his social station cannot be deduced exactly from this evidence. It is very likely that he received minor orders and held several positions as a clerk (*clerc*). In the late fifties of the thirteenth century Maerlant moves northward to the island of Voorne (in the estuary of the River Maas in the southern part of the county of Holland). He takes his name from the village Maerlant (near Brielle) on that island. He became sexton (*coster, custos*) of the local church of St. Peter (if *Coster* is not his family name), a profession that agrees perfectly with his activities as an author. During his stay in Maerlant he was possibly a tutor to young Floris V (d. 1296), count of Holland. Circa 1270 he returned to Flanders, to Damme near Bruges. There he earned his livelihood as a civil servant (at toll regulations) and continued his writing. Tradition has it that he was buried circa 1290 "under the bells" of the church of Our Lady in Damme (an indemonstrable theory).

Shadowy though the details of his life may be to us, we are fortunately better informed about his works.[11] Some of these we only know from references, made by Maerlant in other of his works, such as the *Sompniarijs* (presumably a book on dream interpretation) and a *vita* of St. Clare of Assisi. From his *Lapidarijs*, an early work on the mineral qualities of stones and for a long time thought lost, only a fragment remains. It is to be noted that Maerlant's authorship of some works still is a matter of dispute. In the following survey of his oeuvre I discuss the *Spiegel Historiael*—on which this article focuses—more in detail. The order of discussion is largely chronological.

The oldest surviving work is *Alexanders Geesten* (ca. 1260, 14,277 verses). Maerlant wrote this history of Alexander the Great at the commission of an unidentified noblewoman, whom he gives the pseudonym Gheile. The text is a translation and adaptation of the *Alexandreïs* of Walter of Châtillon. But it is not a slavish translation. Maerlant uses a broad range of additional sources, like the *Vulgate*, the *Historia Scholastica* of Petrus Comestor, Ovid's *Metamorphoses*, the *Disciplina Clericalis* of Petrus Alfonsi, the *Secreta Secretorum* and (probably) one of the same sources used by Honorius of Autun for his *De Imagine Mundi*. For Albrecht of Voorne, Maerlant wrote (in 1261) the *Merlijn*, a title which, in fact, encompasses two separate texts: the *Historie vanden Grale* (1,926 verses) and *Merlijns boeck* (8,472 verses), adaptations of Robert de Boron's *Joseph d'Arimathie* and *Roman de Merlin*. The *Torec* (ca. 1262) is Maerlant's second exercise in the field of Arthurian romance. This text (ca. 3,800 verses) has only been handed down to us in an abridged form, included in the vast *Lancelotcompilation* of The Hague. The *Historie van Troyen* (ca. 1264, 40,880 verses) renders the history of the Trojan War, complete from its preparatory stages to its aftermath, as is evident from the sources Maerlant used. His principal source was the *Roman de Troie* of Benoît of St. Maure, but additions from (among others) the *Achilleid* of Statius, the *Aeneid* of Virgil, Ovid's *Metamorphoses*, and his own *Alexanders Geesten* were meant to complete the history. The patron behind this work is not (yet) known, but it is likely that it was intended for an audience of noble men and women. Maerlant's "mirror of Princes," the *Heimelijkheid der Heimelijkheden* (ca. 1266, 2,158 verses), was possibly written on behalf of the young count of Holland, Floris V. This translation of the *Secreta Secretorum* of Pseudo-Aristotle, is one of those texts of which Maerlant's

authorship is disputed. *Der naturen bloeme* (ca. 1266, 16,670
verses) is the first bestiary in the vernacular, in which the books
of Aristotle on biology were assimilated. This does not imply
that Maerlant himself was familiar with the writings of Aristotle,
rather that he derived this knowledge from his immediate
source, the *Liber de natura rerum* of Thomas of Cantimpré. *Der
naturen bloeme*, in which Maerlant inserted quite a lot of social
criticism, was commissioned by the nobleman Nicolaas of Cats
(d. 1283). In 1271 Maerlant finished his *Scolastica*, an abridged
adaptation of Petrus Comestor's *Historia Scolastica*. To this book,
running to 27 thousand verses, he added an adaptation of
Flavius Josephus's *De bello Judaïco*. Maerlant considered this work
of almost 35 thousand verses as a unity. In all probability it was
commissioned by a noble patron and intended to serve an
audience of noble laymen (whereby one should understand
"laymen" to mean *illiterati*). Even though it is not a translation of
the Bible, the *Scolastica* marks the beginning of the
popularization of the Bible in the Dutch language. In the early
seventies, and having completed the *Scolastica*, Maerlant wrote
his *Sente Franciscus Leven* (10,545 verses). This fairly literal
translation of the *Legenda Maior* of St. Bonaventure is perhaps the
first *vita* of St. Francis in the vernacular. Maerlant wrote it at the
request of the *fratres minores* in Utrecht. During his career as a
poet, Maerlant composed several shorter stanzaic poems. These
lyrical texts (with a didactic aim) show a fervent devotion to
Mary and a strong critical attitude toward society. For the sake
of brevity I will not discuss these poems—of which date and
authorship are not undisputed—separately.

Maerlant's *magnum opus* is undoubtedly his *Spiegel
Historiael*.[12] He worked from 1283 until 1288 on this world-
chronicle, which is dedicated to count Floris V of Holland. The
main source is the *Speculum Historiale* of Vincent of Beauvais,[13]
but Maerlant consulted and absorbed many more sources,
among others the *Vulgate*, again the *Secreta Secretorum*, *De
Hormesta Mundi* of Orosius, *De origine et rebus gestis Getarum* of
Jordanes, two works of Martin of Braga (the *Liber de Moribus* and
De quattuor virtutibus cardinalibus), Paulus Diaconus's *Historia
Miscella*, the *Historia regum Brittanniae* of Geoffrey of Monmouth,
as well as the crusade chronicles of Albert of Aken and

(probably) William of Tyre. As it has come down to us, the *Spiegel Historiael* (ca. 91,000 verses), is not solely from the hand of Maerlant. He had planned a work in four parts (which he called *partïen*) and of these he himself wrote the first, the third, and three "books" of the fourth part. The second part, containing the years A.D. 54–367, he had skipped provisionally, but he never got back to writing it.[14] Apart from the lacuna of the second part and the remaining "books" of part four, Maerlant wrote a history from Creation through to the year 1113. The *Spiegel Historiael* was to be completed by two of his younger contemporaries, Philip Utenbroeke and Lodewijc van Velthem. The latter added a fifth part, containing the history up to the year 1316.

The part of the *Spiegel Historiael* on which this chapter focuses, was undoubtedly written by the master himself,[15] who throughout his oeuvre reveals himself as an exceptionally erudite and critical author of European stature.

The Image of Islam in the *Spiegel Historiael*

In book 8 of the third part of the *Spiegel Historiael* Maerlant devotes all of chapters 13 to 18 to Muhammad and Islam. But at the end of chapter 12 he gives a prelude to the discussion proper. He explains the rise of the Saracens as a political and military factor in the Middle East by connecting their appearance with the decline of the Byzantine empire under Heraclius (d. 641). Toward the end of his life, Heraclius indulged in theological speculations and became a supporter of monothelitism. Maerlant considers the triumphs of the Saracens over the Byzantines as a divine chastisement for Heraclius's unorthodoxy: "For God, on account of his heresy, had allowed his enemies to plunder him, and visited defeat upon him everywhere, in every battle."[16] In this way Maerlant acknowledges the Saracens as a part of history as God designed it. He subsequently emphasizes this by elucidating the origins of the Saracens: "For the Saracens that descended from the union of Abraham and Hagar, those are called Agarenes."[17] This explanation has the same background as the lines quoted previously from the *Scolastica:* Genesis 16:12, the image of the divided world. Maerlant did not derive this explanation from Vincent's *Speculum Historiale,* a fact that gives no cause for an in-depth search for its putative source: It is a commonplace from the encyclopedic tradition. Already in the *Etymologiae* of Isidore of Seville we find a similar explanation of the name "Saracens."[18] But Maerlant's phrasing of it is remarkable. From this we may infer that he was well aware of the name "Saracens" as a generic name for several Oriental peoples. Perhaps that is why he closes chapter 12 with an explicit reference to Ishmael as the progenitor of Muhammad. In this way he also sets the tone for the rest of his exposition: Muhammad belongs to the wrong part of the divided world, the camp of the enemy.

Maerlant's actual biography of Muhammad opens in chapter 13 with a reference to the profession of the Prophet: trade.[19] The frequent traveling that this profession entailed is adduced by several medieval authors as an explanation for Muhammad's knowledge of Christian and Jewish doctrine (both evidently present in the *Qur'ân*).[20] Maerlant also makes the connection between "traveling" and "knowledge", but he does not posit any explicit relationship of cause and effect:

> Often he made his way with camels to Egypt and he knew Jews and Christians too in many cities. And from them he learned in due time the New Law and the Old, in such measure that he could speak well about it, if necessary, on many an occasion.[21]

It is striking to see that in his biographical sketch Maerlant almost completely ignores the early life of Muhammad; he could have found ample data about it in the *Speculum Historiale.* Vincent of Beauvais did not hesitate to underpin his negative image of the Prophet with references to his humble parentage, orphanhood, and former idolatry.[22] Maerlant simply mentions his orphanhood with one word and his former idolatry gets two verses (to follow). Obviously he regarded Muhammad's occupation as a merchant—in Maerlant's days an accepted vocation, but morally not stainless[23]—in glaring enough contrast with his arrogant pretensions. To his mention of Muhammad's trade, he moreover adds that he was a famous and powerful magician, which might explain his extraordinary knowledge, but at the same time reeks of sulphur . . .

When traveling as a merchant to the land of Cordes, Muhammad makes acquaintance with Lady Cadigan. He courts her by flaunting his merchandise, but moreover, through cunning and magic, he leads her to believe that he is the Messiah, long expected by the Jews.[24] In this Maerlant sees the beginnings of Muhammad's career as a fraudulent founder of a new religion: "Then, at that place, he also started to invent new laws and he brought forward many a statement from the New Law and the Old one."[25] Maerlant severely discredits Muhammad by ascribing to him the pretension of being the Jewish Messiah. First, by so doing Muhammad implicitly denies an important aspect of the Christian faith, namely the belief in Christ's incarnation. Second, he thus ascribes to Muhammad the presumptuous claim of being a messenger from God. In imitation of Vincent of Beauvais, Maerlant proclaims a traditional opinion: Most of the learned authors knew and acknowledged that Muhammad did not claim to be (a descendant of) God, his only claim was that of divine prophethood.[26] This claim, meticulously refuted in his exposition, does not keep Maerlant from frequently referring to Muhammad as "the Prophet." Finally, Maerlant implies here, as elsewhere in his discussion, that the Qur'ân is a derivative of the Old and New Testaments, which disqualifies it as original divine revelation.[27] This supposedly new religious doctrine exerts a great attraction for Jews as well as Saracens, to that very day— according to Maerlant—the descendants of Ishmael call Muhammad the proclaimer of their faith. Lady Cadigan sees the increasing number of adherents and she too is convinced of God's working through Muhammad. She decides to have him as her husband, whereby Muhammad ultimately gains control over the Land of Cordes. When he subsequently rises to power over all Arabs, he steers toward an offensive war against Persia (which puts up a strong resistance).

Maerlant's account becomes more detailed when he describes Muhammad's epilepsy—which he calls "the great serious disease"[28]—and Lady Cadigan's reaction to it. When one day she watches Muhammad falling down in an epileptic fit, she sadly realises that she has married an unclean man. Muhammad succeeds in reassuring her:

> It is not the disease you think it is, that made me fall. It is the angel Gabriel, coming to me. For I am human; when I see him my carnality cannot bear his brightness; I must fall down.[29]

Lady Cadigan believes his words and so do the Arabs and Ishmaelites.[30] Maerlant explains their credulity as follows: "For they found in old books and believed that it was at God's bidding that His angel Gabriel told him [= Muhammad] his law, which he then wrote down."[31] By having Muhammad invoke the appearance of Gabriel in order to obscure his epilepsy, Maerlant gives a subtle reference to the improper use of "miracles," an evidently blasphemous act. Surely of equal interest are the last quoted verses, added by Maerlant to his source. In these he refers to a fundamental aspect of the controversy between Christianity and Islam. Several Christian authors include in their argument a plea against an alleged accusation (by Muslims) of having altered the text of the Bible, especially those places in the Gospels where Christ supposedly announced the coming of Muhammad.[32] Maerlant reduces this dispute to very simple proportions by using an ambiguous phrasing: the Middle Dutch *ouden viten* can be understood as "the Old Testament," but also as "old books" in an unspecific sense.

Chapter 14 relates the previous history of Muhammad's prophethood. The evil genius behind his aspirations is the Nestorian monk Sergius. In the relevant passage Vincent of Beauvais gives an aside on the nature of Nestorianism.[33] Maerlant amplifies this for the benefit of his audience:

> (Sergius) was a Nestorian monk. That is a special kind of Christian, who interpret the Bible in a wrong manner. They do not want to accept that Mary was the mother of God and (they believe) that her son was only human, not God and man at the same time.[34]

This Sergius, after being expelled from the Church, went to Mecca where he encountered Muhammad, who, like his fellow countrymen, was an idolator. This is significant for Maerlant's position as author: he only mentions Muhammad's status as an idolator, he does not equate Islam with idolatry; as is common practice in the literary tradition.[35] Sergius succeeded in converting Muhammad to Nestorianism.[36] Maerlant then describes the Jews' reaction to Sergius's meddling with Muhammad: Fearing that he would effectively convert Muhammad to Christianity, they offered themselves as his supporters, thus hoping to gain control over him. This part of the exposition might be intended to explain the presence of Talmudic influences in the Qur'ân. Maerlant, however, explicitly states that the Qur'ân was written under direction of Sergius: "By this Nestorian monk his book, called Alcoraen, in which his law is written, was first given to the Arabs."[37] In essence Maerlant's view is the same as Vincent of Beauvais's,[38] although at a single glance it is evident that he shortens and simplifies Vincent of Beauvais's argument strongly, a valid observation for the whole of Maerlant's discussion. He also changes the internal order of his source text, a point to which I consider in the next paragraph.

In chapter 15 Maerlant continues his biography of Muhammad, following the Sergius episode. After Muhammad finishes his "education" by Sergius, he starts to cheat peasants and other simple folk. The use of the verb "to cheat" is significant, for it betrays his assessment of Muhammad's mission. The main point in this deceit, according to the poet, is Muhammad's false prophethood:

> And he said that he was a prophet, sent to them at God's bidding and for their salvation, in order that he might sufficiently soften the Old Law—which the Jews found too oppressive—and thereafter the New Law—which similarly the Christians found burdensome—so that they (these laws) would be mild enough for men to bear.[39]

Maerlant combines the severe accusation of falsely claiming to be God-sent with the equally blasphemous softening of Jewish and Christian doctrine that was traditionally attributed to Muhammad. This alleviation of the religious and moral prescriptions of both religions may well be intended as an explanation for the tremendous rise of Islam among the simple folk (though not exclusively among them): Moral criticism is thus incorporated into an effort to explain the Islam as an historical phenomenon.

The poet then continues with a description of Muhammad's miracles. First, he has a trained dove pick a grain from his ear, thus suggesting that the dove came whispering the divine word to him. Second, Muhammad fixes his law (the Qur'ân) between the horns of an equally well trained bull. At a public meeting the bull appears as an envoy from God, offering the Qur'ân to Muhammad. The third miracle consists of barrels filled with milk and honey, buried beforehand on a meeting place, in order that the Prophet can point them out at the proper moment:

> And he said that those who received his law would always abound in earthly goods and be satisfied. And because he wanted them to believe his words, he thereupon had them dig where they would find the milk and honey, and he said that was a sign.[40]

Such descriptions of Muhammad's "fake miracles," designed to contest his prophethood and expose it as a deception, are quite common in the medieval criticism of the Prophet.[41] Nevertheless, the fact that the Qur'ân denies that Muhammad had come to perform miracles was well-known to many medieval authors, as Maerlant himself admits in the next chapter (see below). We cannot with certainty accuse him of withholding evidence that would reflect favorably on Muhammad: Such information is also lacking in the corresponding passage in Vincent of Beauvais's *Speculum*.

This presentation of Muhammad's miracles is part of a complex argumentation against his prophethood, a threefold way to judge prophethood or saintliness in general: A person claiming to be God-sent must lead a pure life, must perform valid miracles and must always speak the truth.[42] Maerlant uses two of these touchstones: Muhammad's miracles are "prefab tricks" and by pretending they are real miracles he shows himself to be a liar. The third criterion, purity of life, plays a prominent role throughout Maerlant's biography of Muhammad, either explicitly or implicitly, but always in a self-evident way.

Following the description of the false miracles Maerlant portrays Muhammad as a leader of brigands and robbers of the lowest kind. One detail here merits our attention: according to the poet, Muhammad was wounded in one of his raids. This is perhaps a dim reflection of the (historical) campaign against Uḥud (625), in which the Prophet was indeed wounded in losing a battle.[43] Be that as it may, it is important that Muhammad's human vulnerability is always emphasized in the polemic literature of the Middle Ages[44] and Maerlant, too, alludes to it, implying that the Prophet enjoys no divine protection. The poet finishes this chapter with a brief notice of the Muslim paradise and the evil (and revealing!) death that befell Muhammad, points which he elaborates at a later stage of his exposition. In the closing verses of this chapter, we read the simple mention of Muhammad's orphanhood, which—as I stated before—plays a far more important part in Vincent of Beauvais's *Speculum* as an underpinning of the negative image of Muhammad.

Chapter 16 is entitled "On his morals" and it opens with a reference to Muhammad's age. He is supposed to have lived fifty-three years, forty of which he spent in Mecca. With a classical *brevitas*-formula, Maerlant avoids the obligation of giving a full record of Muhammad's crimes. He contents himself with a short notice on the Prophet's murderous nature, only to continue in a more prolific way with describing his lewdness and voluptuousness:

> During his life he also lusted after all women, so that in his writings he boasted about his unclean nature: he himself had the (sexual) strength of 40 men, and he said that his greatest pleasures were obviously beautiful women and fine aromatic herbs. These are the words of a boorish prophet.[45]

The last quoted verse shows clearly that Maerlant deems such behavior to be unfitting for a prophet. This statement, too, belongs to the previously-mentioned set of standards commonly used to evaluate Muhammad's prophethood: A truly God-sent man leads a pure life, in which there is no room for voluptuousness professed and performed in public.[46] This is not the last word on Muhammad's relationships with the opposite sex. Without naming her explicitly Maerlant relates how Muhammad lent his wife to another man, adding laconically: "There are enough women to be had, and he is not a wise man who attaches himself too much to one woman."[47]

Following Vincent of Beauvais, Maerlant also reproduces Muhammad's self-justification (taken from the Qur'ân, Sura 33: 50–51): By divine revelation Muhammad had been told that his wife would not be held culpable for this organized adultery.[48] But he immediately negates this justification by adding that Muhammad had been lying when he said this, just as he had lied when he claimed that he was able to understand the language of wolves and other animals.

After discussing Muhammad's immoral behavior, Maerlant turns to the attempted assassination of the Prophet. A Jewish women allegedly offers him a poisoned leg of mutton for dinner. Muhammad, his suspicions having been aroused, has a friend eat first. When this man dies instantaneously, Muhammad pretends that he had been warned by the mutton itself. Thus, he claims to be the benefactor of supernatural protection. In his *Speculum*, Vincent of Beauvais sensibly exposes this attempt to lay claim to the gift of providence. Maerlant, with his feeling for "common sense", renders it as follows: "If it was true that he heard this warning, why then did nobody else? And why did not he prevent his friend from touching the food?"[49] This argumentation contra Muhammad is like a double-edged sword: He pretends to have supernatural powers (which is evidently not true) and in order to state his claim he unblushingly sacrifices a friend (which is inhuman).[50]

Next comes a statement by Muhammad—presented as a quotation from the Qur'ân—on his mission on earth:

> This false prophet Mahumet wrote in his Alcoraen: "I was not sent to this world to be known by miracles. On the contrary: I was sent with a sword. Whoever considers it beneath himself to receive what I prescribe, he should be killed."[51]

Whereas Christianity (ideally) only wants to convert by the Word, Muhammad does not hesitate to preach with an iron tongue. The history of the Crusades, however, shows that this objection against Islam is not altogether justified.[52] In this quotation we also meet an example of the generally current, but incorrect opinion that Muhammad himself wrote the Qur'ân.[53] The chapter closes with the statement that Muhammad in his lifetime married fifteen noblewomen and two women of common parentage, but besides these he had concubines at will.

Chapter 17 is largely devoted to the wordly ambitions of Muhammad. Maerlant starts by offering his audience a sort of excuse: "It is a shame to tell a long story about this thief, but this illegitimate tyrant destroyed the country of Persia, such great power he accumulated."[54] Then he speaks again—and this time more thoroughly—about Muhammad's conquest of Persia. This part of the biography is clearly unhistorical: Persia was not conquered and incorporated into the Muslim empire until the forties of the seventh century. At this place Maerlant seems to use a different source, which I have not been able to trace.[55] These worldly ambitions do not suit a prophet: The conquest of Persia and the incursions in the Byzantine empire clearly belong to the outrages of Muhammad, as Maerlant explicitly states at the end of this episode: "Thus the Roman empire was miserably mutilated by Mahumet. His base and vicious deeds and his great atrocities are too grievous to tell."[56] With these verses Maerlant approaches the end of his biographical sketch. He repeats that Muhammad reached the age of fifty-three and then fell victim to a serious disease.[57] Maerlant does not reveal exactly which disease killed Muhammad,[58] but he follows Vincent of Beauvais closely in his description of Muhammad's last days. Muhammad supposedly orders his followers not to bury him for three days after his death, because on the third day he will be carried to heaven. Completely robbed of his senses by his illness, he dies after a sickbed of fourteen days. "His body swelled enormously and death made his little finger bend backwards. His friends kept him (unburied) for three days as he had ordered, and they washed and dressed him."[59] His friends obeyed his commands, but after three days the corpse started to stink. Expectant onlookers awaiting Muhammad's ascension flew into a rage and, having disrobed the corpse, tossed it ignominiously aside. It was buried by one of Muhammad's cousins. To the medieval audience this announcement of an ascension after three days must have sounded very blasphemous indeed: Muhammad identifies himself with Christ! The swelling of the corpse immediately after his death and the distortion of one of the little fingers, must have been a proof of his mendacity. That his body was not carried heavenward, but buried (accompanied by decay and stench), was only to be expected: false prophets do not ascend to heaven.

Chapter 18 constitutes the last part of Maerlant's exposition on Muhammad and Islam and it contains an anthology of Muslim doctrine, derived from the *Speculum Historiale*. The following announcement of the contents of the chapter is remarkable: "Listen to a part of his law, which was issued by the devil, containing neither reason nor grace, full of base acts."[60] Even though Maerlant never tries to explain Muhammad's prophethood in terms of diabolical influence, he here nevertheless posits that Muhammad's law, as written in the Qur'ân, was drawn up by the devil and thus void of reason (*ratio, logos*) and (divine) grace.[61]

The first item of Muslim doctrine treated by Maerlant is the precept of circumcision. According to Maerlant, Muhammad only ordered circumcision in order to lay claim to an apparently legitimate descent from Abraham. But the poet immediately defuses this claim by reminding the audience that Muhammad was a bastard, and descendant of the bastard Ishmael. The precept of circumcision was incorporated "[i]nto his book *Alcoraen*, in which all his commandments are written. And he said in public that his law was so sacred, that neither devil nor man was able to make up such a law."[62]

Initially Maerlant does not comment on the claim Muhammad makes to a divine origin of the Qur'ân by denying it a human or satanic origin. He only adds that according to Muhammad the Qur'ân was so holy that a mountain would bend for it. Moreover, Muhammad presumably stated that his name had been written on God's throne before Creation, a claim to the status of divine missionary which Vincent of Beauvais refutes with an elaborate scholastical argument. Maerlant, in his turn, is very succinct: "This is undoubtedly nonsense."[63] He proceeds with a discussion of the precepts, as laid down in the Qur'ân, for fasting—here represented as a simple imitation of the Christian practice—the ordered times of prayer, and the times of purification. The prohibition of the consumption of pork, on the other hand, has been copied from the Jews. With this Maerlant implicitly returns to a criticism of the derivative character of

Muslim doctrine: By putting Christian and Jewish tenets together, Muhammad created a "religion" that is not austere and which utterly lacks divine origin. At this point Maerlant mentions the Muslim marital practice. Following Vincent of Beauvais he gives a fairly accurate representation of the facts:

> And he [= Muhammad] gave every man permission—if he wanted to and thought it correct—to divorce his wife. But this man should be prohibited from returning to the same woman again, unless she had (meanwhile) been married to another man.[64]

Maerlant—like Vincent of Beauvais—adds no criticism to the precept, even though this codification of marriage is evidently in contravention to Christian precepts. Could it be that Maerlant was restraining himself here because the European nobility left a great deal to be desired in the realm of morality and fidelity in their marital relations? Polygamy, permitted by Islam, occurred only seldom, if at all, among the European nobility, but the large number of noble bastards revealed a great deal about their conjugal ethics. And the frequent annulments of noble marriages, for example, because of too high a degree of consanguinity, cast a slur on European marital practice. Or was this Maerlant's subtle and oblique way of criticizing his own audience for such practices? Whichever this may be, he next speaks about the Muslim paradise. He denies it every spiritual quality, even though the clerical tradition possessed enough sound information on the matter.[65] According to Maerlant, Muhammad's presentation of paradise in the Qur'ân shows that it "is nothing but eating and drinking and stinking in lechery for all eternity."[66] Muslim hell was, in Maerlant's opinion, meant primarily as a place of punishment for the infidel. It is nothing but eternal heat and the only food offered to the inhabitants is the bitter paste from a tree called Assatum.[67] It is here that we again encounter Maerlant the natural scientist. In his *Der naturen bloeme* he had written extensively on flora and fauna, and from his phrasing here I gather that he did not know this tree Assatum. The suggestion, then, is that it was an invention of Muhammad.

He practiced such lies and tricks until such time as he
died, a faithless man. And by means of murder and
robbery he gathered an enormous number of followers,
because he gave every man part of the spoils. This devil
pitifully damaged Heraclius's empire with his incursions,
as I will tell you clearly in the history which follows.[68]

With these verses Maerlant concludes his exposition on
Muhammad and Islam, in order to return to the history of the
Byzantine empire. It is remarkable that in his summarizing
words he calls Muhammad a devil. I doubt whether he really
aims at identifying the Prophet with Satan. It seems that he uses
the word in a rather general and superficial way to indicate
Muhammad's malice, so apparent from the previous verses.

Maerlant's Strategy as an Author

As the analysis clearly shows, Maerlant's exposition on
Muhammad and Islam is firmly rooted in the clerical tradition.
As far as the data are concerned, he follows Vincent of Beauvais
closely, bringing forward hardly any new information on the
subject. The *Speculum Historiale* itself has (at least for Maerlant's
exposition) two main sources. By drawing on the *Historia
ecclesiastica* of Hugh of Fleury it incorporates parts of the famous
Byzantine *Chronographia* of Theophanes.[69] But Vincentius also
made good use of the *corpus Cluniacensis,* a collection of Arab
texts in a Latin translation, which was commissioned by Petrus
Venerabilis in the forties of the twelfth century. This collection
includes the first Latin translation of the Qur'ân, but also a
translation of the *Risālat* 'Abdillāh ibn-Ismā'īl al-Hāshimi ila
'Abd-al-Masīḥ ibn-Isḥāq al-Kindi wa-Risālat al-Kindi ila al-
Hāshimi, an apology for Christianity attributed to 'Abd al-Masīḥ
al-Kindî (d. ca. 870), but more likely the work of an anonymous
author of the tenth century.[70] This text, translated by Petrus of
Toledo and Petrus of Poitiers, and in Latin called the *Epistola
Saraceni* and *Rescriptum Christiani,* forms with the Qur'ân-
translation the foundation of the clerical tradition.

This background of the *Speculum Historiale* and
subsequently the *Spiegel Historiael* does not imply that neither

text has anything in common with the pseudoclerical tradition. With it they share some themes, for example, Muhammad's epilepsy, the role of the (Nestorian) monk and the archangel Gabriel and the bull carrying the Qur'ân.[71]

Maerlant chooses the *Speculum* as his primary source, because he regards Vincent of Beauvais as an author of great veracity and erudition.[72] That is not to say that he does not make full use of his own knowledge and critical capacities, as is apparent from his comments on the tree Assatum.[73] Moreover, he has his own motives and aims in adapting the *Speculum Historiale:* His text is far from being a literal translation of the source. In Maerlant's technique of translating and adapting, two aspects are of particular interest: (1) He abbreviates Vincent of Beauvais's discussion considerably, and (2) He rearranges the data provided by his source.

To start with the first aspect, Maerlant omits almost all of the scholarly background information in Vincent of Beauvais's exposition. When, for instance, the latter goes into the historical context of the first Latin translation of the Qur'ân,[74] Maerlant remains completely silent on this topic. He also neglects scholastically formed (theological) argumentation in his source. Vincent of Beauvais devotes four full chapters to an elaborate *refutatio* of the Qur'ân, examining its genesis, as well as its stylistic and compositional qualities.[75] Maerlant gives only a straightforward rejection of the Qur'ân (aforementioned).[76]

The second aspect of Maerlant's compositional technique concerns his restructuring of the exposition as he encountered it in his source. In my opinion Maerlant aims at writing a narrative text, focusing on the biography of Muhammad and the (implicit) argumentation against Islam resulting from it. An example, Vincent of Beauvais tells us the story of the Nestorian monk Sergius in 23, LI of his *Speculum*. This is the twelfth chapter of his exposition, and the life of Muhammad has at that point already been described from the cradle to the grave. For Vincent of Beauvais the Sergius episode is something like a prelude to his refutation of the Qur'ân. Maerlant, on the contrary, puts the Sergius episode in the second of his six chapters on Muhammad and Islam. He admits that Sergius exerted a strong influence on the realization of the Qur'ân, but his chief aim is obviously to integrate this episode into his biographical sketch of Muhammad, which is thus created out of elements scattered throughout Vincent of Beauvais's biography.

These adaptational techniques are not an end in themselves, but serve a well-considered purpose on Maerlant's part. These adaptations indicate that Maerlant wanted to offer his audience a fluid tale, a narrative with power of persuasion; edifying, veracious, based on a reliable source, but *not* academic. This working toward a narrative text is also apparent from the frequent use of direct speech (compared to the *Speculum Historiale)*, a stylistic device to enliven an exposition known from classical historiography. The polemic import of Maerlant's discussion results from the facts described, not from a sophisticated commentary on these facts, which his audience probably would not understand. That audience, primarily the cultivated but *illiteratus* nobility, asked for an intelligible and transparent story. As was the case for his adaptation of Comestor's *Historia Scolastica*,[77] Maerlant adjusts his literary strategies to the worldview of his audience, which is more accustomed to vernacular texts of the epic genre than to discursive texts in Latin. In this respect Maerlant seems to be an exceptional case among medieval authors writing on Muhammad and Islam in the vernacular.

Maerlant's Exposition in its Historical Context

In the representation of Muhammad's biography by Christian authors of the Middle Ages, the question of Muhammad's divine mission or divine inspiration plays—as we have seen—an important role. Norman Daniel remarks that, with respect to this question, "the popular writers tended to be indifferent; they were certainly more concerned to attract and amuse than to be academic."[78] Maerlant undoubtedly belongs among these "popular writers," in the sense that he addresses an audience of *illiterati*: It is quite obvious that he is not aiming to offer an academic discourse. But that popularizing implies an indifference toward the reliability and veracity of his exposition—and that is how I understand Norman Daniel's statement—does not in my view apply to Jacob van Maerlant. He does not aim at amusing his audience, he is popularizing in the true meaning of the word: offering truthful, scientifically founded information which is understandable and persuasive.

In this respect Maerlant's work appears at a very early stage of history. In the thirteenth century the information on Muhammad and Islam, as transmitted in vernacular texts, is almost exclusively "literary" by nature. That is to say: it is based on prejudices which only contain a paper-thin nucleus of (correct) insight into Islam. In the *chansons de geste*, the pseudoclerical tradition, and similar texts, we mainly encounter a "judging by appearances," which very often goes as far as describing Muhammad and his followers as awfully disfigured, almost inhuman creatures.[79] This imagery is completely subordinated to the narrative structures of the texts. Maerlant, on the other hand, takes the available scientific knowledge concerning Muhammad and Islam as a starting point, and then looks for an "epic" narrative structure in which to present it. Maerlant thus moves from the clerical to the literary tradition, but he treats the data of his source with respect and only looks for a different textual form in which the explicit scholarly refutation is replaced by an implicit narrative refutation.

Just how early is Maerlant's appearance, in fact? He has his chapters on Muhammad and Islam firmly embedded in a vernacular world chronicle, thus giving the phenomenon a (negative) place in history. If we look at other vernacular (world) chronicles in the thirteenth century, we must—again—conclude that Maerlant is among the first to give a serious exposition on Islam and its founder. Within the sphere of English, French, and Scandinavian languages there is nothing that can compare with Maerlant's work.[80] In the area of the German language we find three vernacular (world) chronicles in or before the thirteenth century, but none of these has a presentation of Muhammad and Islam comparable with Maerlant's.[81]

The only vernacular chronicle that has features similar to Maerlant's on the subject of Muhammad and Islam, is the *Primera Crónica General de España*, commissioned by Alfonso X (1221–1284) "the Wise," king of Castile and León. This medieval Spanish chronicle, begun in 1270 as the *Estoria de España* and later continued as the *Primera Crónica General*, contains an extensive biography of Muhammad and some general information on Islam.[82] It is, however, completely interwoven with general Spanish/European history. Some familiar themes also appear in this chronicle, for example, Muhammad obscuring his epilepsy by invoking the appearance of Gabriel, but it is nevertheless obvious that other sources were used.[83] While giving a lot of comparable information, the Spanish chronicle differs somewhat in tone with the *Spiegel Historiael*, but then it was written for a Spanish king who tried to rule a country with a strong Muslim population. To avoid a harsh polemic tone was surely in the king's interest, whereas Maerlant, working in the Low Countries, was not restricted in the same way.

Jacob van Maerlant and his Spanish colleague are exponents of what R.W. Southern has called "the century of reason and hope" in Christian-Muslim relationships during the Middle Ages.[84] The crusader-kingdom in the Holy Land and the diffuse Arab-European borderline on Sicily and the Iberian peninsula offered an opportunity to acquire firsthand knowledge of Islam, albeit this knowledge was determined by local circumstances and the polemic relationship with Islam. This learning about the other half of the divided world was subservient to the intellectual struggle against it, and restricted to the learned, the *litterati*. Maerlant, though living far away from the Arab-European borderlines, unlocked this knowledge— knowledge which was, from our point of view, far from accurate, but which his critical mind deemed truthful—for an audience of *illiterati*. It is exactly this that makes his position in the history of medieval Christian perception of Islam a very interesting one.

NOTES

1. I would like to express my gratitude to Paul W.M. Wackers and John V. Tolan for their critical remarks, to Eileen C.M. Meyer for her help in consulting Vincent of Beauvais, and to David F. Johnson for his

corrections in the English text. The author is Lektor für Niederländisch at the Rheinische Friedrich-Wilhelms-Universität of Bonn, Germany.

2. Jacob van Maerlant, *Rijmbijbel*, vv. 1739–1748 (pp. 43–44):

Sijn [= Ishmaels] gheslachte dat sal comen
—Dus eist bescreven van hem somen—
Hier naer entie werelt duinghen
Harde seere met fellen dinghen.
Papen sulsi te sticken houwen
Ende vercrachten oec die vrouwen.
Hare parde ende hare besten mede
Sulsi stallen in helegher stede.
Aldus sulsi wreken die sonden
Van den vulen kerstinen honden.

Punctuation and some normalizations in spelling are mine. Throughout this article I print the translated verses from Jacob van Maerlant as prose.

3. The crusades contributed greatly to the formation of this concept. There is an enormously expanding use of the term *christianitas*—indicating the good half of this divided world—in the Latin chronicles of the crusades, from the twelfth century onward. See Jan van Laarhoven, "Chrétienté et croisade," 27–43.

4. Comfort, "The Literary Rôle of the Saracens in the French Epic," 628–659; Meredith-Jones, "The Conventional Saracen of the Songs of Geste," 201–225; Daniel, *Heroes and Saracens*.

5. Daniel, *Islam and the West*.

6. This small group includes Embrico of Mainz, *Vita Mahumeti* (ca. 1034–1041?), Walter of Compiègne's *Otia de Machomete* (ca. 1130) and its translation into Old French by Alexander du Pont, the *Roman de Mahomet* (1258), and the Latin *Vita* attributed to Adelphus. These texts are discussed by John Tolan in the introduction to this volume.

7. Cf. Daniel, *Islam and the West*, 175–184.

8. Maerlant lived in the thirteenth century, an epoch in which the crusades still belonged to current events. It is not until well into the fourteenth century that literature in the vernacular manages to treat the Christian–Muslim antithesis in a less black-and-white manner, e.g., in some works of Langland and Gower, as well as in Andrea da Barberino's *Guerrino il Meschino* (as Gloria Allaire shows in her article in the present volume).

9. In other works as well, Maerlant comments on Islam, but not in a systematic way (as in the *Spiegel Historiael)*; therefore these works will not be drawn into my argument.

10. This outline is based on Van Oostrom, "Maerlant tussen Noord en Zuid. Contouren van een biografie," 185–216. This article gives an outstanding and clear synthesis of all the issues concerning Maerlant's biography, with comprehensive bibliographical references.

11. Still a good general introduction to Maerlant's oeuvre is Te Winkel, *Maerlant's werken beschouwd als spiegel van de 13de eeuw*. From the vast body of studies, published since Te Winkel's pioneering book I mention Peeters, "Nieuwe inzichten in de Maerlantproblematiek," 249–285; and Van Oostrom, "Jacob van Maerlant: een herwaardering," 190–197, The latter is preparing a new general study on the subject.

12. This vast text is divided in parts ("partiën"), books, and chapters, which have separate line numberings. I will refer to the text thus: Maerlant, *Spiegel Historiael*, III (= part), viii (= book), 13 (= chapter), 1–13 (= verses); references to the pages of the edition are, for brevity's sake, as follows: (vol. 2, p. 75).

13. Even though it is well-known that the *Speculum*-tetralogy of the learned Dominican is in fact the work of a team of authors under his direction, I shall designate it—again for brevity's sake—as the work of a single author. References are made in the following manner: Vincent of Beauvais, *Speculum Historiale*, 23 (= liber), LX (= caput) (919) (=page number of Beller's edition).

14. It is argued that Maerlant died before he could finish the second part and the remaining "books" of the fourth part. Cf. Te Winkel, *Maerlant's werken*, 75–76. The reason for skipping the second part is perhaps the little interest which the commissioner, Floris V, had for hagiography, the second part being dominated by the lives of the saints.

15. Cf. *Spiegel historiael* 1:viii–liii. See also Te Winkel, *Maerlant's werken*, 72–75.

16. Maerlant, *Spiegel Historiael*, III, viii, 12, vv. 55–58 (vol. 2, p. 74):

> Want God, omme sijn ongeloven,
> Lietene sine vianden roven,
> Ende gaf hem in elker zide
> Onzeghe in allen stride.

Cf. Vincent of Beauvais, *Speculum Historiale*, 23, XXXIX (912).

17. Maerlant, *Spiegel Historiael*, III, viii, 12, vv. 59–61 (vol. 2, p. 74):

> Want die Sarrasine, die quamen

> Van Abrahame ende Agar te samen,
> Diemen heet Agarene.

18. Isidore of Seville, *Etymologiarum* IX, I, ii, 57.

19. In chapter 13 Maerlant follows his source, Vincent of Beauvais, fairly closely, *Speculum Historiale*, 23, XXXIX (Beller, 912–913).

20. Cf. Daniel, *Islam and the West*, p. 88. Daniel poses this as an "alternative explanation" for this knowledge of Muhammad, whereas other explanations posit renegade monks and insidious Jews as the source. But, as Maerlant's exposition already proves, it is rather a complementary explanation: in chapter 14 Maerlant traces Muhammad's knowledge back to his being influenced by the Nestorian monk Sergius.

21. Maerlant, *Spiegel Historiael*, III, viii, 13, vv. 5–12 (vol. 2, p. 75):

> Dicken voer hi sine vaert
> Met kemelen te Egypten waert,.
> Ende was bekent in meneger stede
> Met Jueden ende met Kerstinen mede,
> Ende leerde mettem, alst sijn soude,
> Die niewe wet ende die oude,
> Dat hire wel af spreken conde,
> Alst was te doene, ter meneger stonde.

22. Vincent of Beauvais, 23, XLI (913). On the negative implications of Muhammad's descent and youth see Daniel, *Islam and the West*, 84–87.

23. Cf. Goerevitsj, "De koopman," 241–279, Goerevitsj convincingly argues that by the thirteenth century the merchant was accepted as a necessary part of urban society, but the vocation was always under suspicion: There was ample opportunity for unfair profits and usury. The nobility saw the accumulating wealth in the hands of the merchant class as a threat to the traditional order of society.

24. Cf. Daniel, *Islam and the West*, 53–55.

25. Maerlant, *Spiegel Historiael*, III, viii, 13, vv. 41–44 (vol. 2, p. 75):

> Doe begonsti daer ter stede
> Nieuwe wette veinsen mede
> Ende brochte orconde menechfoude
> Uter nieuwer wet ende uter oude.

26. Cf. Daniel, *Islam and the West*, 18–19.

27. Many medieval authors writing in Latin treat this dependency in an explicit and more elaborate way; cf. Daniel, *Islam and the West,* 48–49.

28. "Den groten evele sere," Maerlant, *Spiegel Historiael*, III, viii, 13, vv. 67 (vol. 2, p. 75).

29. Maerlant, *Spiegel Historiael*, III, viii, 13, vv. 72–79 (vol. 2, p. 75):

> En es niet sulc ongemac
> Als du wanes, daer ic af vel.
> Het doet dinghel Gabriel,
> Als hi comet tote mie;
> Want ic bem mensche: alsicken zie,
> Sone mach mine vleschelijchede
> Niet ghedoghen sine claerhede,
> Ic en moet ter neder vallen.

30. In imitation of Vincent of Beauvais, Maerlant here makes an incorrect distinction between Arabs and Ishmaelites. This shows that he—even though he was aware of the generic character of the name "Saracens"—had no clear insight in the ethnic composition of the Oriental population.

31. Maerlant, *Spiegel Historiael*, III, viii, 13, vv. 84–88 (vol. 2, p. 76):

> Want men vant in ouden viten
> Ende waende, dat God selve bevel
> Sinen inghel Gabriel,
> Hem te seggene sine wet,
> Ende hise in brieve hadde gheset.

32. This aspect of the Christian-Muslim controversy is elaborately treated in Daniel, *Islam and the West*, 53–55.

33. Vincent of Beauvais, 23, LI (917): "erant enim haeretici Nestoriani, qui dicunt Mariam non peperisse Deum, sed hominem tantum."

34. Maerlant, *Spiegel Historiael*, III, viii, 14, vv. 6–12 (vol 2, II, p. 76):

> Dat was een moene Nestoriaen:
> Dats ene maniere van Kerstinen lieden,
> Die de scrifture qualike bedieden,
> Die niet en willen lijen das,
> Dat Maria Gods moeder was
> Ende haer sone was mensce alleene,
> Niet God ende mensche gemeene.

35. Cf. Comfort, "The Literary Role," 639–641 and Meredith-Jones, "The Conventional Saracen," 204–208.

36. That Nestorianism in particular was considered to be an important source of Islam is hardly surprising: The adherents of this current in Christianity shared with Islam the disbelief in the dual nature

of Christ. For them, as well as for the Muslims, Christ was only human. By linking Nestorianism with Islam two birds were killed with one stone: Both were portrayed in an unfavorable way.

37. Maerlant, *Spiegel Historiael*, III, viii, 14, vv. 55–58 (vol. 2, p. 76)

> Bi desen moenc Nestoriaen
> Wart sijn bouc, die heet Alcoraen,
> Daer sine wet in staet gescreven,
> Eerst den Arabienen gegeven.

38. Cf. Vincent of Beauvais, 23, LI (916).

39. Maerlant, *Spiegel Historiael*, III, viii, 15, vv. 9–18 (vol. 2, p. 76):

> Ende seide: hi ware een prophete,
> Hem ghesent bi Gods gehete
> Ende thaerre salicheit geset,
> Omme dat hi die oude wet,
> Die den Jueden was te zwaer,
> Entie niewe wet daer naer,
> Die den Kerstinen te swaer was mede,
> So gevougelike sachten dede,
> Dat si waren also sochte,
> Dat mense wel ghedragen mochte.

Cf. Vincent of Beauvais, 23, XL (913).

40. Maerlant, *Spiegel Historiael*, III, viii, 15, vv. 51–57 (vol. 2, p. 77):

> Ende seide: die sine wet ontfingen,
> Si souden van erdschen dingen
> Ghenouch hebben ende wesen sat.
> Ende omme dat si souden geloven dat,
> Dede hise graven indien stonden,
> Daer si melc ende honech vonden
> Ende seide, dat dat lijctekijn ware.

Cf. Vincent of Beauvais, 23, XL (913).

41. Cf. Daniel, *Islam and the West*, 32.

42. Ibid., 68.

43. For this campaign see Saunders, *A History of Medieval Islam*, 28–29.

44. Cf. Daniel, *Islam and the West*, 91–92.

45. Maerlant, *Spiegel Historiael*, III, viii, 16, vv. 25–34 (vol. 2, p. 78):

> Oec was hi van sinen live
> Onghier up alle wive,
> So dat hi in sire scrifturen

> Beroemde der onreenre naturen,
> Dat hi alleene hadde daer an
> Die macht wel van XL man,
> Ende seide sine genouchte ware
> In scone wiven openbare,
> Ende in cruden die wel roken.
> Dit sijn dorpre propheten sproken.

Cf. Vincent of Beauvais, 23, XLIV (914).

46. The words which Maerlant puts into the mouth of Muhammad (vss. 31–33), belong to the traditional stock of statements ascribed to the Prophet. In his reproduction of Muhammad's excuse for his lechery, Maerlant (in imitation of Vincent of Beauvais) is one of the more severe judges of the Prophet: Originally this statement consisted of three elements (as e.g., in the work of Petrus Paschasius): "[I]t is given to me to delight in three things, the first, unguents, the second, women, and the third, prayer" (quoted in Daniel, *Islam and the West*, 102). Maerlant omits the "prayer," a point in favor of Muhammad.

47. Maerlant, *Spiegel Historiael*, III, viii, 16, vv. 38–40 (vol. 2, p. 78):

> Men vint genouch wijf,
> Ende dat ennes gheen wijs man,
> Diere te vele sins leghet an."

Maerlant did not derive these verses directly from Vincent of Beauvais. Cf. Vincent of Beauvais, 23, XLIV (914).

48. Cf. Vincent of Beauvais, 23, XLIV (914).

49. Maerlant, *Spiegel Historiael*, III, viii, 16, vv. 61–64 (vol. 2, p. 78):

> Oft waer was dat hi horde dit wort,
> Waer omme en heefse el niemen gehort,
> Ende twine haddi sinen vrient benomen,
> Dat hire niet an ware comen?

Cf. Vincent of Beauvais, *Speculum Historiale*, 23, XLVI (915):

> Vellem scire utrum ipse solus, an omnes qui cum eo aderant, vocem illius scapulae audierint: si enim ille solus audivit, quare socium suum inde comedere permisit, si vero omnes audierunt, mirum est quomodo ille comedere ausus fuit, nisi forte de suo propheta sperans, quod etiam mortuum resuscitare potuerit.

NB: Vincent of Beauvais's criticism is more elaborate than Maerlant's.

50. Maerlant aggravates Vincent of Beauvais's phrasing, but he undoubtedly takes the contents of the argument from his source (cf. Vincent of Beauvais, 23, XLVI (915)).

51. Maerlant, *Spiegel Historiael*, III, viii, 16, vv. 65–72 (vol. 2, p. 78):

Dese valsche prophete Mahumet
Hevet in sinen Alcoraen gheset:
"In bem niet ter werelt ghesent,
Datmen mi bi miraclen kent,
Maer ic bem ghesent metten zwerde,
Wie dat maect onwerde
Tontfane dat ic bescrive,
Datmenne doe vanden live."

Maerlant follows Vincent of Beauvais closely (*Speculum Historiale*, 23, XLIII (915). See also Daniel, *Islam and the West*, 73–77, 125–126.

52. On the missionary aspects of the crusades, see Kedar, *Crusade and Mission*.

53. Cf. Daniel, *Islam and the West*, p. 26. Vincent of Beauvais has a more realistic view of the genesis of the Qur'ân (23, LII–LV; 917–918).

54. Maerlant, *Spiegel Historiael*, III, viii, 17, vv. 1–5 (vol. 2, 78–79):

Het es scame van desen dief
Te telne eenen langen brief;
Maer dese onwettege tyrant
Destruweerde Persen lant,
So grote macht haddi te samen.

55. The information given here might—for the most part—have been taken from Vincent of Beauvais (23, XLV; 915), but the *Speculum* does not mention a king Hormisda, against whom Muhammad supposedly fought.

56. Maerlant, *Spiegel Historiael*, III, viii, 17, vv. 33–37 (vol. 2, p. 79):

Daer wart geminct tRoemsce rike
Bi Mahumette jammerlike.
Sine valsche dorperheden
Ende sine grote onmenscelicheden
Ware te telne te swaer.

Cf. Vincent of Beauvais, 23, XLVII (915).

57. According to Vincent of Beauvais, Muhammad is supposed to have lived for sixty-three years: "Vita ergo eius 63 annis extitit." (*Speculum Historiale*, 23, XLVII [915]). A scribal error in the *Spiegel Historiael*?

58. The phrasing "Ende viel in enen evele groot," nevertheless suggests that a fit of epilepsy caused his death. Vincent of Beauvais, in the corresponding passage, speaks of a "morbo pleuretico" (Vincent of Beauvais, *Speculum Historiale* 23, XLVII; 915).

59. Maerlant, *Spiegel Historiael*, III, viii, 17, vv. 50–54 (vol. 2, p. 79):

> Sijn lachame hief hem groot
> Ende hem cromde metter doot
> Sijn mindste vinger achter waert.
> Sine vrient hebbene bewaert
> Drie daghe naer sijn beheet
> Ende gewasschen ende gecleet.

60. Maerlant, *Spiegel Historiael*, III, viii, 18, vv. 1–4 (vol. 2, p. 79):

> Een deel hort van sire wet,
> Die biden duvel was geset,
> Sonder redene ende genaden,
> Vul van dorperlike daden.

61. On accounting for Muhammad's prophethood by machinations of the devil, see Daniel, *Islam and the West*, 69–70.

62. Maerlant, *Spiegel Historiael*, III, viii, 18, vv. 15–20 (vol. 2, p. 80):

> In sinen bouc Alcoraen,
> Daer alle sine gebode in staen.
> Ende seide al openbare,
> Dat sine wet so heilich ware,
> Dat no duvel no mensce vulbrochte,
> Datmen sulke wet ghewrochte.

Cf. Vincent of Beauvais, *Speculum Historiale* 23, L (916).

63. Maerlant, *Spiegel Historiael*, III, viii, 18, vv. 30 (vol. 2, p. 80): "Dit es truffe sekerlike." Cf. Vincent of Beauvais, *Speculum Historiale* 23, LVII (919). On the remark of the mountain bowing before the Qur'ân, Maerlant also adds the commentary that it must be a "boerde" ("lie, invention").

64. Ibid., III, viii, 18, vv. 39–44 (vol. 2, p. 80):

> Ende hi gaf orlof elken man,
> Alse hi wilde, dochtem goet dan,
> Dat hi van sinen wive sciede:
> Maer datmen dien man verbiede,
> Dat hire hem niet kere weder an,
> Eer soe neemt enen anderen man.

Cf. Vincent of Beauvais, *Speculum Historiale*, 23, LIX (919).

65. Cf. Daniel, *Islam and the West*, 148–152.

66. Maerlant, *Spiegel Historiael*, III, viii, 18, vv. 47–48 (vol. 2, p. 80):

Dans niet dan eten ende drinken
Ende euwelike in luxurie stinken.

The four verses that Maerlant devotes to the Muslim paradise stand in marked contrast with the two full chapters from the *Speculum Historiale* (23, LXV and LXVI, 921–922).

67. Cf. Vincent of Beauvais, *Speculum Historiale* 23, LXVII (922).

68. Maerlant, *Spiegel Historiael*, III, viii, 18, vv. 57–66 (vol. 2, p. 80):

Met deser truffen, met derre ghile,
Ghinc hi omme toter wile,
Dat hi staerf sonder gelove,
Ende met morde ende met rove
Versament hadde een groot diet,
Want hi elken gebruken liet.
Dese duvel scorde jammerlike
In sijn incomen Eraclius rike,
Alsic indie ystorie hier naer
U seggen sal al openbaer.

69. Cf. Adelphus, "Ein Leben Mohammeds," 107–108.

70. On al-Kindî's text and its Latin translation, see the article by P. S. van Koningsveld in this volume.

71. See Lepage's introduction to his edition of Alexandre du Pont *Roman de Mahomet*, 19–46; See also Cambier's introduction to his edition of Embrico of Mainz, *Vita Mahumeti*, 6–32. The pseudoclerical tradition has two important themes that are omitted in Vincentius and Maerlant: Muhammad's celestial voyage, and his flying tomb. Perhaps these were too close to the supernatural to be included?

72. Cf. Maerlant, *Spiegel Historiael*, I, 1, prologue, vv. 19–32 (vol. 1, p. 15). In fact, a few lines further on in his prologue, he mentions Vincent of Beauvais by name as the author of his source (vv. 65–66, p. 16).

73. The list of secondary sources for the *Spiegel Historiael* (see intro., pp., 216–217) attests to Maerlant's critical attitude. This attitude, less evident in the chapters analyzed here than in other parts of the *Spiegel Historiael*, sometimes amounts to being hypercritical. Cf. Gerritsen, "Jacob van Maerlant and Geoffrey of Monmouth," 368–388.

74. Cf. Vincent van Beauvais, *Speculum Historiale* 23, XL (913).

75. Ibid., 23, LII–LV (917–918).

76. An important traditional argument against the Qur'ân is based on its form: Whereas the Bible is (largely) in prose, the Qur'ân is metrical. Thus, verse is associated with mendacity, prose with veracity. Maerlant cannot use this argument, for his own text is in verse (an idiosyncrasy of much of the secular Middle Dutch literature, be it narrative or discursive). It would be interesting to see whether there are any connections between this part of the polemic against the Qur'ân and the prose-vs.-verse controversy in medieval vernacular literature.

77. On this see Berendrecht, "Maerlants' *'Scolastica'* en zijn directe bron," 2–31.

78. Cf. Daniel, *Islam and the West*, 19.

79. Cf. Comfort, "The Literary Role," 650–654.

80. I am very grateful to Rolf Bremmer, Jr., Martijn Rus, and Heinrich Beck for their information on the English, French, and Scandinavian situation.

81. I refer to the *Kaiserchronik* (ca. 1147), the *Sächsische Chronik* (ca. 1220) and the *Jansen Enikel Chronik* (ca. 1280). I thank Michael Bohländer, preparing a study on the *Jansen Enikel Chronik*, for kindly sharing his knowledge on this subject.

82. Cf. Alfonso X, *Primera Crónica General* 1:261–275. I am grateful to Barbara Schuchard and Oele I. M. Verhoeven for helping me with the Spanish text.

83. Among the used sources are some works by Rodrigo Toledano, and the world chronicle of Sigebert of Gembloux. Cf. Alfonso X, *Primera Crónica General*, 1:cxxv–cxxvii. Menéndez Pidal (ibid., cxxvi) states explicitly that the Byzantine *Chronographia* of Theophanes was not used.

84. Southern, *Western Views of Islam in the Middle Ages*, 34–66.

CHAPTER 11

Portrayal of Muslims in Andrea da Barberino's *Guerrino il Meschino*

Gloria Allaire

Other chapters of this volume examine the myriad Christian literary response to the spread of Islam in the Middle Ages and beyond. We summarize this ongoing discourse as comprising three categories: biographical data about Muhammad's life, beliefs about Muslim people and culture, and active polemics against Islam as false religion. The Florentine Andrea da Barberino incorporates all three into his fifteenth-century prose romance Guerrino il Meschino.

Andrea da Barberino was an indefatigable compiler and author of Carolingian chivalric prose in the Italian vernacular. A Florentine, he lived from approximately 1371 to 1431.[1] His authorship of six romances is proven, and three others have been attributed to him. I Reali di Francia, L'Aspramonte, Ajolfo del Barbicone, Ugone d'Avernia, and Le storie Nerbonesi have all received modern editions, though the last three leave much to be desired. His best work, Guerrino il Meschino, still lacks a critical edition.[2] Attributions include a lost Prima Spagna and an unedited Seconda Spagna.[3] Finally, the problematic prose romance Rambaldo has also been ascribed to Andrea.[4]

The stylistic feature most pertinent to our discussion is Andrea's almost historiographic verisimilitude, a trait noted by numerous anthologists and critics.[5] While Andrea had inherited the complete baggage of chivalric conventions, and was familiar with the major French cycles, he consciously eliminated most magical and fantastic elements from his narrations. Where giants, exotic beasts or even otherworldly journeys occur, he couches them in naturalistic descriptions with real-world texture and dimensions. Where preexisting narrative traditions conflict, he often discards the more improbable variants or subjugates what he viewed as inaccurate material, such as genealogical relationships, to his own overarching scheme.[6] Thus, with respect to the material concerning Muslims, we may be sure that he would have suppressed anything that may have seemed implausible or unrealistic to himself or his pragmatic readership.

That these works were conceived for private reading and not only for public recitation is discernible from numerous references to the lettore scattered throughout the texts. From copyist and ownership information in the manuscripts, and from other documents such as book inventories and private financial records, we may establish that Andrea's readers were members of unquestionably prestigious Florentine families such as the Visdomini, Salviati, Viviani, Davanzati, Galli, Benci, Doni, Bardi, Nasi, and Orlandini.[7] Thus, we may view Andrea as representative of the reasonably well-educated middle- or upper-class Florentine's beliefs about Islam.

Guerrino il Meschino, more properly (according to the manuscript tradition) Il Libro del Meschino di Durazzo, holds a special place in Andrea's oeuvre, and indeed, in the history of Italian chivalric literature. There are no French or Franco-Venetian models for this work as there are for his other romances. While there are clear sources for many individual elements, the juxtaposition of nonfictional structures and material with conventional chivalric narrative, as well as the mingling of all three "matters" (classical, Arthurian, and Carolingian) on such a vast scale, seems to be a feat unique to Andrea.

Though beginning and ending as a "romance epic," the bulk of Guerrino is structured like a medieval travel account that encompasses elements from numerous popular medieval texts. Source texts and legends include the Alexander Romance, Dante's Comedy, Ptolemy's Cosmographia, the Purgatory of St. Patrick, the Sibyl's cave, bestiaries, lapidaries, and astrological and alchemical manuals. The story takes place during the years preceding and following 824 a.d.[8] The young hero, captured by pirates and sold as a slave in infancy, is in reality a descendent of Charlemagne. His deposed and imprisoned parents await their freedom, and his betrothed maintains her faithfulness for ten years while Guerrino searches the three parts of the medieval world looking for clues to his homeland and identity. In the role of a soldier of fortune, Guerrino variously captains the Persians and Arabs against the Turks, Prester John's armies against the bestial Cinnamoni, the Egyptians versus the Arabs, and finally, his own dynasty's Christian forces against the combined Turkish and Saracen armies.

We have noted Andrea's importance as a cultural representative of Florence. If we consider the transmission of Guerrino, we find that this work spread throughout Italy and abroad in Andrea's own century, and that its popularity endured nearly down to our own day. We have archival evidence that Guerrino was owned by princes and kings outside Tuscany. For example, Borso d'Este commissioned a now-untraceable copy in 1467, and an extant copy in the Bibliothèque Nationale in Paris originally belonged to the kings of Aragon in Naples.[9] Guerrino also enjoyed a long printing history, beginning in 1473.[10] The work was translated into French in 1501 by Jean de Rochemeure and into Spanish by Alonso Hernández Alemán prior to 1512.[11] Official inventories from the sixteenth through the eighteenth centuries show that there were multiple copies of Guerrino, both in manuscript and in print, in the libraries of the kings of France.[12] In the nineteenth and early twentieth centuries, Guerrino was a favorite cycle in the puppet theatres of Naples and Sicily.[13]

Guerrino, with its unique blend of narrative materials, is also a noteworthy example of a nontheological text that contains all three categories of the medieval discourse on Islam. It includes elements of the legendary biography of Muhammad, observations on Islamic culture, and one overt polemical passage against the Islamic religion. Due to Andrea's concern for verisimilitude, the romance contains a more detailed and accurate portrayal of Saracen culture than is normally found in chivalric literature. Surprisingly, Guerrino has, to date, been slighted in studies of the Muslim element in chansons de geste and romances.

Few modern critics are aware of the presence of Muslim material in Andrea's texts. Blochet included Guerrino in his survey of Arabic-inspired otherworldly journeys.[14] D'Ancona mentions the scene in which Guerrino denounces the heretical basis of the Prophet's theological formation.[15] Franceschetti, citing I Reali and L'Aspramonte but not Guerrino, asserts that Andrea was a pivotal figure in the way Muslim figures would be viewed in later Italian chivalric literature. Changes that he initiated "made a substantial contribution to the different attitude toward the Saracens that was accepted by following generations. . . . The development of these circumstances during the course of the fifteenth century shows a definite improvement in the attitude of Italian writers towards the Saracens."[16] Indeed, another study suggests that several sixteenth-century Renaissance epics "have no trace of a sense of European racial superiority over Turks and Arabs."[17] In this chapter, we attempt to investigate the full spectrum of references to Islamic culture and religion found in Guerrino and to decode Andrea's various representations with regard to his own moral attitudes on Islam and those of his society.

We begin by examining the conventional views of Muslims, which Andrea inherited from the chivalric genres. The authors of earlier chansons de geste tended to use the terms pagan or Turk synonymously with Saracen.[18] Thus, to the medieval reader or listener the word Saracen, in effect, denoted non-Christian or unbeliever. Andrea follows the norm in Ugone, Nerbonesi, Ajolfo and in portions of Guerrino. In these texts, Saraini is used most often, followed by *pagani* and much less often, by Turchi.[19] In Andrea's Aspramonte Saracens are referred to as "Turks" only once, and very rarely as pagans, but several times—with a certain geographical sophistication—as africanti (Africans).[20] In Guerrino Andrea explicitly equates saraini with infedeli very rarely (165v).

In several instances in Guerrino where turchi are equated with saraini, it is not immediately clear whether Andrea is merely following loose romance convention or if he considers Turks to be Muslims.[21] His view is clarified when one of the non-Christian characters speaks of "valiant Turkish knights, defenders of the faith of Muhammad against the Christians."[22]

This quote should not give the impression that Guerrino is merely a Crusade-like epic of Christians succumbing to or triumphing over the Saracen host. Andrea does maintain the synonymity of Saracen, pagan and Turk in Books One and Seven, the most conventional portions of the romance; however, within this bracket of standard narrative practice, one finds a radically different approach. In the nonconventional narrative of the central books, Andrea differentiates among non-Christian peoples (arabi, egiziani, persiani, indiani, etc.), not all of whom are viewed as inimical. This approach is based more on real or perceived geographical boundaries and less on religious identifications. Such a shift of emphasis makes possible a representation that echoes the internecine warfare which took place within early Muslim history and, as such, debunks the view of many conventional epics which portray a kind of "united Islamic front" massed to destroy the "true" Christian religion. In one episode, for example, the Turks—clearly identified as Muslims—are the aggressors in a war against Mecca, the seat of Islam itself. To defend his city, the Sultan appoints Guerrino "captain of all the Persian and Arabian people against the Turks" (italics mine). [23]

While Andrea at times follows the convention of equating pagans with Saracens, in one passage in Nerbonesi he draws a clear distinction between the two. In this section, the decorations of an historiated pavilion include a depiction of the four faiths: Judaism, Paganism, Christianity, and Islam. [24] Andrea tells us that Ham, son of Noah, was the founder of the pagan people: "[E]ven though many pagans were of the lineage of Sem and of Iafet, nonetheless we begin with him [Ham] and his son Cush, and Nimrod, son of Cush." [25] Later Andrea cites the legendary biographies which show Muhammad first as a powerful advocate of Christianity and later as its most feared opponent. Andrea's definition, therefore, is predicated on the idea that the pagans preceded Christianity and therefore could not have known about Christ, but that Islam followed the emergence of Christianity, yet rejected its Messiah. [26] The passage, which articulates the histories of the four faiths, is strong evidence that not all medieval Christians viewed Islam as merely a heretical sect, as some critics believe, but granted it the status of an autonomous religion.[27]

When discussing the origins of peoples, St. Isidore notes the falsity of the etymology Saracens < Sara:

> Ishmael, son of Abraham, whence "Ishmaelites," who are now [called] Saracens, by corruption of their name, in as much as [they are considered] descendents of Sarah . . .[28]

This etymology, however corrupt, gained acceptance in medieval lore: we note, for example, its repetition by Mandeville.[29] Andrea would have had access to these texts either in the original or through the numerous Tuscan *volgarizzamenti*, as evidenced by elements of both works, which appear in *Guerrino*.[30] It is interesting that, in the passage of *Nerbonesi* which discusses the history of the *saraini*, Andrea follows Giovanni Villani's lead in citing the false etymology *Saracini* < *Sara* while nonetheless noting the correct historical ancestor of this people: Ishmael, son of Abraham.[31] Andrea includes an additional flourish when he suggests that the name "Sarain" comes, not from "Sara," but from the place where Ishmael first lived.[32]

Although Andrea at times approaches historical accuracy, in numerous instances throughout *Guerrino* he repeats the medieval lore about Islam found in earlier chivalric literature. We find, for example, the misconception that the Saracens worship Muhammad as their God.[33] Likewise, the false trinity of Saracen gods from Old French *chansons de geste* recurs in *Guerrino*, here with the Italian names Macone, Apollin, and Trevigante (68v, 104r).[34] In one instance in *Guerrino*, perhaps viewing the name Apollin as analogous to the Greek god Apollo, Andrea conflates pagan and Islamic practices and treats an oracular shrine—the Trees of the Sun and the Moon—from the *Alexander Romance* as if it were a holy place respected by Muslims.[35] When the romance's Christian protagonist arrives at Mecca, he receives special honors because of a visit previously made to this mystical site. In another passage which speaks of "the priest of the temple of Apollo," the classical deity—here clearly synonymous with Apollin—is accorded godhood by Andrea's Muslims.[36] The faulty conception of an Islamic priesthood, which Andrea endorses had already appeared in the

Dittamondo (Book V, chap. 13, line 61) and thus could not have been invented by Ariosto as Donnelly states. [37]

Perhaps because of his society's familiarity with classical figures, Andrea had no difficulty inserting yet another god into Saracen worship. The formidable warrior Guerrino is repeatedly called "son of Mars, the god of battles" by an admiring Oriental king (65v, 69r). That this comment has more than tropic significance is clear when the king tells the whole camp that Guerrino was a man sent by the gods to help the Persians. [38]

The use of Muhammad's name by Muslim characters in *Guerrino* is conventional and parallels the Christians' use (or misuse) of their own deity's name. Saracen knights vent their rage, pray for help and protection, give thanks for victories, curse defeats, take binding oaths, and begin ambassadorial declamations by calling on the name of their Prophet. [39]

The physical appearance of Saracenic warriors in *Guerrino* also follows earlier narrative norms, but often includes more detail. [40] They are poorly armed (". . . sono male armati . . .") in comparison with Christian knights, a literary convention that does have some basis in historical truth (33v). [41] In another episode, a group of Saracens admire the Christian heroes' armor (182v–183v). Saracens are turbaned, bearded, and possess a great quantity of hair (33r–v, 111r). [42] They use scimitars in contrast to European swords, and some, especially giants, also carry clubs or maces reinforced with iron. Their archers are to be feared. The following brief description of a Saracen, in this case, from Media, may be illustrative:

> Just then, there arrived before her [the queen] one of her war captains with a twisted mass of linen fabric wrapped around his head and a scimitar at his side, a club in his hand, a large beard, and a head of hair so wild that he seemed a bear . . . [43]

Similar images of Moorish Saracens which occur later in *Guerrino* are not so detailed, but regularly feature the stereotypical turban and scimitar (111r–v). One notices that, despite Andrea's broader concept of geography as shown by the use of different adjectives of nationality for his Muslims, in his physical descriptions he relies upon the traditional identifying marks.

In its depiction of other Saracen attributes, *Guerrino* again encapsulates medieval attitudes. As in the tradition of the noble Saracen, Muslims are deemed worthy opponents capable of valor in battle (*"franchi* saraini," 167r). The Saracen host of Old French literature was noted for producing a frightening din with its battle cries: "Gherardo had never seen more Saracens, and those were making such a tumult that he was afraid of those cries."[44] While Andrea's Saracens in *Guerrino* largely observe chivalric practices, at times they seem predisposed to cruelty. In one scene, they threaten to dismember their Christian prisoners in order to distribute various body parts as trophies among different parties to whom the Christians had given offense (179r). One former Muslim champion, turned Christian and now returned to rescue the captured hero, adopts a tone of braggadocio as he threatens to eat the hero's nose (180v). Such descriptions are part of a recurrent emphasis on physical mutilation in the Christian legends about Muhammad, best exemplified by that of his death (being eaten by swine after falling to the ground due either to drunkenness or epilepsy).[45] Other authors present Islam as a religion of the sword, stating that when Muslims preach their religion it is with a sword in hand to kill those who refuse to obey or pay tribute.[46] In this connection, it is comforting to note that while horrific executions are frequently threatened by Saracens in Andrea's works they are rarely carried out.

Next we shall examine the medieval legends of the Prophet himself that are found in *Guerrino*. Various fictional versions of Muhammad's biography circulated in medieval Europe: one included the monk Sergius, and another featured a disgruntled candidate to the papacy named Nicholas. Later, a third variant emerged, which substituted Muhammad himself for the character Sergius. Muhammad's character is thereby considerably blackened, since he is seen as a dangerous renegade rather than a non-Christian in need of religious enlightenment. Andrea alludes to this latter variation in both *Nerbonesi* (1:350) and *Guerrino* (106v). Andrea seems to have consciously chosen among versions, since two fifteenth-century Tuscan miscellanies permit us to establish that both the Sergius and Nicholas stories were still extant in Andrea's day and beyond.[47]

Despite the generally tolerant presentation of Muslims in *Guerrino*, a Christian abhorrence of Islam as a false religion with Muhammad as its false prophet does appear in one episode. Here the protagonist, in no uncertain terms, calls Muhammad a hypocrite who brings damnation on the whole Saracen nation.[48] This attitude is reified in the portrayal of otherworldly journeys which Andrea includes both in *Ugone* and *Guerrino*. In *Ugone* the Christian protagonist reacts violently, spitting at Muhammad when he sees his soul being tortured in Hell (2:115). While the tone of the passage in *Ugone* is quite vindictive, perhaps due to its older source material, in *Guerrino* the hero merely laughs ironically when he thinks of all the Saracens who so fervently followed the teachings of Muhammad to their own damnation (156r). Perhaps following Dante's lead, Andrea humanely allows the possibility for some Saracens to escape the worst infernal torments. But whereas Dante had doomed Saladin to an eternity in Limbo, Andrea goes further and grants a place in Purgatory to one of Guerrino's former opponents.[49] Although this Saracen knight had during his lifetime recognized the falsity of Islamic beliefs, he had not actively sought baptism. Only Guerrino's act of concern in baptizing him *in extremis* and the grace of God had saved his soul from damnation.[50]

While both Dante and Andrea portray Muhammad's soul in Hell, they do so with a difference. Dante's neat *contrapasso*, in which Muhammad's body is split open, emphasizes his function as a schismatic. Even though Andrea apparently subscribed to the same legend of Muhammad as a turncoat cardinal, and though he had earlier quoted Dante in calling Muhammad a "seminator di scandalo" (sower of scandal),[51] the punishment he assigns to Muhammad differs: the soul of Muhammad is torn apart on a Catherine's wheel. Andrea derives this image from a *terza rima* imitation of Dante by the otherwise unidentified "Giovanni Vincenzio Isterliano" which he inserts in *Ugone* (2:83). This image appears in the verse sections of *Ugone*, is glossed in the prose which follows, and is repeated again, with embellishments, in *Guerrino*. While we need not hold Andrea to strict Dantesque requirements, from a comment made in *Ugone* one wonders if Andrea did not indeed have a *contrapasso* in mind, but one with a different emphasis than Dante's. He writes that the instrument used to torture Muhammad was "like the wheel which martyred St. Catherine." In identifying the soul on the wheel as Muhammad's, he offers as reason for his punishment the "fact" that Saracens adore him as their god (*Ugone* 2:115). The connection of the spiked wheel to the worship of false gods may have its roots in medieval martyrologies, which narrate that Catherine was martyred on the wheel because she preached against polytheism. According to medieval thinking, both charges would merit infernal punishment, but it is difficult to say which crime would have been considered more severe. If one considers that, of the two sins, only worshiping false gods is included among the Biblical Ten Commandments, one could argue that the poet Giovanni and Andrea condemn Muhammad on more serious grounds and that Dante's Minos had, in effect, been too lenient.

We have seen how medieval Christians inaccurately projected their own religious concepts such as the Trinity, the clergy, and the Messiah onto the Islamic faith. Yet one thing shared by both faiths is not always acknowledged: their parallel use of houses of worship. While medieval texts abound in polemics against Muhammad and the Muslim faith, I have found none which includes the physical description of a mosque.[52] By structuring the internal books of *Guerrino* along the lines of a medieval travel account, Andrea created the opportunity to include a graphic description of the "tabernacle" of Muhammad at Mecca:

> . . . we went to the "mosque"—that's what it's called— which is round and not very high. It is much smaller than Round Saint Mary's in Rome. The emir entered, took off his shoes and, in the doorway, knelt down; and I, who was near him knelt, not for devotional reasons, but in order to see. And. there inside I saw the Caliph with many high priests—richly robed as is their fashion—and since we were now standing, I raised my head and studied how the false church of Muhammad was constructed. It was up to the halfway point and all round white; and from the midpoint on up it was all black; and running between the white and black was a red stripe; and there were two round windows, one toward the east and the other toward the west; [and there were two doors, the one on the east side and the other

on the west side;] and in the middle of the church is an altar
with a circle of alabaster around. The top of the alabaster
was all of gold, and the altar seemed all of gold; and
around the altar were the most important priests . . . and
one could go around the outside of this choir where the
altar was, but not inside.[53]

Thus, from the pen of a late-medieval romancer, we have a
representation of how medieval-Christian imagination conceived
the interior of the holiest Islamic shrine.[54] Of course, this image
bears no resemblance to the unadorned Ka'ba, the function of
which Andrea's mosque clearly resembles. On first glance, one
may be tempted to dismiss his representation as simply a
Christian projection of a cathedral replete with cupola, choir and
exquisite altar; yet the broad outlines of this description do
reflect actual Islamic architectural features. Since Andrea
consciously strove toward verisimilitude in his romances, it
seems likely that he would have tried to include architectural
details with the proper patina of exoticism. To achieve a certain
realism then, Andrea may have drawn upon accounts of the East
for details.

One decorative feature of Andrea's mosque is the use of
clearly demarcated areas of white and black stone. While Muslim
architecture is not standardized,[55] the alternation of white and
black stone is one recurrent feature.[56] A more important
characteristic of Andrea's mosque is its roundness. With his
specific reference to "Santa Maria Rotonda" (the Pantheon) in
Rome, Andrea indicates both the shape he had in mind as well as
the dimensions. Andrea could have learned of this building from
a pilgrim's guide, such as the *Mirabilia Urbis Romae*, from
merchants or pilgrims returning to Florence from Rome, or
perhaps from a visit there himself. The notion of roundness
prominent in his description may be intended to represent the
revolutionary type of Arabic architecture called "aisled
rotunda."[57]

It is probable that medieval travel accounts of the "Temple
of the Lord" (the Dome of the Rock) in Jerusalem contributed to
Andrea's vision of a mosque. A passage in Theoderich's *Guide to
the Holy Land* may have been a far-off textual antecedent to
Andrea's description:

Its lower part is ornamented as far as the middle with most
glorious marbles, and from the middle up to the topmost
border, on which the roof rests, is most beautifully adorned
with mosaic work. Now, this border . . . reaches round the
entire circuit of the Temple. . . . The upper wall . . . supports
a leaden roof. . . .[58]

Since the entire passage in Theoderich is much more
detailed than Andrea's, mentioning mosaics, inscriptions, an
octagonal bottom, four (not two) doors, and various ranks of
columns, and since Andrea does offer details of mosaic decor,
stairs, and internal columns in describing other exotic buildings,
it seems likely that Andrea did not directly avail himself of
Theoderich's handbook for pilgrims. Looking farther afield, we
find in Mandeville a simplified description of the Temple of the
Lord that corresponds more closely to Andrea's more barren
mosque: "[I]t is alle round and high and couered with leed and it
is wel paued with white marble."[59] The white color appears in
both accounts and the lead roof Mandeville mentions is roughly
equivalent to Andrea's dark-colored upper half. While it is
difficult to say which of the many versions of the account
Andrea may have utilized, it is possible that Mandeville's
abbreviated description of the Temple of the Lord served as
inspiration for Andrea's mosque.[60]

Andrea's view of Islam in *Guerrino* also comprises legends
concerning Muhammad's final resting place. While at least one
Christian author insisted Muhammad was buried in Baghdad,[61]
most (Gauthier de Compiègne, Alexandre du Pont, Mandeville,
the Anonymous Florentine, Giovanni Villani and Andrea) not
unreasonably believed his tomb was at Mecca.[62] In truth, the
grave was dug on the spot where he died in the house of one of
his wives in Medina.[63] Another of these legends concerns
Muhammad's iron coffin, which levitated "miraculously" by
magnet force. This tale was obviously invented by Christian
polemicists to underscore the false nature of Muhammad and his
teachings, for there is no mention of such a sarcophagus in
Islamic writings.[64]

While retaining this legendary motif in *Guerrino*, Andrea
situates the object inside the mosque at Mecca. His choice surely
reflects, not historical accuracy, but Catholic practice of burying

their saints and spiritual leaders in cathedrals. In *Guerrino* Andrea presents us with the most graphic depiction of the coffin of any text I have found. Through the eyes of his virtuous Christian protagonist, he not only describes the scene in detail, but passes moral judgment on the Islamic religion:

> In the middle of this cupola was an urn shaped in the fashion of a evenly-formed iron casket—I estimated almost a *braccio* and a half in length, and a bit less on its other side—and it was suspended and not touching anything. Then I recognized the false Muhammad's deception, since I realized that that part of the false church was from the middle up made entirely of loadstone which is a marine rock that is between black and grey in color and has this property in it: that it pulls iron to it because of its coldness. . . . It's this reason that the ark of Muhammad (which is made of iron) stays suspended: because the magnetic rock holds it; and the obtuse Saracen people don't know what loadstone is: they believe that the ark stays up by a miracle.[65]

Although Andrea did not invent the notion of the "ark" of Muhammad, his account must have had a powerful impact on his readers: two scribes inserted drawings of this object in their copies of *Guerrino*. The illustrations of Riccardian 2226, taken together with the structuring of episodes in *Guerrino*, furnish a clue to the origin of this medieval legend. Just as so many other misconceptions of Islam are merely inversions of Christian tenets, medieval authors may have created the ark as a fictitious Islamic parallel to the holy sepulcher of Christ. Since the supreme pilgrimage destination for Christians was Christ's tomb in Jerusalem, by extension Christians assumed a similar function for the Ka'ba, the recognized goal of Islamic pilgrimages.[66] Andrea seems to heighten this symmetry consciously: just a few folios after Guerrino's dramatic penetration into the mosque to view the ark, the hero passes a night praying at Christ's sepulcher in Jerusalem. The sketches by the copyist of Ricc. 2226 (Jacopo di Lippo Doni of Florence) present a striking parallel between the two sacred objects. That the identical portrayal of both was no simple copying error is seen by the distinctive labels written in the margin by each image: "archas maumettj" (61v) and "sepol[??] christi" (76r).

Thus far we have seen how both romance conventions and popular medieval legends about Muslims are woven into the fabric of *Guerrino*. More remarkable is the variety of details of Islamic religious practice and culture that Andrea included. In the course of the protagonist's journeys, the many exotic peoples he encounters are described in nearly anthropological terms. For the most part, these are reported in the dry tone of a chronicle yet with a feeling of wonderment at beholding such extraordinary sights. At times, exotic practices are decried as morally reprehensible when they conflict with Christian teacings or European customs. It should be noted that, despite Andrea's heavy debt to the *chanson de geste* tradition, he does not automatically impose that genre's vigorous racial antipathy on his portrayal of the Muslim culture. In general, the Saracenic peoples in *Guerrino* are viewed as civilized, albeit with a few immoral practices due to their benighted religious beliefs.[67] Thus, in contrast to the stereotypical portrayals of Muslim culture in earlier epics, and to its "shapelessness" (Donnelly's term) in sixteenth-century ones, Andrea includes many particulars that he believed to be cultural fact.

Immediately after the description of the ark of Muhammad (quoted above), Andrea furnishes additional details concerning Islamic worship:

> . . . at the exit of the mosque—which no woman may enter—I saw certain individuals who had gouged out their eyes; and they were saying that they did it for love of Muhammad and in order to never again see anything since they had seen the ark of Muhammad, that in the world there was no holier thing; and I laughed at their foolishness. And I heard it said that in the year of the pardon, many put themselves under the wheels of carts and kill themselves—and they say that of their own will they give up their bodies for love of Muhammad—and their bodies are carried back to their homes. And they maintain that these are saints in company of Muhammad.[68]

The prohibition of women worshiping in the mosque was not apparently dictated by Muhammad, although among Ḥadith there are two points of view expressed on the subject.[69] Andrea's reference to a year in which Saracens receive pardon is more closely based on the medieval Catholic practice of Jubilee years, but may also contain some notion of the Hajj, the once-in-a-lifetime pilgrimage to Mecca; however, it may be due merely to a preexisting account: the notion that "Indians go on pilgrimage, as we do unto St. Peter" is found in the journal of Friar Odoric of Pordenone.[70]

Christian narrative descriptions of Islamic "idolaters" blinding themselves or committing suicide under the wheels of wagons to attain sainthood are patently false. A description of this sort also appears in the aforementioned account of Indian devotees, but here the devotees are apparently Hindi, not Muslims.[71] These bodies are cremated and their ashes kept as relics. Mandeville repeats and slightly expands upon this description. While reference to blinding does not occur in these earlier travel accounts, in the description of suicides one notices remarkable similarities between Mandeville and Andrea:

> And summe of hem fallen doun vnder the wheles of the chare, and lat the chare go ouer hem so that thei ben dede anon. . . . [A]nd than thei seyn that tho ben seyntes because that thei slowen hemself of here owne gode wille for loue of here ydole.[72]

Thus, although *Guerrino*'s geography does not follow that of thirteenth- and fourteenth-century travel literature, as Bezzola points out, such evidence of borrowings nonetheless demonstrate Andrea's familiarity with these accounts.[73]

Another element of religious practice concerns the direction Muslims face when they pray. According to actual Islamic practice, one of the prerequisites of prayer is "to stand facing the Qibla (the direction of the Sacred Mosque in Mecca)."[74] While medieval authors recognized the significance of Mecca to the Islamic religion, not all their descriptions treat the practice of facing that city to pray. Some specified that Christians face east, Jews face west, and Saracens face south to pray.[75] In *Guerrino*, Andrea omits reference to Jewish practice, but includes the other two faiths with reversed directions: the Christian turns toward the west and the Saracen toward the East (65r). This is no doubt an attempt by Andrea to adjust directions based on realistic geographical location since the hero now finds himself somewhere on the Arabian peninsula.

With regard to marriage and sexuality, the fact of Middle Eastern polygamy was well-known to medievals. Andrea acknowledges this practice in *Guerrino* when clarifying a reference to the "head queen" of the sultan of Mecca:

> ... the damsel ... was commended into the keeping of the principal queen, since according to Saracen custom they take many wives, and the sultan had more than 200 wives and one of them he had crowned queen.[76]

Andrea's account omits the moral outrage which accompanies references to polygamy by authors such as Giovanni Villani and Fazio degli Uberti.[77] This seems remarkable because normally Andrea is only too ready to condemn any hint of *lussuria* in his characters' behavior. He does, however, draw the line at sodomy, another perceived Saracen vice. In one scene, the hero enters the war pavilion of a decadent young Saracen and observes

> ... Lionetto lying on a bed of silk, and in the pavilion were many lords, here three and here four, seated on carpets on the ground. Some played one game and some another. One couldn't tell the disgraceful manner of their positions: Lionetto Meschin had his legs up high and was showing the shameful parts of his person, and so were many others.[78]

We have already noted that the appearance of Andrea's Saracens included a full beard and long hair. In another scene, still in Muslim territory, when one of his messengers is sent back with a shaven head, Guerrino learns that this is a sign of gross disrespect (187r–v). Ever flexible to the demands of local customs, Guerrino pays his enemy back in spades by not only shaving the unfortunate envoy next sent to him, but by singeing all his body hair (188v, 190v). Once again, Andrea's fiction appears to contain a grain of truth gleaned from actual Islamic history. Narayan, in his account of the life and times of the Prophet, relates that one early martyr was tortured with hot irons used to singe his head. In another incident, supporters of 'Â'ishah attacked 'Alî's agent, Othman Bin Hanif, and "cut off his beard and eyebrows, shaved his head, lashed him with forty stripes and arrested him."[79]

The Muslim prohibition on wine was widely recognized and commented upon by medieval authors; however, of the texts under examination, only *Guerrino* mentions accurate details of an alternate beverage. The hero is staying at an inn at the city of Darinda in Persia:

> The innkeeper called his daughter and had her bring something to eat and to drink; and she did not bring wine because their law commands them not to drink wine, but she brought water with spices and ground raisins [in it].[80]

This passage corresponds exactly to the traditional Muslim drink which Muir describes: "Water in which dates or raisins have been steeped or washed is called Nabîdh."[81]

Finally, while Andrea generally depicts his Saracens more humanely than was done in Old French *chansons de geste*, he does mention two methods of punishment that may have seemed cruel to European Christians: amputation and crucifixion. Both of these punishments are mentioned in the Qur'ân.[82] While amputation of the hands was historically prescribed for robbers, in Andrea's fictional world the "saw" (*sega*) was reserved for traitors. He mentions this punishment in *Nerbonesi, Ajolfo,* and *Guerrino*. It is not a very common motif, being mentioned once each in *Nerbonesi* and *Guerrino*, and a few times in *Ajolfo*.[83] Likewise, crucifixion is an extremely rare motif in Andrea's works, occurring once (*Nerbonesi* 1:151) when a young Christian knight is scourged and tied to a cross by Saracen invaders. This may simply have been a borrowing from a source text: in no way is it representative of Andrea's view of Muslims.

While depictions of Muslim life are generally presented in a neutral tone, passages that treat religious beliefs become overtly polemical. We have mentioned Guerrino's laughing at Islamic suicides and at the soul of Muhammad. In another scene, he explains to his Saracen guides the falseness of Islamic beliefs in contrast to the truth of Christian ones (106v). The most intolerant passage occurs during the visit to the mosque at Mecca. Guerrino comments on the indignity of the position assumed by Muslim during prayers (kneeling, with face to ground and buttocks raised) and mocks Muhammad by reversing the direction of his own "worship" so that his buttocks face the holy ark.[84] This, he says, is the "honor" which Muhammad rightly deserves. The frank bigotry of this passage is in line with earlier practice of Christian polemics and *chansons de geste*, which sought to discredit Islamic beliefs and practices by disfiguring or misrepresenting them.[85] Yet *Guerrino* is not a tract against Islam: It is instead an honest attempt to represent the lands and peoples of the entire known world, comprising a vast panorama of doctrines, relics, and shrines of various religions. If Guerrino at times roundly condemns the Islamic religion, at others he participates fully in Islamic culture, even to the extent of fighting to defend Mecca from its attackers. While Guerrino's disrespectful bow smacks of vulgarity, his behavior as captain of the Persian armies demonstrates camaraderie and admiration for the Other.[86] Although the hero defiantly rejects the Saracens' religion, he never allows these feelings to eclipse his awareness of their common humanity. So as Guerrino views the mutilations and suicides of the faithful outside the mosque (cited previously), he feels both spite for their foolish beliefs and sorrow for their lost souls.[87]

More revealing of this bond of humanity is the striking use of the possessive adjective when the Christian hero speaks of "our" Sultan ("nostro soldano" 63r, 65r). In orally performed Italian *cantari*, the expression *i nostri* ("our boys," "our troops") had been used to orient the listener within the competing Christian and Saracen ideologies and to draw the audience's sympathies toward the former by consciously signalling antipathy toward the latter.[88] Given this well-established tradition, Guerrino's close identification with the foreign culture he serves is truly remarkable. Andrea's use of the old formula radically departs from the norm since it now aligns the reader's point of view with that of the Other. In *Guerrino*, despite the lingering presence of conventional antipathies, a new spirit emerges that does indeed make possible revisionary literary depictions of Muslims based on tolerance and understanding.

NOTES

1. Catalano, "La data di morte di Andrea da Barberino," 84–87.

2. I have already conducted preliminary research toward producing such an edition of *Guerrino*.

3. A nineteenth-century copy of rubrics for the now lost *Prima Spagna* may be found in Henri Michelant, "Titoli dei Capitoli della Storia *Reali di Francia*." The Seconda Spagna (MS. II.I.15, Bibl.ioteca Nazionale, Florence) was first attributed to Andrea by Paris, *Histoire poétique de Charlemagne*, 179–190. I have transcribed MS. II.I.15 for a future edition.

4. Palatine MS. 578, Biblioteca Nazionale, Florence. Described in Gentile, *I codici palatini*, vol. 2, fasc. 2, 145–46. While this manuscript contains passages describing the ark of Muhammad that are virtually identical to those in Guerrino (cited in this chapter), I believe the work to be derivative of several of Andrea's romances and not by him at all. The passages in question are found on fols. 38v, 40r, 41r, 43v, 56r, esp. 41v–42r.

5. For example, Rajna (*Ricerche intorno ai Reali di Francia*, 1:94) notes that Andrea's prose resembles a dry chronicle when compared to the exciting adventures of *Fioravante* upon which *Reali* was closely modeled:

> . . . [le] avventure che nel luogo corrispondente narra
> il F[ioravante] ci appaiono sì scolorite, che nulla più.
> Del romanzesco non partecipano proprio punto, ma
> invece hanno tutta la secchezza di una cronaca.

See also Grendler, "Chivalric Romances in the Italian Renaissance," 68–71.

6. Evidence suggests that Andrea even corrected geographical inaccuracies in his sources. See Hawickhorst, "Über die Geographie bei Andrea de' Magnabotti," 689; Colby-Hall, "La géographie rhodanienne des *Nerbonesi*," 658–659.

7. I examine the ownership/readership question in detail in one chapter of my dissertation, "The Chivalric 'Histories' of Andrea da Barberino."

8. Ricc. MS. 2226, fol. 138v, Biblioteca Riccardiana, Florence. Unless otherwise noted, all citations of *Guerrino* are from this

manuscript. I have transcribed Italian quotations from manuscripts with minimal editorial interventions.

9. Bertoni, _La biblioteca Estense e la coltura [sic] ferrarese_, 39 n. 2; Delisle, _Le cabinet des manuscrits de la Bibliotheque Impériale_ 1:244.

10. Osella, "Il _Guerrin Meschino_," 29–37.

11. For a description of the manuscript of the Rochemeure translation, see Wormald and Giles, _A Descriptive Catalogue of the Additional Illuminated Manuscripts in the Fitzwilliam Museum_ 1:41–42. For the Spanish _Guerrino_, see Osella, 164–165.

12. Ministère de l'Instruction Publique, _Anciens Inventaires et Catalogues de la Bibliothèque Nationale_, 1:244, 401; 2:345, 352, 495; 3:12, 109, 136; 4:54.

13. Pitrè, "Le tradizioni cavalleresche popolari in Sicilia," 348–349.

14. Blochet, _Les Sources orientales de la Divine Comédie_, 85.

15. D'Ancona, "La leggenda di Maometto in Occidente," 214–215.

16. Franceschetti, "On the Saracens in Early Italian Chivalric Literature," 207.

17. Donnelly, "The Moslem Enemy in Renaissance Epic," 163.

18. Saracens called "paiens," see _La Chanson de Roland_, lines 484, 692, 940, 974, 1543. "Turk" as an all-encompassing term, see _Chanson d'Aspremont_ 1:205: "Turc, Turcs, nom donné à tous les païens." For similar usage in Italian works, see an annotation to a passage from Andrea's _Reali di Francia_ in Adelaide Mattaini, ed., _Romanzi dei reali di Francia_, I classici Rizzoli, ed. Maurizio Vitale (Milan: Rizzoli Editore, 1957), 35: "_Turchio_: qui sta in genere per Saraceno o infedele."

19. While the Italian forms _saraceno_ or _saracino_ exist, _saraino_ is the most common spelling in manuscripts containing Andrea's texts.

20. Andrea da Barberino, _L'Aspramonte_, 123, 193, 207–208, 214–217, 247–249. Andrea also does this to a lesser degree in _Nerbonesi_ 1:123, 131.

21. _Guerrino_, fols. 6r, 173r, 174v, 175v, 179r, 180v.

22. " . . . valentj turchi chavalierj difenditorj della fè di Maometto chontro a' cristianj" (Ibid., fol. 178v). (All translations in this essay are my own.)

23. " . . . chapitano di tutta la gente persiana e arabesscha chontro a' turchi" (ibid., fol. 63v).

24. The notion of four distinct "laws" or faiths already appears in Giovanni Villani, *Cronica*, book II, chap. 8 as cited in D'Ancona, "Il Tesoro di Brunetto Latini versificato," 274.

25. "Bene che molti pagani fussino del legnaggio di Sem e di Iafet, nondimeno cominciamo a costui, e a Cus suo figliuolo, e Nembrotte, figliuolo di Cusse" (*Nerbonesi* 1:345).

26. The distinction between Saracens and pagans appears briefly in *Guerrino* as well, where Andrea categorizes combatants as "cristiani e ssaracinj e paganj" (fol. 49v).

27. See, for example, D'Ancona, "*Il Tesoro*," 178: "L'islamismo adunque alle menti degli uomini dell'età di mezzo dovette naturalmente sembrare una delle tante aberrazioni dalla verità predicata da Cristo." The same idea is expressed more recently: "The medieval mind conceived Muhammad not as the founder of a new religion but as a schismatic and apostate" (Al-Sabah, "*Inferno* XXVIII: The Figure of Muhammad," 148).

28. Isidore of Seville, *Etymologiae IX*, p. 47.

29. *Mandeville's Travels* (Seymour, ed.), 102–103. Mandeville seems somewhat confused on this point: "ther ben Sarazines that ben clept Ishmaelytenes; and some Agaryenes, of Agar, and the othere propurly be clept Sarrazines, of Sarra." On *Mandeville's Travels*, see Frank Grady, "'Machomete' and *Mandeville's Travels*" elsewhere in this volume.

30. *Mandeville's Travels*, [Anonymous medieval Italian translation], 1:172–73. For this edition, Zambrini used two Florentine exemplars of Mandeville in Italian: Magliabechiano XXXV, cod. 221 of the Biblioteca Nazionale, and Ricc. 1917 of the Biblioteca Riccardiana.

31. Villani, cited in D'Ancona, "*Il Tesoro*" 272; *Nerbonesi* 1:350.

32. *Nerbonesi* 1:342: "E come Ismaelle prese da poi moglie, di cui nacque la generazione chiamata Sarain per lo nome del luogo dove prima abitò Ismaelle. . . ."

33. ". . . Maometto ch'è nostro idio . . ." (Guerino, fol. 70r); " . . . Maumetto . . . è 'l loro grande iddio . . . " (fol. 106v); "nostro grande idio Maometto" (fol. 197v).

34. *Chanson de Roland*, see esp. ll. 2580–2590. Other texts such as *La Chanson d'Aspremont* (ll. 3700, 3704, 8228–8229) represent Islam as having four gods: Mahon, Tervagant, Apolin, and Jupiter. See also Meredith Jones, "The Conventional Saracen of the Songs of Geste," 206–08; and Zink, "Apollin," 503–509.

35. Anon., *The Greek Alexander Romance*, 134–135.

36. " ... uno sacerdote del tenpio [sic] d'Apollo ... " (*Guerrino*, fol. 113r). In *Ugone* 2:125–126, Andrea still more explicitly describes "Apolline" in terms equivalent to the classical god Apollo.

37. Donnelly, 164. In another of his romances, Andrea illustrates the belief that priests served the god Muhammad: " ... un satrapo, ch'era prete di Maometto ... " (*Ajolfo* 2:180).

38. " ... e llo re Aginapar rienpie per queste parole tutto il chanpo che Guerrino era huomo mandato dagli dej in aiuto de' persianj, ch'eglj era figliuolo di Marte, idio delle battagl[i]e ... " (*Guerrino*, fol. 65v).

39. Prayer for help "Maometto c'aiutj" (Ibid., fol. 184v); asking for protection on sea voyage (fol. 104r); thanking for answered prayers "O Maumetto vendichatore de' turchi ... " (fol. 180v); cursing (fols. 68v, 111v, 119r, 182v passim); taking oath or greeting "per Maometto" (fol. 114r passim). For similar usage in *chansons de geste* see Meredith Jones, "Conventional Saracen" 206–207.

40. For earlier examples of Saracen turbans and war cries, see Pastre, "Étranges sarrasins," 331–332.

41. This is also noted in *Mandeville's Travels* (Seymour, ed.), 48: "And thei beren but o scheld and o spere withouten other armes." However, Christians are "bene armati" (*Aspramonte* 9).

42. For Saracens wearing turbans, see also *Mandeville's Travels*, (Seymour, ed.), 44, 73.

43. "i ... in questo g[i]unse dinanzi da llei uno suo chapitano di guerra chon uno cercine di tela lina avolto al chapo e una iscimitarra allato chon uno bastone in mano, barba grande, ed una chapegliaia piloso [sic] che parea uno orso ... " (*Guerrino*, fol. 33r).

44. Since Ricc. MS. 2226 contains an error in word order here, I now quote from Ricc. MS. 2267, fol. 132r: "Gherardo non avea maj veduto piu saracinj e quelli facieno si grande il romore ch'elli avea paura di quelle grida."

45. Al-Sabah, 150.

46. Fazio degli Uberti, *Il Dittamondo e Le Rime*, Book V, chap. XII, ll. 22–24, 61–66. The medieval misconception of "Islam as a religion of violence and the sword" was held even by Aquinas and persists almost to our own day (Watt, *The Influence of Islam on Medieval Europe*, 75).

47. Magl. MS. XXXV, 169, fol. 60r–v (early fifteenth century) and Magl. MS. II.IV.279, fol. 41r–v (finished copying in 1478), both at the Biblioteca Nazionale Centrale in Florence. The first follows the "Sergio" tradition while the second preserves that of "Niccholao." I include

mention of these two manuscripts for the reader's information since they have not been cited in any of the Italian studies known to me and appear to be unknown with respect to the European discourse on Muhammad.

48. "Maometto . . . chome ipochrito fa perdere tutta la generazione sarraina . . . " (*Guerrino*, fol. 106v).

49. Dante, *Inferno* IV, 129.

50. ". . . io fuj re e ffuj chiamato Palidor da Polismagna d'Egitto il quale tue facesti battezzare. Per la grazia di dio sono salvo, ma io sono gudichato [sic] di stare mille annj in purgatorio per la iscienza ch'io aveo che lla nostra fede sarraina era falsa e vana, e none avevo cerch[at]o di farmj battezzare" (*Guerrino*, fol. 148r).

51. *Inferno*, XXVIII, 35; Ricc. Ms. 2226, fol. 62r.

52. For Christian conceptions of mosques in Old French *chansons de geste*, see Meredith Jones, "Conventional Saracen," 209–210. In Italian texts surveyed, brief passing references to mosques occur with the variant spelling "meschite" (*Inferno* VIII, 70; Fazio, Book V, chap. XII, l. 44). The earliest occurrence of the word *moschea* recorded by Battaglia, *Grande dizionario della letteratura italiana* (10:986) is in Pulci's *Morgante*, a fifteenth-century Florentine work which postdates Andrea. Earlier unrecorded occurrences are found in Andrea's *Ugone* (2:180) and, as we shall see, in *Guerrino*.

53. " . . . andamo alla moschea ch'è chosi chiamata la quale ène tonda e non è molto alta; molto ène minore che sSanta Maria Ritonda di Roma e dentro entrò l'almansore ischalzò e 'nsulla porta s'inginochiò ed io ch'egli ero apresso m'inginochiaj non per divozione ma per vedere. E vidi là dentro l'argaliffa chon molti sacerdoti a lloro modo richamente adobatj e poi che noj fumo ritti, alzai el viso e posi mente chome era fatta la chiesa falsa di maometto. Ella era insino al mezzo dintorno biancha e dal mezzo insu era tutta nera e intorno intorno tra 'l biancho e 'l nero era una listra rossa ed àvi due finestre tonde l'una verso levante e ll'altra verso ponente [Ed evi due porte l'una dal levante e ll'altra da ponente] e nel mezzo della chiesa è uno altare chon uno circhulo d'alabastro intorno la sonmità dello alabastro era tutto d'oro e ll'altare parea tutto d'oro, e intorno dell'altare erano i magorj sacerdotj, . . . e intorno a questo choro dove era l'altare si poteva andare ma dentro no." Citation taken from Ricc. MS. 2226, fol. 61r–v, with additional material (indicated between square brackets) from Conventi Soppressi MS. C. 1, Camaldoli 720, fol. 42v, Biblioteca Nazionale Centrale, Florence.

54. For a fifteenth-century Florentine artist's conception of the mosque's exterior, see MS. Camaldoli 720, fol. 41, a design which bears a striking similarity to the thirteenth-century lead *bulla* of the Knights Templar.

55. Barker, "The Crusades," 62.

56. Gulick, *Muhammad the Educator*, 88.

57. Briggs, "Architecture," 160.

58. Theoderich, *Guide to the Holy Land*, 25.

59. *Mandeville's Travels*, (Seymour, ed.), 60.

60. A census of MSS in various languages is found in Bennett, *The Rediscovery of Sir John Mandeville*, 263–334.

61. Enrico Cerulli, *Nuove ricerche sul "Libro della Scala,"* 42–43 n. 3.

62. D'Ancona, "*Il Tesoro,*" 194, 267, 274.

63. Muir, *The Life of Mohammad from Original Sources*, 504.

64. The legend is first found, it seems, in Embrico of Mainz's *Vita Mahumeti*. See Eckhardt, "Le cercueil flottant de Mahomet.," 77–88. The persistence of this myth is demonstrated by an engraved illustration in the De Bry edition of the *Acta Mahometis* printed at Frankfort as late as 1597 (Cerulli, plate 7).

65.

> Nello mezzo di questa chupola era uno vaso ritratto a modo d'una chassetta di ferro pulita istimai di grandezza uno bracco e mezzo e alchuna chosa meno per l'altro verso e istava sospesa e non tochava niente. Allora chonobi lo 'nganno del falso Maometto inperò ch'io chonobbi che quella parte di quella falsa c[h]iesa era dal mezzo insu tutta di chalamita la quale ène una pietra marina ch'è di cholore tra nero e bigo e à questa propieta in sé ch'ella tira il ferro a sse per la sua frigidezza . . . . e questa chagone l'archa di maometto ch'è di ferro ista sospesa perché lla chalamita la tiene, e lla grossa gente sarraina non sanno che chosa sia chalamita chredono che ll'archa che ista in altura istia per miracholo. (*Guerrino*, fol. 61v).

66. See, e.g., *Mandeville's Travels*, (Seymour, ed.), 29: "Also the cytee of Methon, where Machomet lyth, is also of the grete desertes of Arabye; and there lith the body of hym fulle honourabely in here temple that the Sarazines clepen *musketh.*"

67. In another of his texts, Andrea portrays a large number of his Saracen characters as having good qualities. They are aristocratic, brave, proud and loyal and some become Christian. See Schmidt, "Ein Vergleich," 123.

68.

> E all'uscire della moschea nella quale non può entrare nessuna femmina vidi certi che s'avevano chavati gli occhi e dicevano che llo facevano per amore di Maometto e per non vedere mai nessuna chosa dapoi ch'egli aveno veduta l'archa di Maometto che al mondo non era la più sancta chosa. Ed io mi ridevo della loro stoltitia E udi dire che ll'anno che fanno il perdono molti si mettono sotto le ruote de' charri e fannossi uccidere e dicono che danno di lor volunta il chorpo per l'amore di Maometto e loro chorpi ne sono portati ne' lloro paesi e tenghono che sieno sancti in chonpagnia di Maometto." (Camaldoli 720, fols. 41v–42r).

69. One Ḥadith recorded by Ahmad Ivn Hanbal advises women to perform prayer in their houses (Wensinck, *Handbook of Early Muhammadan Tradition,* 193) while a larger group states that women should not be prevented from visiting the mosque (ibid., 255).

70. A translation of Oderic's work is found in the collection *The Travels of Sir John Mandeville* and *The Voyage of Johannes de Plano Carpini; The Journal of Friar William de Rubruquis; The Journal of Friar Odoric* from Hakluyt's *Navigations, Voyages, and Discoveries* (New York, 1964), 333.

71. Ibid.

72. *Mandeville's Travels* (Seymour, ed.), 129–130. An equivalent passage in Italian is found in the Italian translation of Mandeville 2:43–44.

73. Bezzola, "L'Oriente nel poema cavalleresco del primo Rinascimento," 395.

74. Faridi, *Everyday Practice in Islam,* 16.

75. Rambaldis da Imola, *Comentum super D. Alighierii Comoediam* 2:352. Fazio, Book V, chap. XII, ll. 46–51.

76. " . . . la danmigella . . . ffue rachomandata alla reina magore inperò che alla loro usanza sarraina egli tolgono molte mogl[i]e e 'l soldano n'avea piu di cc.° mogl[i]e e una n'avea inchoronata reina . . . " (fol. 63v).

77. G. Villani in D'Ancona, "*Il Tesoro*," 273; Fazio, Book V, chap.
XII, l. 25.

78.

> Lionetto insu uno letto di seta a g[i]acere e nel
> padiglone era' moltj tappetj in terra e moltj signorj
> dove tre e dove quattro a ssedere chi g[i]uchava a uno
> g[i]uocho e chi a uno altro. Non si potre' dire lo
> scellerato modo chome egli istavano e lLionetto
> meschin avia le ganbe alta e mostrava le disoneste
> parte della sua persona; chosi moltj altrj. (fol. 182v)

79. Narayan, *Mohammed the Prophet*, 40, 172.

80. ". . . l'ostiere chiamò la figliuola e ffece rechare da mang[i]are e
da bere e non rechò vino perché la lege loro chomanda non beino vino
ma rechò aqua chon ispezerie chon uve seche macinate (*Guerrino*, fol.
69r).

81. Muir, 475 n. 1.

82. Qur'ân, 5:33, 38; 7:124; 20:71.

83. ". . . lui farà segare come traditore" Nerbonesi 2:651;
"bando . . . della sega" Ajolf*o* 2:12; "meritava la forca e la sega" *Ajolfo*
2:17; "segati per mezzo" *Ajolfo* 2:233, 239; "ssegato pello mezzo" Ricc.
2226, fol. 97v.

84.

> si gittò l'almansore tre volte in terra chol viso dicendo
> non essere degno di vedere e ffannogli p[rop]io
> l'onore che merita inperò ch'egli naschondono a
> Maomeometto [sic] la più bella chosa che idio facessi
> al mondo inperò ch'egli naschondono il viso e
> (m)mostrògli il chulo ch'è lla disonesta parte della
> persona. Alora vedendo gittare ognuno in terra, volsi
> le spalle all'archa e missi el viso in terra e ingegnamj
> d'alzare l'anche per suo sprego chome à chosi fatto
> inganno si chonvenia; e lla mia orazione fu questa: "O
> maladetto seminatore di schandolj, la divina potenza
> dia a tte debito merito dell'anime che ttu ài fatto e ffaj
> perdere per la falsa operazione. (*Guerrino*, fol. 61v–
> 62r)

85. Meredith-Jones, 201–203.

86. For more on the historical role of European knights in the employ of foreign princes, see Frank Grady, "'Machomete' and Mandeville's Travels" elsewhere in this collection.

87. ". . . ed io di queste pazie aveo tra (n)me medesimo piacere e inchrescevamj dell'anime loro" (*Guerrino*, fol. 62r).

88. Cabani, *Le forme del cantare epico-cavalleresco*, 76.

CHAPTER 12

"Machomete" and *Mandeville's Travels*

Frank Grady

The one thing we know for sure about *The Travels of Sir John Mandeville*—which was probably composed about 1357, in French, probably on the continent—is that it was "the most popular secular book in circulation" in its day,[1] a fact attested to by about 250 surviving manuscripts and 35 incunabular editions (in a total of ten languages). The *Travels*—written by an unknown author who may never have left his library, much less Western Europe—recounts the thirty-odd years spent by one "Sir John Mandeville," an English knight from St. Albans, in traveling through the known world, from the Holy Land and the Eastern Mediterranean to India and China, and almost to the shadow of the Earthly Paradise. Equal parts pilgrimage guide, encyclopedia, and universal chronicle, the *Travels* exerted considerable influence over European conceptions of the world beyond Christendom even into the sixteenth century, after which time the text's obvious inaccuracies—or, perhaps better, its lack of susceptibility to scientific and empirical confirmation—left it to languish in a state of malign neglect, punctuated by an occasional editor's diatribe about its status as plagiarism and forgery.

For whatever its generic affiliations,[2] the *Travels* is above all a text woven out of other texts, a careful and stylish conflation of earlier travel accounts, exotic romances, miraculous legends, and stories of marvels, all drawn together by the conceit of Sir John's lengthy "voiage" and his frequent evaluation and comment on the state of the world. Nowhere is this conflation of sources more adeptly handled—and nowhere does Sir John play so important a role—as in the *Travels'* account of the state of Islam and the nations under "Saracen" rule, which occupies several chapters in the first part of the text. Here, as with many of the topics he treats, the author of the *Travels* waxes encyclopedic, making his text an irresistible source for the study of Christian perceptions of Islam in the mid-fourteenth century. In *Western Views of Islam in the Middle Ages*, R. W. Southern says of Islam that

> As a practical problem it called for action and for discrimination between the competing possibilities of crusade [which the author of the *Travels* calls for in his Prologue], conversion [which the Travels ultimately promotes, and also sees as inevitable], coexistence [embodied in Sir John's two years' service as a soldier of the Sultan of Egypt], and commercial interchange [which the author of the *Travels* inextricably ties to informational exchange, in the form of espionage].[3]

And there's more: The author of the *Travels* gives the Saracens a voice of their own in the figure of the Sultan of Egypt, with whom Sir John has an unusual private conversation in chapter 15.

Sir John prepares for this extraordinary private colloquy by previously establishing for us his close relations with the Sultan: "I duelled with him as soudyour in his werres a gret while ayen the Bedoynes," he claims in chapter 6, adding that "he wolde haue maryed me full highly to a gret princes doughter yif I wolde han forsaken my lawe and my byleue, but I thanke God I had no wille to don it for no thing that he behighte me" (6:24). Later he asserts that he was able to travel freely in the Sultan's lands because "I hadde lettres of the Soudan with his grete seel, and comounly other men had but his signet; in the which lettres he commanded of his specyalle grace to alle his subgettes to lete me seen alle the places and to enforme me pleynly alle the mysteries of euery place and to condyte me fro cytee to cytee . . ." (11:60); on and on he goes, reminding us again at the end of the passage that other (lesser) men who ask for the Sultan's grace receive only the signet, in case that distinction escaped us the first time.[4] Having established himself as a favorite and intimate of the Sultan, it is thus perfectly reasonable that Sir John would pause to illustrate his observations on the Saracen faith (derived from William of Tripoli's *De Statu Saracenorum* [1273][5]) with a revealing personal anecdote (derived from Caesarius of Heisterbach's *Dialogus Miraculorum* [1223][6]). That the rebuke which ensues closely resembles the dialogue between one Brother William of Utrecht and a Saracen emir from Caesarius's early thirteenth-century collection of *exempla* does not diminish the originality of the author of the *Travels* in inserting it into an already sympathetic account of Saracen beliefs, and the flourish with which he ends the episode— which I will defer discussing for the moment—renders it one of the most arresting passages in the book.[7]

The passage begins after Sir John has concluded that the Saracens "han many gode articles of oure feyth, alle be it that thei haue no parfite lawe and feyth as Cristene men han" (15:100). The Saracens are monotheists, believing in the Creation and Doomsday, and they venerate both the Virgin Mary and Jesus, whom they acknowledge as the Word of God. In fact, they might be easily converted due to this proximity to the Christian law, although they are mired in a literal rather than spiritual understanding of the Scriptures.[8] In a characteristically thorough report, Mandeville acknowledges that the Saracens themselves think that both Jews and Christians fail to fulfill their own laws: Jews "han defouled the lawe that God sent hem by Moyses," and Christians "ben cursed. . . . for thei kepen not the commandementes and the preceptes of the gospelle that Ihesu Crist taughte hem" (15:100). And here he digresses, that the Christians might be cursed in person:

> And therfore I schalle telle you what the Soudan tolde me vpon a day in his chambre. He leet voyden out of his chambre alle maner of men, lordes and othere, for he wolde speke with me in conseille. And there he asked me how the Cristene men gouerned hem in oure contree, and I seyde him, "Right wel, thonked be God. (15:100)

The convention that informs Mandeville's hapless reply renders it utterly disingenuous. When confronted with a similar question in the *Dialogus Miraculorum*, William of Utrecht, "unwilling to

say what the truth was," played it cagily: "Well enough," he
answered, "*Satis bene*."⁹ Here, as there, it precipitates a diatribe
excoriating everything from Christian gluttony, irreverence,
belligerence, deceit, avarice, and lechery to their prideful slavery
to fashion: "thei knowen not how to ben clothed, now long, now
schort, now streyt, now large, now swerded, now daggered, in
alle maner gyses" (15:100). And the Sultan firmly attaches his
rebuke to the prevailing theme of sin and dominion already
established by Sir John in the Prologue, where he himself had
described the sinfulness and depravity of Western Christian
lords as responsible for the loss of the Holy Land.¹⁰ The Sultan
agrees:

> And thus for here synnes han thei lost alle this lond that
> wee holden. For for hire synnes here God hath taken hem
> into oure hondes, noght only be strengthe of oureself but
> for here synnes. For wee knowen wel in verry soth that
> whan yee seruen God, God wil helpe you, and whan He is
> with you, no man may ben ayenst you. (15:101)

It would be a mistake to dismiss these words, which Sir John
deems "a gret sclaundre to oure feith and oure lawe," as simple
ventriloquism on the part of the author. Whenever Sir John's
major themes are placed in the mouth of some other
spokesman—the Sultan, in this case, and later the Cathayans and
the Brahmans—this stand-in is always invested with sufficient
moral authority to criticize freely and legitimately. And the
source of that authority is evident to us, thanks always to Sir
John's own long and close acquaintance with the character and
customs of this other culture. The conceit of travel permits Sir
John to found his critique on close study and personal
knowledge, gained through that travel, and to go beyond the
simple satirical paradigm of the Prologue. Thus both the Sultan's
"trouthe," that is, his and his people's faithful adherence to their
law, and the effectiveness of his political administration, that is,
his ability to manage his realm effectively and magnificently,
render him fit to pass judgment on his Christian counterparts
and their subjects.

"And treuly thei sey soth," says Mandeville of the
Saracens' critical estimation of Christian morals, "For the

Sarazines ben gode and feythfulle, for thei kepen entierly the commandement of the holy book Alkaron that God sente hem be His messager Machomet . . ." (15:102).[11] That the Saracens are true to what Mandeville perforce considers an imperfect law scarcely diminishes the respect they merit; in a style fully in accord with fourteenth-century popular theology, Sir John more than once praises fidelity in intention in non-Catholic peoples— as with the Brahmans and Gymnosophists in chapter 32—and refuses to condemn outright most practices that they engage in so faithfully.[12] Although the categories of Christian and non-Christian remain prominent throughout the *Travels*, Mandeville's readiness to judge either is never based on formal doctrinal allegiance, but on individual or corporate morality. This attention to the spirit of performance informs the *Travels'* treatment of rites as diverse as those of the Christians of Prester John's land, who "beleuen wel in the Fader, in the Sone, and in the Holy Gost. And thei ben fulle deuoute and right trewe on to another" even though "thei haue not alle the articles of oure feith as wee hauen" (30:197); to the Jacobites', whose refusal to practice auricular confession is buttressed by citations from Scripture; to the priests of the Church of St. Thomas of India in Jerusalem, who pray without knowing "the addiciouns that many popes han made, but thei synge with gode deuocoun" (10:58); to the Mabaronians', who undertake pilgrimages to the city of their idol "als comounly and with als gret deuocoun as Cristene men gon to Seynt Iames or other holy pilgrimages" (19:128), where they engage in ritual forms of self-mutilation and suicide to achieve martyrdom "for loue of hire god in gret deuocoun."

Even cannibals can mean well in *Mandeville's Travels*, and the firm belief of the people of Ryboth in their own devout, sober, kind intentions must give any reader pause. The passage in which their priests feed the dead man's flesh to the birds, and the son and kin devour the brain and make a goblet of the skull reverberates with overt echoes of Christian services: "as prestes amonges vs syngen for the dede *Subuenite sancti dei, et cetera*, right so tho prestes syngen"; "And of the brayne pan he leteth make a cuppe, and therof drynketh he and his other frendes also with gret deuocoun in remembrance of the holy man that the aungeles of God han eten" (34:225). One critic finds this scene a "grotesque burlesque,"[13] which is only heightened by reference to "the pope of hire lawe that thei clepen *Lobassy*. This Lobassy yeveth alle the benefices and alle othere dignytees . . . And alle tho that holden ony thing of hire chirches, religious and othere, obeyen to him as men don here to the Pope of Rome" (34:224). But Donald Howard, in a more thorough reading of the passage, points out how the practice of cannibalism, earlier repudiated (the inhabitants of Lamory engage in the "cursed custom" in chapter 20), is here "impregnated with filial piety, with tenderness, with dignified family love, and redolent of the Holy Communion. . . ." The passage "asks us to behold a cannibalism not savage or repugnant but tender, dignified, and pious. It subtly reminds us of the Christian rites at which the Body and Blood of the Lord are consumed, but throws attention on the spirit in which men perform such rites."[14]

The author of the *Travels* has here moved many miles beyond the simple "live well to rule well" formula of the prologue, to a point where irony can be both structural and tonal, where not only who speaks but how they say it (or how it is said about them) matters. Sir John makes sure that we note how the Rybothan service explicitly recalls similar Christian procedures, but at the same time also makes explicit how it benefits the Rybothans themselves by giving them an avenue to express their devotion and reverence. And he refuses to condemn the practice, not because he cannot imagine a moral objection, but ironically precisely because he can, and has, and has registered his disapproval in previous chapters.[15]

For Mandeville, then, devotion seems admirable almost regardless of dogma. Partner to this admiration is the approbation Sir John expresses for successful political administration and princely exercise of power, an example of which is his description of the Sultan's administration of his realm in chapter 6. His castle, the five kingdoms under his rule, the thousands of men at arms he commands, his loyal "amyralles," the elegance and richness of his court and the reverence paid him there (which is merely a preview of the magnificence surrounding the Great Chan)[16] all depict a powerful and secure lord whom Mandeville seems proud to have served. The description peaks with a passage about the

Sultan's magnanimity: No stranger who makes a request of the Sultan will be denied its fulfillment, provided that it does not contradict Saracen law. Indeed, all the princes under the Sultan's rule adopt this policy in imitation of him, saying that "no man schalle come before no prynce but . . . schalle be more gladdere in departynge from his presence thanne he was at the comynge before hym" (6:28).[17] In essence, the Sultan is everything that the Christian lords of the Prologue are not, and the account of his kingdom is a sort of projection of a fallen Western ideal onto a Saracen screen. Although the brief history of the Sultanate that precedes this passage tends to belie its peaceful and generous impression—in fact, it is a litany of parricide, fratricide, and assassination[18]—nevertheless the overall picture of the Sultan's kingdom, revealed through the course of several chapters, is a positive one and one of the kindest in all European medieval literature. It establishes a relationship between political and moral authority that is not only rhetorical, but reciprocal, and which makes the phrase "virtuous heathen" seem an ethnocentrism but not an oxymoron.

At the same time, the Saracens' moral authority is subject to several conventional strategies of containment. The very proximity of the tenets of Islam to Christian doctrine undermines Islam's claims to integrity and self-sufficiency, as if by some process of supernatural selection it will simply evolve into orthodox Christianity. The author of the *Travels* inherits this tactic from William of Tripoli, who devotes more than half of the *De Statu Saracenorum* to cataloging the contiguities of Christianity and Islam, concluding from their proximity that "through the simple word of God, without philosophical arguments or military warfare, like simple sheep [the Saracens] will seek the baptism of Christ and pass into the sheepfold of God."[19]

Further circumscribing the moral threat of Islam is the strategic deployment of prophecy throughout the *Travels*, also a technique it shares with the *De Statu Saracenorum*.[20] Evidently even the Saracens believe the Christians are destined to retake the "Lond of Promyssioun," when (not if) they amend. The Sultan admits to Sir John "that knowe we wel be oure prophecyes that Cristene men schulle wynnen ayen this lond out of oure hondes whan thei seruen God more deuoutly" (15:101). Indeed, according to Mandeville, Islam itself shall vanish according to prophecy: "And also thei seyn that thei knowen wel be prophecyes that the lawe of Machomete schalle faylen as the lawe of the Iewes dide, and that the lawe of Cristene peple schalle laste to the Day of Doom" (15:98–99). The recourse to prophecy allows the author of the *Travels* to assert the moral successes of the virtuous heathen while yet containing them within a larger Christian context, and ultimately an orthodox one. Indeed, speculation about the inevitable if historically indeterminate (in fact, infinitely deferrable) demise of Islam not only diminishes the urgency of the call for a crusade or an elaborate program of proselytizing, it also reduces the duty of Christians interested in the intractable problem of the Saracens to the mere maintenance of the orthodox faith, which is bound to triumph by its very nature. All a good Christian really has to do is not become a Saracen. Thus, Sir John's own orthodoxy functions as a sort of boundary for the exposition of Saracen virtues: although he is a self-confessed admirer, he is firm enough in his own faith to dismiss the thought of converting to their law, despite the offer of marriage to "a gret princes doghter."[21]

The author of the *Travels* thus appears to make the Sultan's critique both more than the allegorized fulmination of a conventional moralist by investing him with the ethical authority to speak freely and legitimately, and less than a true threat to the moral integrity of Chrisitianity by creating an overarching structure of prophecy to provide an orthodox, if unusually tolerant, perspective. But Sir John's amazing conversation is not over yet.

To return to the Sultan's chamber: when Sir John asks the Saracen chief where he acquired the information upon which his accusations are based, the latter replies that

> he knew alle the state of alle contres of Cristene kynges and princes and the state of the comounes also be his messangeres that he sente to alle londes, in manere as thei weren marchauntes of precyous stones, of clothes of gold, and of othere thinges, for to knowen the manere of euery contree amonges Cristene men. (15:101)

Chaucer's Man of Law calls merchants "fadres of tidynges" in his Prologue, and the author of *Mandeville's Travels* shows us why. They're spies:

> And than he leet clepe in alle the lordes that he made voyden first out of his chambre, and there he schewed me iiii. that weren grete lordes in the contree, that tolden me of my contree and of manye other Cristene contrees als wel as thei had ben of the same contree, and thei spak Frensch right wel and the Sowdan also; whereof I had gret meruaylle. (15:101)

Perhaps the most striking thing about Sir John's response to this revelation is his utter lack of alarm at the prospect of Arabic espionage perfectly disguised as mercantile activity;[22] he issues no warnings to his countrymen, no call to monitor trade or close the ports. In fact, anxiety about the use of merchants as spies was relatively widespread, especially in xenophobic wartime England,[23] where the ports were closed off and on throughout the Hundred Years' War—although paradoxically "[e]xceptions to the general ordinance were . . . often made, as when the bailiffs and wardens of the ports were instructed to permit 'known merchants' to leave."[24] Later in the century, Philippe de Mézières—perhaps drawing on Mandeville—would claim that

> the spies through whom one might best learn of the state of his enemies are Lombards and other foreign merchants, who because of their trade have occasion in person or through their agents to send from one part to another; and especially those merchants who by means of their trade in precious stones gain access and private friendship with kings and princes.[25]

But Sir John merely expresses "gret meruayle" at the phenomenon, more impressed perhaps by the Saracens' perfect French than by their covert activities.[26]

The key to Sir John's silence and his "meruayle" may lie in the adaptations that the author of the *Travels* has made to this episode as it comes down to him from Caesarius of Heisterbach. In the *Dialogus Miraculorum*, the Saracen emir who is William of Utrecht's companion claims to have learned French in the household of the King of Jerusalem, where he had been sent as a boy in a sort of aristocratic cultural exchange program; his indictment of Christian behavior is limited to the inhabitants of the Kingdom of Jerusalem, although Brother William's "satis bene" clearly implies that the rebuke is meant for Christendom at large.[27] But in the *Travels*, what had been open cultural exchange becomes covert infiltration, disguised as trade and issuing in direct knowledge of Christian depravity. The Sultan's critique of Western mores is not implied, but bluntly stated, and based on immediate and empirical evidence—the testimony of his spies.

This is a strikingly unconventional moment in the *Travels*, for a number of reasons. First, it gives weight to the Sultan's words over and above his carefully elaborated moral authority, suggesting that he has a practical and empirical right to speak about the vicious habits of the Christian West. The superstructure of prophecy and doctrinal proximity created to limit both the integrity and the evaluative power of Islam cannot restrict evaluations based on direct observation—not in a text the very conceit of which is the collection and assessment of information through direct ethnographic study, through the very adventures and travels of Sir John Mandeville. If we accept the premise of *Mandeville's Travels*, we must also accept this fundamental analogy between one kind of discovery and another. It is perhaps no coincidence that one Latin word for spy—*explorator*—has come to mean something quite different for us.

And here arises the second problem. For not only is Sir John like the Saracen merchant-spies in his fact-gathering activities, but the occupation that enables him to travel and learn—mercenary knight—is analogous to theirs as well. Like De Mézières's Lombards, Sir John's private friendship with the Sultan has earned him the privilege of inquiring into "alle the places" and of exploring "pleynly alle the mysteries of euery place" in the Sultan's domain. And it is through these investigations and this participation in the daily business of the Arab world—blending in, taking part, speaking we must presume adequate Arabic (for the Sultan evidently does not break into French until his espionage network has been revealed)[28]—that Sir John's own compatriots learn about the

Arabic world, and beyond. Who else knows French "right wel" in *Mandeville's Travels*? Why, Sir John himself, of course: "And yee schulle vndirstonde that I haue put this boke out of Latyn into Frensch and translated it ayen out of Frensch into Englyssch, that euery man of my nacoun may vndirstonde it" (Prologue: 3–4).

Rather than precious stones, however, Sir John exchanges his services for information and the chance to study the world through which he moves. That the narrator of *Mandeville's Travels* is a knight is the first thing we learn about him: "I Iohn Maundevylle knyght, alle be it I be not worthi, that was born in Englond in the town of Seynt Albones, and passed the see in the yeer of oure lord Ihesu Crist m.ccc. and xxii. in the day of Seynt Michelle, *etc., etc.*" (Prologue: 3). We soon learn that that his knighthood is more existential than it is feudal, that it comes with an allegiance that can be transferred or sold. It crosses national boundaries not because of some inherent quality of transcendence, but because it stands for a set of valuable and sought-after skills—because it can be commodified and rendered as negotiable as a gem and as marketable as cloth of gold.[29] Thus the fourteenth-century Arab historian Ibn Khaldûn notes how, for the Muslims, too, desire for a commodity—in this case Western military technology—overcomes doctrinal impediments.

> The position of the ruler is strengthened by establishing a line formation in support of the fighting men ahead of it. The men in such a line formation must be people who are used to hold firm in closed formation. If not, they will run away like the men who use the technique of attack and withdrawal, and, when they run away, the ruler and the army will be routed. Therefore, the rulers of the Maghrib had to use soldiers from a nation used to hold firm in closed formation. That nation was the European Christians. The line formation around their (army) is formed by European Christians. The Maghribi rulers do this despite the fact that it means utilizing the aid of unbelievers. They do not think much of it, because the necessity (of using such men) exists, as we have shown. They fear that their own line formation might run away, and (they know that) the European Christians know only

> how to hold firm, because it is their custom to fight in
> closed formation. They are, therefore, more suitable for the
> purpose than others.[30]

The role of European and particularly English mercenaries in the
Mediterranean has been explored by several critics and
historians.[31] Norman Daniel describes a conventional stereotype
of "the loyal Christian knight in Arab service" which reflects "a
pattern of employment, especially in North Africa, over a very
long time."[32]

Hence Sir John's service in the Sultan's wars against the
"Bedoynes" in chapter 6 and his fifteen-month stint in the Great
Chan's army "ayenst the kyng of Mancy" in chapter 23
demonstrate that the struggles for succession and the wars of
conquest whose history he relates throughout the *Travels* extend
into the present as well, a present in which Sir John is meant to
be thoroughly implicated, not as a neutral observer or an
itinerant romance knight, but as an historical actor, a role
completely intelligible to a fourteenth-century audience. But
what would that audience have made of such a role? In the
decade or so preceding the composition of *Mandeville's Travels*, it
might have been seen as at the least unpatriotic; at several points
during the 1340s and 1350s Edward III issued proclamations
intended to prohibit English knights from seeking employment
from foreign princes or even from going on pilgrimage.[33]
Suddenly Sir John's address to the knights and lords in his
audience at the end of the Prologue sounds more like worldly
cynicism than conventional authorial obsequiousness:

> But lordes and knyghtes and othere noble and worthi men
> that conne not Latyn but litylle and han ben beyonde the
> see knowe and vnderstonden yif I seye trouthe or non.
> And yif I erre in devisynge for foryetynge or elles, that thei
> mowe redresse it and amende it. (Prologue: 4)

The topos of correction here reaches out and threatens to
implicate the audience, to extract their approval of and mark
their complicity in the account of contemporary European and
Mediterranean history that the *Travels* supplies. Just who are
these "othere noble and worthi men"—and just why have they
been beyond the sea?

Ultimately, then, the real lesson that *Mandeville's Travels* teaches about the philosophical proximity of the West and the East—and the real reason for Sir John's "gret meruayle" and subsequent silence on the subject of Saracen espionage—is that the similarities are in fact deeper and more disturbing than even his charitable evaluations of Saracen doctrine might suggest. Sir John's investigations reveal that it is not interdenominational devotion to the worship of the one God but international complicity in the realm of trade, war, and politics that unifies the world. It is an idea that Sir John backs away from, I think, when he recognizes it—but one that the author of the *Travels* clearly implies.

Sir John registers his anxiety by shifting his attentions quite suddenly from the Mediterranean to parts farther abroad. Chapter 15, which begins with the Qur'ân and the Sultan's interview, ends with the tenets of Islam and the implict suggestion that the mere fact of difference ought not always to imply the necessity or imminence of moral evaluation. Sometimes it's just alphabetical: after setting down a version of the Arabic alphabet, Sir John observes that

> . . . iiii. lettres thei haue more than othere for dyuersitee of hire langage and speche, for als moche as thei speken in here throtes. And wee in Englond haue in oure langage and speche ii. lettres mo than thei haue in hire abc, and that is *Þ* and *3*, the whiche ben clept thorn and yogh. (15:104)

The recognition that the difference between what is English and what is Saracen is both so natural and basic and so trivial as a couple of the symbols in the alphabet evidently proves unnerving, for Sir John quickly mounts up and rides off into parts unexplored at the beginning of the next chapter.[34]

> Now sith I haue told you beforn of the Holy Lond and of that contree abouten and of many weyes for to go to that lond and to the Mount Synay and of Babyloyne the More and the Less and to other places that I have spoken [of] beforn; now is tyme yif it like you for to telle you of the marches and iles and dyuerse bestes and of dyuerse folk beyond theise marches. For in tho contrees beyonden ben many diuerse contrees and many grete kyngdomes that

ben departed by the iiii. flodes that comen from Paradys
Terrestre. (16:105)

Ultimately the emphasis on difference and diversity ("dyuerse
bestes," "dyuerse folk," "diuerse contrees") will again fail to
sustain itself; the farther East, like the nearer East, will turn out
to be home to much that is morally and politically congenial to
Sir John's turn of mind.

That tolerant perspective, however, and the overall
congeniality of the narrator ought not to blind us to the most
dismaying implications of his account of the relationship
between the Christian West and the Saracen Mediterranean. If
anything, the easy familiarity which Sir John invites with his
humane and tolerant outlook ought to evoke in us the same
anxiety he manifests in Chapter 15, when he experiences and
then swallows into silence his "gret meruayle." For in fact things
haven't changed that much in the six-and-one-half centuries
since the composition of *Mandeville's Travels*. The Gulf War of
1991, with its transferring and purchasing of allegiances, its
suppression of doctrinal differences in the interest of larger
political considerations, the massive amount of information its
transactions made available—indeed, unavoidable—in our
contemporary media, and the collective presumption in the West
that there exists in the Arab world a resource that only the West
can properly appreciate and exploit, and must reclaim—*nunc* oil,
olim the sanctity of the Holy Land—all this demonstrates not so
much Mandeville's prophetic modernity as our own inability to
leave the Middle Ages behind.[35]

NOTES

1. *Mandeville's Travels*, xx. Citations from Seymour's edition of the
Cotton manuscript are identified in the text by chapter and page
number. Although the *Travels* was probably first composed on the
Continent, I treat it in this essay almost exclusively as an English book,
in part because of my own field of expertise, but also because the text
was so eagerly adopted by the English, who produced multiple versions

of it in the fourteenth and fifteenth centuries. And even in the original redaction, Sir John represents himself as an English knight.

Malcolm Letts prints a French version of the *Travels* in the second volume of his Hakluyt Society edition (2nd ser., vol. 102, 1953), as does Warner in the Roxburghe Club edition (*The Buke of John Mandevill* (London, 1889). For a full account of the history and reception of the *Travels*, see Bennett, *The Rediscovery of Sir John Mandeville*; Higgins, "The World of a Book of the World"; and Deluz, *Le Livre de Jehan Mandeville*; for bibliography, Ralph Hanna III, "Mandeville," 121–132; and Zacher, "Travel and Geographical Writings, 2235–54, 2449–66."

2. A useful prolegomenon to the study of the various discourses operating in the *Travels* has been articulated by Iain Higgins in "The Multiplicity of Writing in *The Book of John Mandeville*," a paper delivered at the Medieval Association of the Pacific Conference at University of California-Davis, March 2, 1991.

3. Southern, *Western Views of Islam in the Middle Ages*, 3.

4. For a metaphorical approach to Sir John's "passport," see Greenblatt, *Marvelous Possessions*, 38.

5. William of Tripoli, *Tractatus de statu Saracenorum*. William was a Dominican living in Acre in the second half of the thirteenth century.

6. Caesarius of Heisterbach, *Dialogus Miraculorum*, Book IV, chap. 15; see also Letts, ed., *Mandeville's Travels: Texts and Translations*, 97, n. 2; and Chauvin, "Le Pretendu Sejour de Mandeville en Egypte," 237–242.

7. Indeed, the conversation between Mandeville and the Sultan later took on a life of its own, as witnessed by the "Stanzaic Fragment" of Bodleian MS e Musaeo 160, an early sixteenth-century MS containing 313 lines about "[Ser Iohn Mandev]ille and Ser Marc of Venesse," including a report of "The Commonyng of Sir Iohan Mandeville and þe Gret Sowdon" (ll. 185–240). Seymour, who has edited the fragment ("Mandeville and Marco Polo: A Stanzaic Fragment"), sees a general but not certain correspondence between the verse and the Cotton version of the *Travels*. At the very least, the "Fragment" reveals a reader who found Mandeville interesting precisely because of his description of pagan kingdoms: the "Sowdan" and the "Grete Caan" occupy virtually every stanza.

8. In this description the author of *Mandeville's Travels* leans heavily on William of Tripoli; see n. 19.

9. *Caesarius*, Book IV, 187: "Ille dicere nolens quod verum fuit, respondit, 'Satis bene.'"

10. This theme first arises at Prologue: 2–3, and the author of the *Travels* returns to it again and again: "For God wole not that [the Holy Land] be longe in the hondes of traytoures ne of synneres, be thei Cristene or othere. And now haue the hethene men holden that lond in here hondes xl. yere and more, but thei schulle not holde it longe yif God wole" (10:55). And again: "But whan God allemyghty wole, right

als the londes weren lost thorgh synne of Cristene men, so schulle thei ben wonnen ayen be Cristen men thorgh help of God" (10:58). And again: "For withouten ony drede, ne were cursednesse and synne of Cristene men, thei scholden ben lordes of alle the world" (28:88).

11. In the Defective Text (*The Travels of Sir John Mandeville: A Facsimile of Pynson's Edition of 1496*) the Saracens "are trewe for they kepe truly the com[m]andementes of their alkaron" (sig. E3ᵛ); the Egerton text (in Letts' modernized version; see n. 4) calls them "right devout in their law and right true" (99). In addition, the Defective version refers to the Saracens' beliefs as their "trouthe" at the beginning of the chapter (sig. E1ʳ), instead of Cotton's "beleue" (15:96).

12. For a review of fourteenth-century theological opinions on the value of pagan virtue, see, e.g., Coleman, *Piers Plowman and the Moderni*, esp. chap. 4.

13. *Mandeville's Travels*, ed. P. Hamelius, EETS o.s. 153–154 (London, 1919, 1923), vol. ii. 146. The editor here follows Mandeville's source in Odoric of Pordenone, who termed the practice "vile and abominable." See Komroff, *Contemporaries of Marco Polo*, 244–245.

14. Howard, "World," 16. See also Greenblatt, 45, who finds the scene equally remarkable, if less subtle.

15. See, e.g., the account of the people of Lamory in chap. 20, who engage in the "euil custom" of eating human flesh; other instances can be found in chaps. 21 and 31.

16. The extent of the Chan's influence is felt even in the description of Egypt; in making the distinction between the Sultan's Babylon and the biblical "gret Babyloyne" of tower fame, Mandeville notes that the latter lies within the land that pay tribute to the "Grete Chane," who is "more myghty and gretter lord withouten comparsoun than is the Soudan" (6:29).

17. The Cotton version is very garbled here:

> And also no straungere cometh before him but that he maketh hym sum promys and graunt of that the Soudan asketh resonably, be it so it be not ayenst his lawe. And so don othere prynces beyonden, for thei seyn that no man schalle come before no prynce but that the Soudan is bettre and schalle be more gladdere in departynge from his presence thanne he was at the comynge before hym. (6:28)

I have omitted for sense in the text. The French text (quoted by Hamelius [vol. ii.43] and Seymour [*Mandeville's Travels* (Cotton Version), 260n.]) reads much more sensibly, as do the Egerton and Bodley versions (see Letts, vol. i.28 and vol. ii.434).

18. In fact, the account is appalling, albeit delivered in Mandeville's characteristically matter-of-fact style. The effect of such a juxtaposition, as usual, is to force the reader to pause and assess what's

being described; as I suggested previously, the final assessment is a (disturbingly) positive one. On the accuracy of the *Travels'* description of the Arab world see Bennett, 61–64.

19. William of Tripoli, *De Statu Saracenorum*, 597–598.

20. The *Dialogus Miraculorum* episode also contains a prophecy of the Christians' impending (but not immediate) reclamation of the Holy Land. It is possible that Mandeville's use of one formal move toward containment—prophecy—is meant to take the place of another equally conventional one—crusade. Although the Prologue seems to issue a half-hearted exhortation, the passages quoted above could be taken as implicitly deferring the necessity for another "generalle passage."

21. On the level of genre, the rejection of the Saracen princess by the author of the *Travels* represents an embrace of his historical and ethnographic project to the pointed exclusion of any sort of romance perspective. Dorothy Metlitzki describes the importance of the marriage theme in literary treatments of Christian-Muslim relations (see *The Matter of Araby in Medieval England*, 136–176); I argue later, however, that in *Mandeville's Travels*, war and commerce—two sides of the same coin, as it were—bind the two cultures much more closely and permanently than love.

22. For an account of contemporary anxiety about the use of merchants as spies, see Alban and Allmand, "Spies and Spying in the Fourteenth Century," 73–101.

23. On English anxiety about foreigners, both mercantile and clerical, see Hewitt, *The Organization of War Under Edward III*, 165–168.

24. Alban and Allmand, 90.

25. Philippe de Mézières, *Le Songe du Vieil Pelerin* 2:405.

26. In the Bodley version, the Saracens speak both French and Latin, suggesting cultural as well as political literacy. Also, "the Sawdon hath man with him dwellynge of al manere of speche that Cristen men vsen, three or foure of ilke speche"—knowledge of the West is such a priority that the Sultan is constantly surrounded by tutors and translators. See Letts, *Texts and Translations*, 432, and *The Bodley Version of Mandeville's Travels*, 79.

27. In Caesarius's account, the Saracen had been sent as a youth to the court of the King of Jerusalem "ut Gallicum discerem apud illum," while the King's son was sent to the Emir's father "ad discendum idioma Sarracencium." *Dialogus Miraculorum*, iv. 187.

28. Sir John also claims to have often read the Qur'ân, at the beginning of Chapter XV. Evidence of Western travelers fluent in Arabic does not seem to be extensive, although Norman Daniel does cite one anecdote from Geoffrey of Vinsauf's chronicle of Richard I's crusade in the 1190s, which describes both the fluency and the Egyptian clothing of "Bernard, 'the king's spy.'" See Daniel, *The Arabs and Medieval Europe*, 199.

29. For the notion of the "commodification" of Sir John's skills I am indebted to Laura King.

30. Ibn Khaldûn, *The Muqaddimah* 2:80. There are limits to the Maghribi rulers' utilitarianism, he notes:

> However, the Maghribi rulers employ (such European Christians) only in wars against Arab and Berber nations, in order to force them into submission. They do not use them for the holy war, because they are afraid that they might take sides against the Muslims. Such is the situation of the Magrhib at this time. (ibid.)

31. See, e.g., the first part of Terry Jones's controversial *Chaucer's Knight: The Portrait of a Medieval Mercenary*; and for the immediate post-Conquest era, Jonathan Shepard, "The English and Byzantium," 53–92.

32. Daniel, 219. He cites a story that appears in the *Chronique d'Ernoul* about the Sultan of Damascus, who upon his death in 1227 allegedly left his small children to the custody of a Spanish Christian retainer, whose probity was shown not only in his years of faithful service but also in his unwillingness convert to Islam: "And because of the loyalty that al-Muazzam saw in him, that he held and kept his religion, he knew well that he would loyally care for his land and his children." See the *Chronique d'Ernoul et de Bernard le Tresorier*, 358. Note also the uses to which Christian orthodoxy can be put: in the *Travels*, Sir John's refusal to give up his faith functions as a sign of Islam's inherent weakness and eventual decay; the Spanish knight's similar refusal, on the other hand, helps to guarantee the legitimate succession of Islamic rule from one generation to the next.

33. Jones, 63, 99–100, 265–266, cites examples from 1343–1344, 1349, 1353, 1355, and 1358–1359.

34. Greenblatt, 29, also notes the placement and abruptness of this shift, calling it "decisive, peculiar, and unexplained."

35. Even the more moderate suggestion of an economic boycott of Iraq was strikingly anticipated 700 years ago by Fidenzio de Padua, not a source of Mandeville's Travels but one of a generation of crusade propagandists writing in the years prior to the fall of Acre; in 1291—the fatal year—Fidenzio's *Liber Recuperationis Terrae Sanctae* reported that

> I have heard it said that the Sultan receives everyday from Alexandria a thousand 'old besants,' worth more than a thousand florins, which he can spend on equipping many Saracen horsemen . . . If Christians would not go to Egypt [to trade], the Saracens would forego this profit and it would be a great loss to them.

See Golubovich, *Biblioteca bio-bibliographica della Terra Sancta e dell'oriente Francescano* 2:47.

V. The Sixteenth Century

CHAPTER 13

Arredondo's *Castillo inexpugnable de la fee*: Anti-Islamic Propaganda in the Age of Charles V*

John S. Geary

> My intention in this work was to follow that custom of the
> Fathers by which they never silently passed by any heresy
> of their times, not even the slightest . . . without resisting it
> with all the strength of faith and demonstrating, both
> through writings and discussions, that it is detestable.
>
> ———(Peter the Venerable)

This explicit reference to intentionality, which Peter the
Venerable expressed in a letter to his friend Bernard of
Clairvaux,[1] seems a fitting point of departure for a study of anti-
Islamic, and by extension anti-Turkish, propaganda in the work
of the Spanish Benedictine abbot and chronicler, Gonzalo de
Arredondo y Alvarado. Like his predecessor, Arredondo sought
to expose the heresy of Islam and to motivate Europe's Christian
princes to formulate and enact a course of action designed to halt
the spread of the *maldicta secta mahometana* and its tenets. Peter's
polemical writings set the tone for subsequent Christian
apologists, Arredondo included, many of whom perpetuated his

* I owe a debt of gratitude to the Graduate Committee on Arts and
Humanities of the University of Colorado for a travel grant which
enabled me to track down materials on Arredondo and his works in
various Spanish libraries in May 1991.

views on the figure of Muhammad and the interpretation of the Qur'ân.[2]

In the *Castillo inexpugnable de la fe* (Burgos, 1528),[3] an obscure work written at the behest of Charles V, Arredondo espoused many of the standard medieval stereotypes of Islam.[4] That many Renaissance authors, taking their cue from a long list of medievals, resorted to caricature and distortion in their accounts of Islamic religious ideas, is hardly surprising in the light of what Robert Schwoebel, among a host of other scholars, has taught us about typical Renaissance views of the Turk:

> Even under the pressure of momentous change, [Europeans] clung tenaciously to established categories and adapted a large body of new information to the forms of thought and expression developed in the anti-Moslem and crusading literature of the Middle Ages.[5]

Baumer notes, moreover, that in the case of England, the attitude of publicists, the clergy, and statesmen toward the Turk in the sixteenth and even seventeenth centuries differed very little from literary and popular attitudes.[6] The same claim, of course, can be made for Spain, where many of the legendary or literary representations of Muhammad and his religion originated. In this essay I shall demonstrate that the *Castillo* is an important early modern extension of a medieval tradition in which particular perceptions and misperceptions about the prophet and Qur'ânic revelation are rooted in the theological conception of Christian unity.

Not much is known about the life of Arredondo y Alvarado, nor are his works frequently cited.[7] It is generally believed that he was born in the Valley of Ruesga in northern Spain sometime during the first thirty years of the fifteenth century[8] and that he maintained the abbacy at the Benedictine monastery of San Pedro de Arlanza until 1518, when he assumed the priorate at Bohada.[9] We know as well that he served as court chronicler under the Catholic Monarchs, Ferdinand and Isabel, although, curiously enough, one searches in vain for his name in the standard works on their reign. We also know that King Ferdinand commissioned him to write a biography of the "liberator of Castile," the Count Fernán González, whose life and exploits in the tenth century had been commemorated in a thirteenth-century epic poem, the *Poema de Fernán González*, the putative work of an anonymous Arlantine monk. Arredondo wove a significant amount of the material from this text into the fabric of his *Crónica de Fernán González*. He was also the author of a history of the monastery at Arlanza, a chronicle dealing with the famous deeds of the Castilian heroes Fernán González and Rodrigo Díaz de Vivar, popularly known as the Cid, a rhymed biography of Fernán González, and a *villancico* of some 163 lines commemorating the Count's death.[10]

The historical value of much of Arredondo's work has been challenged since the seventeenth century by several critics such as Juan de Ferreras, Justo Pérez de Urbel, and Marcelino Menéndez y Pelayo.[11] They comment on the abbot's extensive utilization of legendary materials, his reliance on falsifications and diverse literary traditions. But as Toscano points out, "the historical character of Arredondo's work is neither better nor worse than that of other chronicles."[12]

The literary quality of Arredondo's prose and verse does not seem to have received any formal attention until the end of the nineteenth century when Manuel Milá y Fontanals referred to their "affectedly archaic" tenor.[13] Other literary scholars have been sharply critical of the author: his style is deplorable, even detestable; his merit as a poet is nugatory. A recent assessment attempts to qualify his work on the basis of fifteenth century poetic praxis by comparing his style to that of poets such as Juan de Mena and those of the *Cancionero de Baena*.[14] In this context Arredondo's manner of presentation seems less offensive since it reflects to a significant degree the medieval rhetorical tradition still operative in Spain at the close of the fifteenth century.

The *Castillo* betrays many of the literary qualities obtaining in Arredondo's other works, and it is the only one to have been published. Despite the disdain with which many of the author's contemporaries and successors viewed Arredondo's creative efforts, the Emperor himself must have valued his ability to compose the kind of propaganda needed to arouse support for a holy crusade.[15] The work bears the rather unwieldy title *Castillo inexpugnable defensorio de la fee y concionatorio admirable para vencer a todos enemigos espirituales y corporales. Y verdadera relación de las cosas maravillosas antiguas y modernas. Y exhortación para yr contra el turco; y le vencer; y anichilar la seta de Mahoma. Y toda infidelidad; y ganar la tierra sancta con famoso y bienaventurado triumpho* [Inexpugnable Castle, Defender of the Faith and Admirable Discourse to Conquer all Enemies, both Spiritual and Corporeal. And True Account of Marvellous Things, both Ancient and Modern. And Exhortation to Pursue the Turk, and to Conquer Him, and to Annihilate the Sect of Muhammad. And Every Heresy. And to Win Back the Holy Land With Great and Joyous Triumph]. The significance of the phrase "impregnable castle, defender of the faith" is explained in a fleeting reference to God at the end of the treatise as the "castillo inexpugnable . . . contra todos los males" [impregnable castle against all evil]. The frontispiece reinforces this metaphor as it bears an image of a three-turreted castle crowned by a red cross. The symbolism is nowhere explicated, but it is clear that early readers familiar with the legendary history of Arlanza would immediately have associated the visual representation with the heraldic arms of the monastery's putative founder, the Count Fernán González. The seventeenth-century historian Prudencio de Sandoval, in his *Historias*, observed that the castle and red cross were the distinguishing emblems of the Count's blazon and that they could be seen on many of the old buildings at Arlanza and on monastic seals.[16] A large silver cross hanging in the monastery's sacristy during Sandoval's lifetime was believed to have served as the Count's standard in numerous battles waged and won against the Moors. Together with the castle it became a symbol of Christian faith, endurance, and invincibility. In the *Castillo* the Emperor is encouraged to follow the model of his illustrious ancestor, Fernán González; hence the significance of the iconography.

Arredondo's treatise is cast in the form of a dialogue between a Benedictine monk, who is both a literary creation and a mouthpiece for the historical author, and the sister of Charles V, Mary, who has just lost her husband, Lewis, King of Hungary and Bohemia, to the forces of Suleyman the Magnificent at Mohács (August 28, 1526).[17] This event intensified the concern of the Habsburg dynasty with the collapse of the eastern frontier between Christianity and Islam. Preceding the dialogue is a "painful and sad" lament by a personified Universal Roman Catholic Church, which presents a bleak picture of the devastation caused by the Ottoman janissaries in order to persuade her Christian allies to rally to her aid. The propagandistic tone of the work is immediately established:

> My enemies prevailed with more than two hundred thousand combatants, and they stole both arms and artillery, they killed and took from me my greatest lords and the innocent, they lacerated the blameless, they raped many virgins and forced married women, they affronted widows, injured poor orphans, trespassed on the holy temples, showing no respect for the holy images, slapping the priests. . . . never refraining in their attempts to convert to their diabolical sect with their false arguments both the sad women and the weak. . . . (fol. 4)[18]

The rhetorical language of this brief passage, like that of many other segments of the *Castillo*, was of course designed to inculcate in the Christian reader a sense of horror and revulsion. The conventional images of the Turk, distorted as they are, betray an irreverent populace given to violence, sexual lubricity, and falsehood.

Participating in the dialectic discourse of the *Castillo*, in addition to the monk and Queen Mary, are numerous secular and ecclesiastical characters. These include various counts, marquesses, bishops and prelates, and even "historians," whose frequent interjections served the political, religious, and ideological posturing of the author. They present a univocal interpretation of events in Hungary as a sign of God's anger in response to the failure of the Papacy and of Christian princes to take seriously the Turkish peril by joining with the Holy Roman Emperor in a holy war.[19] They also view the famous rivalry between Francis I of France and Charles as a grave impediment to this goal. Having lost his bid for the Emperorship, Francis participated in a bitter dispute with Charles over the Duchy of Milan, which the French had maintained since the battle of Marignano (1515). In October 1524, the French army attacked General Antonio de Leyva and his troops at the fortified city of Pavia. The following February the Imperialists successfully defeated the French, and Francis himself was taken to Madrid, where he was imprisoned in the tower of Los Lujanes, and from which he was released as a condition of the Treaty of Madrid.[20]

The Emperor's desire to make peace was further frustrated by Francis's refusal to obey the stipulations of the Treaty and by his association with Charles's former allies, Henry VIII of England, and Pope Clement VII, both of whom conspired with the French King against the Habsburg Monarch in a League signed at Cognac. In an ensuing war against the Pope, Charles sent an army to sack Rome (1527), an act that shocked all of Christian Europe.[21] The same year saw the birth of prince Philip and the convocation of a General Cortes in Castile to which members of the nobility and clergy were invited. At this Cortes the Emperor sought economic support for his campaign, in part to aid his brother Ferdinand of Austria against the Turk in the wake of events in Hungary. Although a holy war was proclaimed, it was evidently difficult to convince both camps that Castile was obligated to play such a major role in the defeat of the Turks and the preservation of Christian unity in Europe.[22] Arredondo was clearly on the side of the Emperor, as were generally members of the religious order of San Benito which donated a significant amount of financial aid to the war effort.

One wonders whether the *Castillo* might have been commissioned by Charles shortly after the Cortes took place in order to persuade the Spanish skeptics and the privileged bodies outside Spain, including Francis and Henry, to submit to the Emperor's prestige and authority. In chapter 40 of the *Castillo* Charles's mother and Queen of Spain, Juana the Mad, composes a letter to Francis begging him to cease his feuding and to emulate the illustrious deeds of his ancestors, among whom she singles out for adulation "the good Emperor Charlemagne," and "the virtuous and Catholic King Pepin." She sends a similar letter to Henry and Catherine of England and another to Charles's brother Ferdinand, whose support she seeks on behalf of her widowed daughter and the Emperor himself:

> Consider, consider, my dearest son, the obstacles with which your blessed ancestors, the kings and emperors of Spain, have had to contend. Remember your glorious progenitors, the good Count Fernán González, and the good Cid of Vivar, and how they, with only a small army, fought the infidels in order to serve God, and how they were assisted in their great and famous conquests by the

> Almighty, the angels, and the saints. . . . Console your sad
> and illustrious sister Mary, and serve and help your
> brother, the great Emperor Charles, so that together you
> may win the Holy Land, and pacify and unite all
> Christendom in peace and love. (fol. 9)

The invention and dramatization of speech illustrated in
this passage was obviously designed to convince the reader of an
important moral or exemplary point. It was also a kind of
literary embellishment commonly accepted by medieval
historians.[23] Arredondo was patently aware of this stylistic habit
since in the Prologue to the *Castillo* he addressed those potential
readers who might have objected to the apparent inauthenticity
of his characters' speeches: "Forgive me if the words I say in
their name are not as scientific as you would like. . . . Suffice it to
say that nothing is said that is untrue." His attitude toward the
praxis of invention and linguistic embellishment was
commonplace, for as Morse has pointed out,

> The omission of part of a narrative which ought to have
> been included, the turning of historical events to
> recognizable narrative patterns, the insistence that agents
> did or said things which accorded with ideas about their
> status, or reign, or character—all these possibilities could
> be manipulated in order to convey complex impressions of
> the past and its relevance to the present.[24]

A modern reader can quite naturally relate the dialogic
structure of the *Castillo* to the dramatization and stylized
presentation of emplotted events[25] as a kind of plausible
construction rather than as a true depiction of reality.[26] By
medieval standards this type of presentation was clearly
acceptable in chronistic literature, and Arredondo himself even
referred to the *"cartas fingidas"* [invented letters] that he had
Suleyman write to the Grand Master of Rhodes. Nonetheless, at
times the author clearly exceeded the limits of plausibility by
indulging in pure literary caprice based on the allegorical
tradition, common legends about the life of Muhammad, and
distorted notions about the teachings of the Qur'ân. These
served to orient the reader's reaction to the Turkish onslaught as
a horrifying event.

While ancestral deeds were upheld as a model of appropriate behavior for Charles, in the case of his nemesis the past and all that it conjured up had only a negative value. In chapter 22 Juana asks the monk to reveal the identity of the seven Turkish captains who, in alliance with the devil and his follower, Muhammad, continue to perpetrate evil and abominable acts against the Christians with whom they come into contact. The monk proceeds to name the seven deadly sins, each of which is accompanied by a host of knights and other cohorts. Sir Avarice, for example, is abetted by Sir Simony, Sir Usury, Sir Systematic Robbery, and Sir Rapine. Sir Pride, leader of all the others, counts among his "worthy vassals" Sir Arrogance, Sir Ambition, Sir Irreverence, and Sir Discord.

The allegorical representation of traits popularly associated with the Turks is reinforced by the monk's conclusion, based on scriptural exegesis, that God has permitted the infidel to succeed because Christians everywhere have neglected their religious and moral reponsibilities by failing to emulate the example of Christ and his holy virtues. As a corrective to this situation the monk suggests that the Emperor enlist the aid of the four cardinal and three theological virtues, all of which appear in allegorized form to challenge the forces of Sir Pride.[27] In this piece of artistry the author seemed to imply not only that Christian princes must search within themselves for the values that would guarantee the survival of a unified Christian Republic. He also made clear that Charles himself must attempt to convince his noble congeners of the need to put aside their dissensions for the welfare of all Christendom. The Emperor's exhaustive efforts to this end had of course been well documented at this juncture in the text, and so the *Castillo* seems to have represented a platform for Charles's political and religious agendas. Indeed, in chapter 6 the Emperor recognizes the imperative of Christian solidarity. Arredondo seems to have conceived of himself as Charles's spokesman and the *Castillo* as an official pronouncement of the latter's view on the Turkish question. In the following chapter Charles expresses his moral responsibility to Christendom, and he issues a plea to the Papacy to join him in his campaign:

> ... and I promise to be the first to go and to employ my
> person and all that God has given me in His service, in
> defense of His Holy Church and the Holy Faith, in order
> to destroy the faithless and spurious Turks,
> Mohammedans, Saracens, and Ismaelites. . . . Let us all
> extol the Holy Catholic Faith like good Christians, and let
> us march against the enemies of our Holy Catholic
> Religion and our immortal God. And this I have begged,
> implored, and exhorted with humility and affection of all
> the Sovereign Pontiffs, Leo, Adrian, Clement, and so forth,
> that as vicars of the Redeemer of this world we might
> unite and obey, like good sheep, the voice of the true
> shepherd, our Lord eternal. (fol. 9)[28]

Whether any of the Christian princes for whose benefit the work
appears to have been written ever had an opportunity to read it
is a matter for speculation, but the historical period immediately
following the Christian defeat at Mohács witnessed a very
different turn of events than that suggested in the *Castillo*.[29]

The words that Arredondo had the Emperor speak betray
a leader whose view of the Turks and whose religious zeal are
never compromised. Yet the chronicler, as the fictionalized
monk, occasionally intervened to remind his patron of the dire
urgency of enacting a holy war. The rhetorical force behind such
exhortations was surely intended to convince the Emperor that
God at least, if not all representatives of the Church, was behind
him and that his goal was a noble one. The most poignant
address occurs in chapter 63, as follows:

> Therefore take, your Majesty, the knife of vengeance
> against evil, lost, and unbelieving Muslims, for they are
> destroying the holy faith of our Lord whose captain is
> your Majesty himself, and they are destroying the lands of
> your empire, and like traitors and perjurers, they
> abandoned the Catholic religion that they once followed,
> pledging allegiance to the bestial sect of that diabolical
> Muhammad, and they rose up against your ancestors, the
> emperors. . . . Exterminate, good Emperor, these
> unbelieving Muslims, these idolaters who worship the
> house of Mecca. . . . Great Christian Emperor, cause these
> blasphemers of the most holy name of Christ, along with
> the Jews, to be stoned, and they will descend into
> Hell. . . . (fol. 58)

The pejorative description of Muslims as "evil, unbelieving, bestial, diabolical, idolaters," carried the weight of several centuries and was no doubt conceived as a strategy by which to convince Christian readers of their responsibility to join the crusading movement. Another technique utilized routinely by Christian authors was the introduction of a distorted and malicious representation of the prophet Muhammad and, by extension, of Islam itself. Watt has shown that the medieval image of Islam was based primarily on the desire to show that Islamic teaching is a falsehood and a deliberate perversion of the truth, that it is a religion of violence and of self-indulgence, and that Muhammad himself is the Antichrist.[30] This image was evidently complete by the time Ricoldo da Monte Croce (d. 1321) wrote his *Improbatio alchorani*. All of these notions inhabit the discursive space of the *Castillo*, and they illustrate the derivative nature of much of Arredondo's thought. The lustful and ambitious Muhammad is seen as the Great Impostor and Islam as a false and erroneous doctrine.

In many respects the text closely parallels the account of the prophet's youth afforded by Ramón de Martí's *reprobatio quadruplex*, including his upbringing as a poor merchant and his acting as agent for the widow Khadijah.[31] Passing reference is made to his having become a skilled *magus*, to leading simple people astray, and to the legend of Sergius, the heretical monk believed by some to have corrupted the Arabs via his protégé Muhammad.[32] In the *Castillo* the prophet is said to have encouraged sodomy among both men and women and to have boasted of his own generative power ("his sexual potency exceeded that of forty men"). The view of Islam as a sect and the mixing of truth and falsehood contained in Muhammad's teachings closely followed Aquinas, although, like many of his predecessors and contemporaries, Arredondo added that "whenever he [Muhammad] said anything true, he mixed in poison which corrupted it." One of the most egregious aspects of Islam, according to what the Benedictine monk claims to have concluded on the basis of unspecified readings, is that it combines the erroneous notions of all previous heresies, including denial of the Godhead. Arredondo's slavish attitude toward his sources is nowhere more evident than in this passage, as his recognition of the Devil's role in plotting Islam as the renewal of the heresies echoes the standard Cluniac position espoused in the *Summa* of Peter the Venerable and later in the work of Ricoldo da Monte Croce.[33]

Arredondo also espoused the Cluniac view of the Qur'ân as a collection of commandments (Span. *mandamientos*).[34] According to this view, as a false prophet Muhammad sought to annihilate the laws of Moses and Christ in order to create his own set of commandments. These include, for example, the idea of fasting by day and feasting by night, washing one's private parts before prayer, and the taking of up to four legitimate wives and as many concubines as one desired, among several others. In the *Castillo* the Emperor himself offers his assessment of these laws:

> "Accursed be such commandments," responded the Emperor Charles, "and many others that he [Muhammad] put [in the Qur'ân], for they all go against the law of nature, against the written law, against the law of grace, and against all good habits. Who should follow such a perverse sect, so full of filth? Even the learned Muslims themselves make fun of such laws, which are beyond all reason." (fol. 25)

Numerous fanciful tales about the death of Muhammad circulated throughout the medieval and renaissance periods, and they often served a discrediting function, unlike the Christian hagiographical narratives which sought to glorify the death of the Christian martyrs. Smith mentions the legend of Muhammad's poisoning by his followers who sought to test his prophetic abilities.[35] Another fable involved the placing of the prophet's dead body in an iron coffin which was then suspended in the air by loadstones in the roof of the temple at Mecca. Daniel records similar accounts involving a poisoned shoulder of lamb, including one version from the *Hadith* literature in which the meat actually utters the words, "I have poison in me, be careful not to eat me in the food."[36] An additional fabrication is considered by Smith to be a parody of the Christian story of the resurrection.[37] According to this version, Muhammad led his followers to believe that after the third day of his death, he would ascend into Heaven. Several different stories about the prophet's death must have appealed to Arredondo, for the account presented in the *Castillo* seems to be a hybrid:

> Consider, consider, answers Lucas of Tuy,[38] the circumstances of Muhammad's death and how they match those of his life, for in the tenth year in which he was made King in Damascus, one of his disciples by the name of Albunor wanted to find out if Muhammad would be resurrected on the third day just as he had said he would. So Albunor gave him poison, and when Muhammad realized he was dying, he said to those present that he would be saved by water and would be pardoned. And he raised up his sword without being able to speak, and then he died. And he gave up his soul to his teacher, the Devil. (fol. 25)

A semiotic interpretation of this report is pronounced by another character, the Empress Isabel, who construes the act of washing the face as a sign that Muhammad must have intended his followers to seek baptism in order to assure their salvation.[39] The raising of the sword, she remarks, must surely signify that the prophet wanted them to view his death as a form of crucifixion. Her comments precede an explanation by Lucas of Tuy of events following Muhammad's death. Here, too, the standard Christian fabrications found their way into the *Castillo*. After a while the prophet's followers could no longer stand "the stench of his cursed body," and they went away confused by what they had failed to witness, that is, the ascension into Heaven. After fifteen days Albunor returned to the site of death only to find that the body had been eaten and the bones gnawed by dogs. As Daniel has pointed out, "The story seemed valuable to those who told it for its disproof of a hoped for miracle, but still more for the contrasts, sometimes explicit, sometimes implicit, between Muhammad and Christ."[40]

The entire discourse on the death of Muhammad and its aftermath betrays an inevitable intertextuality characteristic of historical narratives from the Middle Ages. Because many of the legends referred to were widespread in that era, including that of the dove trained by Muhammad to eat grain from his ear, it is difficult to posit specific sources for much of the material contained in the *Castillo*. Nevertheless, the one authority most frequently cited throughout the work is St. Antoninus of Florence (1389–1459), the Dominican archbishop whose *Summa* of moral theology and treatises on the Christian life were highly influential medieval texts.[41] Arredondo most assuredly borrowed from Antoninus when in chapter 53 he offered an explanation of why God permitted the infidels to possess the city of Jerusalem: "God doesn't want Christians to sin in the Holy City in which the son of God suffered for the sins of mankind." At the same time God takes no offense at the presence of the Muslims in that city because, as the author himself put it, "they are dogs,"[42] and they were allowed to guard the gates of the city by an angry God who was no longer willing to tolerate the sins that had proliferated among His flock. Antoninus's influence is also evident in the sections that depict Muslims as renegade Christians who have been led astray by the Great Impostor.

Whereas Arredondo's efforts to malign Islam and the Turks were based to a significant degree on theological arguments, legendary underpinnings, and the use of opprobrious language, it was primarily by means of portraying the Ottomans as violent and avaricious people that the author's propagandistic goals were achieved. This type of portrayal was commonplace during the period in question, for as Schwoebel has shown, "the unhumanity of the Turks was emphasized above all else, and the stereotyped Turk—savage and bloodthirsty, swooping down upon innocent Christians, and massacring them indiscriminately—was firmly established in the traditions of the West."[43] To this end several chapters of the *Castillo* recounted the events leading to the Christian defeat at the citadel of Rhodes, which was abandoned by the Knights of St. John after a long and dreadful siege. This lengthy interlude served to exemplify the aggressive character of the enemy. Suleyman appears as a deceitful and false leader, having betrayed an oath sworn to the Grand Master of Rhodes that, should the city surrender to the Ottomans, he would see to it that the churches and shrines not be harmed, that no Christian would be forced to adopt the faith of Muhammad, and that those who wished to leave the city would be given ships and sundry provisions. These and other terms, according to the chronicler, were quickly forgotten, and instead of a peaceful settlement, violence and malice ensued:

> ... like a perverse and cruel tyrant, an enemy of truth, on Christmas Day, in order to cause Christians grief, he [Suleyman] tore down the gate to the city, and with his banners and armed men, and with a great uproar, he entered the city and profaned and defiled the Church of St. John, and he destroyed the holy statues and the altarpiece, and he worshiped Muhammad in this same temple, and he had the same done in all the temples and churches, and he didn't uphold a thing that he had promised, like infernal Lucifer. (fol. 46)

The text thus sought to establish a trifold relationship, based on deception, between the prophet Muhammad, his successor, Suleyman, and their mutual agent, the Devil. This notion of the diabolical sect, strategically reinforced throughout the *Castillo*, could hardly have elicited an ambivalent response from a Christian reader living with the threat of invasion from the East. Arredondo's message was clear enough: the Devil and his allies must be annihilated.

The view of Islam as a satanic scheme had its roots in the writings of eighth-century eastern Christian polemicists. Peter the Venerable in turn considered Muhammad in relation to Arius and the Antichrist.[44] In the Prologue to the *Summa* the abbot justified this connection by stating that

> in no way could anyone of the human race, unless the devil were there helping, devise such fables. . . . By means of them . . . this Satan had as his object particularly and in every way to bring it about that Christ the Lord would not be believed to be the Son of God and true God, the creator and redeemer of the human race.[45]

As an imperial propagandist Arredondo coupled his knowledge of history and contemporary European affairs with his rhetorical skill and with undergirding from both literary and theological traditions in order to present a picture of Islam and the Turks intended to make a marked impression on his readers, many of whom, he must have assumed, would consist of Christian princes and noblemen who could perhaps be persuaded to wage the holy war that would put the survival of the Christian Commonwealth on more secure ground. Toward the end of the *Castillo* he issued one last plea on behalf of the Church, reminding members of the nobility of their responsibility to support the Emperor:

> Go, go and defend the holy law of your Lord and God Who gave you the estates, dominions, and incomes that you possess. Now we will see who among you is truly a Catholic knight, how much sincerity you have in serving your God, your King and Emperor, how much you love your country, how much charity you have for your faithful brother Christians and how much hate toward the evil unbelievers. Arm yourselves, oh noble knights, with both material and spiritual weapons so that you may destroy the enemy, these dogs, the Turks. (fol. 61)

The kind of support that Arredondo so zealously sought for his Emperor in the wake of the first Hungarian campaign was not immediately forthcoming despite his appeal to medieval crusading traditions. One doubts that he lived long enough to witness the second (1527–1529) or third (1532) Hungarian expeditions.[46] Be that as it may, Charles's interest in the Ottoman Wars waned over the years as his attention was diverted by the Reformation and by dissensions with his enemies in Europe. If he lived to see these events, Arredondo could hardly have been pleased by them. His patron's ultimate failure to restore the old Holy Roman Empire would also no doubt have been a major source of disillusionment to him as it certainly was to his Emperor.

NOTES

1. James Kritzeck, *Peter the Venerable and Islam*, 37.

2. Peter the Venerable's efforts to provide Europeans with trustworthy information about Islam are too well known to warrant rehearsal here. Suffice it to say that he was responsible for the production of a dozen Latin works, known as the Cluniac corpus, which

included a translation of the Qur'ân by Robert of Ketton and his own treatise on Islamic teaching, the *Summa totius haeresis Saracenorum*, as well as a refutation of Islam entitled *Liber contra sectam sive haeresim Saracenorum*. Much of the information contained in these works is accurate, although distortions abound. The quote with which I began this paper is from the *Epistola de translatione sua*.

3. Published on June 23, 1528, by Juan de Junta, the work was begun sometime during the year 1527, as is evident from the following exchange between Mary of Hungary and her interlocutor (chap. 21): "'Porque conforme a Jeremías, desde el propheta fasta el sacerdote, todos hazen engaño, y como testifica el psalmista, no áy ninguno que haga bien.' 'Bien lo puede dezir aun del presente en este año de mil y quinientos y veinte y siete, y en los passados' . . . , respondió el monje." Since Arredondo also made reference in the *Castillo* to the birth of Charles's son Philip, it is conceivable that the abbot set to work sometime after that date (May 21). Carl Göllner described the work as

> ein Mélanges von den verschiedensten Briefen / Trostbrief der verwitweten Königin Johanna an ihre Tochter Maria, Königin von Ungarn, ein Brief Johannas an ihren Sohn Kaiser Karl V., zwei Briefe Kaisers Karl V. usw. / und Schriften über die Eroberung von Rhodus und die Schlacht von Mohács, um an Hand dieser Schrift zu beweisen, das der Kampf gegen die Türken eine Notwendigkeit sei. Es folgen dann einige Kapitel über den Ursprung der Türken und die Bestimmungen des Korans. Aus dem Schluswort ist ersichtlich, das das Werk in der Priorei von Bohada geschrieben wurde. Das ganze Werk ist in 78 Kapitel geteilt, und enthält vor jedem Kapitel eine kurze Inhaltsangabe.

See *Turcica: Die europäischen Türkendrucke des XVI Jahrhunderts*, 2 vols. (Bucharest-Berlin-Baden, 1961), i. 157.

4. For a thorough treatment of the Turks in Spanish literature from the Golden Age, see Mas, *Les Turcs dans la littérature espagnole du siècle d'or*. A more comprehensive assessment is López-Baralt, *Islam in Spanish Literature*. Dwayne Carpenter's analysis of the legal status of Moors under Alfonse the Learned sheds light on later developments in Spain. See his "Minorities in Medieval Spain," 275–287.

5. Schwoebel, *The Shadow of the Crescent*, x.

6. Franklin L. Baumer, "England, the Turk and the Common Corps of Christendom," 26–48. Of the many additional studies on Islam

and the Turks in England, the most enlightening are Chew, *The Crescent and the Rose*; Smith, *Islam in English Literature*; and Metlitzki, *The Matter of Araby in Medieval England*.

7. For information about the life and works of Arredondo, consult Martínez Añíbarro y Rives, *Intento de un diccionario biográfico*; Gómez Pérez, "Una crónica de Fernán González," 551–581; Labandeira Fernández, "Historicidad y estructura de la Crónica Arlantina en verso," 225–243; Toscano, "Edición crítica de los versos inéditos de Arredondo sobre Fernán González," 321–360; Mercedes Vaquero, ed. *Vida Rimada de Fernán González* (Exeter, 1987); Geary, "The 'tres monjes' of the *Poema de Fernán González*," 24–42; and "The Death of the Count," 321–334.

8. One must question the likelihood of Arredondo's having been born sometime during the first thirty years of the fifteenth century, as is generally maintained. Even if we postpone the birthdate some twenty years, the abbot would have been a very old man (70–80 years) when the *Castillo* was published.

9. Toward the end of the work the author identified himself in the following paragraph:

> La presente obra es acabada intitulada *Castillo inexpugnable defensorio de la fee* por el muy reverendo padre fray Gonçalo de Arredondo, monje del seráphico patriarcha Sant Benito, último abbad perpetuo del monesterio de Sant Pedro de Arlança y también primero ende abbad de la observancia. El qual, movido de zelo divino y por servicio de Dios y aumentación del sobredicho monesterio, renunció en el trienno su perpetuydad ad modum de la célebre Sanctíssima congregación de Sant Benito de Valladolid y dende se transferió al priorazgo de Bohada. . . . (fol. 70)

10. The incomplete *Poema de Fernán González*, probably composed between 1250 and 1270, survives in a unique fifteenth-century manuscript (IV-b-21) at El Escorial library. No edition yet exists in English. An early version of the *Crónica de Fernán González* was written between 1492 and 1504; a second redaction was probably composed between 1513–1514. Various abridged versions of the latter text appeared in the seventeenth century in manuscript form, but the work in any of its redactions remains unpublished. The whereabouts of the *Historia del monasterio de Arlanza* are unknown. For a detailed description of all of Arredondo's works and the various manuscripts in which they have survived, consult Gómez Pérez, "Una crónica."

11. Ferreras, *Synopsis histórica chronológica de España* 4:314; Menéndez y Pelayo, *Antología de poetas líricos castellanos*, vol. 4, chaps. 6, 32; Pérez de Urbel, *El condado de Castilla* 1:102.

12. Toscano, 56.

13. Milá y Fontanals, *De la poesía heroico-popular castellana* 1:258. Ruth Morse has recently described the literary character of much historical writing from the medieval period in her illuminating study *Truth and Convention in the Middle Ages*.

14. Toscano, 58–66. Juan de Mena (1411–1456), translator of the *Iliad*, is considered the greatest Spanish poet of the fifteenth century. His best known work, the *Laberinto de Fortuna* (1444), is a long political poem aimed at winning support for Alvaro de Luna, the Constable of Castile. Through a highly Latinate style, in terms of both vocabulary and syntax, Mena sought to dignify the Castilian language. The *Cancionero de Baena* (1445) is one of the largest and most significant collections of lyric poetry written at the court of King John II. It contains 576 poems by some 54 Spanish poets.

15. It seems feasible that Charles had read at least parts of the *Crónica de Fernán González*, commissioned by his maternal grandfather, and that he had noted the author's clever manipulation of Castilian history to eulogize and sanctify the figure of the Count. In Book ii of the *Crónica*, Fernán González was portrayed as the avatar of Christian virtues, and he became a symbol of Christian unity and faith.

16. Sandoval, *Historias de Idacio Obispo*, 334.

17. On Mary of Hungary, see De Iongh, *Mary of Hungary*. Suleyman the Magnificent and his reign are discussed by Merriman, *Suleiman the Magnificent* and by Bridge, *Suleiman the Magnificent*.

18. All translations of passages from the *Castillo* are mine. For the purpose of this paper, I have utilized a copy of the *Castillo* housed at the Biblioteca Nacional de Madrid (signature R-2.495). The volume forms part of the Luis de Usoz y Río collection given to the BNM by the owner's widow in 1873. Other copies exist at Madrid's Real Academia de la Historia, the Biblioteca de Palacio, the library at the University of Salamanca, and the Hispanic Society of America in New York.

19. Their formal speeches reveal an acquaintance with two styles of rhetoric which can be traced all the way back to Aristotle: deliberative and epideictic oratory. As Morse has noted in *Truth and Convention* (47,57), deliberative speeches concern decisions about a course of future action, while epideictic discourse generally refers to speeches of praise or blame. The latter is closely related to the widespread tradition of exemplary literature in the medieval period.

20. The episode of the battle and of Francis's incarceration are alluded to in the *Castillo* (chap. 11).

21. See Fernández Alvarez, *Charles V*, 64.

22. Ibid., 69. The author notes that the sacking of Rome was attributed by Charles's propaganda machine to the influence of Erasmus, whose view that the Emperor could overrule the Pope was widely accepted in Spain, particularly among members of the order of San Benito. Arredondo clearly supported this view.

23. Morse, *Truth and Convention*, 106 describes the kinds of moral defenses commonly represented in historical writings:

> . . . it is right to remember the deeds of one's forebears; they present the current generation with models of how to act, or of how not to act; and they remind their readers of the vicissitudes of fortune and the stoicism and faith necessary to deal with the turnings of Fortune's Wheel. It is this idea of the past as a moral example which constantly legitimated the embellishing or moulding of earlier accounts, and encouraged the conception of the past as a source of actual moral exempla which ultimately justified the study of secular history.

24. Ibid., 2.

25. Hayden White defined emplotment as "the encodation of the facts contained in the chronicle as components of specific kinds of plot-structures, in precisely the way that [Northup] Frye has suggested is the case with 'fictions' in general." ("The Historical Text as Literary Artifact," 46).

26. See also Morse, 95.

27. Cf., e.g., the allegorical battle between Sir Carnival and Lady Lent in the fourteenth-century *Libro de buen amor*. See Juan Ruiz, *Libro de Buen Amor*. This form of "entertainment" was common in medieval Europe.

28. The monk himself issues a similar plea in the *Castillo*, chap. 50:

> "Despertad, despertad, dixo el monje, pues christianos no estés somnolentos, no estés tibios, no perezosos a orar si vencer queréys al diablo vuestro enemigo capital y a su miembro el espurcíssimo Turco. Si os plaze de ser victoriosos, plega os orar con Moysén, con David, con Salomón, con Daniel, con Thobías, con Matathías, con Judas Machabeo, con Eleazar, que orando a sus adversarios vencieron. . . . Dexad, dexad, vicios, aborreced pasatiempos vanos, considerad que un día que perdáys, cobrar no

lo podéys. Espended, espended, pues los días que
Dios os concede en los emplear en su servicio en
defensa de su sancta fee cathólica, en socorrer a los
afflegidos tristes y cativos de los Turcos. . . . (fol. 52)

29. I noted earlier that the defeat of Lewis of Hungary set the stage
for the *Castillo*'s propagandistic discourse. This event was preceded by
the capture of Belgrade in 1521 and the fall of Rhodes the following
year. Under Suleyman the Magnificent, Turkey was at the height of its
power, having become suzerain of the Moors in North Africa. On
various occasions the Cortes of Castile had petitioned the Emperor to
make peace with the other Christian kings, but by 1525 France had
already begun to establish an alliance with the Turks, and Henry VIII
himself, angry about Charles's determination to marry Isabel of
Portugal, declared war on him in January 1528, the year in which the
Castillo was published.

30. Watt, *The Influence of Islam*, 73.

31. The *reprobatio quadruplex* is a term used by Daniel to describe a
work attributed to John of Wales and printed in 1550 (*Islam and the West*,
13). It was in fact composed by the Dominican Ramón Martí in the
thirteenth century, according to Delgado, "Le 'De seta Machometi' du
cod. 46 d'Osma, oeuvre de Raymond Martin (Ramón Martí)," 351–371;
and Cortabarria, "La connaissance des textes arabes chez Raymond
Martin, O.P. et sa position en face de l'Islam," 279–324. It contains a
fourfold refutation of Islam and a Qur'ânic validation of Scripture.

32. Ibid., 84.

33. Ibid., 186. Arredondo's rendition closely parallels the following
description of Ricoldo da Monte Croce's classification cited by Daniel:

Thus Muhammad denied the Trinity with Sabellius,
and agreed with Arius and Eunomius that Christ was
a creature excelling all others; he taught with
Carpocrates that God could have no son save by the
medium of a wife, and with Cerdonius and the Jews
that if God had a Son They would endanger the world
with Their dissension; and so he continues with the
Manichees, Donatists, with Origen, the Anthroi-
pomorphites, Macedonius, Cerinthus, the Ebi-onites
and the Nicolaites. . . .

34. Ibid. 34. Daniel acquaints the Spanish word *mandamiento* with
the surah, and *preceptum* with divine command, but Arredondo seems
to make indiscriminate use of *mandamiento*, *ley*, and *precepto*.

35. Smith, *Islam in English Literature*, 9.

36. Daniel, *Islam and the West*, 102–108.

37. Smith, 9.

38. Lucas, bishop of Tuy, author of the *Chronicon mundi* (1236).

39. Cf., e.g., St. Pedro Pascual's recollection of a description of how, at the point of death, Muhammad washed and poured water over his face (see Daniel, *Islam and the West*, 103).

40. Ibid., 105.

41. See Morçay, *Chroniques de Saint Antonin*, and Walker, *The "Chronicles" of St. Antoninus*.

42. The author attempts to drive home the point by offering the following rather obscene analogy: "Mucho desplazería al rey y mucho se indignaría si sus hijos o los cavalleros si measen o hiziesen polución en su cámara. Mas si el perro se ensuzia, no tiene cuydado" (fol. 52).

43. Schwoebel, 13.

44. See, e.g., Emmerson, *Antichrist in the Middle Ages*.

45. See Kritzeck, 147–48.

46. The dating of the abbot's death is as problematic as that of his birth. According to Martínez Añíbarro, Arredondo probably died in 1518, the year in which he assumed the priorate at Bohada (*Intento de un diccionario*, 58). Gómez Pérez, however, mentions a decree issued to Arredondo by the Emperor in 1520 and another in 1522 ("Una crónica," 552). On March 10, 1520, Charles requested that the abbot continue and finish his work on Fernán González and the Cid. Toscano assumes that Arredondo was still alive in 1522 ("Edición crítica," 48), but it is clear that we must extend that date by at least five or six years in order to take into account that the author was in the process of composing the *Castillo* in 1527 (see n. 3).

CHAPTER 14

Las Guerras civiles de Granada: The Idealization of the Assimilation

Rhona Zaid

The year 1568 was one of great crises for Philip II's reign; Muslims were still a major threat in the Mediterranean, and adding to his problems, in an atmosphere of mounting anger, Christmas Eve of that year saw the initiation of the second rebellion of the Alpujarras. As contemporary historian-soldier Diego Hurtado de Mendoza reported, this was a religious war, and not merely a war between enemies but between enemy civilizations that touched the deepest of human emotions, spreading rapidly across a terrain paved with hate and misery.[1] If Hurtado de Mendoza's use of hyperbole qualifies as Spanish propaganda, his interpretation of this conflict as a clash between two irreconcilably different faiths has a passion that is absent from the work of writer-historian Ginés Pérez de Hita. For all that the latter decried the conflict and war itself, the absence of an elaborate defense of Spain—and Catholicism—characterizes *Las Guerras civiles de Granada*.

At first Philip tried to keep the conflict quiet, lest his enemies use it to their advantage. Communicating with his viceroy in Naples, he wrote in the margin of a letter, "it is best to keep Granada a secret."[2] As an uninterrupted chain of relays functioned between Madrid and Istanbul, however, even without counting itinerant and fugitive Moriscos who were indefatigable merchants and travelers, Spanish galleys were alerted to patrol the coast, and Philip asserted that, were war to continue, and especially if other Morisco regions entered the

313

fight and the Turks intervened, Spain was at risk of returning to Muslim power. How real this risk was must be measured not only objectively, but also in terms of Philip's desire to turn the situation to his advantage. Part of this strategy was designed to persuade the pope to reestablish the crusade indulgence so that those contributions might help defray the costs of the war. Pius V acceded to his wishes. The rebellion was not fully suppressed until 1571, the conflict having been conducted with savagery on both sides. Approximately sixty thousand Moriscos were killed and several thousand more were sold into slavery.[3]

The Morisco uprising of the Alpujarras provided Ginés Pérez de Hita with both impetus and material for his extensive work, *Las Guerras civiles de Granada*. The first volume discusses Arab customs, language, and culture, and paints an accurate picture of the internecine discords that helped assure Spanish victory over Granada. Volume II is devoted almost exclusively to a detailed eyewitness account of the Alpujarra uprising and its aftermath. Although Pérez de Hita was a poet and dramatist, he is best known for this largely historical work—indeed, he is called by literary historians Spain's first historical novelist. Perhaps the most intriguing aspect of this literary effort is the author's blatant Morisco sympathies as well as his almost protopacifistic sentiments, both unorthodox attitudes for any Golden Age writer. Few concrete biographical facts are known about the author; thus, we must rely on somewhat sketchy and speculative information, drawing most of our conclusions about him from the work itself.

The author was born between 1544 and 1550, probably in Murcia, if he were between the ages of nineteen and twenty-five at the beginning of the Morisco uprising. No doubt he studied in one of Murcia's famed learning centers, sent there by his mentor, Luis Fajardo, Marqués de los Vélez, who exerted a great influence over Pérez de Hita. The Fajardos were both warriors and poets, and from the time of Juan II and Enrique IV, this illustrious family figured prominently as patrons of the arts in the kingdom of Murcia.[4] It is likely that those who fought under the Marqués de Vélez's standard also attended the social gathering of his court.

As Shasta M. Bryant notes in her recent introduction to Volume I of the *Guerras civiles*, "it seems certain that his interest in literature began quite early and that he had a good education."[5] This theory is substantiated in an entry of June 26, 1568 of the records of the municipality of Lorca, where we find the first reference to Hita, a writer:

> And to enliven the festivities, and from henceforth that they serve and honor said festival of the sacrament, it was ordered that Ginés Pérez de Hita and the Master of the Chapel create the principal entertainments, each one to be paid eight ducats.[6]

By early 1572, after serving as a soldier against the Moors in Granada, and subsequently as a guard, guarding Moorish prisoners in Lorca, he presented a book of verses to the municipality of Lorca: "The People and Deeds of the most Noble City of Lorca." In 1595, some twenty-five years after the fact, he brought out the first volume of the *Guerras civiles*, waiting nine years to publish the second volume.[7] Still officially listed as a resident of Murcia in 1619, he is thought to have died sometime in the third decade of the seventeenth century.[8]

One of the most intriguing facts about Pérez de Hita's early years and the mystery that surrounds them, is the fact that his official occupation invariably is listed as *zapatero*, or cobbler. Obviously belonging to the lower social class (and we see that it is necessity which prompted him to join the army), how did he come to the attention of the Marqués de los Vélez? It is unusual, although not impossible, that an individual born into a class which enjoyed small social standing could attain the patronage of someone so highly placed. Given the author's somewhat tenuous social position, his outspoken views strike an even more incongruous chord.

Although there is controversy in categorizing the work—literary authorities claim it is too historical, while historians allege that it is too literary—the author is a first-rate storyteller. Pérez de Hita's talent consisted of his abilities to gather information from popular traditions and amplify the texts and chronicles of historians. He infused his somewhat austere presentation of facts with a poetic sensibility. But as Paula

Blanchard-Demouge, an early twentieth-century editor of the
Guerras civiles, has noted, he invented little. [9]

Perhaps one of the most entertaining features of the first
volume is his detailed and colorful descriptions of Moorish
customs and culture. Certainly these were more acceptable than
his politically controversial observations in the second volume.
As literary historian Giorgio Valli has remarked, the world
described by Pérez de Hita is a symphony of colors within a
framework of tournaments and battles, love and duels. [10] It is
history filtered through the poet's lens, even if the author has
taken liberties and westernized some elements of the Arab
world. Chivalry is much in evidence here and the love themes
show the definite influence of courtly love. In the same vein, the
imprecations against Muhammad and the lauding of the
Christian religion attributed to various highly placed Arabs
sound contrived at best. Given the author's attitude in the
second volume, however, this literary license is more easily
understood, and the author may have employed this stylistic
device as a clever means to couch his interest in toleration.
"Those writers who sympathized with the Morisco cause,"
comments literary historian José María Delgado, "used
euphemisms to avoid prosecution." [11]

One aspect of Western chivalric literature that is absent in
Pérez de Hita is any mention of the supernatural. Can this
absence be interpreted as complimentary in the sense that he
wished to portray Arab culture with a less urgent need to rely on
outside forces? [12] A more obvious explanation is Pérez de Hita's
complete lack of humor or whimsy. While other contemporary
writers might have injected a note of veiled laughter, or even
satire or ridicule, particularly when dealing with love potions or
flying dragons, Pérez de Hita's work, even the first volume, is
characterized by an assiduous seriousness, perhaps emanating
from his wish to have both volumes accepted as history. The
atmosphere he creates and the characters who people the *Guerras
civiles* are real, as is the author's extolling of morality and virtue.

While the gallant chivalric spirit is the basis for most of the
chapters, especially in the first book, the author may have a
secondary motive in relating these tales. Personal combat speaks
to the issue of arms and armor, and Pérez de Hita's detailed

description of how these splinter and crack as they succumb to the blows of the combatants may be, at bottom, another example of his dislike of armed conflict. In one aspect, however, he remains almost unerringly true to the chivalric example: the physical characteristics of the place of combat inevitably include a fountain where the wounded can take refreshment and sometimes, as in the incident involving Abayaldos and Ponce de León, where the moribund pagans receive baptism.

He reveals a penchant for historical detail in his discussion of colors and descriptions of shields, standards, flags, devices and other paraphernalia of the battlefield. Unlike other writers of the genre, the society he depicts, if not entirely realistic, is not completely a product of his imagination.

Pérez de Hita influenced various other writers such as Luis Vélez de Guevara, Pedro Antonio Alarcón, Jerónimo de Contreras, and Castillo de Solórzano, as well such Golden Age luminaries as Lope de Vega, Calderón de la Barca, and Cervantes.[13] But these writers differ from him substantially in the question of presenting the Moorish point of view. The pain, physical and emotional, of a Christian held captive by infidels is a common element running through Cervantes's "Story of a Captive" which appears as a chapter in the *Quixote*, Jerónimo de Contreras's story of Caluman and Lazman in his *Jungle Adventures*, or in "Liberty Deserved" from the *Comic Acts* of Castillo de Solórzano. The horrors of captivity serve to underscore the Christian point of view.[14] The only exception to this theme is the "Story of Ozmin and Daraja" which Mateo Alemán included in his novel *Guzmán de Alfarache*. This work more closely parallels Pérez de Hita's owing to its detailed descriptions of festivals and jousts and its general historical accuracy.[15] The relations between Moors and Christians are less amicable than in Pérez de Hita as these protagonists deceive their Christian protectors. Love between people of different religions, in this case the unrequited feelings don Rodrigo entertains for Daraja, was an element scarcely visible in Golden Age literature with the exception of dramatic works, and this aspect makes Alemán's work exceptional.

Both Pérez de Hita and Alemán were inspired by the first "Moorish novel," *La Historia del Abencerraje y la hermosa Jarifa,* written by Antonio de Villegas and published at mid-century. This short novel depicts a westernized and valiant Moorish knight, one of the last members of the star-crossed Abencerrajes of Granada. According to the story, the knight Abindarraez is apprehended by the mayor of Alora, Rodrigo de Narvaéz.[16] Abindarraez spins such a beautiful and melancholy tale about the Abencerrajes in general and Abindarraez's personal love for his lady, Jarifa, that don Rodrigo is moved to let Abindarraez continue on his journey under the solemn promise he will return. When the young Moor keeps his word and returns, with Jarifa, rather than incarcerating them, don Rodrigo receives them as guests, and subsequently intercedes with the king of Granada so that Jarifa's father is forced to accept Abindarraez as a son-in-law. Although the novel makes some attempt to show Moors as individuals, the framework is decidedly western. It avoids mention of religion or religious differences, and the real hero is don Rodrigo de Narvaéz, who embodies the Christian chivalric virtues of honor, wisdom, and nobility.

At the beginning of Volume II of the *Guerras civiles*, Pérez de Hita includes an episode that, while apparently fictitious, is an historical account. He relates the story of Albexani and Almazora, which closely parallels that of Abindarraez and Jarifa, even though a central element, the generosity of the Christian overlord, and by tacit implication the Christian faith, is absent.

Golden Age literary historian María Soledad Carrasco maintains that, despite certain appearances to the contrary, Pérez de Hita did not really sympathize with the Morisco cause, and that he primarily confined his praise to superficial cultural aspects, especially equestrian exercises and appeal, and that these did not constitute any sensitive area of friction.[17] Viewed in general terms, her opinion is accurate, as the depiction of the Moor in Spanish literature as gallant and chivalric was a poetically appealing image. For all that he represented as a once-brilliant and refined civilization, he also represented as a defeated race, this element being necessary and beneficial to inspire melancholy. Rather than denigrating the Moor, now a conquered enemy, chroniclers now can present him in a prototypical chivalric image: a knight errant almost as capable of acts of derring-do and courtly love as his Christian counterpart.

What makes Pérez de Hita's accounts differ from the literary norm, however, are his portrayals of Moorish suffering, depicted in vivid and generally historically accurate terms, and his evident compassion for the Moors as a disinherited race. Juan Martinez Ruíz advances the theory that Pérez de Hita's concerns with morality and justice are rooted in the plight of the *conversos* who, nearly a century earlier, had faced a like dilemma.[18] The similarities between the cases were many, as the Jews were subjected to the indignities and abuses that inevitably accompanied campaigns of forced conversion. Although this comparison is valid, it is nonetheless illogical that Pérez de Hita should have made these views public. For an historian writing under Philip II, the inherent dangers of expressing sympathy beyond the most general of sentiments for an enemy of Spain, especially a non-Christian enemy, were manifold. If the fifteenth-century Inquisition had prosecuted, almost exclusively, *conversos* and crypto-Jews, the sixteenth-century Inquisition was equally vigorous in its prosecution of Old Christians whose conduct was in any way questionable. We must surmise that it is only Pérez de Hita's friendship with the Marqués de los Vélez that protected him from inquisitional prosecution.[19] José María Delgado in his study on Moorish literature offers a partial explanation for a "sentimentalized" picture of Moorish life, and by extension an explanation of Pérez de Hita's attitude. The chivalric exaltation of the Moor, noble in all virtues except perhaps the most important ones that derive from professing the Christian religion, contrasted with the quotidian treatment meted out to the flesh-and-blood Moriscos of the sixteenth century.[20] These individuals were prohibited from maintaining their cultural identity, and the consensus among some Old Christians was that they were worthy of ridicule, if not open hatred. These abuses endured by "outsiders" in Spanish society, particularly when perpetrated by members of the lower orders, generally obeyed economic, rather than racial, motives. It is not illogical that the inhabitants of Granada felt impotent at being forced to abide under a system of government that was not only alien but also oppressive. The only signs of cultural identity and unity—dress and language—proved double-edged swords, for if the continued use of these provided some small comfort, this immediate form of identification only served to aid the inquisitors in their task. Most of the proceedings in the second half of the century, especially against less affluent individuals, came as a result of denunciations. A good number of these were the product of personal, rather than religious motivation. The use of Moorish dress and the Arabic language only enhanced the differences between the two communities, and feuds and personal quarrels helped fuel inquisitional denunciations.

It is not surprising that anti-Spanish feeling characterized Moorish thought, and Morisco ballads, such as the following attributed to the Andalusian Morisco, Juan Alonso Aragonés, were famous for celebrating Spanish vices:

> Cursed crow of a Spaniard
> Fetid Cerberus
> You are with your three heads
> In the doorway of hell.
>
> Others of my beloved homeland
> I know have responded
> In the Latin language
> As well as romance and rhyme.[21]

For all that Pérez de Hita apparently wished to provide a bridge between the cultures and thus lessen the feelings of rage and hostility, he did seek refuge in a literary device, claiming to be only the translator of Volume I of the *Guerras civiles*. Ironically, this pretense is abandoned in the second volume, which contains more sensitive material. Blanchard-Demouge maintains, however, that he did use Arabic sources, including written sources.[22] The only mention that Pérez de Hita makes of the supposed author is in chapter 3, where he alleges that the book was written by the Moor Aben Hamin, an historian of the era of the Moorish arrival in Spain (Vol. I, 24). Pérez de Hita presumably took the name from the real individual who had existed in the era of Peter the Cruel. According to the chronicle of don Pedro, after the battle of Nájera was won, he sent letters to a certain Moor of Granada in whom he had great confidence, and who was a great scholar and philosopher. His name was Benahatin.[23]

Pérez de Hita was not alone in using this literary device, as it was common among authors of chivalric romance. Cervantes himself invented Cide Hamete Bengali for the same purpose. The style of the book is somewhat reminiscent of chivalric Oriental novels, as it was Arabic custom to use poetry to prove the veracity of the recorded events. Pérez de Hita followed this tradition and included many ballads, not only as literary decoration but also as proof of authenticity. The *Jhata* of Aben Aljatib follows this style, and served as a source for him particularly in his meticulous recording of genealogy. The tribes he traces comprise the Arab nobility, whose factiousness and internal discords contributed to the fall of Granada. A dramatic difference exists between Pérez de Hita and other contemporary chroniclers and historians in his exploring of the causes and effects of this dissension. Almost all other accounts of the fall of Granada and the subsequent Moorish uprisings were written from the exclusive Christian point of view, and barely devoted any mention to the internal unrest.

Volume I of the *Guerras civiles*, which enjoyed great popularity, most probably due to its elements of chivalric romance, not only relates the internal strife and intrigues that culminate in the fall of Granada, but also describes the Moorish culture in colorful and vivid detail. Pérez de Hita opens his history by saying that Granada was well governed especially by Boabdil, the "Rey Chico," the last Moorish king of that realm. He traces the lineage of various noble families, the Abencerrajes, Gomeles, Zegries, and Mazas, but pays particular attention to the history of the Abencerrajes (Vol. I, 24). They represent a powerful militia originating in Africa, and their name means "son of the saddle maker." They are the best horsemen in the kingdom of Granada. Pérez de Hita especially praises them for not having changed their name because "the Moors do not deprecate their nobles who come of working-class fathers" (Vol. I, 24). This detail perhaps is an insight into the author's recognition of his own limited social standing in a culture not noted for its generous treatment of sons of working-class fathers. He may also have desired to present an object lesson to his Spanish readers.

His descriptions of love, both requited and unrequited, are courtly in flavor, such as the love professed by Zayde for Zayda: "[I]t was decided between them that if Zayde went to Granada, she would love him and accept him as her knight" (Vol. I, 47). Zayde is an Abencerraje, and is described as possessing great qualities and talents. In a long ballad following this episode, Pérez de Hita extols all of Zayde's many attributes.[24] The Abencerrajes, who the author seems to favor, were hated by the Zegries, Gomeles, and Mazas, among other reasons, because of the Abencerrajes' good fortune with women (Vol. I, 56).

He describes the growing tyranny between the Abencerrajes and the Zegries, always showing the first tribe as composed of valiant knights whose conduct is above reproach, while the second tribe is seen as duplicitous and perfidious. The intrigue culminates in a calumny of adultery against queen Moraycela, wife of Boabdil, and the Abencerraje Albinhamete, circulated by the Zegries. This results in the king's ordering that the throats of all Abencerrajes be cut. The nobles of Granada rebel against a sovereign turned tyrant, and they acclaim his father, Muley Hacen as their king. Boabdil's brother Muza, placates them and combat is prepared between the four Zegries (depicted as Castilians), who continue to sustain the accusation, and Moraycela's four champions. Although her honor emerges triumphant in the combat, the internal situation in Granada worsens as the three kings continue to dispute sovereignty.

An interesting encounter ensues when a Christian knight, who turns out to be Manuel Ponce de León, passes through la Vega. Gazul, a Moorish knight, praises Ponce de León to the king, informing him that the Christian is stouthearted and brave (Vol. I, 68). It was, however, not uncommon for enemies to laud each other's attributes as warriors in order to enhance their own valor in defeating those enemies in combat.

Ultimately the knight challenges Ponce de León to combat because the Christian has killed the Moor's cousin and he, Abayaldos, demands satisfaction (Vol. I, 119). What strikes the modern reader as uncommon are Pérez de Hita's descriptions of the pre-combat preparations: before the two combatants do battle, they engage in pleasant conversation. The author views this scene with dismay in that two apparently civilized people, who have more in common than they are willing to admit, are forced by circumstances to try to kill each other. What is more typical in the account is the fact that Abayaldos, mortally wounded by Ponce de León, converts to Christianity before he dies (Vol. I, 123). Abayaldos asks for mercy as he has given offense by persecuting Christians and now he asks to be forgiven, as he understands that forgiveness is a part of Christian belief. In this scene, we see Pérez de Hita in the uncharacteristic role of Christian propagandist. The ballad that follows this story sings the praises of Abayaldos's conversion and how, having lost his body, he regains his soul. Pérez de Hita records the death scene almost as an event between friends, rather than the result of combat between enemies, and although Abayaldos's conversion is duly noted and praised, the author registers a tacit dissatisfaction that the result of hate often is paid in blood.

Venturing onto still shakier ground, he makes his Moorish sympathies quite evident when he notes, somewhat offhandedly, that it was Moorish custom to have six or seven women (Vol. I, 250). While it was no secret that Christian men enjoyed the favors of women other than their wives, officially polygamy was not looked upon with favor in Christian Spain. Pérez de Hita refused to be scandalized by this practice, and boldly added that it was better to engage in this custom and provide for the women as opposed to having one wife only to abandon her.

His dwelling on the issue of internal discord as a primary factor in the fall of Granada takes an unexpected and suggestive turn. When Pedro Fajardo scores a decisive victory over the Moors in Murcia, Abdili, Muley Hacen's brother, rejoiced that his brother was taken prisoner because he, Abdili, wanted to be the sole sovereign of the realm. Pedro Fajardo, at first presented as generous, gives Muley Hacen his freedom without requiring a ransom. Muley Hacen's mother, however, sends him ten thousand doubloons which the governor returns "so that her son might use the money in the war he will wage against his brother" (Vol. I, 251). While on the surface don Pedro's gesture seems noble, given the circumstances, this might be interpreted as a less than flattering presentation of a Christian governor and soldier. Although he refuses the money for himself, he is more than willing to see it used to continue the internal war among the

Moors and thus for the (eventual) benefit of the Christian cause. Rather than praising Christian generosity, Pérez de Hita appears to condemn hypocrisy disguised as nobility.

Volume I ends with the fall of Granada, and again Pérez de Hita makes an ambiguous statement as to his feelings on the outcome: "The Christian queen, greatly impressed with the beauty and splendor (of Granada) desired to claim it for her own." This purposeful ambiguity, as seen in the episode of Pedro Fajardo, again surfaces in his apparent desire to damn Isabella with faint praise. On the one hand she is the most Christian of queens, yet her avarice is apparent in her anxiety to assert physical claim to Granada.

There are fewer ambiguities, and far less pageantry in Volume II of the *Guerras civiles,* which relates the details of the Morisco uprising of 1568. Pérez de Hita expresses profound humanitarian sentiments in this volume, and does not hesitate to voice unorthodox opinions, especially regarding the cruelties which his compatriots were capable of inflicting on their enemies. Perhaps Blanchard-Demouge's assertion that the book is an energetic protest is overstated; however, the position he assumes toward war, and its attendant horrors, is a criticism, if indirect, of Spain's official policy toward Arabs.

His attitude of repulsion toward the Christian soldiers dominates Volume II, as in this ballad that ironically commemorates the battle of the Marqués de los Vélez in Guécija:

> All the soldiers
> on the cross of swords swear
> to leave no thing living
> on another journey there. (Vol. II, 66)

In this battle the Marqués's soldiers ran amok due to their covetousness, swearing to leave no man, woman, or child living. Pérez de Hita relates that this particular battle had its origin in the great cruelty the Moors had inflicted on the residents of the Augustinian convent in Guécija where all the friars had had their throats cut and had been thrown into a pool of oil. The convent was burned to the ground, the altars and holy objects destroyed (Vol. II, 76–77). "For these and other cruelties the Christians were determined to leave no Moorish man or woman alive, and aside from this cause, they were angry with the Marqués who had not given them a greater share of the booty" (Vol. II, 77). Pérez de Hita cheapens the cause of the Christians' anger, making their legitimate outrage at the destruction of the convent take a secondary position to their greed. In describing the Christian soldiers as self-seekers first and avengers of the faith second, he reflects a point of view rarely shared, at least not openly, by his contemporaries.

Pérez de Hita's view of the Spanish army was colored by his personal experiences. What he avoids, however, and somewhat unjustly, is any discussion of the root cause of avarice on the part of the rank and file soldiers. Problems with, and of, the soldiery were one of the chief social ills in sixteenth-century Spain, and should have been taken into account by the author.

In April of 1569 the town council of Lorca met to recruit three hundred men for the army then being raised for the Marqués de los Vélez to combat the Moorish uprising. Each man was to be paid a stipend of two *reales* a day until he became incorporated into the army.[25] This amount, even when measured against the officially established wages of new recruits, three ducats a month, was low.[26] The real problem, beyond the low wages, was Philip's handling of the military situation, and his theory that soldiers should be paid "when it pleased God." Juan de Pineda, a contemporary Franciscan historian and moralist, considered Philip's attitude detrimental in the extreme, and commented that the worst enemy of the Spanish armies, and perhaps of Spain herself, was the mistreatment of the soldiers.[27]

Apparently the recruits for the Granada uprising, as in the Lorca example, were not even promised a regular salary beyond the two *reales* per day for traveling. They were told only that "His Majesty has sufficient supplies that all will eat."[28] Since soldiering, particularly among the lower classes, was a profession that enjoyed scant regard, those who entered this occupation generally did so with the idea of enlarging their opportunities through some illegitimate means.[29] If Pérez de Hita found this situation untenable, he seems less concerned with the source of this conduct than with its unfortunate consequences. His quick, almost unilateral, indictment of the Spanish army is puzzling. Joaquín Espín offers a possible explanation for this attitude: "Pérez de Hita did not refer to war as war, but as cruelty, assassination, and thievery, and whoever says this, especially in an era when such sentimentality was uncommon, reveals an innate common sense and spiritual refinement."[30]

Of the three hundred men finally recruited and sent to the Marqués de los Vélez from Lorca, number ninety-five on the official roster corresponded to Ginés Pérez de Hita, who was to receive five ducats in addition to an unspecified salary "which he was owed."[31] He apparently had joined the army out of necessity, being paid by one Gonzalo Cazorla to take his, Gonzalo's, place.[32] While this underscored Pérez de Hita's precarious financial situation, and may explain his disgust that wealthier men could shirk their duty, as well as his lack of affection for the *artes* of war in general, it still provides no insight as to why the sufferings of the Moriscos, rather than the Christians, moved him to compassion.

Certainly the war produced myriad atrocities against the Moriscos, particularly involving women and children. The author describes how he found a Moorish woman run through more than ten times by swords, around whom were lying her six dead children. The unfortunate woman had been running for her life when she was discovered by the Spanish army. Moribund, she had fallen on top of a seventh and smallest child, a boy, who, although wounded, survived (Vol. II, 80). Pérez de Hita seems genuinely amazed at the lack of Christian charity evinced by the soldiers as they passed on all sides of the child without being moved to see if he could be saved. "For ill or good fortune I walked by at that moment and moved to pity, I took the child myself" (Vol. II, 80).

He describes the attitude of the Moorish women who were terrified at the advance of the Spanish forces, as they knew no prisoners would be taken. Unable to withstand the attack, they went out on a cliff overlooking the sea and, embracing each other, and shouting their pain and sorrow, plummeted to their deaths (Vol. II, 79). Others sought to put the idea of Christian mercy to the test and constructed crude crosses not out of pieces of wood. Kneeling before the soldiers they would cry, "I Christian sir, I Christian" (Vol. II, 79). But no one in that squadron offered any Christian charity, and the Moorish women were forced to jump from the cliffs.

Pérez de Hita is relentless in his descriptions of the cruelties practiced by the soldiers, providing no hint of explanation as to their conduct, choosing to report only their bloodthirstiness, plundering, looting, and stealing. The fact that the author focuses on these atrocities committed by the Spanish armies even while he demonstrates compassion for the ancestral enemies of Spain and the church, makes his account of the uprising even more untypical. Rather than register dismay at the nominal Christianity of the Moriscos, he shows regard for their customs and traditions as well as their reluctance to abandon their cultural heritage in order to adopt Spanish ways. [33]

The unorthodoxy of the *Guerras civiles*, and particularly Volume II, is owed to the author's Moorish sympathies which cannot be relegated to mere compassion for a conquered foe, and to the almost complete lack of references to the superiority of the Christian belief system. While it is true that individual Christians are described as valiant, noble, and honorable—in short, afforded all the praises attendant in chivalric literature—little interest is focused on Christianity as the true faith. And although the *Guerras civiles* is secular literature, due to the topics involved, the absence of a discussion of the merits of Christianity is conspicuous. But Pérez de Hita is, with few exceptions, far from a Christian propagandist. In describing the aftermath of the battle of Felix, he notes that the Spanish forces, in addition to other atrocities, had cut the throats of many "creatures," a word he employs to describe the children who died in that battle (Vol. II, 97). These particular children were unbaptized (through no fault of their own as there were no clerics to baptize them), but speaking metaphorically Pérez de Hita claims that they were baptized—in their own blood (Vol. II, 96). As if this sanguinary imagery were insufficient to prove his point about Christian cruelty, he adds, somewhat venomously that, as these were the children of baptized parents, "I am unsure as to the meaning of this, and I submit to the findings of the Doctors of Holy Mother Church" (Vol. II, 96). For all of Pérez de Hita's humorlessness, this comment appears to contain more of sarcasm than humility.

If this statement is purposely ambiguous, the stirring note on which he concludes the work is straightforward: "Finally, the Moriscos of the kingdom were removed from their lands, and it was better that they had never been removed however much His Majesty had lost, even if all his realms" (Vol. II, 353). This statement, for all that it might be defended as literary hyperbole, is still treasonous in the Spain of Philip II. The fact that Pérez de Hita was not prosecuted by the Inquisition supports the theory that his friendship with the Marqués de los Vélez protected him.

The feeling of quasi tolerance, rather than acceptance, which most sixteenth-century Spaniards harbored toward the Moriscos was owed to the Moriscos' permanent subjugation and a tacit understanding of Christian superiority, both religiously and culturally. The expansiveness shown to the Moriscos in literature almost always sprang from these sentiments, and if Christians living among Moors and Moors living among Christians had been able to break down some of the barriers, this acceptance disappeared in the immediate threat of treachery or revolt. Pérez de Hita's work does not conform to this literary formula. Whether his views reflect protopacifism, a somewhat unlikely possibility in the mid-sixteenth century, or merely heightened compassion for a foe whom he respected, he broke with existing literary conventions. The *Guerras civiles* is an impassioned defense of the Moriscos, which audaciously questions the veracity of the official contemporary view that the Reconquest and wars against the Moors were "holy wars."

NOTES

1. Hurtado de Mendoza, *Guerra en Granada*, 71.

2 MS. Simanacas, E. 1057, folio 105, Madrid, January 20, 1569, cited by Braudel, La Méditerranée 2:360.

3. Payne, *A History of Spain and Portugal* 1:287. The Moriscos were sold into slavery despite a prohibition against selling baptized Christians as slaves. This is in some measure attributable to the cultural

differences, and to a desire for profit which Pérez de Hita describes in extensive detail in Volume II of the *Guerras civiles de Granada*. See also Kamen, *The Iron Century*, 412–413.

4. Pérez de Hita, *Guerras civiles*, (Blanchard-Demouge, ed.) 1:xiii.

5. Ibid. (Bryant, ed.) 1:x. The text, according to Bryant's introduction, is based upon the oldest authentic version known, the edition published in Zaragoza in 1595, as reproduced by Blanchard-Demouge in 1913. An introduction, list of previous editions, explanatory footnotes, glossary of archaic and uncommon words, and an appendix have been added to the Bryant edition.

6. Cited by Espín Rael, *De la Vecindad de Pérez de Hita*, 18.

7. For a complete list of editions of both volumes, see Pérez de Hita, *Guerras civiles* (Bryant, ed.) 1:xxiii–xxiv.

8. Ibid. (Blanchard-Demouge, ed.) 1:viii.

9. Ibid., 1:ix.

10. Valli, "Ludovico Ariosto y Ginés Pérez de Hita," 23.

11. Delgado Gallego, "Maurofilia y maurofobia," 20.

12. Valli, 27.

13. Pérez de Hita, *Guerras civiles* (Bryant, ed.) 1:xix. See also Carrasco Urgoiti, *El Moro de Granada*, 70.

14. See Cervantes, *Los baños de Argel*.

15. Alemán based his historical descriptions on those found in Pulgar's *Crónica*.

16. Villegas, *Historia del Abencerraje y la hermosa Jarifa*, 508. The author includes an extensive and detailed description of Rodrigo's achievement and exalts him as a great leader. Thus from the outset he states, if tacitly, Christian superiority.

17. Carrasco Urgoiti, "La Cultura popular de Ginés Pérez de Hita."

18. Carrasco Urgoiti, *El Moro de Granada*, introduction of Juan Martínez Ruíz, p. xxiii .

19. For a more detailed explanation of the Inquisition and privileged immunity from prosecution, see García Cárcel, *Orígenes de la Inquisición española*.

20. Delgado, "Maurofilia," 11.

21. Ibid., 14

22. Pérez de Hita, *Guerras civiles*, (Blanchard-Demouge, ed.) 1:xxx.

23. *Crónica del Rey don Pedro*, D. Pedro Lopez de Ayala, 18th year, chap. 23, p. 567; cited by Blanchard-Demouge, *Guerras civiles*, 1: xxxiii.

24. Pérez de Hita, *Guerras civiles* (Bryant, ed.)1:53. The editor notes that since this ballad does not appear in any of the earlier collections, Pérez de Hita may be the author.

25. By mid-century inflation was rampant, and two *reales* per day, even if the sum were paid, was scarcely an inducement for a man to go soldiering, particularly if he had a family to support. For a detailed study of the problems of inflation in the latter half of the sixteenth century, see Fernández Alvarez, *Economía, sociedad y corona*, 280–285.

26. Díaz Plaja, *Sociedad española*, 34.

27. Pineda, *Diálogos familiares de la agricultura cristiana*, p. lxii.

28. Espín, 19.

29. Ibid., 20. The author notes that of the three hundred *cédulas* (identification documents) which had been delivered to the town council and represented all the men eligible for service, only one hundred men appeared to register.

30. Ibid., 55.

31. Ibid., 23.

32. Ibid.

33. Carrasco Urgoiti, *El Moro*, 63–66. The author comments on this anomaly in her study on the *Guerras civiles*.

CHAPTER 15

The Myth of Shah Ismail Safavi: Political Rhetoric and "Divine" Kingship

Palmira Brummett

Introduction

In 1501 a boy-king, hereditary sheikh of the Safavid dervishes mobilized his forces in Azerbaijan and conquered the old Mongol capital of Tabriz, unearthing and desecrating the bones of his Ak Koyunlu (White-Sheep) Türkmen predecessors and cursing the names of the Sunni caliphs from the pulpits of the city. Thus came Ismail Safavi to power, avenging the deaths of his brother and father at the hands of Ak Koyunlu rulers.[1] Within ten years, he had conquered Baghdad, united Iran under his sway, and begun the process, often forcible, of conversion of his heretofore Sunni populace to Shi'ism. Ismail taunted the Mamluk sultan in Cairo, warning him that the seal of his title to hegemony in the Muslim world, possession of the holy cities of Mecca and Med ina, would soon be lost. As further testament to his claims to universal Islamic sovereignty, in 1510 Ismail sent to Ottoman sultan Bayezid II (ruled 1481–1512) in Istanbul, a gift: the head of the defeated Central Asian Uzbek monarch, Shaibânî Khân. Ultimately, Bayezid's son Selim I (ruled 1512–1520) would succeed in deposing the Mamluks and establishing Ottoman hegemony in Mecca, but first he had to contend with Ismail Safavi.

Transformed from an essentially unknown teenager in 1499, hiding out in Ardebil near the Caspian Sea, to a warrior-king of mythic proportion, Ismail suddenly became the object of furious speculation on the part of European Christendom.[2] But in these early years, little was known of Ismail—his beliefs, the source of his might, or the extent of his forces. So the European sources recreated Ismail Safavi, a Muslim monarch, in their own image: a Christian-like holy man, a warrior endowed with divine qualities by his army of *Sufis*, the long-awaited savior who would free Europe from the scourge of the Ottoman Turks.[3]

Representations of Ismail

Once upon a time, a rosy youth, pious and brave, united the *kızılbaş* fierce Türkmen warriors, into an army of *Sufis* who fought for the glory of Allah and for the love of their leader, Ismail. (The kızılbaş, red heads, were so named because of the twelve-peaked red caps they wore, symbolizing their allegiance to Ismail and to the twelve ithna ashari Shi'ite imams.) Thinking him immortal and invincible, these warriors would hurl themselves into battle unarmed, emerging victorious by virtue of their leader's skill and religiosity and their own valor. The youth, wise, handsome, generous, and beloved by all, distributed the booty and wealth among his followers, keeping none for himself. His mortal enemies were the Ottoman Turks, whom he despised as heretics and blasphemers and whose eradication was as vital to him as was his faith. Ismail's closest advisors were priests and he viewed the Christians as his brothers and as partners in a struggle to the death against the Turks.

This is the story of Ismail Safavi, a hero constructed for a Christian audience by Christian authors, the external Ismail, the polemical Ismail, the Shi'ite sheikh represented as savior of Christendom. The elements of this composite story both moved and emanated from the narratives of the tellers—a creation myth with Persian, Turkish, Italian, and Portuguese antecedents, among others, created, concocted, affecting even the protagonist himself, and, above all, a motive force for policy formation in an era when communication was both slow and costly.

The foreign policy decisions of states contending for power in the Levant and beyond could not wait for the assembling of comprehensive intelligence on Ismail's beliefs and troop strength. Round-trip journeys by envoys required a year or even two; and European states had no formal diplomatic channels to Iran. Ismail would be long dead in his grave before European diplomatic missions would begin to flesh out information on the Safavid state.

Muslim states, like the Ottoman and Mamluk empires, had irregular diplomatic exchanges with Ismail, but even the effectiveness of these was limited by antiespionage precautions such as keeping envoys sequestered, and by the ritualized insults employed by sovereigns against the envoys of their Muslim competitors.[4] Thus, the Venetian doge or the Portuguese king, like the Ottoman sultan, relied on letters, rumors, stories, and the accounts of merchants and sometime-spies to gauge the threat and the promise of Shah Ismail. These sources constituted the early sixteenth century's natural order of the transmission of information. Narrative convention freely mixed observation and hearsay, seldom including editorial notation on source "validity." "What was heard" was assumed in the telling— authority sometimes cited and sometimes not. None of the early tellers actually saw Ismail. Hence, layers of story intermingled with literary convention, entertaining anecdote, rumor, observation, official report, trope, and commercial information. The determination to include (everything), rather than the mode of inclusion, decided the starting and ending points of the narrative. Often, too, these accountings of Ismail were designed to define and highlight the nature of the European self.

> [Ismail is known as] the Equalizer or Sufi. [In this realm] . . . the whole of Europe is known as the people behind the wind . . . There is no doubt that those who wear the red cap are more like Portuguese than like people from anywhere else. . . . The Sheikh Ismail spends most of his time in Tabriz which is fifty days' journey on camels from Hormuz.[5]

In this statement, the Portuguese agent, Tomé Pires, located Ismail in time and space for the European "other."[6] He was included and excluded, tangible and intangible, reachable and unreachable. This distance could be measured in something as solid as days by camel from the Persian Gulf, where

Portuguese fleets were attempting to consolidate their control
over the revenues of the oriental trade. Yet Ismail was separated
"by the wind" from the peoples of Europe. His raconteurs had
not seen him. Tomé Pires' audience had to imagine that the
kızılbaş were more like themselves than like anyone else. The
Portuguese accounts represent the outer rim of representations
of Ismail, approaching from the greatest distance by sea, round
the African cape, and not possessed of the longtime familiarity of
commercial and political intercourse with Iran to which Italian
city-states like Venice and Genoa were accustomed. The Italian
accounts, benefiting from long-standing familiarity with the
eastern Levant and from the proximity of resident agents at the
confines of Iran, had more and better opportunities for
information gathering. Still, the stories of merchants, culled from
dialogues in the urban trade *entrepôts* and transported with
caravans to Damascus and Alexandria, or the accounts of
escaped captives and of soldiers from defeated armies, had a
logic of their own not necessarily responsive to the wished-for
knowledge of Ismail required by European policy makers.

Some of the earliest rumors of Ismail, reaching Venice in
1501, referred to him only as "the new prophet" without
additional details.[7] Then, from "persons coming from Persia" in
December 1501, a "deposition concerning the new prophet"
(called here Exeth rather than Ismail) was enscribed in the
official records of the Venetian republic.

> His father, who is dead, was said to be descended from
> Muhammad . . . and he says "my father was not my father
> but he was my slave" and he [Ismail] claims to be god
> himself; and he has with him 40 administrators, who are
> called Caliphani [deputies] who perform and celebrate the
> service (*ufficio*) in his name, because he says he is god. And
> he has goods distributed to everyone, to Christians as to
> infidels; and so all the assassins and men of bad sort go
> with him. To these who go with him he gives money,
> telling them "spend this in the name of Exeth." . . . Exeth
> demanded of a captured Turk, "Where is god?" and he
> responded, "God is in heaven." And quickly Exeth had
> him cut to pieces. Then he asked a Christian, an Armenian

priest, "Where is god?" and he answered, "In heaven, on earth and here," pointing out him who listened. And Exeth replied, "Let him go, because he knows where god is."[8]

This early representation of Ismail contains the germs of images which would be more fully developed in the accounts reaching Europe during the next few years: a prophet claiming to be god, a charismatic leader whose generosity attracted followers, an enemy of Turks and Muslims, and a friend of Christians. His "divinity" subordinated at once his father, Muhammad, and Islam. How Ismail would direct his divinely inspired forces remained unclear for the European audience and its informants, but portents appearing in the heavens linked the power struggles within Europe to those between the monarchs of Islam and Christendom.

[A]bout two miles distant from Bergamo a multitude of creatures appeared in the air: black eagles, falcons, ravens and some others such as have never been seen, nor their form and nature described by any author. As large as a vulture . . . [these latter] had the head and legs of a dog, and claws of incredible length. These creatures fought for the space of about two hours until there were thirty-three corpses of one sort and another, but only two dead from the unfamiliar species. . . . The eagles signified the Christian emperor, the falcons the French monarch, the ravens the Turks, and the unknown others, Ely, the prophet.[9]

This animal tale draws the mysterious and unknown prophet of the earliest Ismail rumors into the contest for Levantine and continental hegemony—a miraculous creature with the ferocity to destroy all the military powers bordering the Italian peninsula—Muslim and Christian alike.

More concrete information reached Italy in 1502 via a Venetian spy report. The spy, Costantino Lascari, pretending to be engaged in trade, contacted Ismail and reported to the Venetian senate on the shah and his troops. Lascari's mission was to see if Ismail was preparing to support a revolt in southern Anatolia by the Karamanid pretender, against the Ottomans:

This Sufi is much loved by those of his sect, which is a
certain religion, catholic after their fashion, discordant
with the opinion of the prophet Muhammad, and with
Umar and Abu Bakr, who were his disciples. The Sufi
adheres to the opinion of Ali, Hasan (Esse) and Husain
(Ossem) who were also disciples of the prophet. In their
articles of faith, they were, however, as one might say, like
the Arians and Manicheans at the time of St. Peter and the
other popes, that, though they claimed to be Christians,
were heretics . . . this religion of the Sufi . . . always bore
great hatred toward the Ottoman house, and counts them
as heretics . . . and this religion of the Sufi has always
made war on the Ottomans. . . . Having seen, in so short a
time, his great success, it seems to me an incredible thing.
. . . Dear Prince, I wished to make this declaration,
because many, many people have asked me about this
Sufi, [whether] he is a prophet and an important person,
these things seeming miraculous. . . . I told them he is a
natural leader and his ancestors are from the Persian royal
house; and it is true that this Sufi, in his faith is very
catholic. [10]

Lascari tried to order the earlier representations of Ismail,
denying his divinity and emphasizing instead his Christian
affinities, his military prowess, and his enmity toward the Turks.
Through this process of distinction and counterdistinction, the
boundaries and limits of both Ismail and the Ottomans could be
articulated, in space and in the imagination of the European
audience. This ordering of evidence and of rhetorical elements
assumed an as yet ill-defined set of options for constructing the
identities of self, opponent, and ally. Furthermore, this process
coincided temporally with a period between 1502 and 1515
during which Venice would redefine the Ottoman state from
enemy (during the Aegean wars of 1499–1502) to ally:
replacement for the Mamluks as middlemen for the eastern trade
and defender of Venetian commercial interests against the
inroads of the Portuguese in the Red Sea and Indian Ocean.
Before this transformation occurred, however, Ismail had to be
translated into the paradigm of Levantine relations. Initially, he
would be constructed as a messianic figure, bounding Ottoman
expansion on the east while the Europeans were uncertain that
they themselves could bound it on the west.

Yet Lascari's sorting of prerogatives did not prevent further representations of Ismail's divinity. An anonymous Italian merchant writing in 1508 of Ismail (called the "Great Sufi") explained:

> The Sufi is loved and reverenced as a god especially by his soldiers many of whom enter into battle without armor expecting their master Ismail to watch over them in the fight. Others go into battle without armor, being willing to die for their monarch, crying "Sheikh, Sheikh." The name of God is forgotten throughout Persia and only that of Ismail remembered. Everyone, and particularly his soldiers, considers him immortal.[11]

Neither solely warrior king, nor merely benevolent and saintly, Ismail was shown inspiring fanatic devotion. His name replaced the name of god. This characterization went beyond the boundaries of sainthood.

> He is adored as a prophet and the rug on which he knelt for Easter was torn to pieces to be used by his followers as Christians use relics. The Turks referred to the Persians as Azamini (*acem*) before the reign of the Sufi, Ismail, but now they call the Persians kızılbaş. After Ismail's first victory, the members of his sect flocked to join him because in their books they found it foretold that a prophet of their religion would come and they must support and exalt him.
>
> It is said that Ismail was sent by God to announce that his sect [twelver Shi'ism] was the only true sect whose members would be admitted to paradise and from this it results that the army of Shah Ismail is unpaid just as when we Christians fought the Crusades. They [his army] fight neither for gold nor for the state but for their religion and they believe that if they die they will go straight to paradise and thus they fight most valiantly.[12]

The messianic representation of Ismail in this account is striking, particularly in view of the Christian distaste for false messiahs and the Muslim insistence that there would be no prophets after Muhammad. There is, however, a clue here to the nature of Ismail's role as "savior"—the fact that followers "flocked" to Ismail's standard only "after" his first victory. Victories were

necessary to sustain such a savior—whose message, for the
Christian audience at least, required not so much a divine
directive as a sword. There were indeed prophecies of Ismail's
coming, but Shi'ite legitimacy was not the concern of Christian
observers who were generally not cognizant of the exact
distinctions between Sunni and Shi'i within Islamic practice.[13]
Ismail fulfilled a different sort of prophetic mission in the
Christian accounts. He became, however briefly, the equivalent
of Prester John, the mythical warrior king whose intervention
was expected to shift the weight of victory to the Christian side
at the time of the crusades.[14] For this reason, the Italian
narratives granted him the accoutrements of Christian
sainthood—the relics and the sacramentals.[15]

The mythology of divine kingship, in sources produced in
Asian and European courts alike, drew on the image of
Alexander the Great as representing the unstoppable force—the
world hegemon who either claimed divinity or was granted it by
his troops. With a deified king, the size of armies alone could not
be counted upon to determine the outcome of battles. Thus,
according to one Venetian account, Yahya Pasha, the Ottoman
general sent against Ismail in 1507, felt himself inadequate to the
task, not for want of soldiers but for want of reputation. He
notified his master, Sultan Bayezid II, that he should come *in
person* to challenge the Safavid shah because, " the people follow
Ismail, as if he were a god."[16]

That same year Zuan Moresini, in Damascus, sent a
lengthy account to Venice which assembled the elements of
Ismail's mythology, including the image of Alexander, in a
striking and impressionistic fashion:

> [T]hese, in their way adore the Sufi, and he is called not
> king or prince but holy and prophet. He is a handsome,
> beardless youth, learned, just, and devoid of greed, and
> much more generous than Alexander. . . . [W]hen money
> comes in he quickly distributes it such that he seems a god
> on earth; and so, as people make offerings in the temples,
> so all in Persia offer to Ismail what they have and are
> grateful that, all holy, he deigns to accept it. . . . He is the
> holy of holies, full of divinatory power, for he takes counsel
> from no one, nor did he as a child, and because of this all
> believe that the Shi'i in his every act is divinely inspired.[17]

Then Moresini presented the vehicle for Ismail's divine inspiration, the shah's miraculous cat.

> [W]ith him always he has a cat, and woe to him who gives it any offense. [Ismail] has a tent, with 365 or 366 entrances, round like the world, and, in the morning, no portal is opened save the place through which the cat every day passes . . . It is said that [Ismail] has as his guide, a spirit, in that cat, who counsels him and works many miracles . . .

Moresini observed that he had heard this story of the cat from some Persians, too, but that it was not told "all in the same way" as this particular version.[18] Although he noted that he heard of "other miracles which one cannot entirely put faith in," he selected, among the representations of Ismail's cat, that which he found most worthy for the retelling to a Venetian audience. There, Ismail in his world-tent awaited each morning his communication with the divine which no mere human was permitted to transmit. With such signs as Moresini recounted, the representations of sacral kingship wove in and out of the Ismail stories, drawing witnesses from the shah's troops, visitors to his camp, and from the European hearers and observers. In this process, past signs and prophets were picked up or placed into the narratives to construct the monarch/sheikh/warrior as something more than Alexander—demon or deity. Moresini's account continued:

> and though they are inferior in military art to the Turks and mamluks, by their faith in this new prophet and by the victories attained, and by the belief that they have that those who die for the faith will go to heaven, they are indomitable and always victorious. . . .[along with Safavid prophecies] some of the friars of Jerusalem believe, as a result of his stupendous and miraculous acts, that [Ismail] is the Antichrist . . . I leave it to Your Magnificence to judge about these things, and will not rest, if I hear of any news , writing [to you] his every progress.

Moresini, protesting his own reluctance to determine which was the "true" Ismail, Antichrist or prophet, erred firmly on the side of allowing multiple possibilities. Yet he left no doubt that Venice would do well to take Ismail seriously. Noting that there were further claims too fabulous to relate, Moresini narrated one final claim that echoed both the ancient glory of Solomon and the awaited glories of the millennium and of Judgment Day: "[T]he Sufi has said that he wishes to entirely destroy Jerusalem, and build it once again." And Moresini warned his listeners not be believe those "crazy" people who reported to Venice that Ismail was weak and a savage:

> [S]ince Xerxes and Darius there has never been a king of Persia, neither so adored, nor so loved by his people, nor so bellicose, nor with such a great army, nor so graced with fortune. The heavens have, in our own time, made a miracle, that exceeds all miracles, that a youth of 12 years and not of royal blood, was so courageous, by force of arms and of followers, to defeat the scions of the Iranian royal house, expel them and seize Tabriz, and to subdue all of Iran in such a way that Alexander [himself] never had such success.

Such was the magnitude of Ismail in the tales spreading out from his camp into the trading centers of Syria and Anatolia, and on into the council chambers and courts of Europe. The assembling and ordering of elements in European representations of Ismail emerged from his location, on the frontier, and from his function as definer of boundaries. A power to rival or surpass Alexander required a target to absorb the force of his energies and a rationale to suggest who his friends and adversaries would be. The European narratives provided Ismail with both target and ideology. Although Ismail's military energies were also directed at his eastern frontiers against the Uzbeks, it was the Safavid western frontier against the Ottomans that concerned European reporters. "The Sophi religion has always fought against the Ottoman royal house because the Ottomans are heretics and usurpers of the territories of many Muslims."[19]

The primary role of Ismail, then, in the European narratives, was as the man to stop the Turk. As Andrea Moresini wrote from Aleppo in 1503, "Great is his fame, and if he launches an attack against the Turk, happy Christianity. . . ."[20]

Christian affinities accrued to or were inserted into the narratives to emphasize and certify Ismail's legitimacy as

Christian ally and as nominal, if not titular, defender of the faith. There is a naive acceptance in this Christianization of the Ismail myth, found, for example, in the following account:

> [He was not] a king nor the son of a king but only the son of a Xeque [Sheikh] of the lineage of Ali. He, being yet a child when his father died, went to live with an Armenian friar, who brought him up. Being then of the age of twelve years he fled away, lest he [the friar] should slay him as a Moor, . . . he began to take to himself other Moorish youths and gathered together many people. Little by little he began to take villages, and to make gifts of the goods and the wealth which he found therein to those who followed after him in such ventures, keeping nothing for himself.[21]

Here we find a fable of a fatherly Christian monk incorporated without benefit of artifice into Duarte Barbosa's account of Ismail. The explanation that the monk might suddenly discover when Ismail was twelve that he was a Muslim ("Moor" used indiscriminately for all Muslims) took no account of the custom by which young children, when "adopted," were readily converted to the faith of their stepparents, and assumed that all Ismail's antecedents, including history and kin, had conveniently, if mysteriously, disappeared. Of course the avenues to and away from the device of the monk require no logical explanation. His insertion into Ismail's life story serves a polemical purpose, to explain intellectual influences and the formation of the young Ismail's beliefs. In this context, the probability that Ismail was raised by a monk becomes irrelevant.[22] What was important was documenting the early development of sincere Christian sympathies that could be acted upon once Ismail mobilized an army. Like the early account in which Ismail was said to deny his father, this story dispenses with history and kin as immaterial when compared to the shah's current mission. It was Ismail's present—the here and now of his charismatic personality, whether deity or man, that captured the imaginations of the European tellers of his tale.

The story of childhood Christian influences was repeated by Tomé Pires, who claimed that Ismail's mother was an Armenian Christian, and that he was raised by Christians from

whom he learned "what was good." He also noted that one-tenth
of Ismail's original two thousand horsemen were Armenian
Christians. [23] Further, Tomé Pires suggested that the Shi'ites and
their first imam Ali, the prophet's son-in-law, were somehow not
really Muslims, contrasting them to the Sunnis, whom he called
"Moors."

> All these things he does by the advice of these Christians.
> They say that he never destroys any Christian dwelling or
> kills any Christian. [Every day many Muslims are
> converted to Ali's side] . . . which the Moors consider a
> bad sign. . . . Many Moors say he is a Christian. [24]

This suggestion was produced in the following Italian accounts,
fleshing out the Christianization of Ismail to enhance the process
of differentiating Ottoman from Safavid, in 1502:

> [A]mong [Ismail's] notable acts, to show his contempt for
> the Muslim faith he brought horses into the Turkish
> mosques [in Erzincan] and tied up dogs inside, then he
> destroyed the mosques down to their foundations. He
> ordered the restoration of a Christian church, half ruined
> previously by the Turks, and adorned it in all
> solemnity. . . . he ordered all the Muslim books burned,
> persuading the people that they must abandon the vain
> and false Muslim tenets and adore the living God . . .[5]

and in 1504: "He is the bitterest enemy of the Muslim
sect . . . and he shows the greatest affection to the Christians. . . ."[6] For this reason, noted another account, the Ottoman
sultan called together all the teachers and wise men and judges
of his faith to determine if he could "without sin" according to
the laws of god proceed with his army against Ismail and these
councillors reassured him

> that he should leave all other operations and all other
> enemies of god and of Muslims, and proceed against this
> reckless man who alone had usurped the dignity and
> office of the great god.[27]

These narratives made it clear that Ismail, if not actually a
Christian, was at least the mortal enemy of the Sunnis, and
mobilized all his military might against them:

> [Some merchants say that the Safavid shah] has sixty
> thousand horsemen, and they are all white people and
> warlike. . . . [Ismail] was going through the country
> putting everything to fire and flame; and especially he put
> to the sword all those who believed in [the sunni caliphs]
> Bubachar and Othman and Aumur [Abu Bakr, Uthman
> and Umar].[28]

The European representations of Ismail's motives can be
contrasted to Muslim sources which were aware that Shi'ite
ideology did not make Ismail any less Muslim. The event, the
cursing of the caliphs, was the same in both sets of sources, but
its interpretation and implications varied according to the
political objectives, religious sentiments, and audience of the
observer, as witnessed by the Persian chronicle of Ḥasan Rūmlū:

> [When Ismail took Tabriz he commanded] . . . that Abû
> Bakr, 'Umar, and 'Usmân, should be cursed in the bazars,
> on pain of death to him who refused. In those days men
> knew not . . . of the rules of the twelve Imams [but]. . . day
> by day, the sun of the Shîa' faith rose higher and lightened
> the dark places of the earth.[29]

It was this animosity toward the Sunnis that observers expected
to translate into an assault on the Ottoman Turkish empire, the
official religion of which was Sunni Islam.[30]

Representations of Ismail in the European sources range from
Christian, to Christian-like, to liker of Christians, to Christ-like.

> [A Venetian officer] reports that a holy man of the Turks
> came to him secretly saying that he had come representing
> the Sufi. He said that Ismail was the friend of the
> Christians and would come to destroy the army of the
> Turkish sultan with an innumerable army. He felt good
> will toward Venice because of his love of their patron
> saint, St. Mark, and [Ismail himself] had his own
> evangelists.[31]

This Venetian account not only equated the political interests of
Venice and the Safavids but also assumed the natural affinity of
Ismail and Venice by virtue of shared religious sentiments. The
affinities were at once produced and labeled as essential. But

here it is notable that Ismail was not himself the evangelist, like St. Mark, but the sender of evangelists, like Jesus—again a projection of divine status.[32]

In fact, it was Ismail's sending of men (to proselytize for shi'ism and to recruit troops for the Safavid army) into Ottoman territory that prompted the Ottoman sultan's mobilization against him. The Ottomans, like the Italians and Portuguese, were spurred to action by the speed and finality of Ismail's victories. None had an accurate idea of the size of Ismail's army, but his accomplishments, in terms of scope of conquest in a very short span of years, could not be denied.

The European narratives complemented the image of the saintly "Christian" Ismail with one of a terrible and vengeful warrior-king. Caterino Zeno, for example, lent considerable drama to the story of Ismail's conquest of Tabriz in 1501 by elaborating on Ismail's contemptuous treatment of his defeated enemies.

> and then, in order to avenge his father on those captains and chiefs who were said to have a hand . . . in his death, he caused their bodies to be disinterred and burnt in the market place. And, while they were carrying them there, he drew up a procession before them of two hundred harlots and four hundred thieves; and to show a greater indignity to those chiefs, he ordered the heads of the thieves and harlots to be cut off and burnt with the bodies. And not satisfied with this, he had his stepmother brought before him, who after the death of his father had married a certain great lord, . . . abused her to her face, insulted her in every possible way, and at last commanded that she should be decapitated as the vile and worthless woman she was, in revenge for the slight estimation she held his father in.[33]

Zeno's account shows that all portraits of Ismail were not drawn in a rosy light. Nonetheless, Zeno did not bemoan Ismail's violence, nor was he moved to sympathy by Ismail's punishment of his stepmother. Rather, Zeno pointed out that the shah's victories and slaughters greatly enhanced his reputation. Further, once Ismail had put his enemies to the sword he "caused all the booty to be collected and divided among his men without keeping a single thing for himself," thus attracting more recruits to his cause. The slaughter was also cost-effective, for it so terrified the surrounding chieftains that they submitted and declared their allegiance to Ismail. In the end, it was this invincible warrior persona, rather than that of the deified Ismail, that dominated in the European tales of divine kingship. Not until he was beaten by the Ottomans at Çaldıran in 1514, did Ismail's importance in the European sources diminish. Once projections that his army would redeem Christendom from the Turks proved false, narratives of Ismail shifted to his hunting expeditions and to his failure ever to lead his troops again into battle. Rumors of the massing of Safavid armies at the Ottoman frontiers lost their messianic language. Between 1502 and 1514, however, since no Christian power managed to mobilize any substantive resistance to Ottoman expansion, Ismail remained the hoped-for savior of record.

Narrative and Political Boundaries

Warrior saints, armies of the faithful, and sword-wielding divines inhabit the pages of late medieval Christian mythology with the ease and familiarity of long habit, but divine kingship belonged to Christ alone. Where then, in the religio-political rhetoric of the early sixteenth century could a Muslim *Sufi* sheikh with pretentions of immortality find his articulation? The explanation for Christian-authored accounts representing Ismail as quasi-divine resides in a combination of theological ignorance, the desire to legitimize "illegitimate" alliances, the available universe of symbols, and the incorporation of the warrior/ sheikh into the canon of images used to differentially articulate Muslim opponents and Muslim "friends."[34]

It is clear that the European writers of many early sixteenth-century Ismail stories were ignorant of the distinction between Sunni and Shi'i belief. Yet ignorance, as a single explanation for the European construction of Ismail, fails to account either for conscious motivation in the tellers, or for a complex set of symbolic conventions in the tales. Sixteenth-century European writers were prone to lump together all of the history of Islam (as had Dante) under the rubric of unabashed heresy, culminating in the Ottomans Turks being cast as the scourge of god. One such writer was Richard Knolles who, in his general history of the Turks, represented a sinful Christendom, groaning under the "divine" punishment implemented by the Ottomans and likely to succumb at any moment.[35] Such representations contain much of moral and political polemic and were contrived not merely to inform but to incite their audience, particularly European rulers, to certain types of action. This was also the case in the composition of accounts of Ismail Safavi. Among the objectives of the composers was the impetus to conquest and to defense—not to mention the impetus to share in the revenues of the Iranian silk trade. Reflected in these accounts there was not the will to see the Safavids become dominant in the eastern Levant. There was, rather, the wish to see them stay the military expansion of the Ottomans and to provide a sympathetic ally and trading partner in the territory between the Indian Ocean and the Mediterranean. For this purpose, the delineation of a uniform Islamic world was inadequate. The Islamic space, from the Mediterranean to India, had to be differentiated.

The tradition of Muslim-Christian alliance formation predates the sixteenth century, but that era continued to require the fiction of a certificate of legitimation when the energies of the "holy war" were turned against those who were, at least nominally, coreligionists.[36] Venice, in particular, found itself under attack from other European states (often competitors for commerce or territory) for its cordial relations with the Ottomans after the Aegean wars of 1499–1503. Thus, although several states (Venice, France, Portugal, Rhodes, Rome) initiated correspondence with Ismail to explore the possibilities of establishing more formal relations, an actual alliance required legitimation. As is evident from some of the previous accounts, one avenue of legitimation was simply to state that the Safavids were, in fact, Christian, or, at worst, a Christian-like sect. An alternative was to suggest that, if not Christian, Ismail was at least advised by Christians and thus acted in the best interests of Christendom. The particulars of his religious ideology could be deferred if his actions furthered the political objectives of interested European states. Ismail's myth, then, was constituted not merely in symbols but at once derived from and constructed its political context.

Ismail was establishing his hegemony in western Persia just as the Portuguese navigations to India threatened to compromise the commercial interests of states like Venice in the Levant.[37] Ismail's successes suggested to Venice that he might reach the Mediterranean.[38] For the Ottomans, it was unclear whether Ismail would be a real contender for control of Anatolia or simply a threat on their eastern frontiers. The softening of Ottoman policy toward Venice, leading to peace in 1503, was mediated by the rise of Ismail and his initial successes.[39] The combination of Safavid expansionism and the Portuguese naval threat to the Red Sea also prompted the Ottomans to send military aid to the Mamluks in Egypt. This aid did not signify a rapprochement between the two long-term enemies, but provided some insurance of Mamluk neutrality if Ismail launched a major offensive against the Ottomans. Thus, the emergence of Ismail on the Ottoman eastern and the Mamluk northern frontiers required a rearticulation of the struggle for hegemony in the eastern Levant, in terms of policy, arms, and rhetoric. The European states like Venice stood by, awaiting the outcome of this power struggle. Their participation was diplomatic and rhetorical rather than military. Yet this rhetorical function operated to delineate policy no less than did military action.

The boundaries between the intelligence/entertainment/rhetorical processes of the European narratives about Ismail were like the sixteenth-century boundaries between contending empires: flexible, porous, not drawn in lines but scattered in points which could be altered, renegotiated, and lost as easily as they were captured. Contenders for power in the Levant employed differential articulations of enemies and allies which, although employing a language of religious legitimation, were not reducible to polarizations of Muslim/Christian or orient/occident. Rather, identities like Ismail's were constructed in a process that was dependent neither upon the "validity" of narration nor upon the "authority" of narrator.

Diplomatic exchanges point up this differential articulation of enemy and ally and the religious affinities employed. Stories and reports, like those cited earlier, formed the basis for these diplomatic exchanges, particularly in the absence of more formal avenues for the conduct of foreign affairs. Thus the Grand Master on Rhodes wrote to the pope urging him to: "send an envoy to the Sufi, whose coming signals the ruin of the Turks and of the infidels."[40]

For his part, Ismail was willing to suspend the fictive necessity of holy war against the Christians in order to further his own expansionist objectives. The language employed in his solicitations of Christian state support is both revealing and illustrative of the easy recombination of religious and political symbolism. In 1505 the shah sent a letter to the doge in Venice.

> [From] Sultan Ismail Sufi, whose reign God makes eternal, to the sultan of the Venetians, our great friend, may God perpetuate his reign. Words cannot explain, nor pen write, nor intellect comprehend the love that we bear you. Great is our desire to see you in person. We hope in the mercy of God, and in him who controls all, that we soon will meet you and that we will be good friends. Be advised that I have conquered all of Iran with great success; and we hope in the all powerful God that we will persevere every day, achieving great victory . . . and in the strength of his arm we will triumph over our enemies.[41]

Here, the god of Ismail was the god of the Venetians and his victories, insofar as they circumscribed Ottoman power, were the victories of Venice. The nature of this affinity formation is illustrated by a later communication between the shah and the doge. Ismail followed up his conquest of Baghdad with efforts to acquire from Venice the founders and artillery needed to properly challenge the Ottomans. He sent an embassy to the doge, via the Venetian consul Zeno in Damascus.[42] The letter of Ismail to the doge commenced with lengthy declarations of friendship and brotherly love. Safavids and Venetians were compelled to fight the Turks, he wrote, "for the love of God." Ismail proposed that they launch a joint attack on the Ottomans. He concluded with a direct request: "Send an excellent bombardier, a master craftsman."[43] The language of brotherhood and the love of god thus inscribed a message that the desire for cannon could overcome the obstacles of religious difference.

Ismail's messenger suggested that Venice send artillery masters by way of Syria and that the Venetian navy engage the Ottoman sultan, Bayezid, off the coast of Greece while Ismail attacked him in Asia Minor.

Venice, however, was not interested in jeopardizing its trade agreements with the Ottomans and Mamluks. Nor did Venice wish indirectly to aid the Portuguese by providing artillery to Ismail that might be used in some joint Safavid-Portuguese action against the Signoria's trading partner, the Mamluk sultan, in Egypt. Venice offered words instead of guns, assuring the envoy of its great friendship for Ismail and animosity against the Turks.[44] These words of friendship, like those of Ismail, adhered to the conventions of Levantine diplomacy where the language of religious legitimation was a requisite emblem of the articulation of sovereignty.[45] Friendship did not mean trust and "for the love of god" did not need to take into account sectarian differences between sovereigns who both recognized the god of the Old Testament, regardless of how many prophets they counted.

The Ottoman sultan, Selim, also used the differential articulation of ally and enemy to mobilize internal support and to intimidate his opponents. Selim took the Hungarian ambassador, Bélay, with him on his campaigns against Ismail in 1514 and against the Mamluks between 1515 and 1517, representing this envoy as the Hungarian king

> ... so that Bélay would see his might and the vast number of his men and report it to his master and the lords of his country. And then, [Selim] started to make war on the King of Egypt ... during all that time he carried Bélay along, calling him, and having him called, the King of Hungary before all the peopl e living there. He had some six thousand men, Bosnians and Serbians, dressed in Hungarian fashion, with flags written in Hungarian, to show that the Hungarian King was on his side and had come to his help.[46]

Thus, Selim used his own brand of affinity formation in confronting the peoples of the Mamluk and Safavid sovereigns, as well as his own armies, with the vision of Hungarian support.

The power of one's allies, actual or imagined, here took precedence over the specific delineation of their theology. Where the audience, however, required a differentiation of ally and enemy on religious grounds, that, too, was forthcoming. So, in 1515, after having Ismail's ambassador to the Ottoman court beaten, Sultan Selim sent his own envoy to the shah, advising him that he could achieve peace if he would "be a Muslim."[47]

The nature of political confrontation was thus subordinated to legitimizing images of sovereign power and to the rhetoric of alliance formation. The representation of Ismail as "messiah" for external European consumption mirrored an image of divine kingship promoted internally by the Safavids.[48] European narratives reconstructed the rhetoric of prophetic warrior/sheikh and of *kızılbaş* religious fanaticism without taking into account the political dynamic of the Ottoman-Safavid frontier. Much of Ismail's support came from the eastern Anatolian frontier *begs* (provincial governors and military commanders) whose allegiance to central governments, either in Tabriz or in Istanbul, was often nominal at best. European observers capitalized on the apparent heterodox religious currents in the frontier area to describe Ismail's followers as an army of *Sufi* devotees. Such an army of the faithful could then be readily transposed into an analog of the Christian crusaders. This rhetorical transformation, in the sources, of hardened frontier Türkmen cavalry units into an army of religious fanatics was nothing short of remarkable. Whereas the motivation of these *kızılbaş* tribal *begs* could be explained adequately in terms of mercenary political interests (maintaining their independence from the Ottomans), instead it was characterized in the European accounts as the flowering of Shi'ite religious fanaticism, inspired by the charismatic leadership of Ismail, in opposition to the Sunni Islam of the Ottomans. The political ambitions of the *kızılbaş* and of Ismail himself were translated into religious terms, thereby serving the political interests of the authors of the European accounts.

To this end, Ismail Safavi and his *kızılbaş* supporters were portrayed as brothers of Christianity—enemies of Sunni Islam. The Ottomans were called heretics (usurpers of the territories of brother Muslims). The Ottomans employed the same terms, representing the Shi'ite Safavids as heretics. Each side justified its military aggressions by charging the opposition with heresy. Christian European writers, in turn, justified their attempts at alliance with Ismail by describing the Shi'ite as somehow not really Muslims, but rather more "Christian" than otherwise. The *kızılbaş* were warriors for the faith (*gazis*) just like the crusaders and their military prowess was the result of religious zeal.[49] They were also willing martyrs for the faith. The mystical aspects of heterodox Islam were emphasized, to show an affinity with Christian supernaturalism; and the messianic and millenarian content in representations of Ismail was emphasized to suggest affinities with contemporary Christian beliefs.

The Shah became a Christ-like figure: celebrating Easter, distributing his wealth, and inspiring his followers to martyrdom. His dress and the things he touched were "relics." Another point of affinity emphasized in Christian accounts was the devotion of heterodox Shi'ism for Fatima, Muhammad's daughter and the wife of the fourth caliph Ali, comparable to the Christian cult of the Virgin Mary.[50] Forging affinities between the mystical aspects of Islam and Christianity was not, however, the primary motivation for these representations of Ismail and the Shi'ites. The elaboration of Ismail's mythology in Europe served the practical purpose of justifying negotiations with a Muslim state. The European accounts brought to the fore the *Sufi* saint persona of Ismail, distancing him from the dangerous and compromising persona of Islamic sovereign which he shared with the Ottoman sultan.

Political opportunism, nonetheless, did not require the deification of Ismail that was suggested in some of the European sources. The images of divine kingship, rather, derive from the symbolic repertoire of the early sixteenth century, and from the inclination to make fantastic the still generally inaccessible territory of Iran. With Shah Ismail Safavi, the notion of divine kingship was appropriated by foreign observers and directed at an audience neither subject to that sovereign nor formally sympathetic to the taking on of divine attributes by mortals. The authors of these representations of Ismail were both transmitting information and creating an image of the exercise of sovereign power in Iran. Yet they remained detached from the immediate exercise of that power; and the effect of their message was dependent upon the removal of their target audience from actual events in Iran. Sympathy for the idea of the deified king is difficult to measure; and it could be argued that the Italian city-states in 1501 were concerned not with articulating divine kingship but with determining the possibilities of classical and republican forms of rule (or with a Machiavellian pragmatism). Yet the notions of "secular" Prince and of one mortal and divine god-king, Jesus Christ, existed in a literary and philosophical context of mythic images of divine sovereignty. In the process of transferring representations of Ismail, the message of divine kingship selected mythological elements from their Perso-Turkish context and added elements calculated to enhance the entertainment value, and the political and rhetorical objectives of the narratives. Some narrators could not seem to resist the impulse to magnify their subject. It was not sufficient that Ismail share his wealth, he had to give it all away. He was not just divinely inspired, but god on earth and his soldiers, to a man, impassioned by explosive piety. Ismail became Prester John, a prophet, Alexander, Jesus, and the heroes of the Persian epic *Shahnamah* (a lavish edition of which he commissioned from his court artists) all rolled into one mystical and mythic sovereign.

The construction of Ismail was not automatic—the early stories of Ismail show the recombinant options for narrative emerging from the frontier space between Ottoman sultan and Safavid shah. Political opportunism alone could not forge Ismail's myth whole. As illustrated by the narrations of Moresini and Lascari, the process of distinction was selective, without ruling out the possibility of alternatives. The contrasting messages of material "evidence" and of narrative representation did not require an absolute, unchanging deciphering of Ismail. Thus the inscription on coins minted in Ismail's name, brought to Venice and transcribed ("There is no other God than the one God, and Muhammad is the messenger of that God . . ."), did not obliterate the narration of Ismail as Christianized or divine.[51] The minting of coinage and the reading of the ruler's name in the Friday prayer service were primary signs of sovereignty in the Islamic kingdoms. Yet the inscribing of Islam in Ismail's coins was subordinated to his cursing of the Sunni caliphs in the *khutbah*, and this in turn, in the European accounts, became a starting point for producing affinities between the shah and Christianity. Christian Europe could claim Ismail without condoning him. It could will to suspend judgment if the end result of Ismail's religious devotion would be a defeat of the Ottoman armies which imperiled the possessions of European states. So, the message of divine kingship, shouted by armies of dervishes, breathed into the ear of a child by Armenian priests or slipped miraculously through tent portals by a spirit cat, wove its way through the narratives of nobles and merchants and spies, there to make mythic history and diplomacy alike.

NOTES

1. N.B.: Names in this article have given preference to Turkified versions (Ismail not Isma'îl) where plausible, using the transliteration based on modern Turkish usage. The Safavids were a Turkish-speaking dynasty and most of the *kızılbaş* were Turkish-speaking as well. On the general history of the Safavids and Ismail see: Jackson and Lockhart, eds., *The Cambridge History of Iran, Vol. 6: The Timurid and Safavid Periods*; Arjomand, *The Shadow of God and the Hidden Imam*; Ross, "The Early Years of Shah Ismâ'il," 249–340; Mazzaoui, *The Origins of the Safawids*; Savory, "The Consolidation of Safavid Power in Persia," 87–124; Haneda, *Le Chah et les Qizilbâs*.

2. Ismail's exact age is unclear. Rûmlû, (Ashanu't–Tawârîkh, 69:15) states that Ismail was thirteen in 905 A.H./1499–1500 C.E. H. R. Roemer, "The Safavid Period," in Jackson and Lockhart, *Cambridge History of Iran*, 6:196, gives Ismail's birth date as July 17, 1487, which would make him fourteen at the conquest of Tabriz.

3. *Sufis* were followers of the mystical path, so called for the coarse woolen cloth (*suf*) worn by some ascetics. *Sufi* was also used as a general term for followers of Ismail, Ismail himself, or for the *kızılbaş* in general without reference to membership in any mystical order. See also Jackson and Lockhart, 6:636 on variant uses of the term.

4. Sovereigns also regularly delayed envoys for months, refused to see them or treated them contemptuously or brutally. For example,

see Sanuto, *I Diarii*, 4:431–432, from Pera in September of 1502, a Venetian account of the maltreatment by Sultan Bayezid of Ismail's envoy to Istanbul; or in 1507, when Ismail served Selim's ambassador a meal of wine and pork and forced him to kill a man who had rebelled against the shah, 7:15. Note that a collection of references to Ismail in Sanuto's *Diarii* has been assembled and collated with an autograph manuscript copy from the Biblioteca Marciana in Amoretti, *Sâh Ismâ 'îl I nei Diarii di Marin Sanudo.*

5. Pires, *Suma Oriental*, 23, written 1512–1515. At this point the Portuguese were still consolidating their control in the Indian Ocean. They had failed in attempts to dominate the Red Sea and Persian Gulf, but had defeated a joint Mamluk and Gujarati naval force in the Indian Ocean in 1509. There are many similarities between the account of Tomé Pires and that of Duarte Barbosa (cited later). Western accounts in this article derive from the sources cited. Where sources are not translated into English (Sanuto, Sansovino), the translations are mine.

6. The use of the terms Europe, Italian, Portuguese, etc., in this article should in no way be construed as imposing an anachronistic notion of nation-state or of continental identity upon the sixteenth-century Levantine world, in which identities were predominantly local and boundaries between states were often unmarked, fluid, and changeable. Sources here are identified by language rather than by geographic origin. The sources compiled in Sanuto (reports, letters, *relazioni*) are sent from all over the Levantine area, by authors of varying ethnic origin and city-state allegiance. In Ottoman, Mamluk, and Safavid sources, Europeans, or nonsubjects of the Middle Eastern muslim empires from the "West" were routinely designated simply as "Frank," emphasizing that inclusion or exclusion from the category "us" (however that was construed), or indications of tax status, often took precedence over considerations of ethnicity, religion, language, or political allegiance. The Ottoman Empire at this time comprised parts of what is now Europe, so "European" accounts, in this work, are understood as those written in European languages that were attempting to delineate both Ottomans and Safavids by virtue of their affinities to or differentiation from "self."

7. Sanuto, 4:255, 258.

8. Ibid., 4:191–192.

9. Ibid., 268–270. This narrative, after describing the strange creatures (*animali*) as "as large as a vulture," characterized them as "*di pena beretina.*" The meaning of this is unclear to me but it may be suggesting that this unknown part-bird, part-beast, had a feathered

headpiece reminiscent of the peaked caps which distinguished Ismail's followers.

10. Ibid., 4:281, 351–357. Ismail was descended from the Ak Koyunlu monarch Uzun Hasan (d. 1453) on his mother's side. Another spy named Murad was also sent to gather information on Ismail; he returned in August 1503 (Ibid., 5:196–197).

11. "Travels of a Merchant in Persia," 206. See Arjomand, 105–110 on the *kızılbaş* allegiance to Ismail. Also, Babinger, "Mario Sanuto's Tagebücher," 28–50. Rûmlû (*Aḥsanut'-Tawârîkh*, 69:26) says that many of Ismail's original force of cavalrymen were "without armor" but he does not attribute this to religious fanaticism. Alternate explanations are lack of equipment and the limited armor employed by Türkmen cavalry.

12. Theodoro Spandugino, *La Vita di Sach Ismael et Tamas Re di Persia Chiamati Soffi*, in Sansovino, *Historia Universale dell'Origine et Imperio de Turchi*, 98–100, this source compiled after Ismail's death.

13. Ross, 328–331, 336, using the anonymous chronicle "Tarîkh-i Ismâ'îl," Ms. OR 3248, British Library (called "Ross Anonymous") notes the prophecy of Ismail's coming in the tale of Dede Muhammad, which recounts a dervish's vision that Ismail would be sent by the Twelfth Imam who personally girded Ismail and gave him his own sword.

14. Prester John's kingdom was first "located" in the East (Central Asia) but he came eventually to be equated with the king of Ethiopia— this legend surviving well into the sixteenth century. See, e.g., Barros, *Da Asia*, v. 2, pt. 8: 278–285, on the Portuguese general, d'Albuquerque's conquest of Kamran in the Red Sea, which noted that d'Albuquerque took time to try and "gather information about Prester John."

15. The story that the shah's troops believed they would go straight to paradise if killed in battle has a familiar ring. Nearly 500 years after Ismail's time this same characterization was employed by the Western media to characterize Iranian troops during the Iran-Iraq war. In both cases the characterization of armies of religious fanatics served the requirements of political rhetoric.

16. Sanuto, 7:171. When Bayezid's son Selim conquered Syria in 1516, his envoy Mehmed Bey, nephew of the general Sinan Pasha, claimed his master was "another Alexander" who had taken Ismail's capital Tabriz (in 1514) and would soon take the Mamluk sultan's territories (23:361).

17. Ibid., 7: 526–535. Moresini, a merchant, claimed the accounts of Christian "slaves"/captives, who had been in Ismail's camp, as partial authority for his narrative. These men, who had escaped from the

Ottoman camp, said they were well treated by Ismail when he found out they were Christians. He invited them to join his army and, when they declined, gave them a ducat and allowed them to go on their way. See also Berchet, *La Repubblica di Venezia e la Persia*, 153–157.

18. In this story the cat is the intermediary with the divine since it is assumed that a king requires counsel from someone or somewhere—a function which in other stories is served by the priests.

19. Berchet, 23–24. This report is dated 1502 from a Venetian residing in Cyprus.

20. Sanuto, 5:25.

21. Barbosa, *The Book of Duarte Barbosa*, 83–87.

22. Roemer, "The Safavid Period," in Jackson and Lockhart, *Cambridge History of Iran* 6:197–198. Ismail, rather, was under the protection of the ruler of Gilan, Kârkiyâ Mîrzâ 'Alî, for about five years before he launched his career and after escaping from Ak Koyunlu's supervision. This mentor saw to Ismail's religious training by a Shi'i teacher.

23. There is no evidence for this claim. See, e.g., Haneda, 67–100, on the composition of Ismail's early supporters, complete with analysis of names and titles (relying on the "Ross Anonymous" mss.). Another account, from 1507, claimed that Ismail numbered 15,000 Christian men among his troops; see Sanuto, 7: 268.

24. Tomé Pires, 26–29. This account attempts to place Ismail living with Christian relatives from the time he was ten years old until he was twenty one: ". . . so that he grew up in goodness and discretion." This author also notes that the *kızılbaş* were allowed by Ismail to drink wine, like Christians, but that the Muslims were forbidden it.

25. Sanuto, 4:485–489, from a letter from Cyprus. This letter also recounted the story of Ismail's Armenian priest advisors, adding that they also taught him the Armenian language.

26. Ibid., 6:68–69.

27. Ibid., 4:498–500.

28. Ludovico d'Varthema, *Itinerary*, 43–44.

29. Rûmlû, 26–27.

30. On the Ottoman-Safavid conflict see Brummett, "Transformations in Political and Commercial Hegemony"; Bacqué-Grammont, "Ottomans et Safavides au Temps de şah Isma'îl"; Allouche, *The Origins and Development of the Ottoman-Safavid Conflict*.

31. Sanuto, 7:659. Written regarding the *provveditore* (administrator for Venice) of Napoli di Romania, September 27, 1508. An earlier Italian account, 4:308–310, from 1502 equated Ali and St. Mark, the patron of Venice.

32. The stories of Ismail's childhood are often aligned with and reminiscent of the stories of the Christ-child. Wise, studious and attentive to the learning of the wise men, Ismail, like Jesus, went public as a youth—Ismail declaring his message and Jesus remaining in the temple to amaze the doctors of theology and law.

33. Zeno, *Travels in Tana and Persia Book II*, 52. Rûmlû, 26 is more reserved in his account of the taking of Tabriz, noting a great slaughter in the battle and Ismail's command that the names of the twelve *imams* be read in the *khutbah*.

34. The Ottoman origin myth of their founder Osman's marriage alliance with the daughter of a sheikh, linking military and mystical-religious legitimacy, is one example of this symbolic repertoire—the *gazi* (warrior for the faith)/*Sufi* synthesis.

35. Knolles (1550–1610), *The General Historie of the Turkes*.

36. See, e.g., on the Ottoman legitimation for attacking the Muslim Mamluks, Abou-El-Haj, "Aspects of the Legitimation of Ottoman Rule," 371–383.

37. For Ismail's extension of his power bases in western Persia see Sümer, *Safevi Devletinin Kuruluşu*, 15–40.

38. On the machinations of Venice with Ismail's predecessor Uzun Hasan as ruler in western Iran, see Woods, *The Aqquyunlu*, 127–128; Minorsky, "La Perse au XVe Siècle entre la Turquie et Venise," 12–13, 15–16.

39. D'Lezze, *Historia Turchesca*, 268. D'Lezze says that nothing of moment occurred between the Ottomans and Venetians in the years after the peace of 1503 because of the threat from the Safavids.

40. Sanuto, 7:490–491, in 1508.

41. Ibid., 6:269, 301–303. This letter to the doge, Leonardo Loredano, was written in Persian, transcribed into Latin, then into Italian in Sanuto's compilation. So, it can be considered three times removed from Ismail, whose own language was Turkish, by its construction at his court and by the two translations into European versions.

42. Ibid., 8:232, 432.

43. Luchetta, "L'Affare Zen in Levante nel Primo Cinquecento," 183–184; Tansel, *Sultan II Bayezit'in Siyasi Hayatı* 245–246.

44. Berchet, 25; Bacqué-Grammont, 165–167; Sanuto 9:166.

45. For the articulation of Ismail et al. in the diplomatic correspondence, see Kerslake, "The Correspondence between Selim I and Kânsûh al-Gawrî"; Bacqué-Grammont, 167–174; Berchet, 158; Setton, 3: 138; Tekindağ, "Yeni Kaynak," 49–76; Schimkoreit, *Regesten Publizierter Safawidischer Herrscherurkunden*, 110–125.

46. From the account of Ferenc Zay translated and cited in Tardy, *Beyond the Ottoman Empire*, 116–117.

47. Sanuto 20:40.

48. In the early Safavid sources there are various reasons for divine attribution, and considerable interweaving of characterizations of the deity, the *imam* and the king. The problems created by this cross-representation and referencing to the divine resurfaced in modern Iran when the Ayatollah Khomeini was charged with claiming to be the *imam* rather than an intermediary (*mujtahid*). Arjomand, 85–102, has discussed the conventions of "sacral kingship" as do Jackson & Lockhart, 6:629, 633–639, discussing the heterodox milieu of the *kızılbaş* and of *Sufi* practice at the time of Ismail. Modern scholarship has attributed Ismail's "heretical" claims to youthful enthusiasm for Islam and for pre-Islamic Iranian heroic epic, or, more generally, linked them to a climate of heterodoxy among the *kızılbaş*. Assessments such as this reflect the multiplicity and composite nature of religious practice in eastern Anatolia and western Iran, while simultaneously privileging religious over political and economic motivations—for Ismail as well as for his followers. To admit the availability of a repertoire of symbols of divine kingship, however, is not the same as assuming acceptance of Ismail's divinity. There is a promotional factor to be taken into account, which effected the construction of both Safavid and European narratives. This promotional factor is not "provable" from the fragmentary evidence of Ismail's millenarian poetry or from the fragmentary accounts of the few Safavid chronicles. Still, it is firmly suggested. Vladimir Minorsky, "The Poetry of Shah Isma'il I," 1006a–1053a.

49. On images of *gazis* in the Ottoman context see Fodor, "Ahmedî's Dâsitân as a Source of Early Ottoman History," 41–54. Fodor points out (51) from this early fifteenth-century work:

> Strangely enough, this, in turn, seems to confirm the idea of a sacred commitment to the holy war . . . [which] crystallized within the Ottoman dynasty since Murâd I during the fights against their

coreligionists [rather] than against the Christians, and came to constitute the ideological legitimation of the dynasty's claim to power.

50. Berchet, 265. The link between Mary and Fatima was carried into modern orientalist scholarship as well. Gibb's obituary on fellow orientalist Massignon says he pursued "themes that in some way linked the spiritual life of Muslims and Catholics and enabled him to find a congenial element in the veneration of Fatima, and consequently a special field of interest in the study of Shi'ite thought in many of its manifestations . . . (quoted by Said, *Orientalism*, 264–65).

51. Sanuto, 7:269–270. Of course the coinage itself was a representation of Ismail and of his claims to universal Islamic sovereignty.

Bibliography

Medieval Texts

Abû Dâwûd Sulaymân al-Sijistânî. *Sunan Abî Dâwûd*. Muḥammad 'Alî al-Sayyid, ed. Ḥims, 1969–1974.

Abū Qurrah, Theodore. *De cultu imaginum*. I. Arendzen, ed. and trans. Bonn, 1898.

———. *Maymar fī wujūd al-Khâliq wa al-Dîn al-Qawîm*. I. Dick, ed. Jounieh/Rome, 1982.

Abū Yūsuf Ya'qūb b. Ibrâhîm al-Ansârî. *Kitâb al-Kharâj*, 3rd ed. Cairo, 1382 A.H.

Adelphus. *Vita Machometi*. B, Bischoff, ed., in "Ein Leben Mohammeds (Adelphus?) (Zwölftes Jahrhundert)." *Anecdota Novissima: Texte des vierten bis sechzenten Jahrhundert* (Stuttgart, 1984): 106–122.

Alcuin. *Epistolae*. In Ernst Duemmler, ed. *Epistolae Karolini Aevi*. 2 vols. Berlin, 1895.

Alexander Minorita. *Alexander Minorita expositio in Apocalypsim*. Alois Wachtel, ed. MGH, Quellen zur Geistesgeschichte des Mittelalters 1. Weimar, 1955; reprint Munich, 1983.

Alexandre du Pont. *Roman de Mahomet*. Y. G. Lepage, ed. Paris, 1977.

Alfonso X el Sabio. *Primera Crónica General de España que mandó componer Alfonso el Sabio y se continuaba bajo Sancho IV en 1289*. Ramón Menéndez Pidal, ed. 2 vols. Madrid, 1955.

Ammianus Marcellinus, *Res gestae*. John C. Rolfe, ed. and trans. 3 vols. Cambridge, MA, 1935–1939.

Andrea da Barberino. *L'Aspramonte: romanzo cavalleresco inedito.* Marco Boni, ed. Collezione di opere inedite o rare, nuova serie. Bologna, 1951.

———. *Guerrino il Meschino.* Florence, Biblioteca Riccardiana MS 2226.

———. *I Reali di Francia.* Giuseppe Vandelli and Giovanni Gambarin, eds. Scrittori d'Italia, no. 193. Bari, 1947.

———. *Storia di Ajolfo del Barbicone.* Leone del Prete, ed. 2 vols. Bologna, 1863.

———. *Storia di Ugone d'Avernia.* Francesco Zambrini and Alberto Bacchi della Lega, eds. Scelta di curiosità letterarie inedite o rare dal secolo XIII al XIX, dispense 188–189. 2 vols. Bologna, 1882; reprint, Bologna, 1968.

———. *Le storie Nerbonesi: romanzo cavalleresco del secolo XIV.* I. G. Isola, ed. 2 vols. Bologna, 1877.

"L'apocalypse d'Esdras touchant le royaume des Arabes." I.-B. Chabot, ed. and trans. *Revue sémitique* 2 (1894), 242–250, 333–347.

"L'apocalypse de Samuel, supérieur de Deir-el-Qalamoun." J. Ziadeh, ed. and trans. *Revue de l'Orient chrétien* 20 (1915–1917): 374–404.

Aquinas, St. Thomas. *Summa Contra Gentiles.* Anton C. Pegis, trans. London, 1975.

Arredondo y Alvarado, Gonzalo de. *Castillo inexpugnable de la fe.* Burgos, 1528.

al-Ash'arî. *Risâlah ilâ ahl al-thaghr.* Qiwameddin, ed. *Ilahiyat Fakuultesi Mecmuasi* 8 (1928): 80–108.

al-Balâdhurî, Amad b. Yayâ. *Kitâb Futūḥ al-Buldân,* ed. M. J. de Goeje. Leiden, 1866.

Barbosa, Duarte. *The Book of Duarte Barbosa.* Hakluyt Series II, no. 44. London, 1918.

Barhebraeus, *Chronicon Ecclesiasticum.* J.-B. Abbeloos and T. Lamy, eds. *Gregorii Barhebraei Chronicon Ecclesiasticum* Paris, 1874.

———. *The Chronography of Gregory Abu'l Faraj.* 2 vols. E. A. Wallis Budge, ed. and trans. London, 1932.

Barros, João de. *Da Asia.* 24 vols. Lisbon, 1973.

Bernardus Parmensis. *Glossa ordinaria* in *Decretales D. Gregorii papae IX. suae integritati una cum glossis restitutae.* In vol. 2 of the *Corpis iuris canonici.* Venice, 1584.

al-Bîrūnî, Abū Rîḥân Muḥammad. *Les fêtes des Melchites.* R. Griveau, ed. and trans. PO 10.4 (1915).

Bonaventure. *Commentaria in quartum librum Sententiarum. Opera omnia*, vol 4. Quaracchi, 1889.

al-Bukhârî, Muḥammad Ibn Ismâ'îl. *al-Jâmi' al-Ṣaḥiḥ*. M. L. Krehl and T. W. Juynboll, eds. 4 vols. Leiden, 1862–1908.

Caesarius of Heisterbach. *Dialogus Miraculorum*. J. Strange, ed. Cologne-Bonn-Brussels, 1851.

———. *Dialogus Miraculorum*. E. von E. Scott and C. C. Swinton Bland, eds. and trans. *The Dialogue on Miracles*. London, 1929.

Cervantes Saavedra, Miguel de. *Los baños de Argel*. Jean Canvaggio, ed. Madrid, 1983.

La Chanson d'Aspremont, chanson de geste du XIIᵉ siècle. Louis Brandin, ed. 2 vols. Paris, 1923–1924.

Chanson de Roland. Joseph Bédier, ed. Paris, 1980.

Chronicle of Fredegar. The Fourth Book of the Chronicle of Fredegar and its Continuators. J. M. Wallace-Hadrill, trans. London, 1960.

Chronicon ad A.D. 846 pertinens. E. W. Brooks, ed., and I.-B. Chabot, trans. CSCO 3/4 (1904).

Chronicon ad A.C. 1234 pertinens. I.-B. Chabot, ed. and trans. CSCO 81 (1920), 82 (1916), 109 (1937), 354 (1974).

Chronique d'Ernoul et de Bernard le Tresorier. M. L. De Mas Latrie, ed. Paris, 1871.

Cyril of Scythopolis. *Life of Euthemius*. Eduard Schwartz, ed., *Kyrillos von Skythopolis*, Texte und Untersuchungen 49.2 (Leipzig, 1939), 5–85.

Dante Alighieri. *La Divina Commedia*. C.H. Grandgent, ed. Cambridge, 1972.

Da Barberino, Andrea. *Reali di Francia*. In *Romanzi dei reali di Francia*. Adelaide Mattani, ed. I classici Rizzoli, ed. Maurizio Vitale. Milan: Rizzoli Editore, 1957.

Decretales Gregorii IX. E. Friedberg, ed. Leipzig, 1881.

Decretum Magistri Gratiani. E. Friedberg, ed. Leipzig, 1879.

Disputation of Sergius the Stylite Against a Jew, A. P. Hayman, ed. and trans., CSCO 338/339 (1973).

D'Lezze, Donado. *Historia Turchesca*. I. Ursi, ed. Bucharest, 1910.

Doctrina Iacobi nuper baptizati. N. Bonwetsch, ed. Abhandlungen der königlichen Gesellschaft der Wissenschaften zu Göttingen N.F. 12.3 (Berlin, 1910).

———. [Ethiopic version.] Sylvain Grébaut, ed. and trans. *Sargis d'Aberga (controverse judéo-chrétienne)*. PO 4.4 (1909), 13.1 (1919).

———. [Greek version.] F. Nau, ed. & trans., *La didascalie de Jacob: Texte Grec: Original du Sargis d'Aberga: Première assemblée*. PO 8.5 (1911).

Dositheos Notaras, Παραλειπόμενα ἐκ της 'Ιστορίας περὶ τῶν ἐν `Ιεροσολὖμοις πατριαρχθευσαντῶν. A. Papadopoulos Kerameus, ed., in 'Αναλέκτα `Ιεροσολυμιτκης Σταχυολογιᾶς, vol. 1 (Brussels: 1963 reprint of 1891 edition), 247–249.

d'Varthema, Ludovico. *The Itinerary of Ludovico d'Varthema of Bologna from 1502–1508*. John Winter Jones, trans. London, 1863.

Embrico of Mainz. *Vita Mahumeti*. Guy Cambier, ed. *Latomus: Revue d'études latines* 52 (1962).

Eutychius. *Das Annalenwerk des Eutychios von Alexandrien*. M. Breydy, ed. and trans. CSCO 471/472 (1985).

Fazio degli Uberti. *Il Dittamondo e Le Rime*. Giuseppe Corsi, ed. Scrittori d'Italia, no. 206, 2 vols. Bari, 1952.

Frederick II. *The Liber augustalis or Constitutions of Melfi Promulgated by the Emperor Frederick II for the Kingdom of Sicily in 1231*. James M. Powell, trans. Syracuse, NY, 1971.

Gauthier de Compiègne. *Otia de Machomete*. R.B.C. Huygens, ed., in Alexandre du Pont. *Roman de Mahomet*. Y. G. Lepage, ed. Paris, 1977.

Glossarium Latino-Arabicum. C. Seybold, ed. *Semitische Studien 15–17* (1900).

Gospel of the XII Apostles together with the Apocalypses of each one of them. J. R. Harris, ed. and trans. Cambridge, 1900.

The Greek Alexander Romance. Richard Stoneman, trans. London, 1991.

Grigor of Akanc', R. P. Blake and R. N. Frye, "History of the Nation of Archers (the Mongols) by Grigor of Akanc' hitherto ascribed to Magak'ia the Monk. The Armenian Text edited with an English translation and notes." *Harvard Journal of Asiatic Studies* 12 (1949), 269–443.

Hurtado de Mendoza, Diego. *Guerra en Granada*. Madrid, 1970.

Ibn Ḥanbal, Aḥmad. *Musnad al-Imâm Aḥmad Ibn Ḥanbal*. 6 vols. Beruit, 1895.

Ibn Ḥazm, 'Alî ibn Aḥmad. *al-Fiṣal fî al-milal wa-al-ahwâ' wa-al-niḥal*. 6 vols. Cairo, 1964.

Ibn Khaldûn. *The Muqaddimah: An Introduction to History*. Franz Rosenthal, trans. 3 vols. Princeton, 1958.

Iliyyâ al-Nasîbî. K. Samir Majlis, ed. "Entretien d' Élie de Nisibe avec le Vizier Ibn 'Alî al-Maghribî (Introduction, édition critique du texte arabe et traduction annotée)." *Islamochristiana* 5 (1980): 31-117.

Isidore of Seville. *Etymologiarum sive Originum Libri XX*. W. M. Lindsay, ed. Oxford, 1911.

———. *Etymologiae IX / Étymologies Livre IX: Les langues et les groupes sociaux*. Marc Reydellet, ed. and trans. Paris, 1984.

Îšô'yaw III. *Liber epistularum*. R. Duval, ed. and trans. CSCO 11/12 (1904–1905).

Joachim of Fiore. *Expositio in apocalypsim*. Venice, 1527; reprint Frankfurt, 1964.

Johannes Teutonicus. *Glossa ordinaria* in *Decretum Gratiani emendatum et notationibus illustratum una cum glossis*. Vol. 1 of the *Corpis iuris canonici*. Venice, 1584.

John of Biclaro. *Chronicle*. Julio Campos, ed. *Juan de Biclaro, obispo de Gerona, su vida y obra*. Madrid, 1960.

John of Nikiu. *The Chronicle of John, Bishop of Nikiu*. R. H. Charles, trans. Oxford, 1916.

John-Jerome of Prague. *Opera*. Johannes-Benedictus Mittarelli and Anselm Costadoni, eds., in *Annales Camaldulenses Ordinis Sancti Benedicti*, 9 (Venice, 1773).

Josephus. *Flavii Iosephi opera omnia*. S. A. Naver, ed. 6 vols. Leipzig, 1888–1896.

Joshua the Stylite. *The Chronicle of Joshua the Stylite*. William Wright, ed. and trans. Amsterdam, 1968.

Juan Ruiz, Archpriest of Hita. *Libro de Buen Amor*. Rigo Mignani and Mario A. Di Cesare, trans. *The Book of Good Love*. Albany, 1970.

Julian the Apostate. *Orations*. W.C. Wright, ed. and trans. 3 vols. Cambridge, MA, 1913–1923.

al-Khazrajî, Aḥmad ibn 'Abd al-Ṣamad. *Maqâmi'al-ṣulbân*. 'Abd al-Majîd al-Sharfî, ed. Tunis, 1976.

al-Kindî, Risâlat *'Abd Allâh Ibn Ismâ'îl al-Hâshimî ilâ 'Abd al-Masîḥ Ibn Isḥâq al-Kindî wa-Risâlat al-Kindî ilâ al-Hâshimî [The Apology of El-Kindi: A work of the Ninth Century, Written in Defence of Christianity by an Arab]*. A. Tien, ed. London, 1885.

Kirakos Ganjekec'i Patmut'iwn Hayoc" K. A. Melik-Ohanjanyan, ed. Erevan, 1961.

Knolles, Richard. *The General historie of the Turkes, from the first beginning of that nation to the rising of the Othoman familie; with all the notable expeditions of the Christian princes against them.* 2nd ed. London, 1610.

Leontius of Mar Sabas. *Vita S. Stephani Sabaitae Thaumaturgi Monachi,* AASS Julii III (1867), 524–613.

Life of Maximus the Confessor. S. Brock, ed. and trans. "An Early Syriac Life of Maximus the Confessor." *Analecta Bollandiana* 91 (1973): 299–346.

Maerlant, Jacob van. *Rijmbijbel.* Maurits Gysseling, ed. *Corpus van Middelnederlandse teksten,* Reeks II: Literaire handschriften, deel 3, *Rijmbijbel*/tekst. Leiden, 1983.

———. *Spiegel Historiael.* Matthijs de Vries and Eelco Verwijs, eds. *Jacob van Maerlant's Spiegel Historiael, met de fragmenten der later toegevoegde gedeelten, bewerkt door Philip Utenbroeke en Lodewijc van Velthem, uitgegeven door.* 4 vols. Leiden, 1863–1879.

Maimonides. *Dalâlat al-ḥâ'irîn.* S. Munk, ed. *Le guide des égarés.* 3 vols. Osnabruuck, 1856–1866, reprint 1964.

Mandeville's Travels. [Cotton version.] Michael C. Seymour, ed. Oxford, 1967.

———. [Variant, defective Medieval English version.] *The Travels of Sir John Mandeville: A Facsimile of Pynson's Edition of 1496.* Michael Seymour, ed. Exeter Medieval Texts and Studies. Exeter, 1980.

———. P. Hamelius, ed. *Mandeville's Travels.* Early English Text Society o.s. 153–154. London, 1919, 1923.

———. George Warner, ed. *The Boke of John Maundevill.* London, 1889.

———. *The Bodley Version of Mandeville's Travels.* Michael Seymour, ed. Early English Text Society o.s. 253 (Oxford, 1963), 79.

———. [Medieval Italian version.] Francesco Zambrini, ed. *I viaggi di Gio. da Mandavilla: volgarizzamento antico toscano,* Scelta di curiosità letterarie inedite o rare dal secolo XIII al XIX. Vol. 26, disp. 113–114. Bologna, 1870; reprint, Bologna, 1968.

Mar Yaballah. P. Bedjan, ed. *Histoire de Mar Jab-Alaha, Patriarche, et de Raban Sauma.* 2nd. ed. Leipzig, 1895.

Michael the Syrian. *Chronique de Michel le Syrien, patriarche Jacobite d'Antioche.* I.-B. Chabot, ed. and trans. 4 vols. Paris, 1899–1910.

Nicetas Choniates. *Historia.* Jan-Louis van Dieten, ed. *Nicetae Choniatae Historia,* Berlin, 1975.

———. Harry J. Magoulis, trans. *O City of Byzantium, Annals of Nicetas Choniates.* Detroit, 1984.

Nicholas of Lyra. *Biblia sacra cum glossa ordinaria . . . et Postillae Nicolai Lirani necnon Additionibus Pauli Burgensis et Matthiae Thoringi Replicis.* Johannes Meursius, ed. 6 vols. in fol. Antwerp, 1634.

————. *Postilla super totam bibliam.* Strasbourg, 1492 Reprint Frankfurt/Main, 1971.

Olivi, Petrus Ioannis. *Lectura super apocalypsim.* Warren Lewis, ed. "*Peter John Olivi: Prophet of the Year 2000.*" dissertation, Tübingen, 1972.

Paris, Matthew. *Cronica maiora.* MGH SS 28.

Passion of 'Abd al-Masî. Sidney H. Griffith, ed. and trans. "The Arabic Account of 'Abd al-Masî an-Nağrânî al-Ghassânî." *Le Muséon* 98 (1985): 331–374.

Passion of Abo of Tbilisi. K. Schultze, trans. "Das Martyrium des heiligen Abo von Tiflis." *Texte und Untersuchungen* N.F. 13.4 (Berlin, 1905).

Passion of Anthony Ruwah. Ignace Dick, ed. and trans. "La passion arabe de S. Antoine Ruwah néo-martyr de Damas (+ 25 déc. 799)." *Le Muséon* 74 (1961): 109–133.

Paul of Burgos (Pablo de Santa María). *Dialogus Pauli et Sauli Contra Judaeos, sive Scrutinium Scripturarum.* Mantua 1475; Mayence, 1478; Paris, 1507, 1535; and Burgos, 1591.

Pérez de Hita, Ginés. *Guerras civiles de Granada.* P. Blanchard-Demouge, ed. 2 vols. Madrid, 1913–1915.

————. *Guerras civiles de Granada.* Shasta M. Bryant, ed. Newark, Del., 1982.

Petrus Alfonsi. *Dialogi contra Iudaeos.* Klaus-Peter Mieth, ed. "Der Dialog des Petrus Alfonsi: Seine Überlieferung im Druck und in den Handschriften. Textedition." dissertation, Berlin, 1982.

————. *Disciplina clericalis.* J. Jones and J. Keller, trans. The Scholar's Guide. Toronto, 1969.

Philippe de Mézières. *Le Songe du Vieil Pelerin.* G. W. Coopland, ed. 2 vols. Cambridge, 1969.

Pierre Auriol (Petrus Aurioli). *Compendium sensus literalis totius divinae scripturae.* Quaracchi, 1896.

Pineda, Juan de O.F.M. *Diálogos familiares de la agricultura cristiana.* Juan Messeguer Fernández, O. F. M., ed. Vol. 1. Madrid, 1963.

Pires, Tomé. *Suma Oriental.* Hakluyt Series II, no. 89. London, 1944.

Porphyry, *Vie de Pythagore: Lettre à Marcella.* Édouard des Places, ed. and trans. Paris, 1982.

Pseudo-Methodius. *Die Apokalypse des Pseudo-Methodios.* A. Lolos, ed. Meisenheim am Glan, 1975.

———. P. Alexander, trans. *The Byzantine Apocalyptic Tradition.* Berkeley, 1985.

al-Qurubî, Imâm. *al-I'lâm bi-mâ fî dîn al-naṣârâ min al-fasâd wa-awhâm wa-iẓhâr maḥâsin dîn al-islâm wa-ithbât nubuwwat nabînâ Muḥammad 'alayhi al-ṣalâh wa-al-salâm, muqadimmah.* Aḥmad Ḥijâzî al-Saqqâ, ed. Cairo, 1980.

Rambaldis da Imola, Benvenuto. *Comentum super D. Alighierii Comoediam.* William W. Vernon and J. P. Lacaita, eds. Florence, 1887.

Rûmlû, Ḥasan. Aḥsanu't-*Tawârîkh.* C. N. Seddon, ed. *Gaekwad's Oriental Series,* vols. 57 (Persian text) and 69 (English translation). Baroda, 1934.

Sandoval, Prudencio de. *Historias de Idacio Obispo, de Isidoro, Obispo de Badajoz, de Sebastiano, Obispo de Salamanca, de Sampiro, Obispo de Astorga, de Pelagio, Obispo de Oviedo.* Pamplona, 1615.

Sansovino. *Historia Universale dell'Origine et Imperio de Turchi.* Venice, 1582.

Sanuto, Marino. *I Diarii.* 36 vols. Venice, 1880–1887.

Sebēos. *History,* R. Bedrosian, trans. New York, 1985.

Severus. *History of the Patriarchs of the Coptic Church of Alexandria.* B. Evetts, ed. and trans. PO 1.4 (1948).

Sophronius, Patriarch of Jerusalem. "Logos eis to Hagion Baptisma." A. Papadopoulos-Kerameus, ed. *Analekta Hierosolumitikēs Stachuologias,* vol. 5 (St. Petersburg, 1898), 151–168.

———. "Weihnachtspredigt des Sophronios." H. Usener, ed. *Rheinisches Museum für Philologie* N.F. 41 (1886): 500–516.

Synopsis Chronike. Constantine N. Sathas ed., in *Mesaionike Bibliotheke,* vol. 7. Paris, 1894, 303–307.

al-Tabarî, Muḥammad b. Jarîr. *Ta'rîkh al-Rusul wa al-Mulūk.* M.J. de Goeje et al., eds. 15 vols. in 3 series. Leiden, 1879–1901.

Theoderich. *Guide to the Holy Land.* Aubrey Stewart, trans.; introduction and notes by Ronald G. Musto. New York, 1986.

Theophanes. *Chronographia.* De Boor, ed. Leipzig, 1883.

"Travels of a Merchant in Persia." *Travels in Tana and Persia,* Hakluyt Series I, no. 49. London, 1883.

Villegas, Antonio de. *Historia del Abencerraje y la hermosa Jarifa*. Madrid, 1846.

Vincent de Beauvais. *Speculum historiale*. Baltazar Beller, ed. Douai, 1624; reprint Graz, 1965.

William of Tripoli. *Tractatus de statu Saracenorum*. Hans Prutz, ed. *Kulturgeschichte der Kreuzzuge*. Hildesheim, 1883, 573–598.

Zeno, Caterino. *Travels in Tana and Persia Book II*. Hakluyt Series I, no. 49. London, 1883.

Secondary Works

Abel, A. "L'Apologie d'Al-Kindi et sa place dans la polémique Islamo-Chrétienne." *L'Oriente cristiana nella storia della civiltà* (Rome, 1964): 501–523.

————. *Les caractères historiques et dogmatiques de la polémique islamo-chrétienne du VIIe au XIIe siècle*. Paris, 1950.

————. "La polémique damascénienne et son influence sur les origines de la théologie musulmane," *L'Élaboration de l'Islam*. Paris, 1961, 61–85.

————. "La portée apologétique de la 'vie' de St. Théodore d'Edesse." *Byzantinoslavica* 10 (1949): 229–240.

Abou-El-Haj, Rifa'at Ali. "Aspects of the Legitimation of Ottoman Rule as Reflected in the Preambles of Two Early Liva Kanunnameler." *Turcica* 21–23 (1991): 371–383.

Abulafia, David. "The End of Muslim Sicily." In *Muslims under Latin Rule, 1100–1300*. James M. Powell, ed. (Princeton, 1990), 103–133.

————. "The State and Economic Life in the Kingdom of Sicily under Frederick II" (paper delivered at the First International Workshop on Frederick II, entitled *Frederick II and the Mediterranean World: Theory and Practice of Government*, Erice, Sicily, September 18–24, 1989).

Alban, J. R., and C. T. Allmand. "Spies and Spying in the Fourteenth Century." *War, Literature and Politics in the Late Middle Ages*, ed. C. T. Allmand (Liverpool, 1976): 73–101.

Alexander, P. *The Byzantine Apocalyptic Tradition*. Berkeley, 1985.

Allaire, Gloria. "The Chivalric 'Histories' of Andrea da Barberino: A Reevaluation." Ph.D. dissertation: University of Wisconsin-Madison, 1993.

Allouche, Adel. *The Origins and Development of the Ottoman-Safavid Conflict (906–962/1500–1555).* Series Islamkundliche Untersuhungen, no. 91. Berlin, 1983.

d'Alverny, Marie-Thérèse. "La connaissance de l'Islam en Occident du IXᵉ au milieu du XIᴵᵉ siècle." *L'occidente e L'Islam nell'alto medioevo.* Vol. 2: *Settimane di studio del Centro italiano di studi sull'alto medioevo* 12 (Spoleto, 1965): 577–602.

———. "Deux traductions latines du Coran au Moyen Age." *Archives d'histoire doctrinale et littéraire du Moyen Age* 22–23 (1947–1948): 69–131.

———. "Translations and Translators." *Renaissance and Renewal in the Twelfth Century.* Robert L. Benson and Giles Constable, eds. Harvard, 1982. Pp. 421–462.

Amoretti, Biancamaria Scarcia. *Sâh Ismâ'îl I nei Diarii di Marin Sanudo.* Rome, 1979.

Anawati, George. *Polémique, apologie et dialogue Islamo-chrétiens. Positions classiques médiévales et positions contemporaines.* Rome, 1969.

D'Ancona, Alessandro. "La leggenda di Maometto in Occidente." *Studj di critica e storia letteraria,* parte seconda, 2d ed. (Bologna, 1912), 165–306.

———. "Il Tesoro di Brunetto Latini versificato." *Atti della R. Accademia dei Lincei, Classe di Scienze morali, storiche e filologiche,* serie quarta, anno 285, 4 (1888): 111–274.

Angold, Michael. *The Byzantine Empire, 1025–1205: A Political History.* London, 1984.

Arjomand, Said Amir. *The Shadow of God and the Hidden Imam: Religion, Political Order, and Societal Change in Shi'ite Iran from the Beginning to 1890.* Chicago, 1984.

Ashtor, E. *A Social and Economic History of the Near East in the Middle Ages.* Berkeley, 1976.

Avi-Yonah, M. "Greek-Christian Inscriptions from Riâb." *Quarterly of the Department of Antiquities in Palestine* 13 (1948): 68–72.

———. *The Jews of Palestine.* Oxford, 1976.

Al-Azmeh, Aziz. "Barbarians in Arab Eyes." *Past and Present* 134 (1992): 3–18.

Babayan, L. G. *Sotial'no-ekonomicheskaia i politicheskaia istoriia Armenii v XIII–XIV vekakh.* Moscow, 1969.

Babinger, Franz. "Marino Sanuto's Tagebücher Als Quellen zur Geschichte der Safawijja." *A Volume of Oriental Studies Presented to*

Edward G. Browne. T. W. Arnold and R. A. Nicholson, eds. (Cambridge, 1922), 28–50.

Bacqué-Grammont, Jean Louis. "Ottomans et Safavides au Temps de Şah Isma'îl." Dissertation, Université de Paris I, 1980.

Baghdassarian (Baldasaryan), E. M. "La Vie de Georges de Skevra." *Banber Matenadarani* 7(1964), 399–435.

Bancourt, Paul. "De l'image épique à la représentation historique du Musulman dans *L'estoire de la Guerre Sainte* d'Ambroise (*L'estoire et la Chanson d'Aspremont*)." *Au Carrefour des routes d'Europe: La Chanson de Geste.* Aix-en-Provence, 1987.

———. *Les Musulmans dans les chansons de geste du Cycle du roi.* 2 vols. Dissertation: l'Université de Provence, Aix-en-Provence, 1982.

———. "Le visage de l'Autre: étude sur le sens de la *Chanson d'Aspremont*," *De l'étranger à l'étrange.* Aix-en-Provence, 1988.

Baramki, D., and S. H. Stephan. "A Nestorian Hermitage between Jericho and the Jordan." *Quarterly of the Department of Antiquities in Palestine* 4 (1935): 81–86.

Barkai, Ron. *Cristianos y musulmanes en la España medieval (el enemigo en el espejo).* 2nd ed. Madrid, 1991.

Barker, Ernest. "The Crusades." *The Legacy of Islam.* Sir Thomas Arnold and Alfred Guillaume, eds. (Oxford, 1931; reprint, London, 1952), 40–77.

Battaglia, Salvatore, ed. *Grande dizionario della letteratura italiana.* 15 vols. Turin, 1961.

Baumer, Franklin L. "England, the Turk and the Common Corps of Christendom." *American Historical Review,* 50 (1944–1945): 26–48.

Beaujouan, Guy. "Transformation of the Quadrivium," in *Renaissance and Renewal in the Twelfth Century.* Robert L. Benson and Giles Constable, eds. (Harvard, 1982): 463–487.

Beck, Hans G. *Kirche und theologische Literatur im byzantinischen Reich.* Munich, 1959.

Bedrosian, Robert G. "The Turco-Mongol Invasions and the Lords of Armenia in the 13–14th Centuries." Ph.D. diss., Columbia University, 1979.

Bennett, Josephine Waters. *The Rediscovery of Sir John Mandeville.* Modern Language Association Monograph Series 19. New York, 1954.

Benz, Ernst. *Ecclesia Spiritualis.* Stuttgart: Kohlhammer, 1934.

Berchet, Guglielmo. *La Repubblica di Venezia e la Persia.* Turin, 1865.

Berendrecht, Petra. "Maerlants' 'Scolastica' en zijn directe bron." *Tijdschrift voor Nederlandse Taal—en Letterkunde* 108 (1992), 2–31.

Berriot, François. "Remarques sur la Découverte de l'Islam par l'Occident, à la fin du Moyen-Age et à la Renaissance," *Reforme, humanisme, renaissance* 22 (1986): 11–25.

Bertoni, Giulio. *La biblioteca Estense e la coltura [sic] ferrarese ai tempi del duca Ercole I (1471–1505).* Turin, 1903.

Bezzola, Reto R. "L'Oriente nel poema cavalleresco del primo Rinascimento." *Lettere italiane* 15 (1963): 385–398.

Blake, R. P. "La littérature grecque en Palestine au VIIIᵉ siècle." *Le Muséon* 78 (1965): 367–380.

Blanchère, Régis (translation with commentary). *Le Coran.* Paris, 1966.

Blochet, E. *Les Sources orientales de la Divine Comédie.* Les Littératures populaires de toutes les nations, no. 41. Paris, 1901.

Blumenkranz, Bernard. *Juifs et chrétiens dans le monde occidental, 430–1096.* Paris, 1960.

Bonis, Constantine G. "Ὁ Θεσσαλονίκης Εὐστάθιος καὶ οἱ δύο 'τόμοι' τοῦ αὐτοκπάτοπος Μανουὴλ Α' Κομνηοῦ," (1143/80) ὑπὲρ τὸν εἰς τὴν χριστιανικὴν ὀρθοδοξίαν μετισταμένων Μωαμεθανῶν." Ἐπετηρὶς Ἑταιρείας Βυζαντινῶν Σπουδῶν, 19 (1949): 162–169.

Boyle, J. A., ed. The Cambridge History of Iran. Vol. 5: *The Saljuk and Mongol Periods.* Cambridge, 1968.

———. "Kirakos of Ganjak on the Mongols." *Central Asiatic Journal* 8 (1963), 199–214.

Brand, Charles M. *Byzantium Confronts the West, 1180–1204.* Cambridge, MA, 1968.

Braudel, Fernand. *La Méditerranée et le Monde Méditerranéen à l'Epoque de Philippe II.* 2 vols. 2nd ed., Paris, 1966.

Bridel, P., ed. *Le site monastique Copte des Kellia.* Geneva, 1986.

Bridge, Antony. *Suleiman the Magnificent.* New York, 1983.

Briggs, Martin S. "Architecture." *The Legacy of Islam.* Sir Thomas Arnold and Alfred Guillaume, eds. (Oxford, UK 1931; reprint, London, 1952), 155–179.

Brock, S. "An Early Syriac Life of Maximus the Confessor," *Analecta Bollandiana* 91 (1973), 299–346.

———. "Syriac Sources for Seventh-Century History." *Byzantine and Modern Greek Studies* 2 (1976): 17–36.

————. "Syriac Views of Emergent Islam." *Studies in the First Century of Islamic Society*, ed. G. H. A. Juynboll (Carbondale, IL, 1982), 9–21.

Brosset, M.-F., ed. and trans. *Collection d'historiens arméniens. Dix ouvrages sur l'histoire de l'Arménie et des pays adjacents du Xe au XIXe siècle traduits de l'Arménien et du Russe, avec des introductions historiques et des notes critiques, linguistiques et eclairissantes.* Amsterdam, 1979; Reprint of St. Petersburg edition, 1874, 1876.

Brummett, Palmira. "Transformations in Political and Commercial Hegemony: Venice and the Ottoman Expansion, 1503–1517." Ph.D. dissertation, University of Chicago, 1988.

Buc, Philippe. "Pouvoir Royal et Commentaires de la Bible (1150–1350)." *Annales* 44 (1984): 691–709.

Bundy, David. "The 'Anonymous Life of Georg Skewṙac'i' in *Erevan 8356*: A Study in Medieval Armenian Hagiography and History." *Revue des Études Arméniennes* n.s. 18 (1984), 491–502.

————. "The Council of Sis, 1307." *After Chalcedon: Studies in Theology and Church History* ed. C. Laga et al. *Orientalia Lovaniensia Analecta*, 18 (1985), 47–56.

————. "George Warda." *Dictionnaire d'histoire et de géographie ecclésiastiques* 20 (1983), 668–669.

————. "Het'um's 'La flor des Estoires de la Terre d'Orient:' A Study in Medieval Armenian Historiography and Propaganda." *Revue des études arméniennes* n.s. 20(1986–1987), 223–235.

Burman, Thomas. "The Influence of the *Apology of al-Kindî* and *Contrarietas alfolica* on Ramon Lull's Late Religious Polemics, 1305–1313." *Mediaeval Studies* 53 (1991): 197–208.

————. "*Spain's Arab Christians and Islam, c. 1050–1200: The Text of* the Liber denudationis (alias Contrarietas alfolica) and its Intellectual Milieu." Ph.D. dissertation, University of Toronto, 1991.

Burns, Robert I. S. J. *Islam under the Crusaders.* Princeton, 1973.

Burr, David. "The Apocalyptic Element in Olivi's Critique of Aristotle." *Church History*, 40 (1971), 15–29.

————. "Mendicant Readings of the Apocalypse." In *The Apocalypse in the Middle Ages*. Richard K. Emerson and Bernard McGinn, eds., 89–102. Ithaca, 1992.

————. "Olivi's Apocalyptic Timetable." *Journal of Medieval and Renaissance Studies*, 11 (1981), 237–260.

————. "Olivi, the *Lectura super apocalypsim*, and Franciscan Exegetical Tradition." *Francescanesimo e cultura universitaria* (Perugia, 1989), 115–135.

Buytaert, E. "Abelard's Trinitarian Doctrine." *Peter Abelard: Proceedings of the International Conference, Louvain*, May 10–12, 1971, ed. E. Buytaert (Leuven, 1974), 127–152.

Cabanelas Rodríguez, Darío, O. F. M. *Juan de Segovia y el Problema Islámico*. Madrid, 1952.

Cabani, Maria Cristina. *Le forme del cantare epico-cavalleresco*. Luigi Blasucci, ed. *L'Unicorno: Collana di testi e di critica letteraria*, no. 2. Lucca, 1988.

Carpenter, Dwayne. "Minorities in Medieval Spain: The Legal Status of Jews and Muslims in the *Siete Partidas*." *Romance Quarterly*, 33 (1986): 275–287.

Carrasco Urgoiti, María Soledad. "La Cultura popular de Ginés Pérez de Hita." *Homenaje a Vicente García Diego. Revista de Dialectología y Tradiciones populares* 33 (1977): 1–21.

————. *El Moro de Granada y la literatura del siglo XV al XIX*. (Granada, 1989).

Caspar, Robert. *Traité de théologie musulmane*. Vol. 1: *Histoire de la pensée religieuse musulmane*. Rome, 1987.

————. "Les versions arabes du dialogue entre le Catholicos Timothée I et le Calife al-Mahdî (IIe/VIIe siècle)." *Islamochristiana* 3 (1977): 107–75.

Caspar, Robert, et al. "Bibliographie du dialogue islamo-chrétien," *Islamochristiana*, 1 (1975): 125–181; 2 (1976): 187–242; 3 (1977): 255–286; 4 (1978): 247–267; 5 (1979): 299–317; 6 (1980): 259–299; 7 (1981): 299–307; 10 (1984): 273–292.

Catalano, Michele. "La data di morte di Andrea da Barberino." *Archivum Romanicum*, 23 (1939): 84–87.

Cerulli, Enrico. *Nuove ricerche sul "Libro della Scala" e la conoscenza dell'Islam. Occidente*, Studi e testi, no. 271. Vatican, 1972.

Chalandon, Ferdinand. *Les Comnène: Études sur l'empire byzantin au XIe et au XIIe siècles*, vol 2: *Jean II Comnène (1118–1143) et Manuel I Comnène (1143–1180)*. Paris, 1912.

Châtillon, J. "Unitas, aequalitas, concordia vel connexio: Recherches sur les origines de la théorie thomiste des appropriations (*Summa theologiae* 1, a. 39, art. 7–8)." *St. Thomas Aquinas 1274–1974: Commemorative Studies*, no. ed. (Toronto, 1974), 337–379.

Chauvin, Victor. *Bibliographie des ouvrages arabes ou relatifs aux Arabes*. 12 vols. Liège, 1892–1922; reprint Paris (no date).

———. "Le Prétendu Séjour de Mandeville en Egypte." *Wallonia* X (1902): 7: 237–242.

Chejne, Anwar G. *Islam and the West: The Moriscos, A Cultural and Social History*. Albany, 1983.

Chew, Samuel C. *The Crescent and the Rose: Islam and England during the Renaissance*. Oxford, 1937.

Chodorow, Stanley. *Christian Political Theory and Church Politics in the Mid-Twelfth Century: The Ecclesiology of Gratian's Decretum*. Berkeley, 1972.

Colbert, Edward. "The Martyrs of Córdoba (850–859): A Study of the Sources." Ph.D. dissertation, Catholic University of America, 1962.

Colby-Hall, Alice M. "La géographie rhodanienne des *Nerbonesi*: réalisme artificiel ou signe d'authenticité?" *Essor et fortune de la Chanson de geste dans l'Europe e l'Orient latin*. Actes du IXe Congres International de la Société Rencesvals pour l'etude des épopées romanes. Padoue-Venise, 29 août-4 septembre 1982, 2 vols. (Modena, 1984), 2: 655–662.

Coleman, Janet. *Piers Plowman and the Moderni*. Rome, 1981.

Collins, Roger. *Early Medieval Spain: Unity and Diversity, 400–1000*. New York, 1983.

Comfort, William W. "The literary role of the Saracens in the French epic." *PMLA* 55 (1940): 628–659.

Coope, Jessica A. "Religious and Cultural Conversion to Islam in Ninth-Century Umayyad Córdoba," *Journal of World History* 4 (1993): 47–68.

Cortabarria, A. "La connaissance des textes arabes chez Raymond Martin, O.P. et sa position en face de l'Islam." *Cahiers de Fanjeaux* 18 (1983), *Islam et Chrétiens du Midi*: 279–324.

Crone, P., and M. Cook. *Hagarism: The Making of the Islamic World*. Cambridge, 1977.

Crown, Alan D. "The Byzantine and Moslem Period." *The Samaritans*, Alan D. Crown, ed. (Tübingen, 1989), 585–623.

———. "The Samaritans in the Byzantine Orbit." *Bulletin of the John Rylands University Library of Manchester* 69 (1986): 96–138.

Daniel, Norman. "Apocalyptic Conversion: The Joachite Alternative to the Crusades." *Traditio* 25 (1969): 127–54.

―――. *The Arabs and Medieval Europe*. London, 1979.

―――. *Heroes and Saracens: An Interpretation of the Chansons de Geste*. Edinburgh, 1984..

―――. *Islam and the West: The Making of an Image*. Edinburgh, 1962.

De Iongh, Jane. *Mary of Hungary, Second Regent of the Netherlands*. M. D. Herter-Norton, trans. New York, 1958.

Delgado, Hernando I. "Le 'De seta Machometi' du cod. 46 d'Osma, oeuvre de Raymond Martin (Ramón Martí)." *Cahiers de Fanjeaux* 18 (1983), *Islam et Chrétiens du Midi*: 351–371.

Delgado Gallego, José María. "Maurofilia y maurofobia, ¿dos caras de la misma moneda?" *Narraciones moriscas* (Seville, 1986), 20–47.

Delisle, Léopold. *Le cabinet des manuscrits de la Bibliotheque Impériale, Histoire générale de Paris*, collection de documents, 3 vols. Paris, 1868–1881.

Delorme, F. M. and A. L. Trautu. *Acta Romanorum Pontificum ab Innocento V ad Benedictum XI (1276–1304)*. Vatican, 1954.

Deluz, Christiane. *Le Livre de Jehan Mandeville: Une "geographie" au XIVe siècle*. Louvain, 1988.

Dennett, Daniel C. *Conversion and the Poll Tax in Early Islam*. Cambridge, MA, 1950.

Deutsch, A. *Edition drier syrischen Lieder nach einer Handschrift der Berliner Königlichen Bibliothek*. Berlin, 1895.

Devillard, Paul. "Thèse sur al-Qurubî." Thèse de troisieme cycle présenté à la Faculté des Lettres à Aix-en-Provence, 1969.

Díaz Plaja, Fernando. *Sociedad española*. Buenos Aires, 1970.

Dick, Ignace. "Un continuateur arabe de saint Jean Damascène: Théodore Abuqurra, évêque melkite de Harran. La personne et son milieu." *Proche Orient chrétien* 12 (1962): 209–223, 319–332; 13 (1963): 114–129.

La Diffusione delle scienze islamiche nel medio evo europeo. Rome, 1987.

Donnelly, John Patrick, S. J. "The Moslem Enemy in Renaissance Epic: Ariosto, Tasso and Camoëns." *Yale Italian Studies* 1 (1977): 162–170.

Donner, Fred M. *The Early Islamic Conquests*. Princeton, 1981.

Dozy, Reinhart. *Glossaire des mots espagnols et portugais dérivés de l'Arabe*. 2nd ed. Leiden, 1869, rpt., Beirut, 1974.

―――. *Supplément aux dictionaires arabes*. 2 vols. Leiden, 1967.

Du Roy, Olivier. *L'Intelligence de la foi en la Trinité selon Saint Augustin.* Paris, 1966.

Ebersolt, Jean. "Un nouveau manuscrit sur le rituel d'abjuration des Musulmans dans l'Église grecque." *Revue de l'histoire des religions* 54 (1906): 231–232.

Eckhardt, Alexandre. "Le cercueil flottant de Mahomet." *Mélanges de philologie romane et de littérature médiévale offerts à Ernest Hoepffner.* Publications de la Faculté des Lettres de l'Université de Strasbourg, Fasc. 113 (Paris, 1949), 77–88.

Emmerson, Richard. *Antichrist in the Middle Ages.* Seattle, 1981.

Epalsa, M de. "Mozarabs: An Emblematic Christian Minority in al-Andalus," S. K. Jayyusi, ed. *The Legacy of Muslim Spain.* Leiden, 1992, 149–170.

Espín Rael, Joaquín. *De la Vecindad de Pérez de Hita en Lorca desde 1568 a 1577 años.* Lorca, 1922.

Fackenheim, E. "'Substance' and 'Perseity' in Medieval Arabic Philosophy with Introductory Chapters on Aristotle, Plotinus and Proclus." Ph.D. dissertation, University of Toronto, 1945.

Faridi, Shahidullah. *Everyday Practice in Islam.* Karachi, 1970.

Fattal, Antoine. *Le statut legal des non-musulmans en pays d'Islam.* Beirut, 1958.

Fernández Alvarez, Manuel. *Charles V, Elected Emperor and Hereditary Ruler.* London, 1975.

———. *Economía, sociedad y corona.* Madrid, 1963.

Ferreras, Juan de. *Synopsis histórica chronológica de España,* 15 vols. Madrid, 1716.

Fiey, J. M. *Chrétiens syriaques sous les mongols (Il-Khanate de Perse, XIIIe -XIVe s.)* CSCO 362, Subsidia 44 (1975).

———. "Îšō'yaw le Grand: Vie du catholicos nestorien Îšō'yaw III d'Adiabène (580–659)." *Orientalia Christiana Periodica* 35 (1969): 305–333; 36 (1970): 5–46.

Fodor, Pal. "Aḥmedî's Dâsitân as a Source of Early Ottoman History." *Acta Orientalia Academiae Scientiarum Hungarica* 38 (1984): 41–54.

Foss, C. "Archaeology and the Twenty Cities of Byzantine Asia." *American Journal of Archaeology* 81 (1977): 469–486.

Fraher, Richard M. "Conviction According to Conscience: The Medieval Jurists' Debate concerning Judicial Discretion and the Law of Proof." *Law and History Review* 7 (Spring 1989), 23–88.

Franceschetti, Antonio. "On the Saracens in Early Italian Chivalric Literature." *Romance Epic: Essays on a Medieval Literary Genre*, ed. Hans-Erich Keller, Studies in Medieval Culture, no. 24 (Kalamazoo, 1987), 203–211.

Franke, Franz R. "Die freiwilligen Märtyrer von Cordova und das Verhältnis des Mozarabes zum Islam (nach den Schriften von Speraindeo, Eulogius und Alvar)." *Spanische Forschungen des Görresgesellschaft*, 13 (1953): 1–170.

Frend, W. H. C. *The Rise of the Monophysite Movement*. Cambridge, 1972.

————. "Severus of Antioch and the Origins of the Monophysite Hierarchy." *Orientalia Christiana Analecta* 195 (1973): 261–75.

Fritz, V., and A. Kempinski. *Ergebnisse der Ausgrabungen auf der Hirbet el-Mŝâš (Tēl Mâsōs)*, 1972–1975. Wiesbaden, 1983.

Fromherz, Uta. *Johannes von Segovia als Geschichtsschreiber des Konzils von Basel*. Basel, 1960.

García Cárcel, Ricardo. *Origenes de la Inquisición española, el tribunal de Valencia, 1478—1530*. Barcelona, 1976.

Geanakoplos, Deno John. *Interaction of the "Sibling" Byzantine and Western Cultures in the Middle Ages and the Renaissance*. New Haven, 1976.

Geary, John S. "The Death of the Count: Novelesque Invention in the *Crónica de Fernán González*." *Bulletin of Hispanic Studies* 69 (1992): 321–334.

————. "The 'tres monjes' of the *Poema de Fernán González*: Myth and History." *La Corónica* 19 (1991): 24–42.

Gelzer, H. "Josua Stylites und die damaligen kirchlichen Parteien des Osten." *Byzantinische Zeitschrift* 1 (1892): 34–49.

Gentile, Luigi. *I codici palatini. Indici e cataloghi IV. I codici palatini della R. Biblioteca Nazionale Centrale di Firenze*. 3 vols. Rome, 1885–1891.

Gerritsen, Willem P. "Jacob van Maerlant and Geoffrey of Monmouth." *An Arthurian Tapestry. Essays in memory of Lewis Thorpe*. Keith Varty, ed. (Glasgow, 1981), 368–388.

Gervers, Michael, and Ramzi J. Bikhazi, eds. *Conversion and Continuity: Indigenous Christian Communities in Islamic Lands, Eighth to Eighteenth Centuries*. Papers in Mediaeval Studies, 9 (Toronto, 1990).

Gibb, Hamilton A. R. "Arab-Byzantine relations under the Umayyad Caliphate." *Dumbarton Oaks Papers* 12 (1958): 219–233.

Gibbon, Edward. *The Decline and Fall of the Roman Empire.* 3 vols. New York, no date.

Gimaret, D. *La doctrine d'al-Ash'arî.* Paris, 1990.

———. *Les noms divins en Islam.* Paris, 1988.

Ginzberg, L. *Geniza Studies in Memory of Doctor Solomon Schechter.* New York, 1928.

Glick, Thomas. *Islamic and Christian Spain in the Early Middle Ages.* Princeton, 1979.

Goerevitsj, Aron Ja. "De koopman." *De wereld van de Middeleeuwen.* Jaques Le Goff, ed. Amsterdam, 1991, 241–279.

Göllner, Carl. *Turcia: Die europäischen Türkendrucke des XVI Jahrhunderts,* 2 vols. Bucharest-Berlin-Baden, 1961.

Golubovich, G. *Bibliotheca bio-bibliografica della Terra Santa e dell'Oriente francescano. Serie prima: annali.* 5 vols. Florence, 1906–1927.

Gómez Moreno, Manuel. "Las primeras crónicas de la Reconquista: el ciclo de Alfonso III." *Boletín de la Real Academia de la Historia* 100 (1932): 562–599.

Gómez Pérez, José. "Una crónica de Fernán González escrita por orden del emperador Carlos V." *Revista de archivos, bibliotecas y museos* 64 (1950): 551–581.

Gosselin, Edward A. "Bibliographical Survey: A Listing of the Printed Editions of Nicolaus de Lyra." *Traditio* 26 (1970): 399–426.

Graf, Georg. *Die arabischen Schriften des Theodor Abû Qurra, Bischofs von Harrân (ca. 740–820).* Paderborn, 1910.

———. *Geschichte der christlichen arabischen Literatur.* 5 vols. Vatican City, 1944–1953.

———. *Verzeichnis Arabischer Kirklicher Termini.* Louvain, 1954.

Greenblatt, Stephen. *Marvelous Possessions: The Wonder of the New World.* Chicago, 1991.

Grendler, Paul F. "Chivalric Romances in the Italian Renaissance." *Studies in Medieval and Renaissance History,* vol. 10 (Old Series, vol. 20). J. A. S. Evans and R. W. Unger, eds. (New York, 1988), 68–71.

Griffith, S. H. "Greek into Arabic: Life and Letters in the Monasteries of Palestine in the Ninth Century: The Example of the *Summa Theologica Arabica.*" *Byzantion* 106 (1986): 117–138.

———. "The Monks of Palestine and the Growth of Christian Literature in Arabic." *The Muslim World* 78 (1988): 1–28.

Grohmann, Adolf. "Greek Papyri of the Early Islamic Period in the Collection of Archduke Rainer." *Études de papyrologie* 8 (1957): 5–40.

Guiard, J. and L. Cadier, *Les Registres de Gregoire X et Jean XXII.* Paris, 1892–1895.

Gulick, Robert L., Jr. *Muhammad the Educator.* Lahore, 1961.

Haddad, R. *La Trinité divine chez les théologiens arabes (750–1050).* Paris, 1985.

Hailperin, Herman. *Rashi and the Christian Scholars.* Pittsburgh, 1963.

Hanna, Ralph III. "Mandeville." *Middle English Prose: A Critical Guide to Major Authors and Genres.* A. S. G. Edwards, ed. New Brunswick, NJ, 1984, 121–132.

Haneda, Masashi. *Le Chah et les Qizilbâs. Le systeme militaire safavide.* Series Islamkundliche Untersuhungen, no. 119. Berlin, 1987.

Hawickhorst, Heinrich. "Über die Geographie bei Andrea de' Magnabotti." *Romanische Forschungen* XIII (1902): 689–784.

Hefele, C. J. *Histoire des conciles d'apres les documents originaux.* Translated and revised by H. Leclercq. Paris, 1914.

Hewitt, H .J. *The Organization of War Under Edward III, 1338–1362.* Manchester, 1966.

Higgins, Iain. "The World of a Book of the World: *Mandeville's Travels* in Middle English (British Library MS. Cotton Titus C.xvi.)." Ph.D. dissertation, Harvard University, 1988.

Hilgenfeld, H. *Ausgewählte Gesänge des Giwargis Warda von Arbel hrsg. mit Ubersetzung, Einleitung und Erklarung.* Leipzig, 1904.

Hitchcock, R. "Quienes fueron los verdaderos mozárabes?" *Nueva revista de filología hispanica* 30 (1981): 574–585.

Hitchins, Keith. "The Caucasian Albanians and the Arab Caliphate in the Seventh and Eighth Centuries." *Bedi Kartlisa* 42 (1984): 234–245.

Hitti, P. K. *History of Syria.* London, 1951.

Hodges, R., and D. Whitehouse. *Mohammed, Charlemagne and the Origins of Europe.* Ithaca, NY, 1983.

Hodgson, Marshall G. S. *The Venture of Islam.* Vol. 1: The Classical Age of Islam. Chicago, 1974.

Honigmann, E. *Le Couvent de Barsauma et le patriarcat Jacobite d'Antioche et de Syrie,* CSCO 146 (1954).

———. *Évêques et évêches monophysites d'Asie antérieure au VIe siècle*, CSCO 127 (1951).

Housley, Norman. *The Italian Crusades: The Papal-Angevin Alliance and the Crusades against Christian Lay Powers, 1254–1343*. Oxford, 1982.

Howard, Donald. "The World of *Mandeville's Travels*," *Yearbook of English Studies* 1 (1971): 1–17.

Howell, Alfred M. "Some Notes on Early Treaties between Muslims and the Visigothic Rulers of Al-Andalus." *Actas del I congreso de historia de Andalucía* 1 (Córdoba, 1978): 3–14.

Husik, I. *A History of Mediaeval Jewish Philosophy*. New York, 1974.

Hussey, Joan M. *The Orthodox Church in the Byzantine Empire*. Oxford, 1986.

Hyland, William P. "John-Jerome of Prague: A Study in Late Medieval Monastic Intellectual Culture." Ph.D. dissertation, Cornell University, 1992.

Ismaylowa, T. A. "The Syunik School of Armenian Miniatures in the 2nd Half of the 13th and the Beginning of the 14th Centuries [Russian]." *Istoriko Filologisheskii Zhurnal* 81,2 (1978), 182–190.

Jackson, Peter and Lawrence Lockhart, eds. *The Cambridge History of Iran*. Vol. 6: *The Timurid and Safavid Periods*. Cambridge, 1986.

Jellinek, Adolf, ed. *Bet ha-Midrasch: Sammlung kleiner Midraschim und vermischter Abhandlungen aus der altern judischen Literatur*. 6 vols. Leipzig, 1853–1877.

Jones, Terry. *Chaucer's Knight: The Portrait of a Medieval Mercenary*. 2nd ed. New York, 1985.

Kaegi, Walter. "Initial Byzantine Reactions to the Arab Conquest." *Church History* 38 (1969): 139–149.

Kakovkin, A. "Historical-Literary Data Concerning the Jewelry Craftsmanship of Cilician Armenia [Russian]." *Istoriko Filologisheskii Zhurnal* 106, 3(1984), 161–165.

Kamen, Henry. *The Iron Century*. New York, 1971.

Kay, Richard. *Dante's Swift and Strong; Essays on Inferno XV*. Lawrence, Kansas, 1978.

Kazhdan, Alexander, and A. Cutler. "Continuity and Discontinuity in Byzantine History." *Byzantion* 52 (1982): 427–478.

Kazhdan, Alexander, and Giles Constable. *People and Power in Byzantium: An Introduction to Modern Byzantine Studies*. Washington, 1982.

Kedar, Benjamin Z. *Crusade and Mission: European Approaches toward the Muslims.* Princeton, 1984.

———. "Muslim Conversion in Canon Law." *Proceedings of the Sixth International Congress of Medieval Canon Law.* S. Kuttner and K. Pennington, eds. *Monumenta iuris canonici,* Series C: Subsidia 7 (Vatican, 1985), 321–332.

Kennedy, Hugh N. "The Last Century of Byzantine Syria: A Reinterpretation." *Byzantinische Forschungen* 10 (1985): 141–183.

———. "The Melkite Church from the Islamic Conquest to the Crusades: Continuity and Adaptation in the Byzantine Legacy." *The 17th International Byzantine Congress: Major Papers* (New Rochelle, NY, 1986), 325–343.

Kerslake, Celia J. "The Correspondence between Selîm I and Ḳanṣûh al-Ġawrî." *Prilozi za Orientalnu Filologiju* 30 (1980): 219–233.

Khoury, Adel-Théodore. "Apologétique byzantine contre l'Islam (VIIIᵉ–XIIIᵉ siècle)." *Proche-Orient Chrétien* 29 (1979): 241–305; 30 (1980): 132–174; 32 (1981): 14–49.

———. *Les théologiens byzantins et l'Islam 1: Textes et auteurs (VIIIᵉ–XIIIᵉ siècle).* Louvain, 1969.

———. *Les théologiens byzantins et l'Islam 2: Polémique byzantine contre l'Islam (VIIIᵉ–XIII ᵉ siècle).* Leiden, 1972.

———. *Toleranz im Islam.* Munich, 1980.

Komroff, Manuel. *Contemporaries of Marco Polo.* New York, 1928.

Kouymjian, D. "Dated Armenian Manuscripts as a Statistical Tool for Armenian History." T. Samuelian and M. Stone, eds. *Medieval Armenian Culture: University of Pennsylvania Armenian Texts and Studies,* 6 (1984), 425–438.

Krause, F. E. A. "Das Mongolenreich nach der Darstellung des Armeniers Haithon." *Ostasiatische Zeitschrift* 8 (1920): 238–267.

Krey, Philip. "Nicholas of Lyra: Apocalypse Commentary as Historiography." Ph.D. dissertation, University of Chicago, 1990.

———. "Nicholas of Lyra, Apocalypse Commentator, Historian, and Critic." Unpublished.

Kristeller, Paul Oskar. *Iter Italicum: A finding list of uncatalogued humanistic manuscripts of the Renaissance in Italian and other monasteries.* 2 vols. Leiden, 1963–1967.

Kritzeck, James. *Peter the Venerable and Islam.* Princeton, 1964.

Laarhoven, Jan van. "Chrétienté et croisade. Une tentative terminologique." *Cristianesimo nella storia* 6 (1985), 27–43.

Labandeira Fernández, Amancio. "Historicidad y estructura de la Crónica Arlantina en verso." *Revista de archivos, bibliotecas y museos* 82 (1979): 225–243.

Labrosse, Henri. "Biographie de Nicolas de Lyre." *Études franciscaines* 17 (1907): 489–505, 593–608.

———. "Oeuvres de Nicolas de Lyre: Sources bibliographiques." *Études franciscaines* 19 (1908): 41–53, 153–176, 368–380; 35 (1923): 171–187, 400–432.

———. "Sources de la biographie de Nicolas de Lyre." *Études franciscaines* 16 (1906): 383–404.

Ladner, Gerhard. "The Concepts of 'Ecclesia' and 'Christianitas' and their Relation to the Idea of Papal 'Plenitudo Potestatis' from Gregory VII to Boniface VIII." *Sacerdozio e regno da Gregorio VII a Bonifacio VIII = Miscellanea Historiae Pontificiae* 18 (1954): 49–77.

Lampe, G. W. H., ed. *A Patristic Greek Lexicon*. Oxford, 1961.

Landgraff A. *Écrits théologiques de l'école d'Abélard: Textes inédits.* Louvain, 1934.

Lane, E. *An Arabic-English Lexicon*, 8 vols. London, 1874, rpt. Beruit, 1980.

Langlois, Charles. "Nicolas de Lyre, Frère Mineur." *Histoires littéraire de la France* 36 (1927): 355–400.

Langois, E. *Les Registres de Nicolas IV*. Paris, 1905.

Letts, Malcolm, ed. *Mandeville's Travels: Texts and Translations*. Hakluyt Society 2nd ser. 101 (1953).

Levi della Vida, G. "I Mozarabi tra occidente e Islam." *L'occidente e L'Islam nell'alto medioevo* vol. 2 (*Settimane di studio del Centro italiano di studi sull'alto medioevo* 12): 667–695.

———. "Un texte mozarabe d'histoire universelle." *Études d'orientalisme dédiées à la mémoire de Lévi-Provençal* 1 (Paris, 1962), 175–183.

Lévi-Provençal, Evariste. *Histoire de l'Espagne musulmane.* 3 vols., 2nd ed. Paris, 1950.

Levtzion, Nehemia. "Conversion to Islam in Syria and Palestine and the Survival of Christian Communities." Gervers and Bikhazi, eds., *Conversion and Continuity*, 289–311.

Lewis, Bernard. "An Apocalyptic Vision of Islamic History." *Bulletin of the School of Oriental and African Studies* 13 (1950): 308–338.

———. *The Jews of Islam*. Princeton, 1984.

————. "On That Day: A Jewish Apocalyptic Poem on the Arab Conquests." *Mélanges d'Islamologie*, ed. P. Salmon (Leiden, 1974), 197–200.

Liebeschuetz, J.H. G. W, and H. Kennedy. "Antioch and the Villages of Northern Syria in the Fifth and Sixth Centuries A.D. Trends and Problem." *Nottingham Medieval Studies* 33 (1988): 65–89.

Limper, B. "*Die Mongolen und die Völker des Kaukasus; Eine Untersuchung zur politischen Geschichte Kaukasiens im 13. und beginnenden 14. Jahrhundert.*" Inaug.-diss. Universitat zu Köln, 1980.

Lindberg, David C., ed. "The Transmission of Greek and Arabic Learning to the West." *Science in the Middle Ages*. Chicago, 1978. Pp. 52–90.

Løkkegaard, Frede. *Islamic Taxation in the Classical Period*. Copenhagen, 1950.

Lomax, John P. "*Ingratus* or *Indignus*: Canonistic Argument in the Conflict between Pope Gregory IX and Emperor Frederick II." Ph.D. dissertation, University of Kansas, 1987.

López-Baralt, L. *Islam in Spanish Literature, From the Middle Ages to the Present*. A. Hurley, trans. Leiden, 1992.

López Pereira, José Eduardo. *Estudio crítico sobre la crónica mozárabe de 754*. Zaragoza, 1980.

Luchetta, Francesco. "L'Affare Zen in Levante nel Primo Cinquecento." *Studie Veneziani* 10 (1959): 109–209.

Lupprian, K.-E. *Die Beziehungen der Päpste zu islamischen und mongolischen Herrschern im 13. Jahrhundert anhand ihres Briefwechsels*. Vatican, 1981.

Lux, U. "Der Mosaikfussboden der Menas-Kirche in Riâb." *Zeitschrift des Deutschen Palästina-Vereins* 83 (1967): 34–41.

Maccarrone, Michele. *Vicarius Christi: Storia del titolo papale*. Lateranum, n.s., 18 (1952).

McGinn, Bernard. "Awaiting an End." *Medievalia et Humanistica*, n.s. ll (1982), 263–289.

————. *The Calabrian Abbot*. New York, 1985.

————. *Visions of the End*. New York, 1979.

Magheri-Cataluccio, M. Elena. *Biblioteca et Cultura a Camaldoli*. Studia Anselmiana 75 (1979).

Mango, C. *Byzantium: The Empire of New Rome*. London, 1980.

Manselli, Raoul. *La "Lectura super apocalypsim" di Pietro di Giovanni Olivi.* Rome, 1955.

———. *Spirituali e Beghini in Provenza.* Rome, 1959.

Martinez, F. J. "Eastern Christian Apocalyptic in the Early Muslim Period: Pseudo-Methodius and Pseudo-Athanasius." Ph.D. dissertation, Catholic University of America, 1985.

Martínez Añíbarro y Rives, Manuel. *Intento de un diccionario biográfico y bibliográfico de autores de la provincia de Burgos.* Madrid, 1889.

Mas, Albert. *Les Turcs dans la littérature espagnole du siècle d'or.* 2 vols. Paris, 1967.

Mazzaoui, Michel. *The Origins of the Safawids: Si'ism, Sûfism and the Gulât.* Wiesbbaden, 1972.

Menéndez y Pelayo, Marcelino. *Antología de poetas líricos castellanos.* 10 vols. Santander, 1944.

Meredith-Jones, C. "The Conventional Saracen of the Songs of Geste." *Speculum* 17 (1942): 201–225.

Merriman, Roger. *Suleiman the Magnificent, 1520–1566.* Cambridge, MA, 1944.

Metlizki, Dorothee. *The Matter of Araby in Medieval England.* New Haven, 1977.

Mews, C. "The Development of the Theologia of Peter Abelard." Rudolf Thomas, ed. *Petrus Abaelardus [1079–1142]: Person, Werk und Wirkung* (Trier, 1980), 183–98.

Meyendorff, John. "Byzantine Views of Islam." *Dumbarton Oaks Papers* 18 (1964): 115–132.

———. *Imperial Unity and Christian Diversity.* Crestwood, NY, 1989.

Michelant, Henri. "Titoli dei Capitoli della Storia *Reali di Francia.*" *Jahrbuch für romanische und englische Literatur* 12 (1871): 65–72, 217–232, 396–406.

Milá y Fontanals, Manuel. *De la poesía heroico-popular castellana.* Martín de Riquer and Joaquín Molas, eds. 2 vols. Barcelona, 1959.

Ministére de l'Instruction Publique. *Anciens Inventaires et Catalogues de la Bibliothèque Nationale.* 4 vols. Paris, 1908–1913.

Minorsky, Vladimir. "La Perse au XVe siècle entre la Turquie et Venise." *Publications de la Société des Études Iraniennes* 7 (1933): 1–23.

———. "The Poetry of Shah Isma'il I." *Bulletin of the School of Oriental and African Studies* 10 (1939–1942): 1006a–1053a.

Mittmann, S. "Die Mosaikinschrift der Menas-Kirche in Riâb." *Zeitschrift des Deutschen Palästina-Vereins* 83 (1967): 42–45.

Montet, Edouard. "Un rituel d'abjuration des musulmans dans l'église grecque." *Revue de l'histoire des religions* 53 (1906): 145–163.

Moorhead, John. "The Earliest Christian Theological Responses to Islam." *Religion* 11 (1981): 265–274.

———. "The Monophysite Response to the Arab Invasions." *Byzantion* 51 (1981): 579–591.

Morçay, Raoul. *Chroniques de Saint Antonin.* Paris, 1913.

Morewedge, P. *The Metaphysica of Avicenna.* London, 1973.

Morse, Ruth. *Truth and Convention in the Middle Ages: Rhetoric, Representation, and Reality.* Cambridge, 1991.

Moutzegyan, K. H. "Money Circulation in Armenia during 9th–14th Centuries." *Istoriko Filologisheskii Zhurnal* 55,4 (1971), 41–60.

Muir, William. *The Life of Mohammad from Original Sources.* T. H. Weir, rev. ed. Edinburgh, 1923.

Muldoon, James. *Popes, Lawyers, and Infidels: The Church and the Non-Christian World, 1250–1550.* Philadelphia, 1979.

Narayan, B. K. *Mohammed the Prophet of Islam: A Flame in the Desert.* New Delhi, 1978.

Nasrallah, Joseph. "Regard critique sur I. Dick, Th. Abû Qurrah, De l'existence de Créateur et de la vraie religion." *Proche-Orient Chrétien* 36 (1986): 46–63; 37 (1987): 63–70.

Oostrom, Frits P. van. "Jacob van Maerlant: een herwaardering." *Literatuur* 2 (1985): 190–197.

———. "Maerlant tussen Noord en Zuid. Contouren van een biografie." Frits P. van Oostrom, *Aanvaard dit werk. Over Middelnederlandse auteurs en hun publiek.* (Amsterdam, 1992), 185–216.

Osella, Giacomo. "Il *Guerrin Meschino.*" *Pallante* 10 (1932): 11–172.

Ostrogorsky, George. *History of the Byzantine State.* New Brunswick, NJ, 1969.

Pakter, Walter. *Medieval Canon Law and the Jews.* Abhandlungen zur rechtswissenschaftlichen Grundlagenforschung 68. Ebelsbach, 1988.

Paret, Rudi. "Toleranz und Intoleranz im Islam." *Saeculum* 21 (1970): 344–365.

Paris, Gaston. *Histoire poétique de Charlemagne.* Paris, 1905.

Pastre, Jean-Marc. "Étranges sarrasins: le luxe et l'exotisme dans le *Willehalm* de Wolfram." *De l'Étranger à l'Étrange ou la Conjointure de la Merveille*, (En hommage à Marguerite Rossi et Paul Bancourt), Senefiance no. 25. (Aix en Provence, 1988), 329–340.

Payne, Stanley G. *A History of Spain and Portugal*. 2 vols. Madison, 1973.

Peeters, H. C. "Nieuwe inzichten in de Maerlantproblematiek." *Handelingen van de Koninklijke Zuidnederlandse Maatschappij voor Taal- en Letterkunde en Geschiedenis* 18 (1964): 249–285.

Peeters, P. "S. Antoine le néo-martyr." *Analecta Bollandiana* 31 (1912): 410–450.

Pelikan, Jaroslav. *The Growth of Medieval Theology (600–1300)*. Vol. 3 of *The Christian Tradition: A History of the Development of Doctrine*. Chicago, 1978.

Pelliot, P. "Les Mongols et la Papauté." *Revue de l'orient chrétien* 23(1922–1923), 3–30; 24(1924), 225–235; 28(1931–1932), 3–84.

Pérez de Urbel, Fray Justo. *El condado de Castilla: Los 300 años en que se hizo Castilla*. 3 vols. Madrid, 1970.

Pitrè, Giuseppe. "Le tradizioni cavalleresche popolari in Sicilia." *Romania* 13 (1884): 348–349.

Powell, James, ed. "The Papacy and the Muslim Frontier." In *Muslims under Latin Rule, 1100–1130*. pp. 175–203.

———, ed. *Muslims under Latin Rule, 1100–1300*. Princeton, 1990.

Rajna, Pio. *Ricerche intorno ai Reali di Francia*. 2 vols. Bologna, 1872.

Reinhardt, Klaus. "Das Werk des Nikolaus von Lyra im mittelalterlichen Spanien." *Traditio*, 43 (1987): 321–358.

Reinink, G. J. "Der Edessenische Pseudo-Methodius." *Byzantinische Zeitscrift* 83 (1990): 31–45.

Rivera Recio, Juan Francisco. *Elipando de Toledo*. Toledo, 1940.

———. "La iglesia mozárabe." *Historia de la iglesia en España*. Vol. 2.1. (Madrid, 1982).

Rodinson, Maxime. *La Fascination de l'Islam*. Paris, 1989. Trans. by T. Veinus, *Europe and the Mystique of Islam*. Seattle, 1987.

———. "The Western Image and Western Studies of Islam," *The Legacy of Islam*. 2nd ed. Oxford, 1974.

Ross, E. Dennison. "The Early Years of Shah Ismâ'il, Founder of the Safavi Dynasty." *Journal of the Royal Asiatic Society* (1896): 249–340.

Runciman, Steven. *The Byzantine Theocracy*. Cambridge, 1977.

———. "Charlemagne and Palestine." *English Historical Review* 1 (1935): 606–619.

———. *A History of the Crusades*. 3 vols. Cambridge, 1955–1957.

Russell, J. "Transformations in Early Byzantine Urban Life: The Contributions and Limitations of Archaeological Evidence." *The 17th International Byzantine Congress, 39–62: Major Papers*. (New Rochelle, NY, 1986), 137–154.

Al-Sabah, Rasah. "*Inferno* XXVIII: The Figure of Muhammad." *Yale Italian Studies* 1 (1977): 147–161.

Sahas, Daniel J. "The Art and Non-Art of Byzantine Polemics, Patterns of Refutation in Byzantine Anti-Islamic Literature." in M. Gervers and R. Bikhazi, eds., *Conversion and Continuity*, 55–73.

———. *John of Damascus on Islam: The "Heresy of the Ishmaelites."* Leiden, 1972.

———. "John of Damascus on Islam. Revisited." *Abr-Nahrain* 23 (1984–1985): 104–118.

Said, Edward. *Orientalism*. New York, 1978.

Samir, Khalid. "Entretien d'Éle de Nisibe avec le vizir ibn 'Ali al-Magribi, sur l'unité et la trinité." *Islamochristiana* 5 (1980): 31–117.

Sanjian, A. K. *Colophons of Armenian Manuscripts, 1301–1480: A Source for Middle Eastern History*. Cambridge, 1969.

Saunders, J. J. *A History of Medieval Islam*. London and New York, 1987.

Savory, Roger M. "The Consolidation of Safavid Power in Persia." *Der Islam* 41 (1965): 87–124.

Schick, Robert. "The Fate of the Christians in Palestine during the Byzantine/Umayyad Transition, 600–750 A.D." Ph.D. dissertation, University of Chicago, 1987.

Schimkoreit. Renate. *Registen Publizierter Safawidischer Herrscherurkunden*. Berlin, 1982.

Schmidt, Barbara. "Ein Vergleich zwischen der Chanson de geste von *Aiol et Mirabel* und der italienischen Prosabearbeitung: *La storia di Ajolfo del Barbicone*." dissertation, Berlin, Humboldt-Universität, 1949.

Schmolinski, Sabine. *Der Apokalypsenkommentar des Alexander Minorita: Zur frhen Rezeption Joachim von Fiore in Deutschland*. MGH Studien und Texte, Band 3. Hannover, 1991.

Schwoebel, Robert. *The Shadow of the Crescent: The Renaissance Image of the Turk (1453–1517)*. New York, 1967.

Sdrakas, E. D. *Hê kata tou Islam polêmikê tôn Buzantinôn Theologôn.* Salonika, 1961.

Seymour, Michael. "Mandeville and Marco Polo: A Stanzaic Fragment." *Journal of the Australasian Universities Language and Literature Association* 21 (1964): 39–52.

Shepard, Jonathan. "The English and Byzantium: A Study of Their Role in the Byzantine Army in the Late Eleventh Century." *Traditio* 29 (1973): 53–92.

Sherwood, Polycarp. *An Annotated Date-List of the Works of Maximus the Confessor.* Rome, 1952.

Sibery, Elizabeth. *Criticism of Crusading: 1095–1274.* Oxford, 1985.

Simonet, Francisco X. *Historia de los mozárabes de España.* Madrid, 1903.

Simonsen, J. B. *Studies in the Genesis and Early Development of the Caliphal Taxation System.* Copenhagen, 1988.

Sinor, Denis. "Les relations entre les Mongols et l'Europe jusqu'a la mort de Arghun." *Cahiers d'histoire mondiale* 3 (1956), 39–62.

Smith, Byron. *Islam in English Literature.* 2nd. ed. New York, 1977.

Sophocles, E. A. *Greek Lexicon of the Roman and Byzantine Periods (from B.C. 146 to A.D. 1100),* 2 vols. New York, 1887.

Southern, Richard W. *Western Views of Islam in the Middle Ages.* Cambridge, MA, 1962.

Starr, Joshua. *The Jews in the Byzantine Empire, 641–1204.* Athens, 1939; rpt. New York 1970.

Stickler, Alfons. "Concerning the Political Ideas of the Medieval Canonists." *Traditio* 7 (1949–1951): 450–463.

————. "De ecclesiastica potestate coactiva materiali apud magistrum Gratianum." *Salesianum* 4 (1942): 2–23, 96–119.

————. "De potestate gladii materialis ecclesiae secundum 'Quaestiones Bambergensis ineditas.'" *Salesianum* 6 (1944): 113–140.

————. "Il 'gladius' nel Registro di Gregorio VII." *Studi Gregoriani* 3 (1948): 89–103.

————. "Il 'gladius' negli atti dei concilii e dei RR. Pontfici sino a Graziano e Bernardo di Clairvaux." *Salesianum* 13 (1951): 414–445.

————. "Magisti Gratiani sententia de potestate ecclesiae in statum." *Apollinaris* 21 (1948): 36–111.

————. "Il potere coattivo materiale della Chiesa nella Riforma Gregoriana secondo Anselmo di Lucca." *Studi Gregoriani* 2 (1947): 235–285.

————. "Sacerdotium et Regnum nei decretisti e primi decretalisti: Considerazioni metodologiche di ricerca e testi." *Salesianum* 15 (1953): 575–612.

————. "Sacerdozio e regno nelle nuove ricerche attorno ai secoli XII e XIII nei decretisti e decretalisti fino alle Decretali di Gregorio IX." *Sacerdozio e regno da Gregorio VII a Bonifacio VIII = Miscellanea Historiae Pontificiae* 18 (1954): 1–26.

————. "Der Schwerterbegriff bei Huguccio." *Ephemerides Iuris Canonici* 3 (1947): 1–44.

Sukiasyan, A. G. *Istoria kilikiiskogo armonskogo gosudarstra i prava IX–XIV BB*. Erevan, 1969.

Sümer, Faruk. *Safevi Devletinin Kuruluşu ve Gelişmesinde Anadolu Türkmenlerinin Rolu*. Ankara, 1976.

Tachau, Katharine H. *Vision and Certitude in the Age of Ockham: Optics, Epistemology and the Foundations of Semantics 1250–1345*. Albert Zimmermann, ed. Studien zur Geistesgeschichte des Mittelalters 22. New York, 1988.

Tansel, Selhattin. *Sultan II Bayezit'in Siyasi Hayatı*. Istanbul, 1969.

Tardy, Lajos. *Beyond the Ottoman Empire: 14th–16th Century Hungarian Diplomacy in the East. Studia Uralo Altaica*, 13. Szeged, 1978.

Tekindağ, M.C. Şehabeddin. "Yeni Kaynak ve Vesikaların Işiği altında Yavuz Sultan Selim'in Iran Seferi." *Tarih Dergisi* 22 (1967): 49–76.

Ter-Minassiantz, E. *Die armenisches Kirche in ihren Beziehungen zu den syrischen Kirchen bis zum ende des 13. jahrhunderts nach den armenischen und syrischen Quellen*. Leipzig, 1904.

Tolan, John V. *Petrus Alfonsi and His Medieval Readers*. Gainesville, Florida, 1993.

————. "Anti-Hagiography: Embrico of Mainz's *Vita Mahumeti*." *Journal of Medieval History* (forthcoming).

Toscano, Nicolás. "Edición crítica de los versos inéditos de Arredondo sobre Fernán González." *Boletín de la Institución Fernán González* 195 (1980): 273–326; 196 (1981): 53–110; 197 (1981): 321–360.

Tournebize, F. *Histoire politique et religieuse de l'Arménie depuis les origines des Arméniens jusqua'à la mort de leur dernier roi (l'an 1393)*. Paris, 1910.

Tritton, A. S. *The Caliphs and Their Non-Muslim Subjects: A Critical Study of the Covenant of 'Umar*. London, 1930.

Vaquero, Mercedes, ed. *Vida Rimada de Fernán González*. Exeter, 1987.

Valli, Giorgio. "Ludovico Ariosto y Ginés Pérez de Hita." *Revista de Filología Española* 30 (1946): 23–32.

Valois, Nol. "Pierre d'Aureoli." *Histoire littéraire de la France* 33 (1906): 479–528.

van Dieten, Jan-Louis. *Niketas Choniates: Erläuterungen zu den Reden und Briefen Nebst Biographie.* Berlin, 1975.

Van Engen, John. "Faith as a Concept of Order in Medieval Christendom." In *Belief in History: Innovative Approaches to European and American Religion.* Kselman, Thomas A., ed. (Notre Dame, 1991), 19–67.

———. "The Christian Middle Ages as an Historiographical Problem." *American Historical Review* 91,3 (June 1986): 519–552.

van Koningsveld, P. S.J. "La Apologia de Al-Kindi en la España del siglo XII. Huellas toledanas de un 'animal disputax,'" *Estudios sobre Alfonso VI y la reconquista de Toledo (Actas del II Congreso Internacional de Estudios Mozárabes [Toledo, 20–26 Mayo 1985]* (Toledo, 1989), 107–129.

———. *The Latin-Arabic Glossary of the Leiden University Library. A Contribution to the Study of Mozarabic Manuscripts and Literature.* Leiden, 1976.

———. "La Literatura Cristiano-Arabe de la España medieval y el significado de la transmissión textual en árabe de la *collectio conciliorum.*" Unpublished paper.

———. "Petrus Alfonsi, een 12de eeuwse schakel tussen islam en christendom in Spanje." *Historische betrekkingen tussen moslims en christenen,* ed. P. van Koningsveld (Nijmegen, 1982), 127–146.

Vodola, Elisabeth. *Excommunication in the Middle Ages.* Berkeley, 1986.

von den Brincken, A.-D. *Die "Nationes Christianorum Orientalium" im Verständnis der Lateinischen Historiographie von der Mitte des 12. bis in die zweite Hälfte des 14. Jahrhunderts* Kölner Historische Abhandlungen, 22 (1973).

von Schönborn, Christoph. *Sophrone de Jérusalem: Vie monastique et confession dogmatique.* Paris, 1972.

Vryonis, Speros. *The Decline of Medieval Hellenism in Asia Minor and the Process of Islamization from the Eleventh through the Fifteenth Century.* Berkeley, 1971.

Walker, James B. *The "Chronicles" of St. Antoninus. A Study in Historiography.* Washington, 1933.

Wasserstein, David. *The Rise and Fall of the Party Kings: Politics and Society in Islamic Spain, 1002–1086*. Princeton, 1985.

Watt, J. A. "The Theory of Papal Monarchy in the Thirteenth Century: The Contribution of the Canonists." *Traditio* 20 (1964): 179–317.

Watt, W. Montgomery. *The Influence of Islam on Medieval Europe*. Islamic Surveys, no. 9. Edinburgh, 1972.

———. "Muḥammad in the Eyes of the West." *Boston University Journal* 22(3) (Fall, 1974): 61–69.

———. *Muslim-Christian Encounters: Perceptions and Misperceptions*. London, 1991.

Wensinck, A.J. *A Handbook of Early Muhammadan Tradition*. Leiden, 1960.

White, H.G. Evelyn. *The Monasteries of the Wadi'n Natrun*. 3 vols. New York, 1926–1933.

White, Hayden. "The Historical Text as Literary Artifact." *The Writing of History. Literary Form and Historical Understanding*. Robert H. Canary and Henry Kozicki, eds. (Madison, 1978), 41–62.

Williams, John. "Purpose and Imagery in the Apocalypse Commentary of Beatus of Liébana." Bernard McGinn and Richard K. Emmerson, eds. *Apocalypse in the Middle Ages*. Ithaca, 1992: 217–233.

Winkel, Jan te. *Maerlant's werken beschouwd als spiegel van de 13de eeuw*. The Hague, 1892; rpt. Utrecht, 1979.

Witakowski, W. *The Syriac Chronicle of Pseudo-Dionysius of Tel-Maḥrē* Uppsala, 1987.

Wolf, Kenneth Baxter. *Christian Martyrs in Muslim Spain*. Cambridge, 1988.

———. *Conquerors and Chroniclers of Early Medieval Spain*. Liverpool, 1990.

———. "The Earliest Latin Lives of Muhammad." *Conversion and Continuity*. M. Gervers and R. Bikhazi, eds., 89–101.

———. "The Earliest Spanish Christian Views of Islam." *Church History* 55 (1986): 281–293.

Wolfson, Harry. *The Philosophy of the Kalam*. Cambridge, MA, 1976.

Woods, John. *The Aqquyunlu: Clan, Confederation, Empire*. Minneapolis, 1976.

Wormald, Francis and Phyllis M. Giles. *A Descriptive Catalogue of the Additional Illuminated Manuscripts in the Fitzwilliam Museum acquired between 1895 and 1979 (excluding the McClean Collection).* 2 vols. Cambridge, 1982.

Xac'ikyan, L. S. *XIV Dari Hayeren Jeragreri Hisatakaranner.* Erevan, 1950.

Ye'or, Bat. *Dhimmi: The Dhimmi Jews and Christians under Islam.* Revised edition and translation by David Maisel. East Rutherford, NJ, 1985.

Zacher, Christian K. "Travel and Geographical Writings." In *A Manual of the Writings in Middle English 1050–1500.* 9 vols. Albert E. Hartung, gen. ed. New Haven, 1986, vol. 7: 2235–2254, 2449–2466.

Zayat, H. *Signes distinctifs des chrétiens et des juifs en Islam* Reprinted from *Al-Machriq.* Beirut, 1950.

Zink, Michel. "Apollin." *La Chanson de geste et le mythe carolingien: mélanges René Louis,* publiés par ses collègues, ses amis et ses élèves à l'occasion de son 75e anniversaire. Emmanuèle Baumgartner, Jean-Charles Payen and Paule Le Rider, eds. 2 vols. Saint-Père-sous-Vézelay, 1982), 1: 503–509.

Contributors

Gloria Allaire
Department of Modern
Languages
Ohio University

Palmira Brummett
Department of History
University of Tennessee,
Knoxville

David Bundy
Library
Christian Theological Seminary

Thomas Burman
Department of History
University of Tennessee,
Knoxville

David Burr
History Department
Virginia Tech

Geert H. M. Claassens
University of Nijmegen
Netherlands

John S. Geary
Department of Spanish and
Portuguese
University of Colorado at
Boulder

Frank Grady
Department of English
University of Missouri—St.
Louis

Craig L. Hanson
Department of Religion
Muskingum College

William P. Hyland
Department of History
Benedictine College

Philip Krey
Lutheran Theological Seminary

John Lamoreaux
Department of Religion
Duke University

John Phillip Lomax
Department of History and
Political Science
Ohio Northern University

John V. Tolan
Department of History
University of North Carolina,
Greensboro

Kenneth B. Wolf
Department of History
Pomona College

Rhona Zaid
University of California,
Los Angeles

Index